JEWS IN AMERICA

The First 500 Years

JEWS IN AMERICA

The First 500 Years

Matthew B. Schwartz

RESOURCE Publications · Eugene, Oregon

JEWS IN AMERICA
The First 500 Years

Copyright © 2019 Matthew Schwartz. All rights reserved. Except for brief quotations in critical publications or reviews, no part of this book may be reproduced in any manner without prior written permission from the publisher. Write: Permissions, Wipf and Stock Publishers, 199 W. 8th Ave., Suite 3, Eugene, OR 97401.

Resource Publications
An Imprint of Wipf and Stock Publishers
199 W. 8th Ave., Suite 3
Eugene, OR 97401

www.wipfandstock.com

PAPERBACK ISBN: 978-1-5326-4411-5
HARDCOVER ISBN: 978-1-5326-4412-2
EBOOK ISBN: 978-1-5326-4413-9

Manufactured in the U.S.A.   06/20/19

Contents

Acknowledgements | vii
Preface | ix
Abbreviations | xi

Introduction | 1
1492–1802: **Colonial Days** | 3
1802–1850: **German Jewish Immigration** | 38
1850–1881: **Civil War and Expansion** | 71
1881–1924: **Eastern European Immigration** | 119
1924–1945: **Americanizing** | 199
1945–1980: **Cross-Currents** | 243

Index | 287

Acknowledgements

It is my joy and pleasure to record here my gratitude to some people who have given help and encouragement in producing this book: to librarians Kitty Allen of the Southfield Library and Sarah Bell of the Midrasha Library, to Professor Kalman Kaplan, Rabbi Binyamin Sendler, Thomas Schwartz, Asher Schwartz, Dr. Zuki Gottlieb, Amanda Sue Donigian, the staff at Wipf and Stock, and especially to my editor Margalit Gottlieb for both her skills and her wisdom.

Dedicated to my Grandchildren.

Preface

ON AUGUST 3, 1492, Christopher Columbus set sail from Palos, Spain on the voyage that brought Europeans to the Americas. On his ships were several conversos, Jews who had converted to Christianity under threat from the Spanish Inquisition. On that very same day, the last citizens of Spain's once glorious Jewish community were driven from their native land amid frightful tribulations, forced into exile by the monarchs Ferdinand and Isabella and the Inquisition, to seek uncertain refuge in Morocco, Italy, Turkey or wherever they could. The proud Jewish community of Spain ceased to exist. Yet on the same day, Columbus's voyage sowed the first seeds of another great Jewish community—in the future United States of America.

In the Middle Ages and in the early Modern Era of history, the Jews of Europe faced incredible hardships. They were driven at one time or another out of France, England, Spain, Portugal and many of the German principalities. They were never welcomed in Switzerland. Jews suffered massacres by mobs of crusaders, or by Cossacks, or simply by their neighbors, in which thousands were slain and whole communities wiped out. Anti-Jewish riots stain the records of many old European cities. Jews were also typically excluded from most crafts. Nor could they often own land. Even so-called enlightened rulers like Frederick the Great of Prussia in the eighteenth century still enforced old restrictions on a Jew's right to marry or to earn a living. The Inquisition in Spain and Portugal remains to this day infamous for its sadistic torture of innocent and helpless people. In many countries, Jews could dwell only in ghettos, confined and walled in to narrow quarters.

The charge of ritual murder was often raised. Jews, whose religion strictly prohibits the consumption of blood, were regularly accused of killing Christian children to use their blood in holiday rituals. The charge was both ridiculous and false but it resurfaced again and again even into the twenty-first century, and often resulted in anti-Jewish violence.

PREFACE

At the very time when Jews were first settling in North America, in 1654, the Jews of Eastern Europe were suffering the slaughter of many thousands during the war between Poland and the Cossack armies of Bogdan Chmielnitski, which devastated the large Jewish communities in their path. When Russia under Catherine the Great took possession of Belarus and the Ukraine in the late eighteenth century, it incorporated large numbers of Jewish residents into its empire for the first time. Predictably, the czarist government perpetrated all sorts of cruel pressures and restrictions on the Jews hoping to convert them to Orthodox Christianity or else to drive them into exile or to death. A decree of the Czar Nicholas I ordered the drafting of little Jewish boys into prolonged military service, which many did not survive. Schools and trades were largely closed to Jews, and few Jews were allowed to live in Moscow or St Petersburg or indeed anywhere outside their Pale of Settlement.

The Jews of Europe survived all this, despite terrible losses and hardships, dedicated to their Faith and their ideals. Indeed, they were generally more educated and hygienic than their neighbors, and they built strong family lives. Yet, many looked for something better. America began to seem like the land of freedom and opportunity, the golden land where people who loved to study could go to school and even university, where people willing to work could enter businesses and professions, and where the law guaranteed freedom from religious persecution, pogrom and inquisition.

Even as Jews migrated to the United States in large numbers during the great immigration wave around the turn of the twentieth century, their brethren left behind would face worse torments than ever before in World War I, the Russian Revolution and the civil war that followed and finally in the Nazi era.

Rarely in history has a nation offered so much opportunity to its citizens as has the United States, especially to its Jews. While the road to full participation even in the U.S. has not lacked its rough spots, American Jews owe a great debt to the founding fathers. People like Franklin, Jefferson, Washington and others were remarkably free from prejudice, and they built a government in which freedom of religion was an important principle.

This book tells something of the story of how the Jews came to the "golden land" and what they have done here — men and women, scientists and athletes, soldiers and merchants, gangsters and scholars. It is indeed a remarkable story.

Abbreviations

AJA	American Jewish Archive
AJHQ	American Jewish Historical Quarterly
AJYB	American Jewish Yearbook
CAJ	Colonial American Jewry
EAJ	Early American Jewry
EJ	Encyclopedia Judaica
JE	Jewish Encyclopedia
PAJHQ	Proceedings of the American Jewish Historical Quarterly
PAJHS	Proceedings of the American Jewish Historical Society
UJE	Universal Jewish Encyclopedia
USJ	United States Jewry

Introduction

FOR OVER TWO CENTURIES after the War for Independence, America's Jews have lived in a Golden Age. Like Athens in the time of Pericles and like Italy in its Renaissance, a blissfully fortunate conjunction of opportunities provided American Jews with nearly unlimited potential to develop and to produce, and the Jews responded magnificently in every area of science, culture, politics and business. The Jews brought to the United States a faith in the importance of human activity and of hard work both mental and physical. They believed that life is serious enough not to be frittered away on short term frivolities.

In the centuries when European settlers built the American colonies, the Old World was still beset with deep religious differences and intolerances that often erupted into bloody wars between factions or nations—Catholic against Protestant, like the brutal Huguenot wars in France or the devastating Thirty Years War in Germany. Spain and Portugal suffered the cruel tyranny of the Inquisition. For the Jews particularly, there were hardship, restriction and persecution. Jews were forbidden to live in England until the 1650's, or in Spain and most of France, and they were often expelled from German towns. In Eastern Europe, they were subjected to persecution, and they suffered through traumas like the 1648 Cossack War and the Sabbatian heresy a few years later.

The first settlers in America came out of this milieu, and that America has been largely free of religious strife and oppression is due to a high minded group of founding fathers like George Washington, Ben Franklin and Thomas Jefferson who wrote laws assuring that the United States government would not countenance religious persecution. Also, the very diversity of immigration to America has made it difficult to single out one group for long term harassment of the sort which dyed Jewish History in Europe. And so far, although there has been anti-Semitism in the United States, it has been largely quiet, repressed and, most important, not violent.

The accomplishments of American Jews are far more than most people realize. They are indeed astonishing. This book presents pictures of some leading people and events in the history of American Jewish life—politicians, soldiers, scientists, athletes, people who sought to run away from Judaism or to come closer to it. Generation after generation of Jews migrated to the new world and made their way into American life—the Sephardim, the Germans, the Eastern Europeans. The challenges of adjustment to the American environment were usually met successfully within one or two generations. The greater internal challenge has not yet been resolved. The Jew has shown that he can live well as an American. But how does he maintain his Jewishness? As he became more Americanized, he sometimes paid less attention to those sources of internal strength that had sustained him through the ages. As America moves into the 21st century, it is clear that while the Jews must remain watchful of outside threats, the greater danger to the Golden Age of American Jews may be internal.

This book is constituted in the form of questions and answers aimed at depicting interesting people and events that are usually not well known but are worth knowing. The question and answer pattern is both ancient and widely used in Jewish literature harking back at least as far as the *Passover Hagada* and the *Talmud*. As a study method, it is highly recommended by expert educators both for focusing attention and as a memory aid.

1492–1802

Colonial Days

IN LATER CENTURIES, AMERICA would become a land of incomparable opportunity. However, in colonial times it still consisted of a few small weak colonies sitting along the Atlantic seaboard. Although distant from Europe, the colonies were ruled from the old country and were bound as well by its established social and religious prejudices. Most Jews who came to America in those days were of Sephardic roots, looking for a land where they might settle and work, and where they might rejuvenate a sense of an identity wounded and distorted by generations of persecution.

As late as the American Revolution, there were no more than 3,000 Jews in the 13 colonies. Charleston, South Carolina held the biggest Jewish community with New York and Philadelphia catching up. Some Jews were still devoted to their traditions, but many were not. In smaller towns, especially on the frontier, it was hard to keep up a Jewish life or to find a Jewish spouse and raise a Jewish family, although some did. There were no permanent rabbis, although a learned traveler would occasionally pay a brief visit.

Church and state were not separate, and laws often excluded Jews, Catholics, Quakers and other outsiders from holding political office or even voting. However, many did military duty, and colonists of different racial and religious backgrounds mingled in unaccustomed though not idyllic peace. Jews joined other colonists in business and trade both in towns and on the expanding frontier. A good percentage of Jews were educated, though more in secular than in traditional Jewish studies .

Above all, there was a sense of freedom provided by the promise of the endless frontier and the inkling of some feeling of fair play that was only beginning to develop. There was perhaps a sense in the air that when one stepped off the boat onto the shores of this New World, he had cast off the choking restraints and rigidities of the Old World.

After the American Revolution, the government of the new United States took an amazing and important step by guaranteeing, in its new Constitution, the basic human freedoms of its citizens, including the freedom of religion. While the constitution did not eliminate all anti-Semitism from people's minds, it did assure the Jews the rights to vote, to hold Federal office, and to practice their faith without hindrance. This was a big step ahead of most European governments of that day, including England, where the Jews were still oppressed and constrained by restrictive laws and ancient prejudices. Frederick the Great of Prussia, supposedly one of the more cultured and enlightened of European monarchs, enforced anti-Jewish measures including old laws restricting their rights to conduct business, to live outside ghettos and even to marry. American Jews still faced problems at state and local levels, but a basic pattern of freedom had become part of the new nation's way of life.

Q. Who were the first Hebrew speaking residents of America?

A. One prominent historian and archaeologist, Professor Cyrus Gordon, has claimed that certain ancient inscriptions found in eastern Tennessee and always thought of as Cherokee are actually Hebrew and were likely written by Jewish refugees from the Bar Kochba War in Judea in the early second century. In fact, however, most authorities agree that the first residents of North America fluent in Hebrew were Massachusetts Puritans like John Cotton, who were graduates of Oxford or Cambridge and very knowledgeable in Hebrew as well as Greek and Latin. When the first expedition was sent to New England to find a suitable site to settle a colony, the explorers reported to John Winthrop and his committee that they had found an excellent spot which the Indians called Naumkeag. Winthrop responded that this sounded like a fortunate place for a town because Naumkeag sounded like the Hebrew words *Khek Nahum*, which means bosom of consolation.

For Further Reading:

Cyrus H. Gordon, *Before Columbus: Links Between the Old World and Ancient* America, New York, Crown Publ. Inc, 1971.
Samuel Eliot Morrison, *Builders of the Bay Colony*, Boston, Houghton-Mifflin Co. 1930

Q. Was Christopher Columbus a Jew?

A. The question of Columbus' national and religious background has long been a matter of debate and remains so. American diplomat Oscar Straus discussed the topic with Spanish historians during a visit to that country in 1914, and biographers of Columbus today support a variety of points of view. Robert Fuson, translator of Columbus' ship's log, finds much evidence, albeit circumstantial, that points to a Jewish background. The *Encyclopedia Judaica,* while also not entirely sure, lists a number of strong indicators of a Jewish background. Columbus' signature can be read as Hebrew letters, and he specifically instructed his son to sign his name the same way. He left money in his will to a Marrano beggar in Portugal. He was apparently in contact with Jewish leaders in Spain like Don Abraham Seignor and Don Isaac Abravanel. His real family name was Colon, a name used often by Spanish and Italian Jews. A leading Italian rabbi of Columbus' time was Joseph Colon. Columbus was always very reticent about his family background, a behavior which would well suit a man of Jewish origin during the heyday of the Spanish Inquisition.

Salvador Da Madariaga, in his 1939 biography, finds the evidence for Columbus' Jewishness overwhelming. In addition to proofs listed above, Da Madariaga points out that Columbus showed no loyalty to Genoa and even fought against it. This would indicate that he had no deep roots in Genoa and was likely of Spanish background. Also, Catalan Jews had long been interested in geography and map making. Columbus often discussed religion in his extant writings, citing Jewish sources and seeming, in Da Madariaga's view, to be seeking a safe position between Jewish and Christian thought.

Gianni Granzotto, while generally praising Da Madariaga's work, totally dismisses his views on Columbus and Judaism, arguing that the admiral's family had lived in Genoa, where there were few Jews, for at least several generations, and that his father had been a keeper of the city gate and therefore not possibly Jewish. Samuel Eliot Morrison, in his *Admiral of the Ocean Seas,* has no doubt at all that Columbus was simply a Genoese. His ruddy coloring indicates a probable descent from the Teutonic invaders that toppled the Roman Empire a millenium before.

Kirkpatrick Sale too, in *The Conquest of Paradise,* 1990, writes that Columbus was probably Genoese and not of Jewish origin. However, he notes that there have been literally hundreds of articles offering different opinions on the matter, including claims of Greek, French and Polish background.

Famed Nazi-hunter Simon Wiesenthal offers a very innovative theory in his book, *The Secret Mission of Christopher Columbus,* 1979. Columbus sailed from Spain on the very day that the Jews had been ordered by the government to quit the country. Perhaps, argues Wiesenthal, he was hoping, desperately, to find a place where Jews would be accepted and could live safely. He took the Hebrew speaking Luis De Torres with him in the hope of reaching Asiatic lands where Hebrew was known. It is curious too, Wiesenthal claims, that there were no churchmen on Columbus' ships, and

Columbus' first message upon reaching the Canary islands en route back to Spain was sent not to King Ferdinand and Queen Isabella but to two *conversos*, Luis de Santangel and Gabriel Sanchez, who had strongly backed the expedition. Also Columbus' first wife seems to have been of Jewish descent.

For Further Reading:

Robert Fuson, *The Log of Christopher Columbus*, Camden Maine; Internal Marine Publishing Co., 1987.

Samuel Eliot Morison, *Admiral of the Ocean Sea: A Life of Christopher* Columbus, Boston; Little Brown and Co., 1942.

Salvador Da Madariaga, *Christopher Columbus*, London; Hollis and Carter 1949.

Simon Wiesenthal, *Sails of Hope: The Secret Mission of Christopher Columbus*. New York; MacMillan Publ., 1973.

Q. When was the first auto da fe in America?

A. The Spanish Inquisition established itself in Mexico all too quickly after Hernando Cortez's conquest of Montezuma's Aztec kingdom, and it soon began its gruesome work of seeking out and punishing enemies of the faith. Several crypto-Jews had served in Cortez's army and, in 1528, two of them, Hernando Alonso and Gonzalo De Morales, were publicly burned at the stake, accused of Judaizing activities. Alonso had received 80 acres of land as part of his share of the booty from the conquest of Mexico, and he had built up a very successful cattle ranch. Although himself of Jewish background and married to a daughter of Jewish converts to Christianity, it is unlikely that Alonso was much involved in Jewish practices.

Gonzalo De Morales was accused of having flogged a crucifix, based on testimony taken from his sister while under torture. Two other Jews on trial were reconciled with the church. Some historians have argued that Alonso and De Morales were burned for political reasons. Increases in trials and punishments of conversos beginning near the close of the sixteenth century attest both to the increasing immigration of conversos and to the growing reach of the Inquisition.

For Further Reading:

Seymour Liebman, *The Jews in New Spain: Faith, Flame and the Inquisition,* Coral Gables, University of Miami Press, 1970.

Q. Who was the first Jew to set foot in an English colony in North America?

A. Joachim Gaunze (Gans), a mining engineer from Prague, came to England in 1581, at a time when Jews were not permitted to live there. He accompanied the expedition sent by Sir Walter Raleigh to found a colony on Roanoke Island in 1585, 22 years before the founding of Jamestown. Several years later, back in England, he revealed his Jewish identity and spoke in Hebrew during a conversation with a clergyman. Gaunze was sent to be tried before the Privy Council in London, led by Lord Walsingham, for whom Gaunze had worked. The results of the hearing are unclear, but Gaunze soon left England and ultimately returned to Prague, where he died in 1619.

For Further Reading:

Jacob Marcus, *United States Jewry*, I:21.

Q. What strange product did Dr. Rodrigo Lopez sell in America?

A. Dr. Rodrigo Lopez, a converso of Portuguese birth, became private physician to Queen Elizabeth I of England. In addition, he was apparently a close supporter of Sir Francis Drake, helping him to maintain contact with the queen despite the intrigues of the court. About 1593, English ships captured two Spanish vessels bound for Peru, carrying a cargo of papal indulgences—documents by which the Roman church granted their holders absolution from sins. Elizabeth made a gift of these to Lopez who outfitted a ship to carry the documents to Spanish America, where they were sold at a good profit. Lopez was also granted monopolies in the import of aniseed and sumac.

All through his stay in England, Lopez involved himself in a variety of diplomatic intrigues and made his share of enemies. In 1596, he was accused, probably falsely, of trying to poison the queen. He was drawn and quartered after a trial which aroused great public interest at the time. Some scholars believe that William Shakespeare molded Shylock, the Jewish moneylender in his *Merchant of Venice*, after Dr. Lopez. The play appeared only a few months after Lopez's execution.

For Further Reading:

Cecil Roth, *History of the Jews of England*, 1941.

Max Kohler, "*Dr. Rodrigo Lopez: Queen Elizabeth's Physician and His Relationship to America*," PAJHS. XVII, 1909, 9–25.

Q. An early church in the village of Amozoc, Mexico has 4 crosses and 4 six-pointed stars on its dome. Why?

A. It is probable that conversos lived in some numbers around Amozoc in the 17th century. They probably had to contribute to the church so as to maintain their outward pose as good Catholics. However, they may also have used the six-pointed stars to alert converso travelers to the possibility of hospitality for Sabbaths and holidays.

For Further Reading:

Seymour B. Liebman, *The Jews in New Spain: Faith, Flame and the Inquisition,* Coral Gables, University of Miami Press, 1970, p. 207

Q. Were there any Jews on the Mayflower?

A. No, although there are records of an occasional Jew staying briefly in Massachusetts in the colonial period. In 1649, when a Jew, Solomon Franco arrived on a Dutch vessel, the Great and General Court of Massachusetts allowed him six shillings per week for ten weeks for his sustenance until he could find passage back to Holland. He eventually made his way to London where he lived as a Christian and married a Christian woman. A certain Rowland Gideon was listed as paying eighteen shillings in taxes for 1674. Gideon too, finally moved back to London and became a prosperous merchant. Probably the first permanent Jewish resident was Moses Michael Hays (1739–1805), who moved there in 1782, shortly after the American Revolution. He apparently hosted a small congregation in his house.

For Further Reading:

Isaac Fein, *Boston—Where It All Began.* Boston, 1976.
Lee Friedman, "Boston in American Jewish History," *PAJHS.* XLII, 1953, 333–340.

Q. Who was Maldonado Da Silva?

A. Dr. Francis Maldonado Da Silva was burned as a Judaizer in a great auto-da-fe in Lima, Peru in 1639. Raised in Argentina as a Christian by parents of Jewish descent, he returned to Judaism, which he practiced secretly until he was betrayed to the Inquisition. His career closely parallels that of the more famous Luis de Carvajal in Mexico four decades earlier.

For Further Reading:

Marcus, *CAJ,* I, 60

Q. Who was Gonzalo Diaz Santillan?

A. Portuguese born Gonzalo Diaz Santillan was murdered by fellow conversos in Mexico in 1648. He had been extorting money from them by threatening to denounce them to the Inquisition for their Judaizing practices. His body was exhumed and burned by the Inquisition on April 11, 1649. The Holy Office was busy enough in Mexico, persecuting crypto-Jews as well as a variety of Lutherans, blasphemers, witches and others. Informers like Santillan have been a problem for Jews through the ages, whether the tale-bearing was in matters of religion or politics. The Talmud refers to the dilatores of the Roman period.

For Further Reading:

Arnold Wiznitzer, "Crypto-Jews in Mexico in the Seventeenth Century," *AJHQ*, LI, 1962, 222–268

Q. Who was the first Jew in New York?

A. The honor is usually accorded to Asser Levy and a small group of refugees, who came to what was then called New Amsterdam in 1654, fleeing from Brazil after it fell to the Portuguese. However, in fact, Jacob Bar Simon, a Dutch Jew, was sent to New Amsterdam from Holland by the Dutch Jewish leaders, a few months earlier, to determine the possibilities for Jewish settlement and arrived some weeks before Levy's group. Another Jew, Solomon Pieterson, had preceded even Bar Simon. by a short time.

For Further Reading:

Marcus, *EAJ*, I, p. 24f.

Q. Why did few Jews settle in colonial Virginia?

A. A certain John Levy owned land in James Town City County in 1643, and some early settlers with Spanish names may have had Jewish antecedents. Moses Nehemiah, in the 1650's, is the first Jew to have permanent residence in Virginia. The colony, however, did not attract many Jews for two reasons. First, Virginia was largely rural, and there were few business opportunities other than in farming. Williamsburg, the capital, had only about 722 white residents at the time of the American Revolution. Second, the Anglican Church dominated the colony and made life difficult for non-Anglicans including other sorts of Protestants.

For Further Reading:

Jacob Marcus, *The Colonial American Jew. 1492–1776*. Detroit: Wayne State University Press, 1970.

Q. Who was the first owner of Labrador?

A. Several ships belonging to Joseph De La Penja, a Jewish merchant of Rotterdam, touched shore in Labrador in 1677, and he claimed the as yet unexplored land for his ruler, William of Orange, who was also about to become the King of England. Some years later, De La Penja happened to save the King's life when the latter's ship foundered in a storm. As a reward, King William granted Labrador in perpetuity to De La Penja. No effort, however, was ever made by De La Penja or his heirs to follow through on the gift. Only in the early twentieth century did his descendants, including Isaac De La Penja, a cantor, apply to the British government to verify the family's title to the land.

For Further Reading:

B.G. Sack, *History of the Jews in Canada*, Montreal, 1965.

Q. What Jew was a governor in the West Indies in the 17th century?

A. Jews settled in the Danish owned island of St. Thomas as early as the 1680's, and from 1684 to 1686, its governor was Gabriel Milan, a Jewish adventurer who had converted to Christianity. Milan's despotic rule led to his removal from office and his execution in Copenhagen in 1689.

For Further Reading:

Jacob Marcus, *The Colonial American Jew*, I, p. 143.

Q. Did any Jews sail with Captain Kidd ?

A. In 1696, Captain William Kidd set out from New York in the Adventure to round up pirates, but soon turned pirate himself, one of history's most notorious. Benjamin Franks, related to the well known colonial Jewish Franks family, had joined the crew of the Adventure when it first sailed from New York, planning to journey to India and try to recoup some large business losses he had incurred while living in the West Indies. After Kidd turned pirate, Franks persuaded the captain to let him go ashore at Carwar, about 350 miles from Bombay, by giving him a beaver hat. The crew was growing unhappy with Kidd, and he hesitated to let anyone go ashore.

Franks' version of the story was presented in a legal deposition taken in Bombay, October 20, 1697. Franks swore to the truth of his statements on the "Old Testament." He later settled in New York.

For Further Reading:

Samuel Oppenheim, Notes, *PAJHS*, XXXI, 1928, p. 229-236.

Q. What is the earliest known document to mention a Jewish religious functionary in North America?

A. On September 13, 1710, Abraham Haim De Lucena of New York, "Minister of the Jewish Nation," sent a petition to Governor Robert Hunter mentioning that De Lucena's predecessors had been exempted from civic and military service, and presumably he should be too. Thus, the Jewish spiritual leaders probably as early as the 17th century held a position comparable to the Christian in at least one of the English colonies.

For Further Reading:

Abraham J. Karp, *Haven and Home*, New York, Schocken Books, 1985, p. 67.

Q. When was the first mass immigration of Jews to America?

A. The honor of being the first mass migration should probably be bestowed on the hundred or so Jews who came from England to Savannah, Georgia in 1733, shortly after the colony was founded. The leaders. including founder James Oglethorpe, were not thrilled about having so many Jews in their midst, although they were preferable to Catholics. Many soon moved on to more welcome sites. Others like the Sheftall family stayed on to play a notable role in the history of early Georgia.

For Further Reading:

Marcus. *EAJ*. II, 392-393.

Q. Who was the first Jew to graduate from an American college?

A. Judah Monis received an M.A. from Harvard in regard of a Hebrew teaching textbook which he wrote. Monis went on to teach Hebrew at Harvard; however, to qualify for that position he had to convert to Christianity, which he did. His book, *The Grammar of the Hebrew Tongue*, was published in 1735.

Monis was valued by the Puritans for his knowledge of Hebrew. However, students complained that he was a poor teacher and that his book, which he used as a classroom text, was too expensive. In the copy that still survives, the title page was amended by a student: "Composed and accurately corrected by Judas Monis, M.A." was changed to "Confuted and accurately corrupted by Judah Monis. Maker of Asses."

For Further Reading:

Marcus *EAJ*, . 107 f.
Arthur Hertzberg, *The Jews of America: Four Centuries of an Uneasy Encounter: A History*, NY; Simon and Schuster, 1989.

Q. How did the great Puritan minister Cotton Mather begin his book, *Magnalia Christi Americani*?

A. Overcoming a childhood speech defect, Cotton Mather became a leading preacher and theologian in early New England like his father and grandfather before him. Study of the classical languages was fundamental to a Puritan education, and Mather studied Greek, Latin and Hebrew.

The Magnalia was a history of the church in America aimed at serving the enhancement of Faith in Europe as well as in the colonies. It begins with the Hebrew letters, *aleph*, *yod*, *heh*, the abbreviation for "*im yirtze hashem*" (God willing). This was equivalent to Latin D.V. (*deo volente*), which was often placed at the start of a book and which expressed the author's reliance on divine grace.

Mather cites Jewish biblical commentators in the *Magnalia*. For example, in explaining the Hebrew word *kippod*, used in Isaiah 14:23, he relates that Rashi (1040–1104) translates it as owl and that R. David Kimchi (1160–1235) as snail, although Mather prefers bittern. In this instance Mather was not wholly accurate. Rashi in fact, translates *kippod* into Old French *hericon* or hedgehog, while R. David Kimchi, referring to both Arabic and French, says that his father R. Joseph translated *kippod* as turtle, while he himself believes *kippod* to be a desert bird. Mather's chapter on the worthy men of New England carries a Hebrew expression, *baalei nefesh* (worthy men) in its title.

The Puritans thinkers had a strong sense of the Hebrew scriptures and likened their own settlement in the American wilderness to the forty years of the Israelites' wandering in the Sinai Wilderness. This did not necessarily mean any special love toward Jewish contemporaries, of whom few if any lived in Massachusetts in Mather's day.

For Further Reading:

Ralph Boas, Cotton Mather: *Keeper of the Puritan Conscience*, New York, Harper, 1928
Robert Middlekauf, *The Mathers. Three Generations of Puritan Intellectuals,* New York, Oxford University Press, 1971.

Q. What is the oldest known extant Jewish structure in the thirteen colonies?

A. According to historian Rabbi David De Sola Pool, it is a trading post built about 1720 near Newburgh, New York and operated by the Gomez family, the most influential Jews of New York in those days.

Family tradition maintains that Isaac Gomez, a converso and a Spanish nobleman, managed to send his wife and infant son, Moses, to France just before he was himself seized and imprisoned by the Inquisition. The name Lewis was added to baby Moses' name in honor of King Louis XIV of France, who gave the Gomez family asylum in his kingdom. Lewis Gomez arrived in New York with his large progeny about 1703 and prospered in the import-export business. Expanding into trade with the Indians, the Gomezes bought large tracts of land up the Hudson River, building a trading post of stone six miles north of the present day Newburgh about 1720. Several Indian trails converged there on a spot they believed to be sacred. The nearby brook was for years called Jew's Creek.

For Further Reading:

David De Sola Pool, *Portraits Etched in Stone,* NY; Columbia University Press, 1952.
Marcus. *USJ 1776-1985*, I:35

Q. In what American colony were Jews first formally permitted to vote?

A. The charter for Carolina written by philosopher John Locke in 1663, allowed Jews to vote, and Jews voted in Charleston at least as early as 1702. However, in 1721 South Carolina enacted new voting laws which made it impossible for Jews to vote or be elected to the Assembly. In early New York, Jews voted for some years but lost their franchise in 1737. Jews throughout the colonies did not begin to gain full political rights until after the American revolution.

For Further Reading:

Lawrence Fuchs, *The Political Behavior of American Jews.* Glencoe, IL; The Free Press, 1956.

Q. Who was the first Jewish criminal to be executed in North America?

A. In New York in 1727, a certain Moses Susman was brought to trial for stealing "Gold Silver money rings etc." (sic.) from Moses Levy. The court appointed an interpreter since Susman spoke no English. Apparently, Susman's guilt was very clear, for the jury pronounced him guilty without leaving the courtroom. Susman was executed by hanging several weeks later, not an unusual punishment by the harsh standards of the times.

For Further Reading:

Morris Schappes, *A Documentary History of the Jews in the United States, 1654–1865*, New York, Schocken Books, 1971.

Q. Why did Sir Alexander Cuming, a Scottish nobleman, want to settle 300,000 Jewish families on the American frontier in 1750?

A. Professor Jacob Marcus reports a letter written in 1750 by Sir Alexander Cuming to King George II of England, proposing to settle 300,000 Jews in the Cherokee Mountains (probably meaning the Southern Appalachians). Cuming claimed ownership of the mountains based on his visit there twenty years before. The Jews, as honest and industrious subjects of King George would, he argued, help pay off England's national debt of £80,000,000. Another £50,000 would go to Cuming and pay his way out of debtor's prison in London where he was when he wrote the letter. Cuming's scheme was outlandish even in an age of discovery when utopian literature was much in vogue. There is no reason to believe that the government ever answered his letter.

For Further Reading:

Jacob Marcus, *American Jewry: Documents, Eighteenth Century.* Cincinnati, Hebrew Union College Press, 1959. p. 203f.

Q. What is "Jacob and the Indians"?

A. Stephen St. Vincent Benet (1898–1943) wrote a short story entitled "Jacob and the Indians." It recounts the life of Jacob Stein, a fictional Jewish immigrant who traveled among the Indians in the mid-18th century. Although Stein is fictional, parts of the story are based on historical events. For example, Chapman Abraham, a Jewish trader, was captured by Pontiac's Indians in 1763 and tied to a stake to be burned to death. As the heat grew more intense, Abraham called for a drink of water, but it was too hot, and

Abraham spat it in the Indian's face. Thinking that Abraham was either very brave or very insane the Indians released him.

For Further Reading:

Jacob Marcus, *EAJ.* I p.229

Q. What was the first Jewish day school in America?

A. In the great upsurge of day schools in the latter part of the twentieth century, it should be remembered that Congregation Shearith Israel of New York conducted a day school as early as 1755. The pupils studied three hours of Jewish subjects and two hours of Spanish, English, and arithmetic. Jews well versed in Judaism were few in the United States, but by 1762, the school had secured the services of a good scholar, Abraham Israel Abrahams. His yearly salary was £20 for teaching poor students plus tuition payments from the well-to-do. The school lasted until the revolution, when most Jews left New York during the British occupation. There may have been some formal teaching even before 1755, but no record remains. The Shearith Israel opened schools twice in the 19th century, 1808–1821 and 1855–1856. In 1842, Reverend S.M. Isaac reorganized the afternoon school of New York's Congregation Bnai Jeshurun into a religious and secular day school which, despite a good scholastic showing, closed in 1847 due to financial difficulties. In 1847–1848, three Orthodox German synagogues opened a school for 250 students under the leadership of Rabbi Max Lilienthal, but the school fell apart after a year. The synagogues opened their own separate day schools, one of which lasted till 1857.

This was all at a time when most children were educated either at parochial or private schools. General public schools were not yet the norm. Day schools declined as public schools grew and became secularized by about 1860.

For Further Reading:

Hyman Grinstein, *The Jewish Community of New York. 1656–1850.* Philadelphia, JPS, 1945.

Q. Who was the first Jew in Canada?

A. As a French colony until 1756, early Canada was French in culture, language, and in its attachment to the Catholic Church. Jews were forbidden to settle in French colonies, although there may have been a few early settlers in Canada with some sort of Jewish ancestry. Some historians believe that the first viceroy of New France, Henri de Levy, Duke of Ventadons, may have been of Jewish descent. His distant descendant, General de Levis, was the second in command to General Marquis de Montcalm during the French-Indian War.

A case in 1738 provides the first clear record of a Jew in Canada. A young sailor by the name of Jacques La Fargue landed in Quebec. In fact, she turned out to be Esther Brandeau, a Jewish girl from Bayonne, France, who told a fantastic story. She had been shipwrecked en route from Bayonne to Amsterdam in 1733. Resolved not to return to the restrictions of her parental home, she assumed the guise of Jacques and served as a sailor on several ships before coming to Quebec.

Canadian archives go on to tell that her case became a real problem for the authorities. Unsuccessful in their efforts to force her to convert to Catholicism, they sought instructions from the government in France. King Louis XV himself intervened and ordered Brandeau returned to France at royal expense. She had been in Canada for about a year. The second clear reference to a Jew is the story of a Dutch Jew who, in 1752, took ship for Canada and was forcibly baptized en route.

In 1732, Colonel David Dunbar, commander of the English Fort Frederick, in Maine, wrote to headquarters that six French men of war full of Jews were arriving in Louisburg, an important French fortress. Dunbar's information was, of course, ludicrous and probably received as good a laugh from the British generals as it might from a reader of a later age.

For Further Reading:

B.G. Sack, *History of the Jews in Canada*, Montreal; Harvest House, 1965.

Q. Who organized the Society of Canada?

A. One of the greatest problems faced by the French settlement in early Canada was the corruption of its own leaders, from Governor Pierre Vaudreuil and superintendent Francis Bigot on down. In 1748, Abraham Gradis, a Jewish merchant of Bordeaux, formed the Society of Canada. The Society sought to maintain open, honest trade between France and its possessions in North America and the West Indies. When the war with England broke out, Gradis was probably the leading supplier of French Canada, and the British destroyed many of his ships. General Marquis de Montcalm's gratitude to Gradis is mentioned in several of his letters. He preferred to communicate directly with Gradis rather than through Vaudreuil and his cronies, with whom Montcalm was constantly at odds. Also at personal expense, Gradis helped bring supplies and comfort to French prisoners of war incarcerated in England. The family received little compensation from the French government for their losses, and the destruction of their properties in San Domingo and Martinique during the period of the French Revolution brought about their economic ruin.

An added note. Historian Francis Parkman in his *Montcalm and Wolfe* writes that the French government arraigned 17 Canadian officials for fraud. Count de Bougainville, an honest officer, named only four Canadian officials as exceptions to the demoralization, commenting that they were "not enough to have saved the wicked city of Sodom."

For Further Reading:

B. G. Sack, History of the Jews in Canada, 1965.
Stuart Rosenberg, *The Jewish Community of Canada*. Toronto, Mclelland and Stuart, 1970.

Q. Did Jews fight in the French-Indian War?

A. The war between the French and British in the New World, 1758–1763, was part of a larger conflict in Europe which also involved Frederick the Great of Prussia, the Hapsburg Empire, Russia, Sweden and Spain. In America, the British and their colonial allies completely defeated the French, acquiring Canada as a prize of their victory.

A number of Jews fought on the British side in the colonies. One of the most prominent was Aaron Hart of New York, who organized and led a battalion in the 60th Royal American Regiment out of New York. After the war, Hart settled in Trois Rivieres, Quebec, where he and his descendants prospered and later held high office in Canada's government.

Sir Alexander Schomberg, 1727–1804, the son of Dr. Mayer Low Schomberg of London, commanded the frigate Diana in General James Wolfe's campaign against Quebec, Canada's capital. Schomberg had helped lead the capture of Montmorency, which cleared the way to Quebec. Schomberg's memoirs offer an important view of the war. He liked America so much that he once asked his friend, actor David Garrick, to use his influence to secure a post for him there. Garrick wrote a poem about Schomberg:

> *Make him the tyrant of a fort*
> *He'll ask no more of you or faith Surrounded by his scalping court*
> *What monarch would be half so great?*
> *Send him where oft he fought and bled, Again to cross th' Atlantic sea.*
> *To tomahawk and wampum bred, He's more than half a Cherokee.*

Major Jewish families of Philadelphia and New York, like the Gratzes, were important suppliers for the British troops. Historian Francis Parkman, in his *Montcalm and Wolfe*, recounts the heroics of Captain Moses Hazen of the Rangers. Some of Hazen's men believed that he was Jewish because of the name, but apparently he was not. Hazen survived a serious wound at Quebec to fight again in the American Revolution.

Two other names have a Jewish sound. The decisive battle of the attack on Quebec took place on the Plains of Abraham before Quebec, where both General Wolfe and the French commander, the Marquis de Montcalm, lost their lives. Abraham Martin, an early French trader after whom the plain was named, was not Jewish, as some think.

Jews were not permitted to live in French colonies. However, the Chevalier de Levis, Montcalm's second in command, was a descendant of Henri de Levy, the governor-general of Canada in the early seventeenth century. The family may have had some distant Jewish roots. An able soldier, de Levis led a force from Montreal that almost retook Quebec several months after Wolfe's victory. The British were saved only by the timely arrival of their fleet. Levis' defeat spelled the end of French power in Canada.

For Further Reading:

B.G. Sack, History of the Jews in Canada, 1965.
Marcus, *EAJ. II.* p.203.

Q. What was the Lindo Packett ?

A. The Lindo Packett was a ship acquired in 1757 by Moses Lindo of Charleston, South Carolina in 1757. Of Portuguese-Jewish background, Lindo came to South Carolina from England in 1756 and prospered in the indigo (a blue dye) trade. First cultivated in South Carolina in 1744, indigo was second only to rice as an item of export. Lindo became a "Surveyor and Inspector General of Indigo" in 1762. For a small percentage, he would inspect and certify the quality of indigo being sent overseas. This was not a government office, and the inspection was not required by law, but Lindo's imprimatur was still valuable to the sellers, as Lindo was well respected in England.

Lindo was apparently a Sabbath observer, advertising himself as closed to business on Saturdays as well as the usual Sundays and public holidays.

Interested in scientific experiment, Lindo once observed a mockingbird eating what were called pouckberries, and he noticed later that the bird's droppings were crimson, showing the pouckberry to be a good crimson dye. To this pouckberry dye, Lindo added some lime juice and produced a new yellow dye. The story is preserved in a letter sent by Lindo to Emanuel Mendes da Costa, librarian of the Royal Society of London, and was published in *Philosophical Transactions* in 1763. In a letter to a local gazette, Lindo claimed to have concocted a herbal medicine which would cure "that grievous and common disease among the Negroes called the Yaws."

For Further Reading:

Barnett Elzas, *The Jews of South Carolina*, Philadelphia; J.B. Lippincott Co., 1905

Q. What notable Jewish "first" was registered in Halifax, Nova Scotia?

A. In 1749, most of Canada was still under French rule, and Jews were not permitted to live there. However, at least a few Jews settled in the British town of Halifax. Samuel Hart, coming from Newport, Rhode Island, was elected to the Nova Scotia legislature, probably the first Jew to sit in any legislative assembly in North America. By the middle 1770's, the Halifax settlement seems to have petered out as most of its members departed either to England or to the thirteen American colonies.

For Further Reading:

Stuart A. Rosenberg, *The Jewish Community in Canada*, Toronto; MacLelland & Stewart, 1970. p. 25–26.

Q. Who introduced the tomato as a salad vegetable in colonial America?

A. English born Dr. John de Sequeyra, 1712–1795, came to Virginia in 1745 with a medical degree from the University of Leiden and opened a practice in Williamsburg. Thomas Jefferson credits him with introducing the tomato to the American salad plate. First brought to Europe from Spanish America in the early sixteenth century, the tomato was variously thought to be a poison (it is related to nightshade), a love potion, or "simply more a flower than a vegetable." But De Sequeyra believed that regular eating of tomatoes could greatly lengthen one's life span. It was not until about 1900 that the tomato achieved its current popularity.

The doctor's family, of Portuguese Jewish background, had settled in England in the seventeenth century and had produced a number of physicians. John's brother, Joseph Henry, was a physician in the West Indies.

Dr. John De Sequeyra also served as the physician and a member of the board of directors of the first mental hospital in America, at Williamsburg, in 1773. In his regular practice, he treated a number of well known people including members of George Washington's family.

In early colonial Virginia, there were few Jews, and they seem to have been tolerated as long as they kept their religious practices and opinions quiet. De Sequeyra was known to his contemporaries as a Jew, but he did not practice his religion openly. The doctor's house on Duke of Gloucester Street near Botetourt Street in Williamsburg is today restored as a historic exhibit.

For Further Reading:

Robert Shostek, "Notes on an Early Virginia Physician," *AJA. XXII.* 1970. 198–212

Q. Who was the first meshulach (fund raiser) from Israel to visit America?

A. In 1759, Rabbi Moses Malki arrived as a messenger from the devout but poor Jewish community in Eretz Israel to collect funds in America. Haim Maduhy came in 1761 to raise funds to help repair the damage to Safed from the earthquake of October, 1759.

For Further Reading:

Isaac Rivkind , "Some Remarks About Messengers from Palestine to America," *PAJHS*, XXXIV, 288–1879.
Jeanette and Salo Baron, "Palestinian Messengers to America 1848–1879," *Jewish Social Studies*, V, 115–162 and 225–292.

Q. What unusual show did Hyam Myers produce?

A. Hyam Myers, a Canadian Jewish merchant, having lost heavily in the fur trade in the 1760's came up with a novel scheme to recoup his fortunes. He took a number of Mohawk Indians to Europe and charged admission for people to see them. Apparently Myers accomplished nothing and ended up adding the Mohawks to his list of creditors.

For Further Reading:

Marcus *CAJ*, p. 814.

Q. Who was the first Jew to come to Detroit?

A. The honor of being the first Jew to come to Detroit generally has been accorded to Chapman Abraham. He was an enterprising merchant who traded with the Indians of the Great Lakes area and settled in Detroit when it was a small frontier outpost in 1762, only a year after the British had taken it from the French.

However, there may have been one earlier Jewish visitor. In the days of the French and Indian War, British General Henry Bouquet, in command of the army near Fort Pitt (modern Pittsburgh), makes frequent mention in his papers of an able engineer officer, Captain Elias Meyers of the Royal American Regiment. Little is known of Meyers' origins, but judging from his name and from the fact that he came from Germany, he may well have been Jewish, one of a number of Jews in the British army.

In 1761, General Bouquet sent Captain Meyers west to build a small fort for the British garrison at Sandusky, Ohio. Meyers went on to visit Detroit as well, at least a year or so before Abraham arrived.

For Further Reading:

Papers of Colonel Henry Bouquet, Harrisburg, Pennsylvania Historical Commission, 1949.

Q. Why were the Jews expelled from New Orleans in 1769?

A. Spain took possession of New Orleans from France as a result of the secret Treaty of Fontainebleu 1762, and there was immediate friction between the new Spanish officials and the citizens. Spanish governor, Don Alejandro O'Reilly, cracked down on the populace, and a number of residents were expelled from New Orleans. In a letter of October 17, 1769, O'Reilly informed his superiors of the expulsions and specified the removal of Isaac Monsanto and several other Jewish merchants, probably the only Jews in New Orleans then, "On account of the nature of their business and of the religion they profess." A letter sent to Monsanto in December notes that Monsanto was not involved in illegal activities, but that "the departure which I require of you and your entire family is specifically a consequence of an order of the king which especially forbids all Jews from residing in the state. "

Despite these letters, Dr. Bertram Korn argues that the main motive of the expulsion was not religion, but the desire of the Spanish government to take over full control of their colonies' economic life.

For Further Reading:

Bertram W. Korn, The Early Jews of New Orleans. Waltham, Mass: American Jewish Historical Society, 1969.

Q. How did the U.S. Government come to possess West Point, New York, present site of the United States Military Academy?

A. In May, 1772, Elazar Levy, a Jewish trader, had lent £1,000 with a large plot of land known as West Point as security. During the American Revolution, the American army had moved in and used up much of the timber, diminishing the value of Levy's land. In 1779 and 1783, Levy petitioned Congress for relief but without success. The land remained in government hands, and later the military academy was built there. Levy later served as executor for the estate of Revolutionary War patriot Haym Salomon.

For Further Reading:
Marcus, *EAJ*, II, 146–147.

Q. A copper company owned by American Jews functioned for 175 years. What company was it?

A. Uriah Hendricks (1731–1798), a Jewish immigrant from England, settled in New York and entered into the copper trade by 1764. Copper played a very important role in the growth of American industry. Uriah often did business with Paul Revere and Nicholas Roosevelt, also major copper dealers.

Operating for many years from their main plant at Belleville, New Jersey, the Hendrickses provided the copper for Robert Fulton's steamboats, for the expanding production and export of American locomotives in the 1830's, and for Thomas Edison's inventions. Uriah's son Harmon (1771–1838), subscribed the huge sum of $58,000 in government loans during a difficult time in the War of 1812. Aided by careful planning, the business continued to flourish through the ups and downs of many generations until its closing in 1939.

The Hendrickses remained active members of Congregation Shearith Israel in New York and were firmly observant Jews, deeply involved in Jewish communal life and in civic philanthropies. A letter of Uriah Hendricks tells of how he once in 1790 stormed out of the Newport synagogue when he found that they were reading the weekly Torah portion from a printed book rather than a parchment scroll, as the Jewish Law requires. The Hendrickses typically married into prominent Jewish families like Gomez, Kursheedt and Nathan.

In 1866, a second Uriah Hendricks, grandson of the old Uriah, learned of a plan by six major insurance companies, including Aetna and Hanover, to restrict Jewish merchants from obtaining insurance policies on their properties. Uriah organized a nationwide public protest and forced the companies to back down. Henry S. Hendricks (1892–1959) became a lawyer and did not continue in the family business. However, like his ancestors, he served as president of Shearith Israel and was active in many Jewish causes.

For Further Reading:

Maxwell Whiteman, *Copper for America: The Hendricks Family and a National Industry. 1755-1939*, New Brunswick, NJ, Rutgers University Press, 1971.

Q. What poem did Tom Paine write about a Jew?

A. Tom Paine, whose little book, *Common Sense*, was a best seller among the American colonists rebelling against England, was a liberal in both politics and religion. In 1775, he wrote "A Bigot's Immersion," a poem about a Catholic who refuses help to a Jew who falls through the ice into a lake, unless he will agree to convert to Christianity.

For Further Reading:

David M. Eichhorn, *Evangelizing the American Jew,* Middle Village NY; Jonathan David Publishers, 1978.

Q. Who were the first Jews to attend American colleges?

A. American colleges of the 18th century were small and usually religious affiliated and with less impact on society than in later centuries. Lawyers, physicians and businessmen were likely to learn their trade on the job and not in a school. Still, several Jewish names appear on college student lists. Isaac Isaac, who graduated from Yale in 1750, was of Jewish descent although not himself Jewish. Three brothers, Abraham, Solomon and William Pinto, attended Yale in the 1770's. Isaac Abraham graduated Columbia in 1774. In Philadelphia, one of the more liberal cities in that day, six Jews attended the University of Pennsylvania in the 1760's. Four Jews, including one young lady, Richea Gratz, were among the first students at Franklin College, founded by Benjamin Franklin in Lancaster, Pennsylvania in 1787. In view of the usual Jewish devotion to education, it is not surprising that Jewish names appear on the lists of contributors even to colleges which had no Jewish students.

For Further Reading:

Leon Huhner, "Jews in Connection with the Colleges of the Original 13 States, " *PAJHS*, XIX, 1910, 101-124.

Q. Did any Jews serve with General Francis Marion, the Swamp Fox, during the American Revolution?

A. After the fall of Savannah and Charleston to the British and General Horatio Gates' disastrous defeat at the Battle of Camden in August, 1780, patriot hopes of victory reached a low ebb in the South. The flame of rebellion was kept alive there by several small irregular forces led by the "Swamp Fox" Francis Marion, Thomas Sumter, and Andrew Pickens. They harassed British troops and supply lines and helped lead the way to General Washington's decisive victory over Lord Cornwallis at Yorktown in October, 1781.

At least one Jew in Marion's unit was Captain Jacob Myers, and Abraham Alexander, reader in the Charleston synagogue, served with Sumter. Cushman Pollack carried dispatches between General Marion and General Nathanael Greene. One report claims that Manuel M. Noah fought under Marion and was later at Yorktown. Several dozen southern Jews served with the American regulars or in local militia units.

A number of Jewish citizens left or were banished from Charleston and Savannah during the British occupation. Samuel Levy and Levy Solomon came from Europe as sutlers to the Hessian troops but left them and settled in Charleston.

For Further Reading:

Samuel Rezneck, *Unrecognized Patriots,* Westcott. Conn. Greenwood Press, 1975.
Charles Reznikoff, *The Jews of Charleston*, Philadelphia, JPS, 1950.

Q. Was George Bush Jewish?

A. There was a Major George Bush, a Jew and no relation to former Presidents George Bush, who served in the American army during the War of Independence. The major's brother, Major Lewis Bush, was fatally wounded at the battle of Brandywine in 1777. Dr. George Bush, a Presbyterian minister, was professor of Hebrew at New York University from 1832–1846. Although he loved the Hebrew language, he had less regard for the Jewish people. At NYU during those same years, Charles Nordheimer, a Jew, taught Semitic languages other than Hebrew, although he knew Hebrew well.

For Further Reading:

"Professor George Bush: American Hebraist and Proto-Zionist," *AJ, XLIII,* 1991, 59–70.
UJE. IX. 622.

Q. How many Jews in the 13 colonies remained loyal to Great Britain during the American Revolution?

A. For a long time, American Jewish historians were perhaps a bit shy to say much about the American Jews who remained loyal to King George III. However, like their Christian neighbors, more than a few Jews supported the British cause and were perhaps not less honorable than the Jews on the patriot side.

One such was Jacob Hart of Newport who removed to England after the War, while the Pollocks of Newport moved to St. Eustatius in the West Indies. David Salisbury Franks became an officer in George Washington's army, while his cousin, David Franks, helped to supply and feed the British troops. The Tory Franks cut a memorable figure at a ball given by British General Sir William Howe in Philadelphia shortly before his army departed from the city in 1778.

For Further Reading:

Cecil Roth, "Some Jewish Loyalists," *PAJHS*, XXXVIII, 1945, 81–107.

Q. Who was the Jewish aide-de-camp of notorious traitor Benedict Arnold?

A. David Salisbury Franks was appointed as aide to Benedict Arnold during the dark days at Valley Forge when Arnold was the darling of the patriot army and hero of the recent victory at Saratoga, where he had been severely wounded. Franks was foppish in his dress and habits, but he was described by no less than Thomas Jefferson as intelligent and honest. Franks was aware of a correspondence between Arnold and a certain John Anderson behind British lines but believed that Arnold was merely gathering intelligence.

Arnold was rude and harsh-spoken to his aides, especially as he grew more nervous while his secret plotting deepened. Franks and another aide, Richard Varick, were fed up with Arnold and ready to leave him, and there were several shouting matches. However, Franks and Varick were completely surprised when Arnold went over to the British and tried to betray West Point in upstate New York. Arnold later wrote to General Washington from the British ship Vulture listing Franks, Varick, and several others close to him as totally ignorant of his traitorous activities. Varick and Franks were later exonerated in a court-martial.

For Further Reading:

James Thomas Flexner, *The Traitor and the Spy: Benedict Arnold and John Andre*, Boston, Little, Brown and Co. 1975

Q. How did Ezra Stiles, Protestant minister in Newport, Rhode Island, react to an application to "use" the Newport synagogue?

A. Ezra Stiles (1727–1795), a learned Christian minister with a good knowledge of Judaism, and later president of Yale University, was living in Newport during the American Revolution. A letter from Moses Seixas. a Newport Jew, to Aaron Lopez, a noted Jewish merchant in Leicester, Massachusetts in 1780, refers to an incident in which Stiles was involved. A certain Mr. Channing, a Christian, on several occasions "applied for the use of the synagogue." Channing's purpose is not clear from the letter. Historian Alexander Guttman has speculated that perhaps Channing was a clergyman whose church had been put to use by occupying troops, British (1776–1779) or French (1780–1781), and Channing wanted to use the synagogue for services for his congregation. Whatever Channing's purpose, Dr. Stiles strongly agreed with Seixas that the synagogue could be used only for Jewish services and that the Jews should refuse the request. Dr. Stiles assured Seixas that he would do all within his power to remove any unfavorable impressions that the refusal might create in his own congregation. Seixas went on to write that he would still like to hear Lopez's opinion on the matter.

Stiles took pride in his knowledge of Hebrew and in his friendship with visiting rabbis, especially Rabbi Chaim Karigal of Hebron, with whom he later exchanged letters. At the Yale graduation of September 1781, for which he wrote the original draft of his speech in Hebrew, Stiles said, "I have been taught personally at the mouth of the Masters of wisdom at the mouths of 5 rabbis, Hochams, of name and eminence viz... R. Moses Malchi... R. Moses Askenazi, R. Raphael Hajim Isaac Karigal ... Like Joseph of a comely aspect and beautiful countenance; R, Tobiah Bar Jehuda... sixth Generation from Selomoh Ishaaki (ed. note Rashi)... But as light excelleth Darkness so far doth R. Karigal surpass and excell all the rest...."

For Further Reading:

Alexander Guttman, *"Ezra Stiles, Newport Jewry, and a Question of Jewish Law,"* AJA 1982, 98–102.
Arthur A. Chiel," *The Rabbis and Ezra Stiles,"* AJHQ. LXI, 1972, 294–312.
Abiel Holmes, *The Life of Ezra Stiles.* 1799.
Edmund Moran, *The Gentle Puritan: A Life of Ezra Stiles*, New Haven, Yale University Press, 1962.

Q. Who was Johann Conrad Dohla?

A. Dohla was a mercenary from Anspach-Bayreuth who served in one of the German contingents in the British army during the American Revolution and was with Cornwallis's army at Yorktown. His diary includes his impressions of American Jews. They are "not easily distinguishable from Christians," he wrote. "They are not like the ones we have in Europe and Germany who are recognizable by their beards and clothes, for they are dressed like other citizens, get shaved regularly, and also eat pork, although that is forbidden in their Law. Also Jews and Christians intermarry without scruple. The women also go about with curled hair and in French finery such as is worn by the ladies of other religions. They are very fond of the Germans and obliging toward them."

There may have been a few Jews among the Hessian soldiers. There is record of an Alexander Zuntz who came in 1779 as Commissary and Agent to the General Staff. In May of that year, he married Rachel Abrahams of New York and dwelt there until his death in 1817. An active member of Shearith Israel Congregation, it was his customary privilege to lead the morning service on Yom Kippur.

For Further Reading:

Abraham V. Goodman, "A German Mercenary Observes American Jews During the Revolution," *AJHQ*, LIX, 1969, 227.

Q. What is the biblical background of the great seal of the United States?

A. You need not travel to Washington D.C. to see what the great Seal of the U.S.A. looks like. It's on the back of the dollar bill and has been in use since its adoption by Congress in 1782. However, another seal had been recommended to Congress in 1776 by a committee consisting of Benjamin Franklin, Thomas Jefferson, and John Adams. It portrayed the Egyptian army charging into the Red Sea and Moses, on the far shore, his arms extended, readying their destruction. The inscription reads: "Rebellion to tyrants is obedience to God."

For Further Reading:

Marcus, *USJ*, I, 568–9

Q. How did Dr. Isaac Levy of Cahokia defend himself from a malpractice suit in the 1780's?

A. "Doctor" Isaac Levy practiced some sort of frontier medicine in the earliest days of settlement on the Illinois frontier around the time of the American Revolution. It is reported that Levy sued a Frenchman named Buteau for not paying his medical bill of 400 livres. Buteau claimed, however, that he had not been cured by Levy's treatment, so the court ordered Levy to complete the cure.

Levy then gave Buteau 67 pills to take over a week, but Buteau took them all in two days, figuring that he would be cured that much more quickly. Levy argued that had he truly taken all those pills in two days he could not have come to court to tell the tale. The court found in Levy's favor.

For Further Reading:

Marcus *CAJ*, I . 375. *EAJ*, II 348 f.
USJ, I, 201.

Q. How did the Jews participate in the celebration in Philadelphia on July 4, 1788, which marked the adoption of the Constitution?

A. The celebration was described 80 years later by Naphtali Phillips who witnessed it as a 15 year old boy. A parade moved from Spruce Street north along Third, passing only half a block from the synagogue. Jews marched along with Christians, the synagogue leader arm in arm with two Christian ministers. At the banquet after the parade, the Jews had a special kosher table spread with "a full supply of soused (pickled. ed. note) salmon, bread and crackers, almonds and raisins etc." prepared under the charge of an old cobbler named Isaac Moses. Yet, it was not until the next year that the new state constitution of Pennsylvania gave Jews full political rights at the state level.

For Further Reading:

Edwin Wolf and Maxwell Whitman. *History of the Jews of Philadelphia From Colonial Times to the Age of Jackson,* Philadelphia; Jewish Publication Society, 1957.

Q. Why are there today no Jewish members of the Society of Cincinnati?

A. Established in 1783, the Society of Cincinnati was a super-patriotic organization whose membership was limited to officers of the American army during the American Revolution. It was named for Cincinnatus, an ancient

Roman farmer-general, who saved his city from invaders but refused an offer to continue as dictator of Rome.

In the original membership list of 1783, there was only one member of clearly Jewish origin, David S. Franks. However, Franks never married, and membership is limited to one lineal male descendant at a time for each charter member. Two Christian members married Jewish women, but no known descendants of theirs are members today.

Two other organizations, The Sons of the American Revolution and The Daughters of the American Revolution, founded in the late 19th century, both have Jewish members. These latter include the descendants of civilians as well as soldiers.

For Further Reading:

Samuel Reznick, *Unrecognized Patriots*, Westwood, Conn: Greenwood Press, 1975.

Q. Who was Alexander Levine Hamilton?

A. The face on the American $10 bill is that of Alexander Hamilton, who played so vital a role in the founding of the U.S. government and who served as our first Secretary of the Treasury. Was Hamilton really the son of a Jew named Levine? Almost nothing can be said for certain about Hamilton's birth. However, it is clear that his mother Rachel Fawcett, probably of French Huguenot background, had married a Northern European Jew, John Michael Lavien or Levine about 1745 on the island of St. Croix in the West Indies. Records of the time spell Levine's name about a dozen different ways.

The marriage was unhappy and lasted, according to Hamilton's biographers, only until about 1750, with John accusing Rachel of numerous adulteries. However, other scholars, for example Nathan Schachner, put the separation as late as 1756. Within a few years Rachel was living with James Hamilton, a Scotsman. The date of Alexander Hamilton's birth is also far from certain. One of the few written documents of that time gives the birth year as 1755. Hamilton probably never was sure either of his birth date or his paternity, although he addressed James Hamilton in letters as father. In his childhood, Hamilton attended a school whose teacher was a Jewish woman, and he would later tell his children that he had once memorized the Ten Commandments in Hebrew. A fragment in Hamilton's script has been found among his papers in which he states that Jewish History from the beginning to the present is so extraordinary that it must be providential.

For Further Reading:

Ron Chernow, *Alexander Hamilton*, New York; Penguin, 2004.

James T. Flexner, *The Young Hamilton: A Biography*, Boston; Little Brown and Co. 1978. Nathan Schachner, *Alexander Hamilton*, New York; A.S. Barnes & Co., 1946. Broadus Mitchell, *Alexander Hamilton*, New York; MacMillan, 1962.

Q. Who was Ben Hassan?

A. The first American written play to contain a Jewish character was Susanna Haswell Rowson's *Slaves in Algiers*, which opened in Philadelphia in 1794. A main character was Ben Hassan, a Jew living in Algiers who had converted to Islam. Written during the period of conflict between the U.S.A. and the Barbary pirates of North Africa, the play portrays Ben Hassan as a treacherous and hateful man, who betrays some American captives in fulfillment of a Mosaic command to cheat Gentiles (of course, no such law ever actually existed.) *Slaves in Algiers* played in several American cities for over two years. It was revived at least once, in Boston in 1816.

Many, though not all Jewish stage characters were rather unsavory, in line with the well established practice of the English drama most notably personified in Shakespeare's *Merchant of Venice* and Christopher Marlowe's *Jew of Malta*. Jewish playwrights in the early U.S. never used Jewish characters among their *dramatis personae*.

For Further Reading:

Edward Coleman, "Plays of Jewish Interest," *PAJHS*. XXXIll, 1934, 180–181.

Q. Can salt water be turned to fresh water?

A. This was an important question in the age of sailing ships when transoceanic voyages could go on for many weeks, and it remains, of course, a crucial issue today in countries which are not blessed with an abundance of water. A number of experiments had been tried but with indifferent success. In 1791, Jacob Isaacs, a Jew of Newport, claiming to have discovered a usable method, petitioned Congress for financial help. Congress turned the matter over to Secretary of State Thomas Jefferson as their expert on science. Jefferson reported to Congress that he was not convinced as to the efficacy of Issacs' method, but that experimentation in that area was certainly worthy of encouragement.

For Further Reading:

Herbert Fredenwald, "Jacob Isaacs and His Method of Converting Salt Water To Fresh Water," *PAJHS*, II, 1984, 111–117.

Q. What famous American founding father contributed five pounds to Congregation Mikvah Israel of Philadelphia ?

A. The Mikvah Israel synagogue of Philadelphia had been weakened when many of its members fled the city during the American Revolution and also by the death of Haym Salomon, one of its biggest supporters. Refused permission by the state assembly to set up a lottery, Mikvah Israel issued a general appeal for funds to both Jews and non-Jews. One of the respondents was Benjamin Franklin, already in his eighties, who generously donated five pounds.

For Further Reading:
Peter Wiernik, *History of The Jews of America*, NY: Hermon Press, 1972.

Q. Who was the first Jew to seek a Cabinet appointment ?

A. Solomon Bush, son of Matthias Bush, a prominent Philadelphia merchant, joined George Washington's army and was wounded in a skirmish a week after the battle of Brandywine in 1777. In 1795, he petitioned President Washington for an appointment to the position of Postmaster General to succeed Colonel Timothy Pickering who had just been transferred over to Secretary of War. In 1789, he had sought appointment to a diplomatic post in Britain, after having obtained the freeing of the crew of an American ship which had been seized by the British. Both job requests were turned down. Bush's diplomatic career never did get off the ground, but he rose to high office among the Masons.

For Further Reading:
Jacob Marcus, *EAJ*. II.77-79.

Q. How did Congregation Shearith Israel of New York keep their Torah scroll in good condition in the 1790's?

A. A Torah scroll must be examined carefully and regularly to make sure that every letter is perfect. In 1795, The Shearith Israel synagogue of New York issued an order that its chazan should regularly peruse the "Parza (reading of the week) in the Sefer Torah, which is to be read the succeeding Sabbath or Holiday: and that he be allowed 2/6 (ed. two shillings and six pence) for each error he may find and correct in the same..... and pay a fine himself of 5 shillings for any Error that may be discovered in the same when read in public, by any person." This duty fell to Gershom Seixas, the chazan of the synagogue and leader of New York Jewry from 1768–1815.

Although not deeply knowledgeable in rabbinic literature and not ordained as a rabbi, Seixas was intelligent and well read, and devoted to his synagogue duties, and he could deliver a sermon with all the length and dignity of the best of his Christian contemporaries. Constant fluctuations in Chazan Seixas' salary reflected the uncertain economy of the day. On one occasion, the congregation raised his salary from £200 a year to £50 a quarter, the quarter consisting of three lunar months. This gave the chazan a small raise, inasmuch as the twelve Hebrew lunar months add up to a few days shorter than a full 365 day solar year. The problem was this; on seven years of every nineteen, the Hebrew calendar adds a 13th month, making lunar leap years actually about two weeks longer than 365 days. The trustees asked Seixas if he expected to be paid for the additional month. He replied that under his contract, he had a right to expect the payment, but in consideration of the synagogue's financial difficulties, he would go back to the old salary of 200 per solar year.

Even so, the synagogue could not meet their salary obligations to Chazan Seixas, and in time they came to owe him a considerable sum. Once again the Chazan forgave his rightful claims. While never in poverty, Seixas also never did achieve any great measure of financial comfort.

For Further Reading:

David De Sola Pool, *Portraits Etched In Stone,* New York, Columbia University Press, 1952. pp. 356–359.

Q. Whence did George Washington take the oft quoted phrase, "to bigotry no sanction, to persecution no assistance," which he used in his famous Farewell Address?

A. George Washington was, besides his other achievements, an excellent speech writer. Alexander Hamilton wrote up the original draft of Washington's Farewell Address, but Hamilton's version was ponderous and it was Washington himself who revised it into one of the most notable speeches in American History.

Professor Richard Morris in his *Seven Who Shaped Our Destiny* points out that Washington did not hesitate to borrow a useful phrase. "To bigotry no sanction, to persecution no assistance" was first used in a letter from the Yeshuat Israel synagogue of Newport, Rhode Island congratulating Washington on assuming the office of President in 1789. Indeed, all six American synagogues wrote to congratulate the new president, and his reply to them expressed the importance of religious freedom in the newborn nation.

For Further Reading:

Richard Morris, *Seven Who Shaped Our Destiny*. New York; Harper and Row Publishers, 1973.

Q. Who was David Felt?

A. In the 1790's the new revolutionary government of France, audacious and radical, did not hesitate to send its diplomats to plot against foreign governments. The French ambassador, Citizen Genet, had caused great embarrassment for the U.S. government in a famous incident in 1793. In May of 1797, David Felt came to Quebec disguised as a Jewish merchant. Felt was actually David McLane, an American, who had been sent by M. Audet, the French ambassador to the U.S., to arouse the French population of Canada to rebel against the English and restore French rule. McLane was caught and put to death.

For Further Reading:

B.G. Sacks, History of the Jews in Canada, Montreal, 1965.

Q. What did Thomas Jefferson think about Jews?

A. The eighteenth century was not a time of great religious tolerance, and certainly Jews were not welcomed in most lands. American Jews can be deeply grateful to Thomas Jefferson as the great champion of religious freedom and of separation of church and state. Jefferson felt that the battle he led for full religious freedom in Virginia, in the 1780's, was perhaps the most bitter of his life. Personally, Jefferson believed in a benevolent Creator and Governor of the world, and in life after death. Jesus was, he thought, an important figure, although not divine, but his teachings had been corrupted by those who wrote about him. Letters written by Jefferson to Mordechai Noah in 1818, and to Jacob de Motta of Savannah in 1820, expressed his clear approval of Jews having full civil rights and criticized the history of persecution of Jews by Christians. Nevertheless, in a letter to Dr. Benjamin Rush on April 21, 1803, Jefferson described Jewish doctrines as "degrading and injurious. Their ethics were not only imperfect but often irreconcilable with the sound dictates of reason and morality." Where Greek and Hebrew philosophers dealt with human actions only, wrote Jefferson, Jesus looked into the heart of men. The Jews also either doubted or disbelieved, Jefferson thought, in "the doctrines of a future state which formed so efficacious a part of Jesus' teaching."

In 1813, Jefferson wrote to John Adams that to understand truly the thinking of ancient Israelites, not only the Hebrew Bible in its original, but later works like "their Mishna, their Gemara, Cabala, Jezirah, Sohar, Cosri, and their Talmud must be examined and understood in order to do them full justice." Nevertheless, it seemed to Jefferson that Judaism paid little attention to morals, and Jesus undertook to reform this lack.

In April 1816, Jefferson, again writing to Adams, spoke at length of David Levi's recent book defending Judaism in answer to Joseph Priestly. Levi's ideas are harsh, he said, but he has the advantage over his opponents by his far superior knowledge of Hebrew. Jefferson felt himself a pygmy among giants in these matters and hesitated to offer an opinion of his own. In fact, Jefferson, as he readily admitted, knew almost nothing of Jews or Jewish thought. He had little access to the centuries of Jewish interpretation of the Bible and, as biographer Dumas Malone pointed out in his *Jefferson the President*, (IV, p. 202) he did not realize the extent to which Jesus, whom he so admired, had drawn on the precepts of his own people.

For Further Reading:

Lester J. Cappon, *The Adams-Jefferson Letters* II, Chapel Hill, University of North Carolina Press, 1959 p. 381 and 468.

Joseph Blau and Salo Baron, *Jews of the United States*, Philadelphia, Jewish Publication Society, 1963.

Q. When did American Jews first act in the theater?

A. A Mr. and Mrs. Solomon performed professionally in Boston in the late eighteenth century. One of their plays was called *"Douglas and the Poor Soldier,"* 1792. William Dunlap's *History of the American Theatre*, published in 1832, lists plays by Isaac Harby, Samuel B. Judah, and Mordecai M. Noah, who wrote in the first three decades of the 19th century. The plays appear to have been melodramas, often meticulously patriotic, of a type common in that era. Often very successful at the time, they are hardly remembered today.

For Further Reading:

William Dunlap, History of the American Theater, 1832.

George Kohut, " A Literary Biography of Mordecai Manuel Noah," *PAJHS*, VI, 1897, 113–122.

Q. How did President John Adams and his family feel about Jews?

A. The famous Adams family produced two American presidents and several distinguished statesmen and scholars. Their attitude toward Jews changed over the generations from a clearly philo-Jewish view of John Adams (1735–1826) to the scurrilous Jew-baiting of his great grandson, historian Henry Adams (1838–1918). John Adams was not the type to express great affection for humanity in any form; however, he felt that the Jews had made the greatest contribution of any nation to civilization by teaching the doctrine of monotheism. "If I were an atheist, he wrote to a friend, and believed in blind eternal fate, I should still believe that fate had ordained the Jews to be the most essential instrument for civilizing the nations...I can't say that I love the Jews very much neither, nor the French, nor the English, nor the Romans, nor the Greeks. We must love all nations as much as we can, but it is very hard to love most of them." In 1808, Adams wrote a letter to a good friend, Dr. Adrian Van Der Kamp, in which he expressed his disapproval of the French philosopher Voltaire's hatred of Jews. "I have read this last fall half a dozen volumes of this wonderful Genius's Ribaldry against the Bible. How is it possible this old fellow should represent the Hebrews in such a contemptible light? They are the most glorious Nation that ever inhabited this earth. The Romans and their Empire were but a bauble in comparison of the Jews. They have given Religion to three quarters of the globe and have influenced the affairs of mankind more and more happily than any other nation ancient or modern."

His son, John Quincy Adams (1767–1848) was a brilliant statesman of high intellectual talents and great integrity. However, he was personally dour and strict and never gained a popular following, despite his gifts. Several remarks about Jews in his diaries and letters probably reflect more his personal harshness than any serious anti-Semitism. In 1780, he visited a Jewish community in Western Europe and attended a Friday night service. In his diary, he wrote, "An old man with a long beard read a chapter of the bible in Hebrew after which three of them sung. They seemed to be songs as I believe they were and not psalms. There was a vast congregation. The women have a place up above but no women can go to church without being married but the men can. They say there are a hundred Thousand Jews in this town, I am sure they are all wretched creatures for I think I never saw in my life such a set of miserable looking people, and they steal your eyes out of your head if they possibly could..." Another Jewish community he described as "A Nasty, Dirty, Place indeed, and fit only for Jews to live in."

John Quincy Adams long maintained an active interest in Christian missionary work among Jews and served as Vice-President of the American

Society for Meliorating the Condition of the Jews, at its founding in 1820. The Society's most active missionary was a Jew who had converted to Christianity, Joseph Samuel Christian Frederick Frey. In his diary entry for January 6, 1839, Adams bemoaned the fact that it seemed useless to send missionaries to Jews because "their hatred of Christians is rancorous beyond description." Still, he wrote a letter to Mordecai Manuel Noah expressing hope for a renewal of Jewish settlement in Israel. Another letter, to Joseph Hume, an English politician, says that experience in the United States bears testimony to the advantage of the admission of the Jews to full civil rights and declares that no set of men will be better citizens. It is perhaps ironic that almost a century after Quincy Adams' death, his house became, for a time, the home of a Jewish day school.

Henry Adams, a very distinguished historian, was the son of Charles Francis Adams and grandson of John Quincy Adams. Despite his sister Louisa's marriage to a Jew Charles Kuhn, Henry showed signs of anti-Semitism in both his public and private writing as early as the 1870's. After his wife's suicide in 1884, he poured forth torrents of Jew-hating invective, often in stereotypical resentment of supposed Jewish wealth and the seeming takeover of American business by Yiddish accented immigrants. He read anti Jewish books, and he was almost obsessed with his anger at Alfred Dreyfus. The Boer War between Great Britain and the South African Boers was, he argued, the fault of Jewish interests.

For Further Reading:

Page Smith, *John Adams*, Garden City: Doubleday and Co., 1962.
David Max Eichhorn, *Evangelizing the American Jew*, Garden City, NY.
John Quincy Adams, *Diary*, for August, 25, 1780.

Q. Who was the first Jew to serve as a state governor in the U.S. ?

A. In 1801, David Emanuel, became the sixth governor of Georgia, climaxing a distinguished career which included service as a soldier in the American Revolution (he was captured by the British and made a daring escape as he was being led before a firing squad). He served on the state Constitutional Conventions of 1789 and 1795, and was President of the Senate, 1801.

Emanuel married Ann Lewis, who according to family tradition was Jewish, but his children married Christians. One son-in-law was Benjamin Whitaker, Speaker of the Georgia House. Emanuel's sister married General John Twiggs, also of Revolutionary note. John Twiggs' son, David Emanuel Twiggs, was an American general in the Mexican War and a Confederate general in the Civil War. David Twiggs' daughter married Abraham C.

Myers (1811–1899), a Jewish West Point graduate and career soldier who served in 1862–1863 as the first quartermaster general of the Confederacy with the rank of lieutenant-colonel. His task of providing supplies for the Confederate armies was next to impossible, and yet he met with much criticism, perhaps partly due to his Jewishness. His removal in August, 1863 probably resulted from his wife's public gossiping about President Jefferson Davis's wife.

For Further Reading:

Leon Huhner, "The First Jew to Hold the Office of Governor," *PAJHS*, XVII. 1909, 187–195.
DAB, VII:1, 375–376 and X:1, 83.

Q. What patriot general of the American Revolution donated several Hebrew volumes to the Charleston synagogue?

A. Christopher Gadsden (1724–1805) was a member of the first Continental Congress, a general in the Revolutionary army, and one of South Carolina's most prominent legislators. In 1802, he donated a set of the Mishna and some works of Maimonides in Hebrew to the synagogue in Charleston. The reason for the donation is not clear although, as a liberal man of wide interests, Gadsden probably had Jewish connections. How and why Gadsden came to own these books is also unknown. However, he had studied classical languages as a young man in London and very likely had some knowledge of Hebrew. Perhaps he had bought Hebrew books during his student days and now, reaching his eighties and having no reason to pass them on to his family, he donated them to the synagogue. It seems that Nicholas Trott, the chief justice of South Carolina in those days, also knew Hebrew.

For Further Reading:

Charles P. Reznikoff & Uriah Englemann, *The Jews of Charleston*, Philadelphia; JPS, 1950.

1802–1850

German Jewish Immigration

MANY OF THE LEADING Jews of colonial America had been of Sephardic background, but by the early 19th century most Jewish immigrants were coming out of Central Europe, sometimes pushed by upheavals like the revolutions of 1848. Often they started peddling from a backpack along rural roads, and if their hard work paid off they would move on to peddle from a wagon and finally operate a store where some were indeed highly successful. The upper classes of Jewry, the wealthiest, the professionals, the best educated, were still largely of Sephardic origins, but the new immigrants were working their way up.

Although individual Jews could be found in many out of the way places, the main communities were still along the East Coast. New York replaced Charleston as the leading Jewish center. American Jewish communal life had always centered around the synagogue, and it still did. The synagogue itself was evolving, as the new Reform movement began to make strong inroads. The first rabbis, both Reform and Orthodox, settled in the U.S. in the 1840's. New organizations began to appear in the 1840's as American Jews felt a greater need to organize their reaction to national or international pressures, like the Damascus affair of 1840. The B'nai B'rith was formed in 1843.

Educating Jewish youth in their religion seemed an almost hopeless task. Sunday schools had opened, but were not effective. Day schools were opening in the 1840's, but there were no institutions for advanced Jewish learning. Colleges and universities seemed open to Jewish students, and Jews entered into a variety of professions, By the 1840's, Jews were holding high national office, and they continued to serve in the armed forces as they had since colonial times. Jews in small towns faced strong challenges to holding on to their Judaism, and it was especially difficult to find Jewish mates.

There has always been conflict between races in the United States, sometimes expressing itself in violence. However, anti-Semitism in this period was subdued and was not a major threat.

Q. What sort of synagogue did not exist in America until 1802?

A. Most of the early Jewish immigrants to the New World were of Sephardic origin. Some, indeed, came directly from Spain or Portugal to Spanish America where they lived as crypto-Jews, in constant fear of the Inquisition. Sephardim settling in North America were usually from England or the Netherlands. The first synagogues in North America followed the Sephardic style in prayer and in rituals. Larger numbers of Ashkenazic Jews began to arrive in the eighteenth century. If they joined a synagogue at all, it would have to be one of the already existing Sephardic congregations. Not until 1802 did German Jews form the first Ashkenazic synagogue, Rodeph Shalom, in Philadelphia. The Sephardic immigration remained small, while the German Jewish numbers increased so that most of the new synagogues after 1802 followed the Ashkenazic customs; for instance, Shaare Chesed in New Orleans, 1826, and Anshe Chesed in New York, 1828. There is some evidence that Ashkenazic Jews formed their own congregation in Charleston as early as 1786.

For Further Reading:

Barnett A. Elzas, *The Jews of South Carolina*, Philadelphia, 1905.

Q. Who were the first graduates of the U. S. Military Academy at West Point?

A. In 1802, two men, one of them Jewish, graduated out of the student body of twelve in the year old school. Joseph Gardner Swift (1783–1865) went on to become a brigadier general in the War of 1812. Simon Magruder Levy, was born in 1774 to Levy Andrew Levy and his wife Susannah in Lancaster, Pennsylvania. The family settled in Baltimore about 1799. Simon had served in the army since 1793 and had distinguished himself at the Battle of Maumee Rapids. After graduation, he was stationed in the south as an assistant engineer until his death in 1807.

For Further Reading:

Ira Rosenswaike, " Simon M. Levy: West Point Graduate," *AJHQ*. LXI, 1971, 69–73.

Q. Were there any Jewish Indian chiefs?

A. A number of works published in the first centuries of American history argued that the native Indians were descended from the ten lost tribes of Ancient Israel. Early explorers often claimed to have found Indians practicing Jewish customs. However, this all seems little more than a fantasy. Somewhat more likely is the idea that some Mexican or Southwestern Indians of today may number among their distant forebears converso Jews who fled from Spain or Portugal in the sixteenth century and settled among the Aztecs.

Edward Rose, a mulatto, supposedly Jewish, and former Mississippi River pirate, joined Captain Ezekiel Williams' expedition to the West, the first such venture after Lewis and Clark. West of Yellowstone, Rose deserted the expedition and joined up with the Crow Indians, who made him a chief after his heroics in a battle in which he killed and scalped five Blackfoot warriors.

In New Mexico in 1885, Solomon Bibo married the granddaughter of an Acoma Indian chief and was appointed pueblo governor, equivalent to a chief. The couple later moved to San Francisco so that they could raise their children as Jews.

For Further Reading:

I. Harold Sharfman, *Jews on the Frontier*, Chicago, Regency, 1977.
Kenneth Libo and Irving Howe, *We Lived There Too*. New York, St. Martin's, 1984.

Q. Who was the first native Hawaiian to study Hebrew?

A. Henry Obookiah left Hawaii on an American ship after a difficult childhood in which his parents had been killed in tribal wars. Arriving in New York in 1809, he lived for a while at the home of President Timothy Dwight of Yale College in New Haven, Conn. There he learned English and taught himself enough Hebrew to translate some passages from the Bible. He died of typhus in 1818.

For Further Reading:

Leon Nemoy, "Henry Obookiah," *PAJHS*. XXXIX, 1949, 190–192.

Q. Who was the last victim of the Spanish Inquisition in Mexico?

A. In 1788 Rafael Cristano Gil Rodriguez, a circumcised Franciscan monk, was convicted of practicing Jewish rites and aiding heretics. The evidence against him centered on his will, in which he requested a Jewish burial. Rodriguez was to be burned at the stake, but minutes before the event, he begged for mercy and promised to repent. He was imprisoned until 1821, when Mexico gained its freedom from Spain and permanently abolished its Inquisition. Spain abolished theirs in 1834.

For Further Reading:

Seymour Liebman, *The Jews in New Spain,* Coral Gable; University of Miami Press, 1970, p. 295-297.

Q. The War of 1812 was not very popular in the U.S. How did American Jews respond to the call to arms?

A. Although only a few thousand Jews lived in the U.S. in 1812, they seem to have been amply represented among the ranks of American fighting men. Major Abraham Massias, of New York, was a hero at the battle to defend Columbus Island, Georgia. Joseph Bloomfield may have reached the rank of brigadier general. Captain Mordecai Myers of Richmond, Virginia was wounded at the Battle of Chrysler's Farm and lived to serve as mayor of Schenectady, New York.

John Ordronneaux (1778- 1841) was captain of the Marengo, a French privateer, when the war broke out. Commanding American vessels over the next two years, he captured numerous English merchant ships. An excellent seaman, he escaped pursuit by British warships 17 times. In October, 1814, he captured the Endymion, a 40 gun frigate in a battle near Nantucket. When the British began to board him, Ordronneaux threatened to blow up his own ship if his men did not beat off the attackers. Ordronneaux eventually settled in South America. It was not until some years later that scholars found clear evidence of the captain's Jewish birth.

Several Jewish prisoners were held in the famous Dartmoor Prison in England, including Uriah Phillips Levy. Members of prominent families like Gratz of Philadelphia, Etting of Baltimore, and Seixas of New York joined local regiments. Midshipman Joseph Nones accompanied Senator Henry Clay as his secretary when Clay went to Ghent as part of the American delegation to negotiate the end of the war. A number of Maryland Jews were in Fort McHenry, Baltimore on September 13, 1814. It was on that night that Francis Scott Key, held prisoner on a British ship, witnessed the British bombardment of the fort and wrote "The Star Spangled Banner."

For Further Reading:

Leon Huhner, "Jews in the War of 1812," *PAJHS*, XXXI, 1918, 173-200.

Edwin S. Maclay, *History of American Privateers*, 1899.
Simon Wolf, *The American Jew as Patriot, Soldier, Citizen* , New York; Brenton, 1895.

Q. Who was removed from a U.S. foreign diplomatic post because he was Jewish?

A. In 1813, at age 28, Mordecai Manuel Noah was sent as U.S. consul to Tunis. In those days, Tunis was one of several North African states that enjoyed pirating merchant ships. Also, the U.S. was at war with Great Britain. Noah's post was not an easy one. In July, 1815, Admiral Stephen Decatur arrived at Tunis with the American fleet that had just forced the Bey of Algiers to pay off American monetary claims, to free American captives and to agree to a trade treaty favorable to the U.S. Decatur handed Noah a sealed dispatch from Secretary of State James Monroe . . .

"Sir,

"At the time of your appointment, as Consul at Tunis, it was not known that the RELIGION which you profess would form any obstacle to the exercise of your Consular functions. Recent information, however, on which entire reliance may be placed, proves that it would produce a very unfavourable effect. IN CONSEQUENCE OF WHICH, the President has deemed it expedient to revoke your commission. On the receipt of this letter, therefore, you will consider yourself no longer in the public service. There are some circumstances, too, connected with your accounts, which require a more particular explanation, which, with that already given, are not approved by the President.

I am, very respectfully, Sir, Your obedient servant,

(signed) JAMES MONROE, Mordecai M. Noah, esquire, &c. &c."

Noah was shocked both to see the reference to his Judaism and the suggestion of his dishonesty. He said nothing to Decatur for he depended on the fleet to cow the Bey of Tunis into paying the U.S. some money that he owed them for having allowed two British ships to take possession of two merchantmen captured by the American Albiellino. With this accomplished, Noah headed back to the U.S. Over the next few years he tried to learn exactly why he had been recalled. He never heard anything more in regard to the references to his Judaism. Secretary Monroe did accuse him of going beyond his orders and spending too loosely. After many months of aggravation, Noah received a half hearted letter of exoneration from the State Department plus $5,217 out of over $7,000 which Noah claimed for expenses.

For Further Reading:

Isaac Goldberg, *Major Noah: American Jewish Pioneer*, Philadelphia, JPS, 1936.

Q. What Jewish pirate became an American war hero?

A. It is possible that Andrew Jackson and the American army would have lost the Battle of New Orleans in 1815 had it not been for the help of Jean Lafitte and his pirates, who were courageous fighters and particularly adept artillerists. Lafitte's story has long been part of American historic lore. He established a small outlaw principality on the island of Barataria near New Orleans from where he made a huge fortune largely in smuggling and preying on Spanish shipping. During the War of 1812, the British approached Lafitte to help them take New Orleans, offering him a high salary and a huge bribe. However, Lafitte's sympathies were with the Americans, and he stalled the British while warning Governor Claiborne of Louisiana of the impending attack. Claiborne's answer was to send a fleet to sneak into Barataria and destroy it under a guise of friendship.

When the British army actually came to New Orleans, Claiborne released the pirate prisoners to Lafitte so that they could join Andrew Jackson in the battle. Lafitte and the pirates distinguished themselves over the next few weeks in the series of encounters that saved the city. One of the best of Jackson's cannoneers was a brother of Lafitte, Alexandre, who went by the name of Dominique Youx. The pirates earned high praise from Jackson and a pardon from President Madison. Lafitte later launched a damage suit against the government over his losses at Barataria, but with no result.

Most of this story forms a well known part of American history. Less well known is Lafitte's private life. Much new information was brought to light by historian Stanley Arthur in his 1952 book *Jean Lafitte: Gentleman Rover*. Arthur had access to previously unused family papers and to an unpublished autobiography of Jean Lafitte apparently written in his own hand.

Lafitte was born April 22, 1782 to a French Christian father and a Spanish Jewish mother, Maria Zora Nadrimal, whose father, Abhorud Nadrimal, alchemist of the city of Bilbao, Spain, had died in an Inquisition prison in Zaragoza. The young Lafitte was very close to his maternal grandmother of whom he wrote; "I owe all my ingenuity to the great intelligence of my Grandmother, who saw the times of the Inquisition." Born in France and raised on Santo Domingo, Lafitte married Christina Levine of St. Croix.

After the victory at New Orleans, Lafitte reestablished himself in a new pirate state on an island outside Galveston. There he was much involved in intrigues with Spain and Mexico. At the age of 50 he remarried, his first wife having died years before. There were children by both marriages. One son, Jules Jean, lived until 1924

A painting of Lafitte by an artist Gros (first name unknown) in 1804 shows a handsome man of straight military bearing.

For Further Reading:

I. Harold Sharfman, *Jews on the Frontier*, Chicago, Regnery, 1977.

Q. What unusual object did Joseph Merrick find while plowing his farm near Pittsfield, Massachusetts in 1815?

A. A long letter of November 10, 1815, written by Elkanah Watson to a friend, claimed that Merrick's plow turned up a Jewish phylactery (tefilin). Watson believed that the tefilin may have been left by Indians who continued to practice the religion of their ancestors, the exiled ten tribes of Israel. The leather boxes were worn with age, but the scrolls inside them were fresh. Others believed that they may have been relics of German Jews who had lived in the area a generation or two before.

For Further Reading:

Lee Friedman, 'The Phylacteries Found at Pittsfield, Massachusetts," *PAJHS*, XXV, 1917, 81–85.

Q. Who were the four Polish Jews whose portraits were painted by Washington Allston in 1817?

A. South Carolina born and Harvard educated, Washington Allston was one of a number of young American artists of the early 19th century who went to study in Europe. He spent some time in France and Italy where he was befriended and inspired by the poet Samuel Coleridge, but his main teacher was another American, artist Benjamin West, who was then living in London.

Greatly influenced by Rembrandt's paintings on biblical themes, Allston wrote in 1816 that he too "wanted to paint some splendid subject from the Scriptures uniting brilliant color and expression." Like Rembrandt, Allston's interest in the Bible seemed naturally to grow into an interest in the People of the Book. The four portraits of Jews were painted in 1817. We cannot identify the subjects by name, but they were apparently Eastern European Jews whom Allston had seen in London . Three are full bearded young men with wide-open dark eyes and deeply expressive faces. The fourth is an older man with a long whitening beard. All four give an impression of a benevolence which overlies a deep seriousness. All have their heads covered and are dressed in the traditional Eastern European Jewish garb.

The portrait of the old patriarch was renamed Isaac of York when it was exhibited in the Boston Athenaeum in 1833. Any connection with the character of that name in Walter Scott's Ivanhoe, published in 1819, is uncertain. The portraits hang today in the Corcoran Gallery in Washington D.C., the Museum of Fine Arts in Boston, and in the Hirsch and Adler Galleries in New York.

For Further Reading:

William H. Gerdts and Theodore E. Stobbins, Jr., *A Man of Genius: The Art of Washington Allston* 1779-1843, Boston 1979.
James T. Flexner, *Nineteenth Century American Painting*, New York, G.P. Putnam, 1970.

Q. Have there been white Jewish slaves in the United States?

A. At one time Europeans would sell themselves as indentured servants for a term of years to an American who would pay the cost of their passage across the Atlantic. In 1819, Wolf Samuel, a young Jewish man from Germany, came to Philadelphia as an indentured servant to the ship's captain, and his contract was sold to Stephen Boyd, a non-Jew, for 190 guilders. Samuel was to serve Boyd for three years and two months. However, Boyd treated him roughly and failed to provide him with proper food and clothing so that Samuel took sick and fled his master after 15 months. There is no further record of Samuel, and it is probable that he went to the frontier to start a new life for himself under an assumed name.

For Further Reading:

Marcus, *USJ*, I, 129-130.

Q. Did Sir Walter Scott model the character Rebecca in his novel *Ivanhoe* after Rebecca Gratz?

A. There is an often told story that Washington Irving, famed author of "Rip Van Winkle," once visited Sir Walter Scott in his Abbotsford, Scotland home and sang to him the praises of Rebecca Gratz, a beautiful, cultured and very pious Jewess of Philadelphia. Sir Walter was so enthralled that he modeled the character Rebecca in his new novel *Ivanhoe* after her. Today we lack contemporary evidence to either prove or disprove this tale. In any case, both *Ivanhoe*'s fictional Rebecca and the true Miss Gratz were most admirable figures, deeply compassionate, intelligent, pious, and beautiful.

A second popular story about Rebecca Gratz is almost certainly true. Although much in love with Samuel Ewing, a Christian, she would not marry him because of the difference in religions, and she remained unmarried all her years, 1781–1860. One unlikely but oft repeated version of the story holds that the Christian was Washington Irving himself. Rebecca Gratz led a very useful life, raising 9 children of a sister who died young and busying herself, like Scott's character, with many benevolent and educational works.

For Further Reading:

Edward Wagenknecht, *Daughters of the Covenant*, Amherst; University of Massachusetts Press. 1983.

Q. "Well... Thou art no different from other people." Who made this unusual remark to a Jewish pioneer?

A. In 1817, Joseph Jonas settled in Cincinnati, a bustling new western town, and as the city's first Jew he was something of a curio. One Quaker woman travelled many miles from her farm to look at this member of the chosen people. "Art thou truly a Jew?" she asked. Jonas nodded. The woman looked him up and down and finally said, "Well. Thou art no different from other people."

The world traveler, I.J. Benjamin, who visited Cincinnati in 1860, met Joseph Jonas and relates a slightly different version of the story - - Jonas opened a watch repair shop upon his arrival in Cincinnati. A farmer brought Jonas a watch to repair and, happening to come to town the next Saturday, stopped by the shop to pick up his watch. Finding the shop closed, he feared that Jonas had gone bankrupt and run away, taking the watch with him. But he was comforted when neighbors told him that Jonas, as a pious Jew, did not work on his Sabbath.

Returning home, the farmer told the story to his mother, who was greatly curious to see a member of that nation of whom she had read so much in the Bible. She went with her son when he returned to the watch maker. "Are you really and truly a Jew, a descendant of Abraham?" she asked him. When he answered that he was, she lifted her eyes to heaven and said, "How can I thank thee, O Lord, that I have lived to see one of the descendants of Abraham before my death."

A similar experience is recounted by Rabbi Bernard Drachman out of his visit with a Jewish farm family in a rustic area of Connecticut about 1900. An aged Yankee couple drove up in a buggy and said, "We have heard that there is a Jewish child here. Would you mind showing it to us?" Rabbi Drachman pointed to the farmer's daughter playing on the porch. The couple stared at her with a puzzled expression. Then the man turned to his wife and said "Jee whillekens, Jerushah, she looks like any other kid." Like many rural Americans before the age of television, they had apparently no idea of what the big wide world looked like.

For Further Reading:

I.J . Benjamin, *Three Years in America*, (Trans. Charles Resnikoff), Philadelphia, JPS, 1956, p. 308–309.
David Philipson, "The Jewish Pioneers of the Ohio Valley," *PAJHS*, VIII, 1900, p 43–57.
Bernard Drachman, *The Unfailing Light*, New York, Rabbinical Council of America, 1946.

Q. What great opera librettist of Jewish background later failed as a shopkeeper in Sunbury, Pennsylvania?

A. The imperial Habsburg court in Vienna of the 1780's was very excited about music, and well it ought to have been for this was the heyday of the great Mozart himself, among others. Emperor Joseph II took a strong personal interest in music, employing an official court musician, Antonio Salieri, and supporting all sorts of composition and production. The appointment of Lorenzo da Ponte, 1749–1838, as poet to the Italian Theater indicated a slight liberalizing mood in the Habsburg court, as da Ponte was born a Jew, Emanuele Conegliano, in the ghetto of Ceneda near Venice. Joseph II's predecessor, the Empress Maria Theresa, had been harshly anti Jewish.

An outstanding poet, da Ponte wrote librettos for many works in the 1780's including Mozart's three great operas, *The Marriage of Figaro, Don Giovanni* and *Cosi fan Tutte*. Always harassed by court intrigues, da Ponte left Vienna in 1792, and ten years later, moved to the United States where he failed as a storekeeper both in New York and in Sunbury, Pennsylvania. Back in New York in the 1820's, da Ponte began a new career as a teacher of Italian literature. He played a very important role in the introduction of Italian culture to his newly adopted country. Although born Jewish, da Ponte makes no reference to his Jewish origins in his several autobiographical writings. After he converted to Catholicism at age 14, along with his father and two brothers, Baruch and Anania, he went through religious schooling and was later often referred to as abbe. Nevertheless, he married an English woman, Ann Grahl, who was also apparently born Jewish and converted to Christianity.

A complex and brilliant man, abbe, poet, womanizer, teacher, da Ponte was perhaps, as his biographer Sheila Hodges writes, "influenced by his

Jewish heritage to a far greater extent than he himself realized, or than he wished others to believe."

For Further Reading:

Lorenzo da Ponte. *Memoirs*, (transl. Elizabeth Wyckoff), New York, Orion Press, 1959.
Sheila Hodges, *Lorenzo da Ponte: The Life and Times of Mozart's Librettist*. London, Granada, 1985.

Q. How much money did John Howard Payne earn for writing his famous Song, "Home Sweet Home?"

A. Born of a Jewish mother and a non-Jewish father, John Howard Payne (1792–1851) wrote "Home Sweet Home" in 1823 as part of his opera, "Clari". The song was a phenomenal success. However, because there were as yet no copyright laws for music, Payne had little monetary benefit from his work, and he spent most of his adult life in poverty. He was serving as a U.S. consul to Tunis at the time of his death. In 1873, a statue of Payne was erected in New York's Prospect Park.

For Further Reading:

Kenneth A. Kanter, *The Jews on Tin Pan Alley*, New York; Ktav Publ.. 1982, p.3–4.

Q. Where did Reform Judaism begin in the U.S.?

A. The first effort at organized synagogue reform in the U.S. came in Charleston, South Carolina in 1824. The new American nation had been greatly influenced by the humanitarian thinking of its founders like Jefferson, Madison, and Franklin and by the sense of freedom fostered in its seemingly endless opportunities for movement and growth. Americans, although respectful to their churches, were not typically doctrinaire pietists. Most indeed did not even belong to an organized church, and many leaned toward Unitarianism and Deism.

While there was anti-Semitism, to be sure, Jews were largely accepted into the general society. They worked hard, held public office, and mixed into their Christian surroundings. Many kept up only a nominal loyalty to their faith, while devoting themselves to life in a Christian world in which they could be accepted even at the highest levels. Some Jews married into very distinguished Christian families. Phila Franks married a New York Delancey, and relatives of John Adams and Henry Clay took Jewish mates.

Reform Judaism, first forming at the end of the 18th century in Germany, was beginning to make itself felt in the New World. By 1824 the Jewish community of Charleston included a number of young worldly intellectuals, well educated in the liberal philosophies of their day — Jacob Cardozo, Philip Phillips, Henry M. Hyams and others. They felt uncomfortable with the traditional style of prayer with its Old World sounds and customs. In November, 1824, 47 people petitioned the leadership of the established synagogue for some major changes. The request was rejected, and the reformers organized the *Reformed Society of Israelites for Promoting True Principles of Judaism According to Its Purity,* in which Isaac Harby's name was to become the most prominent.

Holding services in rented quarters, the Society members prayed bareheaded, mostly in English and accompanied by an organ. They rejected belief in a personal Messiah, a return to Zion, and a rebuilding of the Jerusalem Temple, and in effect, sought to replace traditional Judaism with a modern Enlightened approach. Although this particular effort toward Reform was short lived, it had made its point, and by the late 1830's even the Orthodox establishment in Charleston was leaning toward Reform. Professor Robert Liberles has argued that the Charleston Reformers may have been influenced less by European Reform Judaism than by fears of anti-semitism and by a liberalizing process in American Protestant churches in that period.

For Further Reading:

Robert Liberles. "Conflict Over Reforms: The Case of Congregation Beth Elohim in Charleston, South Carolina," in Jack Wertheimer, ed., *The American Synagogue,* Cambridge, Cambridge University Press, 1987, 274- 296.
Marcus, *USJ* 614–637

Q. How did Maryland Jews gain the right to hold state offices?

A. The Maryland constitution of 1776 specified that no office of public trust should be held by anyone who will not make "a declaration of belief in the Christian religion" (article 35). This continued the practice enjoined in the old colonial charter first issued in 1632 at a time when no Jews lived openly in England or in Maryland. One could be put to death for denying the Holy Trinity according to the Toleration Act of 1649. The Act was modified in 1723 to reduce the punishment to branding.

Jews began to settle in Baltimore by the 1770's and although the old punishments were never carried out, the constitution of 1776 remained in force in the early nineteenth century. Then in 1818, Thomas Kennedy, representing Washington County in the Maryland legislature, began a fight for bringing equal rights to the Jews. Based on the report of Kennedy's committee, Delegate William Pinkney drafted a bill ending the use of any religious test as qualification for public office, the so called "Jew Bill" (or sometimes "Kennedy's Jew Baby"). On January 13, 1819 the bill was defeated 50–24 in the legislature. It was not until January 5, 1826 after years of disappointment that the bill finally was passed and confirmed by a vote of 45–32. The final bill did not single out the Jews for equal rights but included all citizens. A few months later, two Jews, Solomon Etting and Jacob Cohen, were elected to public office.

For Further Reading:

Isaac M. Fein, *The Making of an American Jewish Community*, Philadelphia; JPS, 1971.

Q. Which American Jewish naval officer was offered a command in the Brazilian navy?

A. In 1825, Uriah Phillips Levy was aboard the American ship, Cyane, harboring at Rio, when news was brought that a Brazilian press gang was carrying off an American seaman and that an American officer trying to save him was also under attack. Levy, with some others, rushed to the scene and rescued both men. Shortly after this fracas, Emperor Pedro I visited the American fleet and, praising Levy for his zeal and bravery, offered him command of a 60 gun Brazilian frigate. Levy, an excellent officer, had been under constant harassment by Navy brass and by fellow officers, usually touched off by anti-Semitism. He would go through his fifth court-martial soon afterward. Nevertheless, he turned down the opportunity saying that he would rather be a cabin boy in the American service than a captain anywhere else.

Only in his last years did Levy find some peace, finally attaining command of the Mediterranean fleet. From his last cruise he brought a load of soil from Eretz Israel as a gift to the Jews of New York.

For Further Reading:

Donovan Fitzpatrick, *Navy Maverick: Uriah Phillips Levy*, Garden City, NY, Doubleday, 1963.

Q. What was the first national Jewish flag seen in the U.S.?

A. On September 15, 1825, Manuel Mordecai Noah, arrayed in resplendent black and ermine, led a magnificent procession through the streets of Buffalo, New York. At the local Episcopal church, Noah and the Reverend Mr. Addison Searle ceremoniously dedicated the cornerstone of Ararat, a new colony on Grand Island near Niagara Falls, which was to serve as a city of refuge for Jews until the time of the messianic return to the land of Israel. The marchers carried a Jewish flag of which, unfortunately, contemporary sources leave no description. The project was strongly criticized, however, by the very same Western European rabbis whose support Noah had most expected, and Ararat failed before it began.

The idea of an Ararat sounds, perhaps, more strange to the twenty first century mind than it did in 1825. At that time, religious settlements were being tried by other groups for example, the Mormons, the Oneida community in New York, or Brook Farm. It was indeed not far removed from the spirit of the Puritan fathers of the 1620's who built a new settlement in the wilderness of New England. Noah later became a strong advocate of Jewish return to Zion, and he wrote glowingly of his hopes for the coming of the Messiah. Noah had worked for some years on the Ararat project, writing editorials in the *New York National Advocate,* of which he was editor. He had petitioned the New York legislature for ownership of Grand Island in 1820, but failing in that try, he bought up a large part of it himself. Local residents were apparently pleased at the prospects of increased business from Jewish settlers, merchants and tradesmen. The cornerstone of Ararat is now in possession of the Buffalo Historical Society.

For Further Reading:

Selig Adler and Thomas Connolly, *From Ararat to Suburbia,* Philadelphia, JPS, 1960.
Bernard Weinryb, "Noah's Ararat Jewish State in its Historical Setting, "*PAJHS,* XLIII, 1953, 3-4 and 170-191.

    Isaac Goldberg, *Major Noah: American Jewish Pioneer,* Philadelphia, JPS, 1936.

    Robert Gordis, "Mordecai Manuel Noah," *PAJHS,* XLI, 1951, 1-26.

Q. What scientific work did Joseph Nones accomplish?

A. Joseph B. Nones, son of Revolutionary War hero Benjamin Nones, served in the Navy under Admiral Stephen Decatur and again in the Mexican War. His autobiography is as yet unpublished.

Longer sea voyages and huge armies that typified the Napoleonic Wars made the preservation of food a matter of increasing importance in the early 19th century. Canning was introduced about 1810. A letter of Nones to the U.S. Secretary of the Navy, September 1829, offers the Navy first rights to his new discovery, "Nones Life Preservative and Antiseptic-Nutritive Compound," a plan for a concentrated food mixture which would last indefinitely without spoiling. Apparently, nothing came of Nones' work, and the credit for the discovery of concentrated food is usually given to Germans Justus Von Leibig and Max Von Pettenkofer several decades later.

For Further Reading:

Abraham Kanoff and David Markowitz, "Joseph B. Nones: The Affable Midshipman," *PAJHS*, XLVI, 1956, 1-19.

Q. Who funded the founding of Mercer College?

A. Abraham Simons, a Jew of Washington, Georgia, and a Revolutionary War veteran, left his Christian wife, Nancy Mills, a large fortune when he died in 1824. Three years later, Nancy married Reverend Jesse Mercer (1769-1841) the state's leading Baptist clergyman, who helped found Mercer University, a Baptist college, in Macon, Georgia in 1837. Mercer University grew out of a smaller school begun several years earlier and it emphasized agricultural work as well as theological and Classical studies. Much of the early financing of the school came from the original fortune left by Abraham Simons.

For Further Reading:

Leon Huhner, "Captain Abraham Simons of the Georgia Line in the Revolution," *PAJHS*, XXXIII, 1934, 231-236.

Q. Who was the first Jewish professor of medicine in the U.S.?

A. It was probably Daniel L.M. Peixotto (1800-1843) who served as professor of medicine and also as president of Willoughby College, Ohio for several years beginning in 1836. Born in Amsterdam, Peixotto came to New York in 1807 and graduated Columbia College Medical School in 1819. Deeply devoted to his work, Peixotto wrote for medical journals, receiving an award for a study of whooping cough, and he took on many public medical duties beyond his private practice.

A well read and believing Jew, Peixotto was particularly interested in Jewish education. His father Moses Levi Madura Peixotto had led the Shearith Israel Congregation in New York after the passing of Reverend Gershom Seixas in 1816. Refusing to accept payment for his services, he instead gave over his salary to Rev. Seixas' widow.

For Further Reading:

Daniel Peixotto Hays, "Daniel L.M. Peixotto, M.D.," *PAJHS*, XXVI, 1918, 219—230.

Q. After whom did Charles Dickens model Fagin, the Jewish criminal in *Oliver Twist*?

A. Some scholars hold that the model for Fagin was Ikey Solomon, a fraud specialist who escaped from jail in England and came to the U.S. in 1827. Hearing that his wife had been sent as a criminal to Tasmania, Ikey went to join her but was captured and incarcerated in a penal colony in Australia.

For Further Reading:
Marcus, *USJ*, II, 11.

Q. What types of Jewish characters played important roles in early American novels?

A. Henry Ruffner, president of Washington College in Lexington, Virginia wrote two saccharin novels, *Judith,* in 1827, and *Seclusaval*, in 1839 both about a romance between a beautiful English Jewess and an American who meet while traveling. The characters are stylized, and the literary quality is not distinguished. The book presents another in the line of stereotypes of Jews of which Shylock in Shakespeare's Merchant of Venice is probably the best known. The Jews are measured largely in terms of the sort of relationship that they have with Christians. Ruffner had little sense of issues or themes that might have aroused the interest of a Jewish reader. Indeed, there were only a few hundred Jews in Virginia in Ruffner's day. Although attaining some popularity at the time, the two novels are today deservedly forgotten.

For Further Reading:
Curtis C. Davis, "Judith Ben Saddi and the Rev. Dr. Henry Ruffner," *PAJHS*, XXXIX, 1949, 115–142.

Q. Which American synagogue first used gas lighting?

A. New York's Shearith Israel Synagogue replaced the old fashioned candle light with gas lights when it moved from Mill Street to Crosby Street in 1834. Gas lighting had first appeared on the streets of New York City in 1825. The sanctuary featured a large central chandelier with 12 burners and smaller chandeliers of 6 burners in each of the 4 corners. Manufactured in New York, the chandeliers were considered truly elegant by the standards of the time. Five windows added to the illumination in the daytime. The increased use of gas lighting was one of the early signs of a snowballing change toward a brave new world of technology. Changing neighborhoods and the departure of Jews from the Crosby Street neighborhood led to the sale of the building in 1859.

For Further Reading:

David and Tamar De Sola Pool. *An Old Faith in a New World*, New York: Columbia University Press, 1955, p. 537.

Q. Who was the first important Jewish scholar out of the Enlightenment school to come to the U.S.?

A. The early 19th century in Central and Eastern Europe saw the beginning of a new scientific secular study of Judaism under the impetus of scholars like Leopold Zunz, Abraham Geiger, Heinrich Graetz and others. The first of this school to reach the U.S. was Isaac Nordheimer (1809–1842) in 1835. Nordheimer held a Ph.D. from the University of Munich and had studied in the Yeshiva of Pressburg. A student of both ancient and modern languages, Nordheimer soon published two scholarly works on the Hebrew language and several articles on rabbinic literature in the "American Biblical Repository." Most of his students at New York University, where he took a position, were Protestant clergy. He also taught at the Union Theological Seminary.

For Further Reading: Marcus, *USJ*, II.

Joseph Blau and Salo Baron, *The Jews of the United States*, 1790–1840, New York, Columbia University Press, 1963, 419–436.
JE, IX, 333.
DAB VII, 547–548.

Q. Were any Jews with Davy Crockett and Jim Bowie at the Alamo?

A. A number of Jews were among the Texan settlers that rose against the repressive rule of Mexican President Antonio Lopez de Santa Anna in 1835. English born Antony (Avrum) Wolfe of Nagadoches was with the illustrious company of about 183 frontiersmen that died fighting to the last man at the Alamo in March, 1836. One or two young sons of Antony Wolfe were also killed. Another Alamo defender, Galba Fuqua of Alabama, may also have been Jewish.

A Jew, Colonel Edward Isaac Johnson, was killed when Santa Anna massacred 300 Texans of Colonel James Fannin's company after they surrendered at Goliad three weeks later. Three other Jews in Fannin's command escaped the slaughter.

Surgeon Moses Levy, of Virginia, had led a company of 66 Americans to Texas. In a letter home, Levy credits himself, along with Colonel Ben Milam of Kentucky, with organizing the assault which first captured the Alamo in December, 1835 after it seemed that the Texan force must disband for want of both equipment and spirit. Fewer than 300 Texans took San Antonio and the Alamo from 1400 Mexicans under General Cos in five days of house to house fighting. Levy tended the wounded and fought too. He was later captured, but escaped after several months in Mexican prisons.

After the war, Levy opened a popular medical practice in Matagorda, Texas. However, depressed over the estrangement from his family in Virginia, he committed suicide in 1848. In 1986, a historical marker was placed over his grave in Matagorda.

French born Louis Moses Rose, a 51 year old veteran of Napoleon's army and probably Jewish, was also in the Alamo. Refusing to cross Colonel Travis' famous line, he fled the Alamo three days before it fell, eluded the Mexican besiegers and escaped to live another 15 years.

For Further Reading:

Harold Sharfman, *Jews on the Frontier,* Chicago, H. Regnery, 1987.
Daniel Leeson, "In Search of the History of the Texas Patriot, Moses A. Levy," *WSJH,* XXI, 1989, 291–306.
Saul Viener, "Surgeon Moses Albert Levy: Letters of a Texas Patriot," *PAJHS,* XLVI, 1956, 101–113.
Natalie Ornish, *Pioneer Jewish Texans,* Dallas, Texas Heritage Press, 1989.

Q. Why did Uriah Phillips Levy buy Monticello?

A. A career naval officer, Uriah Phillips Levy rose to the rank of commodore in the U.S. Navy in 1860, climaxing a long and controversial career. He is credited with helping to bring an end to the use of flogging as a punishment for sailors. In 1836, 10 years after Thomas Jefferson's death, Levy bought Monticello, Jefferson's beautiful home at Charlottesville, Virginia. Levy claimed that Andrew Jackson, a great admirer of Jefferson, had persuaded him to buy it. An enemy of Levy claimed that he purchased it to block a friend of the Jefferson family. Most likely, Levy had bought Monticello simply out of his own admiration for Jefferson. He maintained it well and left it in his will to the "people of the United States." However, first because of the Civil War and afterward due to endless legal and personal complexities, the U.S. government did not take possession of Monticello until 1924 after the death of Uriah's nephew, Congressman Jefferson Monroe Levy.

For Further Reading:

Charles Hosmer, "The Levys and the Restoration of Monticello," *AJH,* LIII, 1964, 219–252.

Q. Did President John Adams have a Jewish relative?

A. Alexander Bryan Johnson (1786–1867) was descended from learned Jews on both sides. Born in England, he came to Utica, New York with his family in 1801. While earning a livelihood as a banker, he wrote books on religion, philosophy, finance , politics, language and, finally, an autobiography. His works were, in many ways, ahead of his time and drew high praise from thinkers of later generations, including Albert Einstein, Aldous Huxley, and linguist S.I. Hayakawa. Johnson married Abigail Smith, a granddaughter of President John Adams, and he corresponded regularly with his new grandfather as well as with Uncle John Quincy Adams and other leading Americans. He kept his Jewishness hidden and was active in Protestant churches, although he continued to exchange letters with his Jewish relatives in Europe.

For Further Reading:

Charles Todd and Robert Sonkin, *Alexander Bryan Johnson: Philosophical Banker,* Syracuse, Syracuse University Press, 1977.

Q. How was the first minyan (prayer quorum) in St. Louis organized and maintained?

A. According to Isidor Bush, writing in the *Jewish Tribune* in St. Louis in 1883, several recent arrivals from the east organized a minyan for the High Holy Days in 1836 in St. Louis in a rented room at "Max's Grocery and Restaurant" on Second and Spruce Streets. Finding the quorum of 10 men for prayers was always a struggle. Once, they could only find 9 so they called in an Irishman with a biblical name to fill the quorum. Ever afterward, the Irishman punctually attended the Jewish services on holidays.

Fm Further Reading:

"Trail Blazers of the Trans-Mississippi West," *AJA,* VIII, 1956, 61–62

Q. When did Jews first settle in the Williamsburg area of Brooklyn?

A. The first known Jewish settler in Brooklyn was Adolph Baker, who settled in the Williamsburg area in 1837, when it was a mere village of about 300 homes and a few stores. By 1846, there were 9 Jewish men, and they would bring one more across the river every Friday to make a quorum (minyan) of 10 for the Sabbath prayers. The first Brooklyn congregation was established in Williamsburg in 1851.

Williamsburg Jewry took on its strongly Hasidic character only with the arrival of European refugees after World War II. Statistically, the Jewish population declined from 140,000 in 1923 to 33,400 in 1957 as older Jewish residents were moving out even as the Hassidim moved in.

For Further Reading:

UJE, II, 546–548.

Q. What was the first Jewish farm settlement in the U.S.?

A. In 1838 a group of New York Jews, many of whom were members of the Anshe Chesed synagogue, bought land in Ulster County, New York. There they formed a village called Sholem near Montela, but the village seems to have petered out by about 1841. Almost no record remains.

For Further Reading:

Hyman Grinstein, *The Jewish Community of New York. 1654–1860*, Philadelphia, JPS, 1945, 119–123.

Q. Did American Jews fight in duels?

A. What is probably history's most famous duel involved a Jew - David vs. Goliath. In early America, duels were commonly fought over an insulting word or act. Vice President of the USA Aaron Burr killed the brilliant Alexander Hamilton. Future President Andrew Jackson battled Nolichucky Jack Sevier, a noted frontier leader. Duels were a sport of gentlemen and were fought only between social equals. Thus, ironically, the fact that Jews became involved in duels indicates that they blended well into early American society.

In 1836, Leon Dyer, while an officer of the Republic of Texas, fought with a man who insulted his religion. Uriah P. Levy, a proud naval officer, fought several times. August Belmont, the noted financier, politician and horse breeder (Belmont Stakes) was wounded by a William Hayward in Elkton, Indiana in 1841. Judah P. Benjamin challenged Jefferson Davis to a duel because of a public insult, but Davis apologized, and the two became fast friends. On a few occasions, both gentlemen were Jews. In Charleston, ca. 1812, Mordecai Noah wounded a "puppy" named John Canter who had challenged him. In 1834, a Mr. Moise killed a Mr. Cohen in a duel at a race track. Benedict Schwartz slew Moses Feinberg in a duel in San Antonio in 1857. By the post Civil War era, dueling had become outmoded among both Jews and Gentiles.

For Further Reading:

Harold Sharfman, *Jews on the Frontier,* Chicago, H. Regnery, 1977.

Q. Did philanthropist Judah Touro build the Touro synagogue of Newport, Rhode Island, now an official national landmark?

A. A wealthy Jewish New Orleans businessman, Judah Touro (1775- 1854), was well known most of his life for his benevolence to churches, contributing generously to Christ Church, St. Louis Cathedral, the First Baptist Church, and perhaps others in New Orleans. One of Touro's best known gifts was $10,000 which paid half the cost of the Bunker Hill Monument in Boston in 1839.

As a young man, Judah Touro was seriously wounded and left to die on the field at the Battle of New Orleans, 1815. He was saved by a non-Jewish friend, Rezin Shepherd, an ancestor of later Massachusetts Senator Leverett Saltonstal (1892–1979).

Later in life, for reasons unknown, Touro began to show an interest in Jewish philanthropy also, helping to support the building of New Orleans' second synagogue, the Dispersed of Judah, in 1850. By about 1851, Touro seems to have gone through some internal change, for he returned to Judaism in a most determined manner and attended services regularly. In his will, he left large sums for Jewish institutions including $48,000 for The Dispersed of Judah; $5,000 for Shanarei Chessed, another New Orleans synagogue; $40,000 for a Jewish Hospital; $6,000 for Jews in Palestine; $143,000 for a variety of Jewish organizations in the U.S., and a small sum to help the Jewish community of China. $50,000 was left to be distributed by the great English Jew, Sir Moses Montefiore, most of which went to build the first Jewish neighborhood outside of the Old City of Jerusalem, Mazkeret Moshe (or Yemin Moshe) named after Sir Moses. The will contained over 60 bequests, most of them to charities.

The Touro Synagogue of Newport was dedicated many years earlier in 1763 under the name Jeshuat Israel. The name Touro Synagogue came into use late in the nineteenth century. Isaac Touro, Judah's father came from Amsterdam to be its first chazan. The original Jewish community of Newport had petered out by the end of the 18th century.

For Further Reading:

Leon Huhner, *The Life of Judah Touro (1775-1854)*, Philadelphia, JPS, 1946.

Q. Which two American legislatures were led by Jewish Speakers about 1840?

A. David S. Kaufman (1813-51) settled in Nacogdoches, Texas in 1837 and was elected to the Congress of the Texas Republic, where he was named Speaker of the House. When Texas joined to the United States, Kaufman became its first congressman, and he chaired the House Rules Committee. Kaufman County, a cotton and livestock producing area near Dallas, is named for him. A highly educated Princeton graduate, Kaufman was a lawyer by profession and also an accomplished Classicist.

Samuel Judah (1798-1869), scion of a distinguished colonial Jewish family and also an accomplished scholar, attended Rutgers University and was admitted to the bar. In 1818 he moved to Indiana, which was still largely a frontier area. Elected to the state legislature in 1827, he held various public offices over the next years. including speaker of the legislature in 1840.

Judah was well known as a very able lawyer. In his most famous case he represented Vincennes University in a suit to recover certain lands that had been taken over by the State of Indiana. After years of litigation the case went all the way to the U.S. Supreme Court which upheld the university's claim. Judah's retainer for fees and expenses was $26,728.23. The University trustees challenged Judah's bill but the courts sustained him. (Litigation over the property continued until 1909 when the courts ordered the state to pay another large sum to Vincennes University). The case had major political ramifications and became a bone of constant contention between Judah and a bitter personal foe, Indiana Senator John Ewing.

For Further Reading:

Walter Prescott Webb, ed., *The Handbook of Texas*, Austin;The Texas State Historical Association, 1952. I, p. 939. Suppl. Vol. III 465-466.
A Biographical Directory of the Indiana General Assembly, Indianapolis; 1980, p. 213.
Justin Walsh, *The Centennial History of the Indiana General Assembly. 1316-1978*, Indianapolis: 1987, p 127f. *DAB*, V, 2, 227.

Q. What was American Jewry's first major intervention on behalf of beleaguered Jews overseas?

A. In 1840, the disappearance of Father Thomas, a monk in Damascus, Syria, led to the arrest and torture of 13 Jewish residents of that city on a charge of ritual murder. American Jews reacted slowly. A group led by J.B. Kursheedt, meeting in New York, called upon President Van Buren to intervene. Similar meetings were held in Philadelphia and Richmond. The President and Secretary of State John Forsyth ordered American officials in the Turkish Empire to protest the atrocity. Intervention by Sir Moses Montefiore of England and Adolphe Cremieux of France had resolved the matter probably even before the American message arrived. However, the American Jews' reaction to the so-called Damascus libel set a precedent for increased organized interest in the welfare of Jews in other lands.

For Further Reading:

Joseph Jacobs, "The Damascus Affair of 1840," *PAJHS*. X. 1902, 119–128.

Q. Who began the *American Journal of Mathematics*?

A. J.J. Sylvester was denied a degree by Cambridge University in England because he was Jewish, but he was able to find a position at the University of Virginia in 1841 as a professor of mathematics. He fled the university and returned to England a short time later, after stabbing a student with a sword cane during an argument. Sylvester thought he had killed the man, but he was in fact only slightly wounded. In 1876, the new graduate school of Johns Hopkins University in Baltimore hired Sylvester to its faculty, and two years later he founded the *American Journal of Mathematics*.

It was several decades into the twentieth century before Jews were able to compete for university professorships without facing excessive religious discrimination. This even as Jewish students were attending universities in increasing numbers.

For Further Reading:

Lewis S. Feuer, "The Stages in the Social History of Jewish Professors in American Colleges and Universities," *AJH*, LXXXI, 1982, 432–465.

Q. Who wrote the first Hebrew-Sioux language dictionary?

A. A dictionary of the Hebrew and Sioux, or Dakota Indian, languages was compiled in 1842 by Samuel W. Pond. A hard working Christian of old New England Puritan stock, Pond had little formal schooling; however, he had a phenomenal gift for languages. Had a nineteenth century Jewish traveler through the Badlands of South Dakota chanced upon a Sioux synagogue, he might have been honored by being called to read from the *wokicuze* (Torah). And if he had come late to services that would have been *wowantant* (sinful). Pond 's manuscript was never published, and the original rests today among the treasures of the Minnesota Historical Society.

For Further Reading:

W. Gunther Plaut, "A Hebrew-Dakota Dictionary," *PAJHS*, XLII, 1953, 361- 370.

Q. How did the B'nai B'rith begin?

A. Twelve people met at Sinsheimer's Cafe on Essex Street in New York City, October 13, 1843, to form a Jewish Society. According to the minutes of the first meeting (they were written in German) the society's purpose was to help members who had run into difficulties. The members had in mind an organization something like the Masons or the Odd Fellows and, in fact, there had been discussion of forming a Jewish branch of the Odd Fellows. Originally named Bundes Bruder, the new group soon Hebraized its name to B'nai B'rith (Sons of the Covenant).

For Further Reading:

Edward Grusd, *B'nai B'rith: The Story of a Covenant*, New York, 1966.

Q. Who was the first rabbi of Temple Emanu-El in New York?

A. Leo Merzbacher (1810–1856) born in Fuerth, Germany had studied in the yeshiva in Pressburg under the well known Talmudic scholar R. Moshe Sofer, and apparently had been ordained there. His first position in the U.S. was at Anshe Chesed synagogue in New York, 1843–45, where he delivered holiday sermons, taught teenagers 12 hours a week, officiated at various ceremonies, and rendered decisions on question of Jewish law, all for $6 per week. A sermon in which he criticized the traditional practice of married women covering their hair led to his removal from the synagogue a short time later. His supporters broke away from Anshe Chesed and formed Temple Emanu-El, New York's first Reform congregation, with Merzbacher as rabbi at a salary of $200 per year.

For Further Reading:

UJE, VII, 497.

Hyman Grinstein. *The Je\vish Community of New York*, Philadelphia; JPS, 1947, 89 f., and 354.

Q. What Jewish U.S. Senator was the grandson of a vizier of Morocco?

A. David Levy Yulee was one of Florida's first pair of U.S. Senators when that state entered the Union in 1845. His grandfather Elijah Levy-Yuly was reputedly vizier to the Sultan Muhammad ibn Abd-Allah of Morocco, but fled to England from a palace coup in 1799. David's father, Moses Levy, emigrated to the U.S. and bought up 45,000 acres of land in Florida which had just been acquired from Spain and was inhabited largely by Indians. Levy remained a loyal Jew, all the while accumulating great wealth and becoming active in local politics. He often spoke out in favor of the abolition of slavery. His son David was born in 1810 when the family still lived in the West Indies. Rising quickly in the world of the ante-bellum South, David participated in peace talks with the Seminole Chief Osceola in 1834, served in several government positions and married the daughter of Governor Wickliffe of Kentucky. At his wife's suggestion, the family reassumed the original family name, Levy-Yulee, this when he was already serving in the Senate. Strongly pro-slavery, Yulee supported secession in 1861.

When the war ended, Yulee was arrested while en route to Washington to confer about Florida's reentry into the Union. He was released a year later when General Joseph E. Johnston induced General Ulysses Grant to intercede personally with President Andrew Johnson in his behalf. Levyville and Levy County in Florida were named after him.

For Further Reading:

C. Wickliffe Yulee, "Senator Yulee," *Publications of the Florida Historical Society* II: 1 and 2 74

Q. In 1845, R. Max Lilienthal left Russia and made his way to the U.S. Why?

A. Rabbi Max Lilienthal (1815–1882) became one of the major leaders of early Reform Judaism in the U.S. serving as rabbi of the prominent Bene Israel Congregation in Cincinnati from 1855–1882. He was also on the teaching staff of Hebrew Union College when it opened in 1875.

Born in Munich and with a budding reputation as a synagogue preacher, Lilienthal was invited in 1841 by the czarist government to organize a system of state schools for Jewish children in Russia. Well intentioned, Lilienthal did not at first realize that the Russians were merely using him to try to destroy traditional Jewish religious education and generally to find new means of harassing their Jewish citizens. Some Russian rabbinic leaders liked Lilienthal personally, but they were less naive about the czarist government. By 1844, Lilienthal had come to realize the czarist duplicity. He fled Russia secretly and soon after immigrated to the United States.

For Further Reading:

Max Lilienthal, *My Travels in Russia,* published in David Philipson's, *Max Lilienthal. American Rabbi: Life and Writings,* New York, Bloch Publ. Co., 1915.
David Philipson, *The Reform Movement in Judaism,* New York, MacMillan, 1931.

Q. When did the custom of Confirmation begin?

A. Not by any means an ancient tradition, Confirmation was introduced by Reform leaders in Germany in the early nineteenth century. The first Confirmations in the United States were arranged by Rabbi Max Lilienthal in New York in 1845. The resulting protest helped cost Rabbi Lilienthal his rabbinic position. A Reverend Carillon had introduced Confirmation in St. Thomas in the West Indies two years earlier.

Confirmation was for both boys and girls, whereas the established custom of bar-mitzvah applied only for boys. Reform leaders hoped to encourage young women to greater interest in the temples. Bar or bat mitzvah through the centuries had meant only that the boy of 13 or the girl of 12 had reached the age of full responsibility before Jewish law. The late twentieth century practice of large catered parties was probably invented by some caterer. Indeed, Rabbi Moshe Sofer of Pressburg in the early 19th century issued a statement that bar mitzvah celebrations should be limited to a minyan of ten people and that no lavish food, including coffee, should be served. Most bar mitzvahs in the U.S. in the early 20th century were home made affairs with herring, cake, and a drink in the home after services.

The Jewish journal, *The Occident,* carried a series of articles, pro and con, on Confirmation in the 1840's. Isaac Mayer Wise introduced Confirmation in his synagogue in Albany, New York in 1848 and it brought 'a wasp's nest on his ears." Rabbi Wise's health began to suffer both because of the strength of the opposition and because of his own hesitations at taking so major a step.

For Further Reading:

Isaac M. Wise, *Reminiscences,* 1905, p. 10.
Michael A. Meyer, *Response to Modernity: A History of the Reform Movement in Judaism,* New York, Oxford University Press, 1988.
W. Gunther Plaut, *The Growth of Reform Judaism,* New York, World Union for Progressive Judaism, 1965.

Q. From where did American Jews in the 1840's obtain citrons for the Succot (Tabernacles) holiday?

A. Citrons (etrogim) are used by Jews in the ceremonies of the autumn holiday of Succot (Tabernacles). According to Jewish law, the citrons must be of pure stock not grafted with lemons, as they occasionally are.

Rabbi Abraham Joseph Rice, who came to Baltimore from Germany in 1840, was America's first ordained Orthodox rabbi and an accomplished Talmudist. After some research, he declared that citrons from the Caribbean Islands were, in most cases, not grafted and thus they were fit for ritual use. Max Lilienthal, a Reform rabbi in New York, criticized Rice's decision arguing that evidence on the Caribbean citrons was inadequate. This caused some congregations to cancel their Caribbean orders and to send for Mediterranean citrons instead.

The argument came to a head in 1847 when no Mediterranean citrons were available. Articles pro and con began to appear in Jewish publications, like Isaac Leeser's *The Occident*. Rice argued that although the Caribbean citrons differed in size and shape from the Mediterranean, they were still fit for ritual use and that many citron trees grew wild in the forests and were certainly not grafted. A Reverend Isaac Levy of New York wrote that English Chief Rabbi Solomon Hirschell had disqualified them for use in England. This incident of the 1840's is significant in that it was one of the first debates over religious law in which an American talmudist took part. Previously, questions of Jewish law were typically sent to rabbis in England or Holland. It shows also that although Reform in many ways began to break openly with Orthodoxy by the 1840's it yet retained many traditional features. Isaac Mayer Wise, who was beginning to appear as a major spokesman for Reform, criticized both sides in this debate as unenlightened and out of touch with the realities of the day.

Most citrons used in America today come from Israel or the Mediterranean. Efforts to grow them in the U.S. have had little success.

For Further Reading:

Harold Sharfman, *The First Rabbi: A Biography of the Origins of Orthodox and Reform Polemic Warfare in Ante-Bellum America*, J. Simons, 1988.

Q. What Jewish father and son served as physicians during the Mexican War?

A. Jonas Horwitz (? - 1852) graduated from the University of Pennsylvania Medical School and later served as an army surgeon during the Mexican

War at the same time that his son Dr. Jonathan Phineas Horwitz (1822–1904) was in charge of the Naval Hospital at Tabasco. During the Civil War, Jonathan Horwitz was assigned to the United States Bureau of Medicine and Surgery and later became its medical director.

For Further Reading

UJE, V, 461.

Q. Were there Jews in California before the gold rush of 1848?

A. The first Jew in California was probably Louis Polack, an adventurer who deserted his whaling ship there in 1837. He ran a general store in Yorba Buena (the old name for San Francisco) and after joining the army during the Mexican War returned to California during the gold rush as a gambler. At the age of 32, he was shot to death in a house of ill repute in a fight over a woman. His killer, whose attorney was Samuel Heydenfeldt, a Jewish Justice of California's Supreme Court, was pardoned by the governor.

Several other Jews had reached California by 1846 including Jacob Frankfurt and Jacob Adler. Stevenson's Regiment of First New York Volunteers serving in California during the Mexican War included 17 names which sound more or less Jewish, like Moritz Cohen, Antone Rosenthal, Emil Bergman, and Jacob Posneer.

Dr. Samuel Sussman Snow (1818–1892) came from Germany to New York as a child, became a physician, and moved to Wisconsin, where he traded for furs with the Indians. In 1850, he led a wagon train, including his wife and new born son, to El Dorado County, California and settled there. Snow was active in Jewish life in California and his daughter Carrie married Rabbi Herman Davidson. By the outbreak of the Civil War in 1861, about 10,000 Jews lived in California.

For Further Reading:

Marcus, *USJ*, II, p. 111–112.
Rudolf Glanz, *The Jews of California: From the Discovery of Gold until 1880*, New York: Waldon Press, 1960, p. 18.
Reva Clar, "Samuel Sussman Snow: A Pioneer Finds El Dorado," *WSJHQ*, III, 1971, 3–25.

Q. Which two gold rushes in the 1840's involved a Jewish connection?

A. The rush to California drew many Jews, although they tended to establish businesses rather than to go out prospecting for gold. In the same years, there was a gold rush to Australia which attracted a number of European Jews. As time went on, the excellent business opportunities in California aroused interest in Australia. Ship passenger lists and city directories from the 1850's record the names of a number of Jews who were migrating from Australia to California. One was a Mr. Solomons, for many years the president of Congregation Sherit Israel in San Francisco.

For Further Reading:

Rudolph Glanz, *The Jews of California*, New York, Waldon Press, 1960.

Q. Why did the U.S. Government send naval expeditions to Palestine in 1848 and 1854?

A. The 1848 expedition, proposed and commanded by Lieutenant William F. Lynch, circumnavigated and explored the Dead Sea, or Lake Asphaltites, as it was often called in those days. Although part of the Turkish Empire, Palestine was a wasteland, and the Americans had to be constantly on their guard against marauding Arabs. Lynch saw his expedition as valuable both for finding information and also for religious purposes, as perhaps helping to regenerate Jewish settlement in the Holy Land. The Americans sailed to the Mediterranean port of Acre on the "Supply" and carried the frame of a smaller boat to the Dead Sea where it was assembled for the exploration. Lynch's book, *Narrative of the United States Expedition to the River Jordan and the Dead Sea* went through at least eight editions in the U.S. and one in Britain. The book is cited even by modern archaeologists (e.g., Nelson Glueck, *The River Jordan*, p. 71).

The second American naval visit was of a different sort. In December 1853 (shortly after the outbreak of the Crimean War), S. Hosford Smith, American Consul at Beirut, reported to Washington on the growing agitation in the region and the possible threat to American citizens and their interests. A 36 gun man-o-war, the S.S. Levant commanded by Captain C.C. Turner, was dispatched from the American Mediterranean fleet and dropped anchor at Haifa on June 3, 1854. During a 5 day visit, Turner met with Turkish officials and local Jews and left some carbines with an American family living near Jaffa who were being harassed by Bedouin raiders. A letter from Warder Cresson, an American convert to Judaism living in Palestine, to Rev. Isaac Leeser in Philadelphia, tells that Turner also apprehended some of the offenders and had them tried and imprisoned by the Turkish courts, "since which occurrence the Americans have been treated with the greatest deference and respect."

For Further Reading:

Carl Alpert, "Two American Naval Expeditions to Palestine 1848 and 1854," *PAJHS*, XL, 1949, 281–287.

Q. Who was the first rabbi to visit an American President in the White House?

A. Rabbi Isaac M. Wise, founder of Reform Judaism in the United States, visited President Zachary Taylor in 1849. Washington D.C. was not very formal in those days, so when Wise stopped in to see his senator, William Seward of New York, Seward offered to take him over to the White House for an unannounced visit to President Taylor. On the same stay, Wise also met the great Massachusetts Senator Daniel Webster and witnessed, from the senate gallery, some of the memorable debates which resulted in the Compromise of 1850. Wise noted in his memoirs his pleasure in having Webster refer to him as a coreligionist. Webster was a Unitarian.

For Further Reading:

Isaac Mayer Wise, *Reminiscences*, Cincinnati, 1905

Q. From where did Rabbi Isaac Mayer Wise receive his rabbinic ordination?

A. In the middle of the nineteenth century, the American Jewish community featured a fair member of "rabbis," "chazzanim," " reverends," "doctors," and indeed "rabbi-doctors," and "chief rabbis," who had no authentic rabbinic credentials at all, and who had created their own titles.

Isaac Mayer Wise was a vigorous leader who did not back away from controversy. As such he successfully launched Reform Judaism in the United States battling both Orthodox traditionalists and ultra-liberal Reformers. Hebrew Union College, which he founded in 1875 and guided for 25 years, produced the rabbis and assured the continuance of a leadership for Reform.

The circumstances of Wise's own rabbinic ordination are unclear. Harold Sharfman's book, *The First Rabbi*, presents a very negative view of Wise and claims that he probably never was ordained. Brandeis University Professor Leon Jick in his *The Americanization of the Synagogue* argues that Wise not only was not ordained but also did not have the university degree that he claimed.

James Heller, in an exhaustive and admiring biography of 800 pages, relates that no existing source tells when Wise was ordained. However, Wise himself wrote that he had received his ordination from his teacher Solomon Judah Rappaport of Prague, a liberal rabbinic scholar, Samuel Freund, head of a yeshiva in Prague, and Ephraim Loeb Teweles. Wise had studied Talmud and rabbinic literature in several yeshivot and had attended universities in Prague and Vienna. Although probably not wholly committed to Reform in his early years, Wise was certainly showing very liberal inclinations. His first position was as teacher in the town of Radnitz near Pilsen, where he delivered sermons in German and attended conferences of Reform leaders.

For Further Reading:

James Heller, *Isaac M. Wise: His Life, Work and Thought,* New York, Union of American Hebrew Congregations. 1965.

Q. What man of Jewish birth was elected to Congress on the anti-Catholic Native American Party Ticket?

A. Lewis Charles Levin (1808–1860) began his political career as a crusader against dueling and alcohol and became an outspoken opponent of the policy of open immigration to the U.S. In 1843, he purchased the Philadelphia Daily Sun and campaigned vitriolically for the exclusion of foreigners and foreign influences from the United States. He claimed that Catholic immigrants, particularly the Irish, threatened to undermine the U..S. by filling it with paupers and felons and by putting obedience to the Pope above loyalty to the nation. Antagonism toward Catholics was common enough in America from the earliest colonial times.

The 1840's saw anti-immigrant riots in Boston, Charleston, St. Louis and other cities. In an outbreak in Philadelphia, several churches were burned. Levin was one of the most violently outspoken anti-Catholics. On May 6, 1844, he helped to whip up a crowd into a riot which left seven people dead. In July, 5000 soldiers had to be called out to quell another nativist anti-Catholic riot.

A grand jury indicted Levin on a charge, later dismissed, of instigating the May outbreak. In October, 1844, Levin was elected by a good margin to Congress, where he often spoke out against Catholics. At different times he backed proposals that immigrants must reside in the US for 21 years before they could apply for citizenship or that only the native born could ever be citizens.

Levin's radicalism helped lead to the break-up of the Native American Party convention in 1847 and to the demise of the party shortly afterward. In 1850, he was defeated in his bid for a 4th term in Congress. By the late 1850's, lonely and troubled, he was incarcerated in mental hospitals. The

Native American Party was predecessor of the Know-Nothings, who followed many of the same ideas in the 1850's.

Levin was born of Jewish parents, and it is not clear whether he ever formally affiliated himself with any Protestant denomination despite his outspoken advocacy of Protestantism over Catholicism. He spent his adulthood in Philadelphia, which had a Jewish community, but there is no evidence of any connection there either. Ironically, Levin's wife and son converted from Protestantism to Catholicism after his death.

For Further Reading:

Ray Billington, *The Protestant Crusade* 1800-1860, New York, Rinehart, 1952.
John Forman, "Lewis Charles Levin," *AJA*, XI, 1959.

Q. Who laid out the site for Waco, Texas?

A. Jacob de Cordova, born in Kingston, Jamaica in 1808, of Sephardic descent and raised in New York, moved to Texas in 1836, shortly after Texas won its independence from Mexico. He became a prominent businessman and land dealer. In 1849, De Cordova was hired by a Jonas Butler as his attorney to lay out a tract of land along the Brazos River for a town. De Cordova, who owned 1/5 of the land, and the other partners wanted to name the town Lamartine, but George Erath, the surveyor, insisted on Waco after a local Indian tribe and so it was. De Cordova helped draw good citizens to Waco. In 1850, he made an attractive offer to persuade officials of the newly formed McLennan County government to make Waco the county seat. That same year, De Cordova acted as agent for the sale and settling of the Tomas de la Vega lands directly across the Brazos.

A man of some accomplishment in Jewish learning, De Cordova wrote several Hebrew ketubot which are preserved in the American Jewish Archives in Cincinnati. He was probably among the founding fathers of Congregation Beth Israel of Houston, Texas' first formal synagogue. Jews settled in Waco in the early 1850's, and by 1869 there was an acting local shohet (ritual slaughterer). Reports of that time indicate that observance of kashrut was prevalent among local Jews.

For Further Reading:

James Day, *Jacob De Cordova: Land Merchant of Texas,* Waco, Heritage Society of Waco Inc., 1962.
Mordecai Podet. "Pioneer Jews of Waco, Texas," *WSJH*, XXI, 1989, 195-219 and 322-344.

Q. Who was the United States' first consul in Jerusalem?

A. Warder Cresson (1798–1869) was descended from Pierre Cresson, who settled in Harlem, New York in the 17th century. Born a Quaker, he was much given to religious thinking, and he interested himself in a succession of religious groups of his day — Shakers, Mormons, Millerites, Campbellites. Meeting Reverend Isaac Leeser, an educated Orthodox Jewish leader in Philadelphia in 1840, Cresson began a serious study of Judaism. In 1844, he accepted the newly created position of United States consul in Jerusalem, feeling that in that holy city he might find spiritual Truth. Taking the name Michael C. Boaz Israel, he inclined ever more strongly toward Judaism and associated himself with the Sephardic community of the city. In 1848, Cresson finally converted to Judaism and returned to Philadelphia to straighten out his finances with the intention of settling permanently in Jerusalem.

His wife and children sought to have Cresson declared legally insane, but after two trials he won his case. Back in Jerusalem, Cresson assumed Sephardic garb, married a Sephardic woman and lived the life of a pious Jew.

The complexities of his mind are expressed in a number of writings including a somewhat autobiographical *The Key of David* and in regular essays in Leeser's journal, *The Occident*. He was involved in an unsuccessful effort to organize a farm settlement in Emek Rephaim. Not for some decades, till the coming of the kibbutzniks, would Jews in Ottoman Palestine function well in organized farming.

For Further Reading:

Frank Fox, "Quaker, Shaker, Rabbi Warder Cresson, The Story of a Philadelphia Mystic," *The Pennsylvania Magazine*, 1971, 147–194.

1850–1881

Civil War and Expansion

FROM THE MIDDLE OF the nineteenth century, the United States was growing quickly in both population and economic strength. New territories had been added after the Mexican War, railroads were being built, and new immigrants crossed the ocean seeking to escape the Irish potato famine, the political upheavals of Europe or, for Jews, the continuing chronic poverty and political disability. Jewish communities were taking root in Western towns, notably Chicago, Cincinnati, and in the far west, San Francisco, each with its own synagogues and communal organizations.

Isaac Mayer Wise emerged as the founder and leader of American Reform creating many of its major institutions, most important the Hebrew Union College in 1875 to train Reform rabbis. Reform leaders debated and instituted many changes in traditional practice.

A few Orthodox rabbis came over from Europe, but they could do little to educate their parishioners and to keep them from joining the Reform or all too often from total assimilation. Reverend Isaac Leeser of Philadelphia {1806–1867} was almost a lone voice in his defense of traditional Judaism. Jewish day schools sprouted up in many communities, but they were all soon displaced by the growth of non-sectarian public schools.

German families, by now well established in the U.S., were becoming the Jewish aristocracy, and immigrants from Eastern Europe were forming small congregations of their own. Family life was stable, and the divorce rate was low. In the large cities, at least, there was a wider choice of Jewish marital partners. As always, Jews loved the freedom and opportunity that America offered, and they responded with hard work and determination to play an important part in American life.

The Civil War {1861–1865} absorbed much of the energy and power of the American people for its 4 years. Jews, both Northern and Southern were involved, both in the battlefield and at home. Some of the tensions of the struggle expressed themselves in anti-Semitism which, however, had neither profound nor long lasting effects.

A later anti-Semitic incident involving tycoon Joseph Seligman at the Grand Union Hotel in 1876 marked the beginning of a more persistent, though non-violent social prejudice against Jews.

Q. Why did Albany. NY police close down Congregation Beth El on Rosh Hashana, 1850?

A. When Rabbi Isaac Mayer Wise assumed the pulpit of Congregation Beth El in 1846 he immediately began to introduce reforms — a mixed choir, substitution of confirmation for bar-mitzvah, and changes in liturgy. The congregation divided angrily. Ironically, the ire of some members was further aroused by Wise's insistence that trustees on the Temple board must close their businesses on the Sabbath. Finally, in July, 1850, the Board, led by Louis Spanier, sent Wise a list of six accusations including that he had been seen writing on Rosh Hashana, swinging in a swing on Saturday, that he had ridiculed the ritual bath, and that he had advocated Reform ideas. Of course, the conflict was as much personal as doctrinal. The tension increased through the summer of 1850.

On the first day of Rosh Hashana, when Wise stepped before the holy ark to take out the Torah scrolls, Spanier stepped in his way and punched him. The services erupted into a donnybrook as Wise's supporters and opponents struggled with each other. The sheriff came with his men and cleared the synagogue. Wise was taken to the police station but soon released. The police closed the building, and worshipers attended services for the second day of the holiday either in private homes or at Albany's other synagogue, Beth Jacob.

By 1854, Wise moved on to Cincinnati and the pulpit of Bnai Jeshurun. There he openly espoused Reform Judaism and over most of the next half century, through his writings and his organizational and political accomplishments, he earned the title of father of American Reform Judaism. Perhaps the culmination of his work was the founding of the Hebrew Union College to train Reform rabbis, 1875.

For Further Reading:

Naphtali J. Rubinger, "Dismissal in Albany," *AJA*, XXIV, 1972, 160–183.
James Heller, *Isaac M. Wise: His Life. Work and Thought,* New York; Union of American Hebrew Congregations, 1965.

1850–1881: CIVIL WAR AND EXPANSION

Q. How reformed was early American Reform Judaism?

A. The first major steps to Reform in American synagogues in the 1840's involved changes in decorum rather than ritual. Men and women still sat separate, heads were covered, and Sabbath and dietary laws were observed. Attempts at innovation often met with strong opposition.

The first instance of mixed seating was in Congregation Anshe Emeth in Albany, New York, the new congregation formed by Isaac Mayer Wise in 1851 after his separation from Beth El. In 1864, Temple Emanuel in New York became the first to introduce worship with uncovered heads. After the Civil War, major change began to accelerate so quickly that by the 1870's Reform temples were even moving their Sabbath services to Sunday.

For Further Reading:

Leon Jick, "The Reform Synagogue," and Jonathan D. Sarna "The Debate Over Mixed Seating in the American Synagogue," in Jack Wertheimer, ed., *The American Synagogue: A Synagogue Transformed,* Cambridge, Cambridge University Press, 1987.

Q. What was the first Russian-Jewish synagogue in the U.S.A.?

A. Twelve Jews, eleven of Eastern European background, founded an Orthodox synagogue in 1852 on 83 Bayard Street in New York. Several German Jews joined, unhappy about the changes Reform was bringing to their own congregations. Increasing membership necessitated several moves to larger premises during the next years. Abraham J. Ash served as rabbi. Rabbi Abraham Rice of Baltimore delivered a sermon at the dedication on the Eve of Shavuot, 1856. Ash gave up the office of rabbi with its small stipend for the higher dignity of parnas, when he made a fortune selling fashionable hoop skirts. However, he later lost his money and resumed the rabbinical position at $25 a month until his death in 1887.

The congregation split several times. One split was precipitated in an argument over whether the windows should be opened on a warm Yom Kippur day in 1861. Parnas Aaron Hershfeld objected on the grounds that a draft might damage the cantor's voice.

For Further Reading:

J.D. Eisenstein, "The History of the First Russian American Jewish Congregation," *PAJHS,* IX, 1901, 63–74.

Q. How many Jews served in the U.S. Congress in the 19th century?

A. The *American Jewish Yearbook* for 1900 lists twenty three. The first, Michael Ash, was elected from Pennsylvania to the 24th Congress in 1835 and served on the Committee on Naval Affairs. Ash was a colonel in the War of 1812 and a law partner of James Buchanan. However, there is, in fact, little reason to believe that he was Jewish. The first professing Jew in the House of Representatives was Emanuel Hart of New York, 1851–53.

Q. What was the medical specialty of Dr. Jacob Mitchell?

A. In an age when people believed in all sorts of unsophisticated medical quackery, Mitchell set himself up as an expert in Indian root and herb remedies, and he is listed in a Nashville business directory of 1853 as an Indian doctor. Mitchell treated patients at his office on Market Street and at an infirmary on Vine and Demonbreun, although he is not known to have had any formal medical training.

In the 1840's, he ran a stage coach line between Little Rock and Hot Springs, Arkansas, where he owned and managed a hotel. He was involved in a long and unsuccessful litigation with the U.S. government over the ownership of the hot springs. Mitchell and his brothers were apparently the first Jewish settlers in Little Rock.

For Further Reading:

Fedora Frank, *Five Families and Eight Young Men*, Nashville, Tennessee Book Co., 1962.

Q. Who was the official photographer of General John Fremont's expedition in 1853–54?

A. Solomon Nunes Carvalho (1815–1897) of South Carolina, from an old Sephardic family, was the photographer for General Fremont's pioneering exploration of the west. Carvalho's book, *Incidents of Travel and Adventures in the Far West*, our best source on the Fremont expedition, describes the many adventures and dangers of the western wilderness. Every time a daguerreotype was made, the expedition had to wait twelve hours while it was put in cold water so it could develop.

Fremont reached California, where Carvalho participated in the founding of the first Jewish communal organizations in Los Angeles. Carvalho was also famed for other photo portraits including Abraham Lincoln and Judah Touro, and he wrote books and articles on Jewish topics.

Carvalho's sons later gained some note. David was a handwriting expert whose testimony helped to prove that documents used to convict

Alfred Dreyfus were forgeries. Solomon became general manager of the Hearst newspaper empire. Jacob S. headed a large lumber company in New York.

For Further Reading:
Solomon Carvalho, *Travel and Adventure in the Far West*, Philadelphia, JPS, 1954.

Q. What Hungarian Jew was involved in the Walker filibuster in Central America in the middle nineteenth century?

A. In the mid-19th century, adventurous Americans moved toward Texas, California or to any place where fortune seemed to beckon. In 1855, William Walker headed a group of soldiers of fortune, filibusters, as they were called, which plunged into the mess of Nicaraguan politics. They joined the democratic forces in their war against the legitimists and made Walker dictator for a few months.

Louis Schlessinger (1825-1900) fled Hungary after taking part in the revolution of 1848 and drifted to Central America where he joined Walker and was given command of a body of mixed German, French and American troops because of his military experience and his knowledge of languages. Surprised and defeated in battle by Costa Rican forces, Schlessinger was condemned to be shot, but he escaped and joined the Nicaraguan legitimists, Walker's enemies. After the wars, he went to Guatemala where he became owner of a coffee plantation. Walker himself was captured and executed while leading a new filibuster invasion of Honduras in 1860.

For Further Reading:
UJE, Soldier, Jew, IX: 612.

Q. Did Karl Marx ever live in the United States?

A. Karl Marx, the father of modern Communism, never actually set foot on American soil. However, from 1852 to 1861 while living in London he worked as a foreign correspondent for the *New York Daily Tribune*. Only one of his signed *Daily Tribune* reports touched on Jews — a blatantly antisemitic article about a new English law allowing Jews to serve in Parliament. Several anonymous *Tribune* articles in 1855-1856, probably also written by Marx, analyzed the powers of an alleged world wide network of Jewish bankers and financiers.

Although descended from rabbinical families on both sides, Marx was converted to Christianity as a youngster so that he could gain admittance to a good school. Later, he regularly attacked Jews both in published works and in his private correspondence in the most narrow-minded, vicious and outspoken manner. Ironically, his daughter Eleanor Marx Aveling openly identified herself as Jewish and devoted herself to helping her poorer brethren.

For Further Reading:

Saul Padover, *Karl Marx: An Intimate Biography*. New York, McGraw-Hill Book Co., 1978.

Q. What was Zion College?

A. In 1856, nineteen years before the founding of Hebrew Union College, some Reform rabbis, led by Isaac Mayer Wise, opened a Jewish Studies college in Cincinnati. There were fourteen students, including two Christians, and five teachers, including Rabbi Wise and Max Lilienthal. The curriculum was Liberal Arts, not only Jewish. The courses of specifically Jewish interest were Hebrew Language, taught by Dr. Rothenheim who also taught German, and Talmud, taught by Mr. Junkerman who also taught mathematics. Governor Salmon P. Chase of Ohio delivered the main address at the school's inaugural dinner. Zion College aroused little interest, much of it negative, and soon closed its doors.

The first advanced school of Jewish Studies to show even a small success was Maimonides College, founded in 1867 under the impetus of the Orthodox Rev. Isaac Leeser in Philadelphia. The school had adequate funding and a capable faculty including Marcus Jastrow, but it attracted few students. Only five finished the first year. Maimonides never issued a diploma although two students who had studied for several years went on to hold rabbinical positions — David Levy in Charleston, S.C. and Samuel Mendelsohn in Norfolk, VA and Wilmington, N.C. By 1873 the college was closed.

For Further Reading:

Bertram Korn, *Eventful Years and Experiences*, Cincinnati; 1964.
James C. Heller, *Isaac M. Wise: His Life. Work and Thought*, New York, Union of American Hebrew Congregation, 1965.

Q. German born Isidor Loewenthal migrated to the U.S. and became a professor. Why did he move to India?

A. Born in Posen, Prussia in 1827, Isidor Loewenthal received a traditional Jewish education and then went on to a German gymnasium school where he studied languages, science and philosophy. In trouble with the police because of an anti-government poem which he wrote, Loewenthal fled to the U.S. There he worked briefly as a peddler and then took a position teaching Hebrew and German at Lafayette College in Pennsylvania. A young man far away from his roots, Loewenthal fell under the influence of a Reverend Gayley and was baptized as a Presbyterian. He went on to take a degree in theology at Princeton and in 1855 went as a missionary to India. There he learned to preach in several Indian languages and translated the New Testament into Pashtu. By the time of his death in 1864, he had nearly completed a dictionary of Pashtu.

There were similar cases. Ephraim Menachem Epstein (1829–1913), who came to the U.S. in 1850 to escape an unhappy marriage, soon after converted to Presbyterianism and was ordained a preacher. After completing medical school at New York University in 1859, he served as a Christian missionary in the Ottoman Turkish Empire for several years, then returned to the U.S. and went on to a fine career as an M.D.

Samuel Joseph Schereschevsky (1831–1906) studied in yeshivas in Russia before coming to New York and converting to Baptism, Presbyterianism, and later Episcopalianism. He went on to spend some years as a missionary in China and translated the Bible into the Wen-Li dialect.

Such cases could be dramatic but, in fact, few Jews were converted by missionaries and perhaps they were fewer than the number of Christians who accepted Judaism. Some who left Judaism soon returned to it. Isaac Mayer Wise often criticized the missionaries in his writings, referring to one of the Hebrew-Christian preachers as an impostor and comedian who was interested only in money.

For Further Reading:

David Max Eichhorn, *Evangelizing the American Jew,* Middle Village, New York, Jonathan David Publishers Inc., 1978.
DAB, VI, 356.

Q. Who was the first American to return to Europe to study for the rabbinate?

A. Simon Tuska (1835–1871), son of Reverend Mordecai Tuska, was born in Hungary and came to Rochester, NY in 1849. He specialized in Greek and Latin at the University of Rochester and studied Judaics with his father. In 1854, Tuska wrote a small booklet presenting a very Reformed view of Jewish prayer, and he began publishing articles in two leading Jewish journals — Isaac M. Wise's *The Israelite* and Isaac Leeser's *The Occident.* After taking courses at the Rochester Theological Seminary, a Christian school, Tuska pursued a life-long dream by going to the Jewish Theological Seminary in Breslau, the center of proto-Conservative, or as it was then often known, Historical Judaism. In Europe, Tuska visited liberal Jewish leaders like Abraham Geiger and Judah L. Rapaport and professed his discomfort at attending Orthodox services.

European student life proved difficult, and Tuska returned to the U.S. in 1860 without qualifying for ordination. His increasingly Reform ideas proved too much for the Jews of Rochester, and Tuska accepted a pulpit in Memphis, Tennessee where he remained until his death in 1871.

For Further Reading:

Abraham J. Karp, "Simon Tuska Becomes a Rabbi." *PAJHS*, 50, 1960, 79–98.

Q. How did a Talmudic scholar and writer come to live in Keokuk, Iowa in the mid-nineteenth century?

A. Founded in 1837 in the Mississippi River near its confluence with the Des Moines River, Keokuk, Iowa became an early center for enterprising traders, some Jews among them. It was not until some years had passed that Des Moines began to move clearly ahead of Keokuk both as Iowa's chief city and as its main Jewish community.

Rabbi Joshua Falk Cohen, a capable Talmudist and author of "Abne Jehoshua" on Avot, had lived for some time in New York where he devoted himself to the study of Talmud in the Beth Hamidrash Shaarey Torah Synagogue. He moved on to Keokuk to live with a daughter and died there in 1864.

For Further Reading:

"Trail Blazers of the Trans-Mississippi West," *AJA*, VIII, 1956, 80–81.

Q. Why did Jews oppose the U.S.'s treaties with the Swiss and with China in the 1850's?

A. In 1850, the U.S. agreed to a treaty with the Swiss in which one clause recognized the right of the Swiss cantons to refuse commercial privileges to foreign Jews. Sigmund Waterman, a prominent New York Jew, wrote two articles sharply criticizing both the treaty and the U.S. minister, A. Dudley Mann, who negotiated it. Notable Americans like Daniel Webster and Henry Clay wrote letters supporting Waterman's position. The treaty passed the Senate in 1855 with the offensive passage removed but the substance little changed.

When the text of the treaty was made public two years later there was a strong protest through the U.S. prompting a detailed note from the U.S. government to the Swiss. Several European governments also protested the disabilities to their own Jewish citizens. The restrictions were finally lifted in 1866.

At almost the same time (1860), the U.S. entered into a treaty with China which allowed residential and commercial privileges to all American citizens without discrimination. However, while the treaty specifically protected the practice of Christianity it neglected to specify the same protection for Judaism. A protest from Rabbi Max Lilienthal to Jewish Senator Judah P. Benjamin (D-Louisiana) was answered in a letter assuring the rabbi that Jews would have the same religious rights under the treaty as Christians.

For Further Reading:

Naomi Cohen, *Encounters with Emancipation: The German Jews in the United States. 1830–1914*, Philadelphia, JPS, 1984.
Jacob Marcus, *USJ.* II, p. 290.
Sol Stroock, "Switzerland and American Jews," *PAJHS*, XI, 1903, 7–51.

Q. What is *Minhag America*?

A. A number of revisions of the prayer book were written by Reform clergy during the mid-nineteenth century. The best known prayer book was Isaac Mayer Wise's *Minhag America*. The traditional liturgy was reworked to reflect the new Reform philosophy. Prayers were changed to eliminate references to the return to Zion, a personal messiah, the sacrificial cult, bodily resurrection, and lamentations over past persecutions. Cabalistic passages were removed, and the weekly reading of the Pentateuch was to be shortened so that the Five Books of Moses were now to be read in a three year cycle rather than the traditional one year cycle.

For Further Reading:

Isaac Mayer Wise. *Reminiscences*, 1905, p. 343f.

Q. What journey did Jacob Mordecai Netter take in the late 1850's?

A. Beginning in Austria, Netter traveled around the world from west to east. His book *Slavim Min Hayam, (Seagulls from the Sea)* recounts his travels with a good dose of history and some poems. He says little about his months in the U.S. other than some sermons he preached at synagogues in San Francisco and Utica, New York. Lured by prospects of freedom and profit, American Jews, he feared, were giving up their Jewishness; surely the time of Redemption could not be far away.

For Further Reading:

Salo and Jeanette Baron, "Palestinian Messengers in America, 1849–1879," *Jewish Social Studies*. V, 1943. 115-162 and 225-292.

S. Joshua Kohn, "Jacob Mordecai Netter: World Traveler," *PAJHS*, XLVII, 1958, 196-199.

Q. What was the Newman Case?

A. In April, 1858, Morris Newman, president of Congregation Bnei Israel of Sacramento, was accused of keeping his tailor shop open on Sunday in violation of the state's closing laws. A Sabbath observer, Newman had been closing on Saturdays instead. Samuel Heydenfeldt (1816–1890), a Jewish former State Supreme Court Justice, served as Newman's attorney. The case went to the California Supreme Court where two of the three justices felt that the closing laws were unconstitutional in showing a religious preference. However, the two soon left the court, their opinion was overruled and the Sunday Closing Laws remained on the books for another century.

A 1908 study found Sunday closing laws in force in 37 states, although 24 made some provision for those who observed Saturday as their Sabbath. The Sunday laws were first challenged in Federal court in 1959 in Crown Kosher Super Market vs. Gallagher. The court declared that the Massachusetts Lord 's Day act violated Federal Law in that it discriminated against Saturday observers and gave special protection to dominant Christian sects which celebrate Sunday as the Lord's Day. That decision was overturned in 1961 by the U.S. Supreme Court under Chief Justice Earl Warren, which decided that this and several other local Sunday closing laws no longer held any religious significance and were therefore not in contradiction to Federal law even in cases which caused hardship to Saturday Sabbath observers.

An additional note. Samuel Heydenfeldt was a southern Jewish lawyer who migrated from Alabama to California in gold rush days and sat on California's Supreme Court, 1852–1857. He was prominent in Jewish communal matters but married out of the faith and left no Jewish descendants. During the Civil War, he was known as a supporter of state's rights, although opposed to slavery.

For Further Reading:

Albert Friedenberg, "Solomon Heydenfeldt: A Jewish Jurist of Alabama and California," *PAJHS*, X, 1902, 129–140.
Albert Friedenberg, "Sunday Laws and Judicial Decisions," *AJYB*, 1908–1909.
William Kramer, "The Earliest Important Jewish Attorney in California, Solomon Heydenfeldt," *WSJH*, XXIII, 1991, 149–161.

Q. How did American Jews react to the Edgar Mortara Case?

A. One night in June, 1858, in the city of Bologna of the Papal States, policemen came into the home of Momola Mortara Levi and took away their youngest child, six year old Edgardo, to be raised as a Catholic. Officials claimed that Edgardo had been secretly baptized by a serving girl and that in the view of the papacy the boy was now Catholic. A storm of anger opened all over Europe including protests to the pope from Emperors Franz Joseph of Austria-Hungary and Louis Napoleon of France. Children had been forcibly removed on similar grounds in the past, but for the first time Jews in some parts of Italy were able to speak out, and they did.

Jews in America were outraged, and letters were sent to President James Buchanan and Secretary of State Lewis Cass asking them to protest to Pope Pius. However, Buchanan and Cass refused, arguing that American citizens were not involved so it was not up to the U.S. to do anything. American newspapers followed the case with interest and their opinions reflected the mistrust and ill-feeling between Protestants and Catholics in the U.S., secular and Protestant publications being very critical of the papacy and Catholics usually defensive.

American Jews were much heartened by the general support for the Jewish viewpoint, and this seemed to them to reflect the great promise of American life for Jews. At the same time, it was clear that the lack of any national Jewish organization had rendered the many local protests ineffective. This spurred the founding, in 1859, of the first national Jewish organization, the Board of Delegates of American Israelites, by delegates from 29 synagogues in 13 American cities. This board was not effective, but it was a start.

Notwithstanding the international tumult, the church kept Edgar Mortara and raised him in Catholic institutions as a ward of the pope. Years later, when the political situation would have allowed him to return home, he was already a devout Catholic. Entering the priesthood, he lived in monasteries until his death in 1940 in Belgium.

For Further Reading:

Bertram Korn, *The American Reaction to the Mortara Case*, Cincinnati; 1957.

Q. What were the Holy Stones of Newark?

A. In 1860 David Wyrick of Newark, Ohio, a printer and a dabbler in ancient languages digging in the remains of the pre-Indian Mound-Builders, unearthed stones on which were inscribed the ten commandments in Hebrew plus a large image of Moses containing his name, *Moshe*, in Hebrew. Three other stones were also found — four in all. According to Wyrick, this find proved the Israelitish origin of the Mound Builders. The authenticity of the find was accepted by many scholars and clergymen. After Wyrick's death, pieces of slate with Hebrew letters on them and a copy of the Moses figure were found in Wyrick's office where he had apparently prepared them himself. The fraud died slowly, and for many years journals carried articles debating the authenticity of the stones.

For Further Reading:

David Philipson, "Are There Traces of the Ten Lost Tribes in Ohio," *PAJHS, XI II*, 1905, 37–46.

Q. Were Jews in the pre-Civil War South typically slave owners?

A. Rabbi Bertram Korn has written the definitive book on Jews in the Civil War as well as shorter articles on the topic. Korn argues that about 1/4 of southern Jews owned slaves, about the same percentage as for non-Jews. However, few Jews owned large plantations. One notable exception was Judah P. Benjamin's Bellechase, 20 miles from New Orleans. A second was Esquiline Hill near Columbus, Georgia owned by Major Raphael J. Moses, who served as chief commissary of General Longstreet's corps during the Civil War. There is also record of one much traveled adventurer, Solomon Polack, who worked as a plantation overseer in Alabama in the 1830's. Most Jews followed business or professional careers in the towns. A number of documents describe acts of kindness, even manumission of slaves by Jewish masters. However, slaves were sometimes sold and in one instance Joseph Cohen of Lynchburg, Virginia murdered a slave, in 1819.

Slavery was a normal part of life all over the south and owning or even dealing in slaves was not unknown for Jews. Israel Jones sold slaves at auction and was also president of the Congregation Shaarai Shamayim in Mobile from 1844–1873. His daughter married Rabbi James Gutheim of New Orleans. Abraham Seixas wrote a poem to advertise slaves he was selling in 1784. Miscegenation is rarely mentioned in existing records.

For Further Reading:

Bertram Korn, "Jews and Negro Slavery in the Old South, 1784–1865," *PAJHS*, L, 1961, 151–201.

Q. Were there any Black Jews in the ante-bellum south?

A. At least one is known, Billy Simons, or Uncle Billy as he was often called (ca. 1780–1859). Uncle Billy delivered papers for his owner at the Charleston Courier in the 1840's and 50's. He was a member of the local Hazel Street synagogue where in his last years he attended services regularly sitting among the white parishioners despite rules to the contrary. Probably born in Madagascar, Uncle Billy claimed to be descended from the Biblical Rechabite clan (see Jeremiah 35) who, he said, had left Judah and settled in Africa in ancient times.

For Further Reading:

Ralph Melnick, "Billy Simons: The Black Jew of Charleston," *AJA*, XXXII, 1980, 3–6.

Q. Who was the first Jew nominated to the U.S. Supreme Court?

A. Historians have given much attention to President Woodrow Wilson's appointment of Louis Brandeis as the first Jew on the U.S. Supreme Court in 1916. It is less well known that in 1853, President Franklin Pierce sought to appoint Senator Judah P. Benjamin (1811–1884) of Louisiana to that position. Benjamin declined, preferring to remain in the Senate. Born in St. Croix to Sephardic parents, Benjamin was raised in Charleston, South Carolina and later moved to New Orleans. A brilliant lawyer and excellent orator, Benjamin was sent to the U.S. Senate where he continued to shine. Senator Jefferson Davis of Mississippi insulted Benjamin on the floor of the Senate, and Benjamin challenged him to a duel, but Davis apologized and the two became close friends. When Davis became president of the Confederacy, he relied heavily on Benjamin, appointing him successively as attorney general, secretary of war, and secretary of state.

Benjamin, alone among the Confederate leaders, advocated bringing Black slaves into the army and rewarding them with emancipation. After the war, Benjamin fled to England where he began a new and highly successful career as an English barrister.

Benjamin had little interest in religion, although he was not a self-hating Jew. There are stories of his appearing in a synagogue in Richmond, and he was close to Gustavus Meyers, a leader of the Richmond Jewish community. Benjamin was looked upon as an extremely charming and witty companion and seemed to be always smiling even when under heavy pressure.

There are several versions of a response Benjamin made to an opponent who ridiculed his Jewish roots: "It is true that I am a Jew, and when my ancestors were receiving the Ten Commandments from the immediate hand of Deity, midst the thunderings and lightnings of Mount Sinai, the ancestors of my opponent were herding swine in the forests of Germany." A similar remark is attributed to Benjamin Disraeli in the English Parliament.

One of Benjamin's most severe critics, and an outspoken anti-Semite, was Senator Henry Foote of Mississippi. In January, 1865, Foote was arrested trying to escape across the Potomac to the north and was expelled from the Confederate Congress. Benjamin remains one of the most intriguing figures of mid-nineteenth century America.

For Further Reading:

Eli N. Evans, *Judah P. Benjamin: Confederate Jew*, New York, The Free Press, 1988.
Robert Douthat Meade, *Judah P. Benjamin: Confederate Statesman*, 1943.

Q. On what important occasion did a rabbi first offer the benediction to open the day for the House of Representatives?

A. On February 1, 1860, after a battle of many weeks, Congressman William Pennington was elected by his fellow representatives as Speaker of the House. That same day, for the first time, a Jewish clergyman gave the benediction in the House. Rev. Morris Raphall of New York, wearing a tallit and yarmulke, intoned a long and impressive prayer. One Congressman joked that after Christian influence had failed for eight weeks to produce a speaker, they had to go for outside help. On the other hand, Parson William Brownlow of Tennessee, a notorious demagogue and anti-Semite, criticized Congress for calling "into their aid one of the murderers of Christ."

Ironically, 50 years later Pennington's house in Newark was torn down to make room for the building of the Oheb Shalom synagogue. The next rabbi to appear in Congress was apparently Marcus Jastrow, in 1871.

For Further Reading:

Bertram Korn, *Eventful Years and Experiences*, Cincinnati: 1948, pp 98f, 118.
Eli N. Evans, *Judah P. Benjamin: Confederate Jew*, New York, The Free Press, 1988.

1850–1881: CIVIL WAR AND EXPANSION

Q. How did America's Jewish clergymen react to the slavery issue as the Civil War began?

A. Jewish spiritual leaders do not seem to have involved themselves in the great debate over slavery, before the outbreak of the Civil War. However, as the war began the clergy did speak out. Rev. Morris Raphall delivered an address in New York on the National Fast Day, January 4, 1861 in which he argued that the Bible itself sanctioned slavery. Great prophets and saints in the Bible, people with whom God Himself spoke, owned slaves. Nor was slavery any more sinful in modern times than in ancient. Nevertheless, he said, this did not give the owners the right to abuse slaves.

Rabbi David Einhorn of Temple Har Sinai in Baltimore was an outspoken opponent of slavery, writing that no human being created in the divine image should be held in bondage. But Baltimore was strongly sympathetic to the south and Einhorn, fearing for his life, fled to Philadelphia. R. Bernhard Felsenthal of Madison, Indiana, and later Chicago, was also strongly anti-slavery, and he refused a rabbinical position in Mobile, Alabama because of his anti-slavery feelings.

Rabbi Isaac Mayer Wise labeled the abolitionists as "fanatics," "demagogues" and "revolutionaries" interested only in power, and he felt they could be as much anti-Jewish as anti-southern. Moses, he argued, had tried to restrict and hinder slavery by passing laws which made its existence nearly impossible. However, certainly it was just to own the labor of savages and place them under the protection and benefits of civilized society. "The abstract idea of liberty is more applicable to the Mosaic system than to the savage, and savages only will sell themselves or their offspring." Like Wise, Orthodox Rabbi Bernard Illowy of Baltimore denounced the abolitionists as selfish and ambitious trouble-makers. He soon took a position in secessionist New Orleans.

Rabbi Max Lilienthal opposed slavery as immoral but saw the abolitionists as "incendiaries" and "radicals." The Jews and their leaders were divided like the rest of the population over slavery and the other great issues of the day.

For Further Reading:
Bertram Korn, *American Jewry and the Civil War*, Philadelphia, JPS, 1951.

Q. What rabbi praised James Buchanan in comparison to Abraham Lincoln?

A. Rabbi Isaac M. Wise had voted against Lincoln in the 1860 presidential election. In January 1861, several months after Lincoln's victory, Wise praised outgoing President James Buchanan as a "full statesman" while berating Lincoln for his "queer appearance" and "primitive manner." Four years later Wise had changed his view, even claiming that Lincoln had said in Wise's presence that he was of Jewish ancestry and "indeed he possessed the common features of the Hebrew race both in countenance and features."

For Further Reading:

Isaac Mayer Wise, Articles in "The Israelite" January 13, 1861 and "Cincinnati Commercial," April 20, 1865.
Isaac Markens, "Lincoln and the Jews," PAJHS, XVII, 1909, 109–167.

Q. Which Jewish businessman was regarded by some as the savior of the Democratic party?

A. August Belmont. Born in the German duchy of Hesse Darmstadt in 1813, he immigrated to the U.S. and became one of the leaders of the Democratic Party from the 1840's into the 1880's. He served as the party's national chairman for 12 years, beginning in 1860 with Stephen Douglas' campaign for the presidency. He was often under unjust, vitriolic and anti-Jewish attacks from opponents like Horace Greeley, editor of the *New York Tribune*, who labeled Belmont an international Jew banker of questionable loyalty to the U.S.

Belmont married Caroline Perry, daughter of Commodore Matthew Galbraith Perry. She was also a niece of John Slidell, a prominent Louisiana politician, who along with James M. Mason was captured by a Union ship during the Civil War in the celebrated Trent Affair. A daughter of Slidell's married Baron Erlanger, a leading French Jewish financier.

For Further Reading:

Irving Katz, *August Belmont*, New York; Columbia University Press, 1968.

Q. What became of the project of New Orleans Congregation Nefutzoth Yehudah and its leader James Gutheim to build a statue in memory of philanthropist Judah Touro?

A. World traveler I.J. Benjamin was in New Orleans in 1860 and recounts in his book that he was at the meeting when the project was first announced publicly. The religious Jews protested strongly that sculpting of the human form was against Jewish law. Benjamin was one of the leaders of the protest. Gutheim refused to back down and bitter feelings were aroused on both sides. One man even threatened to murder Benjamin. Jewish leaders in other American cities expressed their opinions in the Jewish journals of the day.

Finally it was agreed to consult four major European scholars - Solomon Judah Rapaport of Prague, Samson Raphael Hirsch of Frankfort on Main, Nathan Adler of London, and Zachariah Frankel of Breslau. All four ruled that the statue was prohibited by Jewish law. In any case, the project was forgotten shortly after, when the Civil War broke out.

For Further Reading:

I.J. Benjamin, *Three Years in America*. 1859-1862, (transl. Charles Reznikoff), Philadelphia, JPS, 1956, I, 320f.

Q. How significant was the role of the Jews in the Civil War?

A. The Jews on both sides did their patriotic duty and more. However, their numbers were hardly decisive in the huge struggle. About 6000 fought in the Federal armies and about 2000 in the Confederate. About 700 died in battle or in prisoner of war camps.

Lieutenant Jacob Valentine commanded a battery at the bombardment of Fort Sumter which opened the war. Seven Jews won the Congressional Medal of Honor; for example, Sergeant Leopold Karpeles of the 57th Massachusetts won his at the Battle of the Wilderness where he rallied retreating Union troops and checked a dangerous enemy advance. Karpeles was later wounded in a battle near North Anna, Virginia. After the war he lived in Washington D.C. and was active in the Washington Hebrew Congregation.

Isaac Hyams won the Roll of Honor, the Confederacy's highest military award, for his heroics at the Battle of Murfreesboro. At the Battle of Newtonia in Missouri in 1862, Confederate forces led by Colonel Joseph Shelby defeated Union forces under General Frederick Salomon in a sharp bloody fight. Shelby, himself a Christian, was the stepson of Benjamin Gratz, Rebecca Gratz's brother, while Salomon was a full-born Jew.

For Further Reading:

Robert Schostek. "Leopold Karpeles: Civil War Hero," *PAJHS*, LIII, 1963, 70- 75.
Mel Young, *Where They Lie*, Lanham, Md., University Press of America, 1991.

Q. Who were the Cameron Dragoons?

A. A New York Civil War regiment composed largely of Jews. The application of Dr. Arnold Fischel for the chaplaincy of the unit was turned down by Secretary of War Simon Cameron due to the law which allowed only Christians to serve as chaplains. Despite considerable pressure from both Jews and non-Jews, Congress did not change the law until long afterward. Thus there were no Jewish combat chaplains in the Union army during the Civil War. Four Jews, including Fischel, did serve as hospital chaplains.

For Further Reading:

Isaac Marken, "Lincoln and the Jews," *PAJHS*, XVII, 1909, p l 14–116.
Bertram Korn, *American Jewry and the Civil War,* Philadelphia, JPS, 1961.

Q. Who was the first surgeon general of the Confederacy?

A. Dr. David Camden De Leon (1817–1872) was the son of Dr. Mordecai H. De Leon of Columbia, SC. David De Leon served as an army surgeon through the Seminole War and was later twice decorated by Congress for both his medical work and his gallantry in action during the Mexican War. When the southern states seceded from the U.S., De Leon resigned from the U.S. army and reported to Confederate President Jefferson Davis, who assigned to him the difficult but important task of organizing the Medical Department of the new nation. He was soon replaced as surgeon general by another officer, a Dr. Moore, who had held a higher rank in the U.S. army than had De Leon and thus, by the rules, outranked him with the Confederacy too. Continuing in the Confederate service until the war's end, Dr. De Leon, like a number of Southern officers, fled to Mexico and remained there for several years until invited to return by President Grant.

Two of De Leon's brothers also achieved some prominence. Edwin (1828–1901} was a lawyer and editor of the *National Democrat,* a Washington D.C. newspaper. In 1854 President Franklin Pierce appointed him consul to Egypt. When the Civil War began, he resigned his post and was assigned by Jefferson Davis as a special agent for the Confederacy in France and England. He wrote a number of books including *The Khedive's Egypt*, and an autobiographical *30 Years of My Life on 3 Continents.*

A third brother, Thomas Cooper De Leon (1839–1914), served in the Confederate army, stationed in Montgomery, Alabama or Richmond, Virginia, the nation's successive capitals. After the war, he embarked upon a career as a writer of novels, plays and poetry and as a newspaper editor. His observations and experiences during the civil war were recorded in 2 books,

Four Years in Rebel Capitals and *Belles, Beaux, and Brains of the 60's*. His play, *Hamlet Ye Dismal Prince,* ran for over 100 days in New York probably the first American play to do so.

For Further Reading:

Barnett Elzas, *The Jews of South Carolina,* Philadelphia; J.B. Lippincot, 1905.

Q. Was there a Jewish governor in the South during the Civil War?

A. Michael Hahn (1830–1886), a loyal Unionist in New Orleans, was elected to the U.S. Congress in 1862 and to the governorship of Louisiana after the Union armies had occupied the state. After the war, he was voted to the U.S. Senate but declined to serve because he disagreed with President Andrew Johnson's policies for Reconstruction.

After some years as a newspaper publisher, Hahn returned to politics, holding a number of offices, including Speaker of the Louisiana House and U.S. Congressman. Although it seems likely that Hahn was Jewish, there is some doubt about it.

Several Jews were prominent in Louisiana politics before the Civil War. Judah Benjamin served as U.S. Senator and later as Jefferson Davis' Secretary of War and State. Henry Hyams was lieutenant governor in 1859, and Edwin Moise was speaker of the state legislature. The first king of Mardi Gras (1872) was Louis J. Solomon.

For Further Reading:

Vaughn Baker and Amos Simpson, "Michael Hahn: Steady Patriot," *Louisiana History,*
    XIII, 1972, 229–52.
UJE, V, 166–167.
EJ, XI, 517–520.

Q. A bitter political opponent of Abraham Lincoln spoke out several times to help Jews on public issues. Who was he?

A. Articulate and combative, Congressman Clement Vallandigham, a Democrat from Dayton, Ohio, was an outspoken enemy of Lincoln, of the war, and of Lincoln's policy toward emancipating the slaves.

On May 6, 1863, Vallandigham was arrested in his home by General Ambrose Burnside on a charge of treason. According to his biographer, Frank L. Klement, Vallandigham wanted to be arrested, hoping that he would gain publicity toward his planned campaign for the governorship.

President Lincoln, a strong supporter of free speech, felt that the arrest may have been unnecessary. However, now that it was done, the cabinet had to support the general. Rather than put Vallandigham in jail and make a martyr of him, they decided to send him beyond Confederate lines into exile.

While in Congress, Vallandigham had spoken up twice on important Jewish issues: (1) He introduced a resolution declaring that American Jews were entitled to the same rights given other U.S. citizens when traveling abroad, especially in Switzerland where there had been problems. (2) He sponsored an amendment to allow rabbis to serve as chaplains in the U.S. Army. This failed to pass Congress.

Despite his exile, Vallandigham was still a serious candidate for governor of Ohio in 1863. Rabbi Isaac Mayer Wise openly supported Vallandigham, endorsing his crusade for peace and compromise, until some of the leaders of Wise's temple persuaded him to back down. Vallandigham abided in Canada until June, 1864 then returned to Ohio and the practice of law. He sought to regain public office but failed to win an election to the Senate in 1868. He accidentally shot himself in 1871.

For Further Reading:

Frank Klement, *The Limits of Dissent,* Lexington ; University of Kentucky Press, 1970.

Q. How did the Union generals entertain themselves in the evening between days of the Civil War battle of Chickamauga?

A. The first day of the bloody battle of Chickamauga ended in a draw. That evening, Union General William Rosecrans called his corps commanders to his headquarters to discuss plans for the next day's fighting. When the conference ended, Rosecrans called for hot coffee to be served, and General Alexander McCook of the 20th Corps entertained his colleagues by singing a popular ballad of those days, "The Hebrew Maiden's Lament," by C.B. Burkhardt and P. Lindpainter. It was the story of a Jewish girl who loved a Christian youth but who would not marry him because of the religious difference. The girl's father was a pious Jew:

> In that sombre chamber yonder,
> Father's taper still burns bright:
> Bending to his breast his aged,
> Care-worn face he prays tonight.
> Open wide before the righteous,
> Lies the Talmud which he reads . . .

It was well that the Yankees sang while they could, for on the next day, the Confederates charged through a gap in the Union line and routed most of the Union army. Rosecrans and McCook fled with the rest and were both soon relieved of their commands. "The Hebrew Maiden's Lament" is still on file in the Library of Congress.

For Further Reading:

Glenn Tucker, *Chickamauga:Bloody Battle in the West*. Dayton, Morningside, 1961

Q. Was there an outbreak of anti-Semitism during the Civil War?

A. Many Jews fought in both the Northern and Southern armies, including nine Northern generals, and Jewish citizens at home on both sides served their causes loyally. There were no major outbreaks of anti-Jewish violence, and certainly Abraham Lincoln was a deeply humane man and no bigot. Nevertheless, there were some ugly incidents and some unpleasant people.

Union General Benjamin Butler was an outspoken Jew-hater As military commandant in New Orleans after that city's capture, he was harsh to Jews and indeed to the citizenry as a whole, and he earned well the nickname — Beast Butler. Parson William Brownlow of East Tennessee, a well known writer, orator, and politician, also included open anti-Semitism in his steady repertoire of hate mongering. Some like Senator Henry Wilson of Massachusetts turned from the anti-Catholic furor of the 1850's to anti-Semitism in the 1860's. Confederate Congressman Henry Foote of Mississippi was an open anti-Semite. Occasional newspaper articles would attack Jews on the age old canards of monetary greed and lack of patriotism. Sometimes they blamed the Rothschilds for America's problems.

There were also several instances of harassment of Jews by local military commanders including the notorious Order # 11 issued from General Grant's headquarters in Holly Springs, Tennessee, which ordered the expulsion of all Jews from the area within 24 hours. There is mention in General William T. Sherman's letters of the greed of the "swarms" of Jewish merchants who traded across military lines. In small southern towns, Jews were sometimes blamed for the hardships of the war and several were apparently ordered expelled from Thomasville, Georgia in August, 1862 for being unpatriotic.

The increase of anti-Semitism was only one small aspect of the history of the Civil War and seems to have had no long term effects on the standing of the Jews in the American system. It was an irritable and unfair reaction to the pressures of the time.

For Further Reading:

Bertram Korn, *American Jewry and the Civil War,* Philadelphia, JPS, 1951.
Jonathan Sarna, *General Grant Expelled the Jews,* 2012
Louis Schmeier, "Notes and Documents on the 1862 Expulsion of Jews from Thomasville, Georgia," AJA, *XXXII,* 1980, 9–22.
Louis Schmeier, *Reflections of Southern Jewry,* Mercer University Press, 1982.

Q. Did Jews attain high rank in the Confederate Navy?

A. Levy Myers Harby (1793–1870) climaxed a life of naval service at age 68 by being assigned command of a fleet of Confederate gunboats that guarded the Sabine River in Texas. During the War of 1812, Harby served on a privateer and later joined the U.S. Navy. However, advancement to higher rank was very difficult, and Harby left the navy for other adventures, serving with Andrew Jackson in the Seminole Wars, pursuing pirates in the Caribbean and fighting in the Texas War of Independence.

Henry Etting of Baltimore (1799–1876), another old time navy man, re-entered the service for the Civil War on the Union side, retiring for the second time finally in 1871 with the rank of Commodore. In 1832, Etting had been court martialed and publicly reprimanded by the Secretary of the Navy for stabbing a man who had attacked him both physically and verbally calling him "a damned Jewish son-of-a-bitch."

For Further Reading:

Eleanor Cohen, "Jews in the American and Confederate Navies," *Maryland History Magazine.* XV, p. lf.
Marcus, *USJ,* I. p. 103–104.

Q. What Jewish legal (*halachic*) disagreement in New Orleans in 1864 sparked a debate between two major European rabbinic scholars?

A. Rabbi Dr. Bernard Illowy had been ordained by R. Moshe Sofer in Pressburg and was one of the few competent Talmudists in the U.S. in Civil War days. As a rabbi in New Orleans in 1864, he refused to allow the circumcision of a baby born to a Jewish father and non-Jewish mother and threatened to excommunicate anyone who would perform the ritual. Illowy reasoned that the circumcision would be a mockery inasmuch as the mother of the boy would never allow him to be converted to Judaism and raised as a Jew.

Turning to the rabbis of Europe to support his position, R. Illowy wrote to Rabbi Marcus Lehmann, editor of the *Israelite,* a major Orthodox periodical in Germany. Lehmann wrote an article supporting Illowy, as did

R. Azriel Hildesheimer, a leading German rabbinical scholar. A dissenting view from R. Zvi Hirsch Kalischer argued that while it was deplorable that the father had drifted so far from Jewish observance, it was an act of repentance to circumcise the child. A rabbinical court could then easily complete his conversion at a later date by arranging his ritual immersion.

The story demonstrates the laxity in the Jewish ritual observance in mid-19th century America, and it also gives a glimpse of one of the first Orthodox rabbis in the U.S. It is curious that when Illowy came to New Orleans in 1861, not one booth *(succah)* was built for the Tabernacles holiday. The year he left, 1864, fifty *succot* were built, presumably due to Illowy's influence.

For Further Reading:

David Ellenson, "Jewish Law in the 19th Century in New Orleans," *AJH*, LXIX, 1979, 174–195.

Q. Was it possible for a Confederate soldier in the Civil War to keep kosher?

A. The Confederate army, of course, did not provide a kosher food service; however, some soldiers did manage. Private Isaac Gleitzman, who served in the cavalry under General Nathan Bedford Forrest, later claimed proudly that he had eaten no non-kosher food during his war service. His family still has his two mess kits, one for meat and one for milk. He also won a Confederate Cross of Honor.

For Further Reading:

Eli Evans, *The Provincials*, New York; Athenaeum, 1973, p. 63–64.

Q. How did David Mayer save his house from destruction during the burning of Atlanta, Georgia in 1864?

A. David Mayer, an Atlanta Jewish merchant, traveled the countryside collecting supplies for the Confederate army. Finding many families destitute as a result of the war, he tried to help them, often giving them shelter in his own house. It is told that when the Union army burned Atlanta, Mayer put a special Masonic sign on the doorposts of both his home and the Masonic Hall. As the signs on the doorposts helped save the ancient Israelites from the angel of destruction on the night of the Exodus from Egypt, so Mayer's signs saved these two buildings from General Sherman's destroyers. This story cannot be verified beyond all doubt, but the two buildings did indeed survive the burning of Atlanta and guards were posted to protect the Masonic Hall from danger.

For Further Reading:

Janice Rothschild , "Pre- 1867 Atlanta Jewry," *AJHQ*, LXII, 1973, 242–249.

Q. Who was the first Jewish chaplain to go AWOL?

A. Rabbi Dr. Ferdinand Leopold Sarner (1820–1878) came from Germany in 1859 and accepted a post as rabbi of Brith Kodesh Congregation of Rochester, N.Y. On April 10, 1863 he became chaplain of the 54th New York Volunteers, a regiment composed of German speaking immigrants including a few Jews. It was probably Sarner's knowledge of German and his Ph.D. from the University of Hesse rather than his rabbinical title which brought him this position. In fact, one contemporary account mistakenly labels him a Lutheran minister. He was present at Chancellorsville in May, 1863 and was severely wounded two months later at Gettysburg. Although Sarner returned to his duties, his health had been damaged, and he was back in the hospital by July, 1864. Because he left the hospital before his discharge papers were formally filed, the government revoked his honorable discharge in 1869 and Sarner was listed as AWOL.

For Further Reading:

Louis Barish, *Rabbis in Uniform*, NY, Jonathan David, 1962.
Bertram Korn, *American Jewry and the Civil War,* Philadelphia, JPS, 1951,
    p. 83f.

Q. Were Jewish soldiers in the Confederate army allowed time off for their holidays?

A. Lewis Leon (1841–1914) along with several other Jews joined a North Carolina regiment, the Charlotte Grays, which served in General Robert E. Lee's Army of Northern Virginia during the Civil War. Leon records in his diary for September 29, 1863, that before the Jewish New Year an order from General Lee had been read out to the troops "granting a furlough to each Israelite to go to Richmond for the holidays if he so desires." Such general furloughs were not the usual practice. In 1861, 1862, and 1864 Rabbi Maximillian Micelbacher sent letters to Lee asking about holiday furloughs. In each instance Lee replied that a general furlough was impractical; however, individual requests would be considered by the appropriate commanding officers, each in terms of his own situation. Leon's statement is our main source for information on the 1863 furlough. He himself did not go to Richmond. His brother Morris did.

For Further Reading:

Morris V. Schappes, *A Documentary History of the Jews in the United States, 1654–1875*, New York; Schocken Books, 1971.

Q. Were any Jews held in the notorious Andersonville prison?

A. Sergeant Elias Hyneman, a pious Jew, was one of a number of Jewish Union soldiers who died in the horrible Confederate prisoner of war camp in Andersonville, Georgia. Surrounded by enemy troops in fighting near Petersburg, Virginia in June 1864, Hyneman gave his horse to one wounded comrade and his shoes to another and was taken prisoner. After six months of starvation and exposure in Andersonville, Hyneman died in January 1865.

In the Baltch Archive in Philadelphia there is a very emotional letter written from Rebecca Hyneman, Elias' mother and a well known poetess, to her son shortly before his capture. The letter never reached him. The most complete biography of Elias Hyneman appeared in an article "An American Hebrew's Heroic Life," written for *The Menorah* in 1888 by a cousin, Alice Hyneman Rhine. Rhine's flowery praise leaves the reader wondering whether she had been in love with the handsome young officer.

Northern prisoner of war camps like the one in Elmira, New York were hardly better for undernourished and disheartened southern boys unaccustomed to northern winters. A number of Jewish Confederates were among those who died and were buried in Elmira.

Information supplied by Lynn Berkowitz, author of *Land That Eats Its Inhabitants*.

Q. What Jewish, former VMI cadet sculpted the "Virginia Mourning Her Dead" monument at VMI?

A. One of the memorable moments of the Civil War was the fight put up by the cadets of Virginia Military Institute at the Battle of New Market in Virginia on June 15, 1864. One of the cadets was Moses Jacob Ezekiel (1844–1917) who was to become the first American Jewish sculptor of international repute. Ezekiel spent the years 1874–1917 in Rome, except for brief visits to the U.S. Still his loyalty to the old South shows in his statues on southern themes including several busts of Robert E. Lee and Stonewall Jackson and the bronze "Virginia Mourning her Dead" dedicated in 1903 on the campus of VMI. Despite his loyalties, Ezekiel was disappointed at the lack of acknowledgment of his work in the South.

Ezekiel was critical at times of Reform Judaism saying that it had failed in its aim of gaining respect for Judaism from intellectual Christians. However, he formed three busts of Rabbi Isaac Mayer Wise, father of the Reform movement in the U.S. There are also several statues on biblical themes, and a memorial to financier Jesse Seligman, and a seal for the Jewish Publication Society was designed by Ezekiel.

He used his influence in European artistic and political circles in the 1890's to facilitate the settlement of Russian Jewish refugees in Palestine and the building of schools and industrial colonies there.

For Further Reading:

Joseph Gutman and Stanley Chyet, eds., *Memoirs From the Baths of Diocletian,* Detroit; Wayne State University Press, 1975.

Q. Was the Confederate army's only Jewish chaplain really Jewish?

A. Charles Goldberg (1820–1890) was born in Fraustadt, Poland, the youngest of 17 children of a rabbi. Fleeing military conscription, he came to the U.S. about 1845 and after being nursed back to health from an illness by a Presbyterian family, he converted to Presbyterianism and became an ordained minister in Texas. Goldberg served in the Confederate army as a Presbyterian chaplain and continued his ministry in Texarkana after the war.

By 1876, the Jews of Texarkana were sufficient in numbers to organize a High Holiday service. They invited Goldberg to conduct it, and he did. He tutored Jewish boys for bar mitzvah without trying to convert them. It is told that on his deathbed Goldberg sent for a local rabbi, said *viddui* and asked to be buried in a Jewish ceremony. His daughter, years later, denied the story, but Goldberg is in fact not buried in the church cemetery.

The descendants of Uriah Feibleman, of Fredericksburg, Virginia, claim that he served as a Jewish chaplain for Mahone's brigade in General Lee's army of Northern Virginia, but there is no documentary evidence to support their claim.

For Further Reading:

David Eichhorn, *Evangelizing the American Jew,* Middle Village, NY; Jonathan David Publ. Inc., 1978.

Q. Whom did Simon Wolf, noted Jewish activist, meet in Washington at the Willard Hotel the morning of Abraham Lincoln's assassination?

A. Wolf claimed that he met John Wilkes Booth, whom he had known years before from an amateur drama club in Cleveland, in which they had both participated. Booth had gone on to become a professional actor. His brother Edwin was one of the great stage personalities of the 19th century, one of his noted roles being Shylock in Shakespeare's Merchant of Venice. Strangely, Wolf chanced upon Booth in the Willard on the morning of Lincoln's assassination. Booth was depressed and told Wolf that the daughter of a United States senator had just rejected his proposal of marriage. The story is from Wolf's own account. Wolf was not shy when it came to talking about his own importance, and the story must be taken with at least a few grains of salt.

For Further Reading:

Simon Wolf, *The American Jew as Patriot, Soldier and Citizen,* New York, Brentano's, 1895.

Q. For what unusual act of hospitality is Abraham Weill remembered?

A. In April, 1865, Abraham Weill, a Jewish resident of Charlotte, North Carolina, performed an act of hospitality following the model of his namesake the biblical patriarch, Abraham. Richmond, the Confederacy's capital, had just fallen to General Grant's army, and Robert E. Lee was about to surrender. Varina Howell Davis, wife of Confederate President Jefferson Davis, was fleeing south from Richmond. An ugly mob of stragglers and deserters threatened Mrs. Davis' party.

Few people in Charlotte were willing to offer her support or hospitality. It was Weill who provided food and other comforts to Mrs. Davis and her party despite threats of later retaliation. The food was carried under cover of darkness to hide from the mob in the streets. Weill would accept no money for his good deed. Several days later, when Davis himself passed through Charlotte accompanied by several other Confederate leaders, Weill played host to Secretary of State Judah P. Benjamin and two companions. He was afraid to take in Davis because Union General George Stoneman had threatened to burn the house of anyone who received Davis. Weill's courage and generosity were acknowledged by Benjamin who presented him with a gold headed cane he had used in his last speech to the Senate.

For Further Reading:

Burke Davis, *The Long Surrender*. New York, Random House, 1985.
Hudson Strode. *Jefferson Davis: Tragic Hero*, New York, Harcourt and Brace, 1964.
  Eli Evans, *Judah P. Benjamin*. New York, The Free Press, 1988.
  Robert D. Meade. *Judah P. Benjamin: Confederate Statesman*, New York, Oxford University Press. 1943.

Q. What happened to the last money in the Confederate Treasury?

A. Jefferson Davis and several other Confederate leaders fled south after the capture of Richmond hoping to escape the victorious Union armies. They took with them important government papers and most of what little was left in the Confederate treasury. By the time the party reached the area of Washington, Georgia, shortly before Davis was finally captured by Union troops, about $143,000 in gold and silver remained and was distributed toward several purposes.

$40,000 in silver was given to Major Raphael J. Moses, a Jewish Georgian who had served with distinction during the war on General James Longstreet's staff. It was to be used to feed impoverished Confederate veterans returning home. Under great pressure both from nearby Federal soldiers and from Southerners made desperate by the war, Moses first turned over $10,000 to the Quartermaster Department of nearby Washington. He brought the remaining $30,000 to General Edward Molineux of the Federal garrison at Augusta, who promised to use it to feed returning Confederate soldiers and to help the needy in local hospitals. It is far from certain how much of this money ever reached those for whom it was intended.

For Further Reading:

Burke Davis, *The Long Surrender,* New York, Random House, 1985.

Q. What unusual vow did Henry Heyneman take?

A. Henry Heyneman, a Jewish native of Munich who had emigrated to Boston before the Civil War, vowed that he would walk from Boston to Washington D.C. to celebrate when the Union Army captured Richmond. The good news came in April, 1865, and Heyneman set out from Boston with a light knapsack on his shoulder and an American flag in his hand. Unfortunately the newspaper that reported his departure does not say how or if he completed his journey.

For Further Reading:

Bertram Korn, "The Jews of the Union," *AJA*, XIII, 1961, 131–230.

Q. What American Jewish actress starred in plays with the great Edwin Booth in the mid-19th century?

A. Rose Eytinge (1835–1911) was born in Philadelphia to a Dutch Jewish family. Her father was a teacher of languages. She made her professional debut in *Old Guard,* by Dion Boucicault, in Syracuse in 1853 and went on to a long career including playing Ophelia to Edwin Booth's Hamlet. In her lively autobiography, *Memories of Rose Eytinge,* she describes Booth's greatness as an actor and his kindness as a human being. Eytinge played in Washington DC before President Lincoln who complimented her.

One of America's most beautiful and talented actresses, Eytinge found little stability in her domestic life. Three marriages failed, including one to Colonel George H. Butler, U.S. counsel general to Egypt. In the 1890's, Eytinge operated drama schools in New York and Portland, Oregon. She seems not to have maintained any connection with Judaism in her adult years.

For Further Reading:

Rose Eytinge, *The Memories of Rose Eytinge,* New York, Frederick A. Stokes Co., 1905.

Q. Two German born Jewish cousins with the same name became American governors. Who were they?

A. Edward Salomon (1836–1913) settled in Chicago where he practiced law. Joining the army in the Civil War he worked his way up to brigadier general, commanding predominantly German speaking units. After the war he was elected clerk of Cook County. Salomon's military connections and his support among German American leaders led to his appointment by President Grant as Governor of Washington Territory in 1870. He resigned two years later, pressed by criticism over his financial maneuverings and his excessive absences. Salomon later moved to San Francisco where he gained prominence as a lawyer and sat in the California legislature.

His cousin, also named Edward Salomon (1828–1909), fled Germany in the political turmoil of 1849 and settled in Manitowoc, Wisconsin. Teacher, surveyor, and finally lawyer, Salomon was elected lieutenant governor in 1861 and replaced Louis Harvey as governor a year later when the latter drowned. A strong supporter of the Union effort in the Civil War, Governor

Salomon made himself unpopular with his strict enforcement of the draft laws, and he lost his bid for re-election in 1864. He moved to New York where he practiced law until 1894 and then returned to his native Germany where he spent the rest of his years.

For Further Reading:

Thomas MacMullin and David Walker. *Biographical Directory of American Territorial Governors,* Westport. Conn.; Meckler Publ., 1984.
Dictionary of Wisconsin Biography, Madison; 1960.

Q. How did U.S. Jews react to the tribulations of the Jews of Morocco during the Moroccan-Spanish Wars that went on from 1859 into the 1870's?

A. Jews suffered great discrimination under Moroccan law. During the war with Spain, hundreds of Jews fled to Gibraltar which was under British rule. In 1863, at the request of the Board of Delegates of American Israelites (BDAI), Secretary of State William Seward instructed the U.S. consul at Tangiers to help. Over a decade later William Evarts, Secretary of State to President Rutherford B. Hayes and helpful to Jews in a number of foreign policy matters, instructed the consul "to shield the Hebrews from oppression." Later, Secretary James G. Blaine continued that policy. The BDAI also sent large sums of money to help the Jews.

The BDAI had been formed in 1859 in the wake of the Mortara case as an organization to represent Jewish interests in a unified way. It achieved some moderate success until it merged with the new Union of American Hebrew Congregations in 1876.

For Further Reading:
Marcus, *USJ,* II, 312-327

Q. How did the Spiegel Catalogue Company begin?

A. Brothers Marcus and Joseph Spiegel from Prussia, settled in Chicago in 1850, and joined the Union army when the Civil War broke out. Marcus, who had risen to the rank of colonel, was fatally wounded in battle near Alexandria, Louisiana in 1864. Joseph, captured in the same battle, returned to Chicago after the war and opened a small dry goods store that the brothers had often talked about. After some years the business developed into the Spiegel Catalogue Company.

Marcus Spiegel wrote a series of letters to his wife which were published in 1985 under the title, *Your True Marcus*, by his descendant Jean Soman. Marcus had married Caroline Hamlin, a Quaker woman who converted to Judaism and raised their four children as Jews.

For Further Reading:
Frank Byrne and Jean Soman, *Your True Marcus*, Kent State University Press, 1985.

Q. Who represented the U.S. in Mexico during the Mexican civil war of the 1860's?

A. The civil war between the republican forces of Benito Juarez and the Emperor Maximilian presented a danger to the U.S. which was then involved in its own civil war. Emperor Louis Napoleon of France had taken advantage of the turmoil in Mexico and of the U.S.'s domestic preoccupation to set up his own puppet, the Austrian Prince Maximilian and his wife Carlotta, as the Emperor and Empress of Mexico with the support of French armies. Sincere and well-meaning, Maximilian had been duped into believing that the people of Mexico really wanted him to rule and that he could do some good for them. However, a rebellion led by Benito Juarez was soon under way. The story was dramatized in a classic 1930's movie starring Paul Muni, Bette Davis and Brian Aherne.

When Mexico's civil war erupted in 1864, the U.S. was represented in Mexico by a consul, Marcus Otterbourg, a German born Jew. Otterbourg was one of the first to realize how desperate the situation of Maximilian's forces was becoming as the French troops began to return home. Not able to trust the mail, Otterbourg went to Washington D.C. to report directly to President Andrew Johnson. The U.S. was going to send Ulysses Grant to Mexico to meet with Juarez, but Grant turned down the job. General William T. Sherman was sent instead, along with Otterbourg and a new ambassador, Lewis D. Campbell. Otterbourg was back in Mexico City late in November, 1866. Campbell came as close as New Orleans and then irresponsibly turned around and went back home to Ohio leaving to Otterbourg the heavy task of ensuring the safety of Americans in Mexico and of helping European nationals as well.

Otterbourg was respected by both sides and was involved in the negotiations between them. He helped to arrange the orderly surrender of Mexico City by General Tabera to the rebel forces under Porfirio Diaz, after Maximilian had been captured and executed by a firing squad. Otterbourg finally was named full ambassador by the U.S. in June, 1867.

For Further Reading:

Ruth L. Benjamin, "Marcus Otterbourg: United States Minister To Mexico," *PAJHS*, XXXll, 1934. 65–98.

Q. Who was the "little Jew" whose bravery at the Battle of Beecher's Island inspired a poem?

A. Sigmund Schlesinger, recently arrived from Europe, joined the U.S. Army in Kansas in 1868 and was immediately sent with a 50 man party under Colonel George Forsyth to scout hostile Indians. At the Arickaree fork of the Republican River, the party was attacked by a large band of Sioux and Cheyenne Indians under the famous chief Roman Nose. The soldiers dug in on Beecher's Island in the river and held out under heavy attack from September 17 to 25 when help arrived.

Although slight of build and with no military experience, Schlesinger earned the respect of Colonel Forsyth and his fellow soldiers by his bravery and his devotion to duty. He also provided a small meal by killing a coyote.

Schlesinger later settled in Cleveland where he became a successful-merchant and a leader in the Jewish community. The Battle at Beecher's Island remained a high point of his life. In early years, he was perturbed when people would not believe his stories about the campaign. Thus, he was glad to see the growing number of written accounts that appeared as the battle became part of the lore of the Old West. The poem about the "little Jew" appeared in 1873.

> "When the foe charged on the breastworks With the madness of despair,
> And the bravest of souls were tested, The little Jew was there.
> When the weary dozed on duty,
> Or the wounded needed care,
> When another shot was called for, The little Jew was there.
> With the festering dead around them, Shedding poison in the air,
> When the crippled chieftain ordered, The little Jew was there."

Rabbi Henry Cohen of Galveston wrote an article about Schlesinger in the *Publications of the American Jewish Historical Society* in 1900.

Schlesinger regularly enjoyed attending reunions of his old unit until his death in 1928.

1850–1881: CIVIL WAR AND EXPANSION

Q. How did Dr. Herman Bendell (1843-1932) become President Grant's Superintendent of Indian Affairs for Arizona?

A. In 1870, President Ulysses S. Grant began a policy of allocating supervision of Indian agencies to different religious denominations. Simon Wolf, a prominent Jewish leader suggested assigning a Jew to one of the jobs and offered the name of Herman Bendell, an Albany, New York physician and a veteran of the Civil War. Despite some anti-Semitic rumblings in the press, Grant sent Bendell to Arizona where he dealt with Apaches, Mojaves, and other tribes (1871-1873). His reports to Washington called for better medical supplies, schools, and water. The Apaches, a warlike people, must be handled fairly but firmly, he suggested, as Generals George Crook and Oliver O. Howard were doing. It is curious that Bendell recommended civilizing the Apaches by sending Christian missionaries out to teach them. Bendell had quite a row with the (Jewish) Goldwater brothers, who complained about him to Washington, when they felt he had unfairly denied them a supply contract.

Bendell returned home in 1873 to get married and served the next year as U.S. consul in Denmark. Returning afterward to medical practice in Albany, he enjoyed a long productive career and became head of the New York Medical Society.

For Further Reading:

Herman Bendell. "The Superintendent of Indian Affairs, Arizona Territory, Annual Reports. 1871 and 1872," *WSJH*, XXII, 1990, 195-206 and 303-316.
Norton Stern, "Herman Bendell: Superintendent of Indian Affairs, Arizona Territory, 1871-1873," *'WSJHQ*, VII, 1976, 265-284.

Q. What U.S. presidential hopeful was named for his Jewish uncle?

A. Benjamin Gratz Brown of Missouri was a grandson of Kentucky's first governor, John Brown, and Senator John Bledsoe. The families were connected with the most prominent in the region — Benton, Blair, Breckenridge, Clay, and Preston. One of Governor Brown's daughters married Benjamin Gratz of the well-known Philadelphia Jewish family. Gratz had moved to Lexington, Kentucky and had been highly successful in business. Benjamin Gratz Brown was born in his uncle Benjamin Gratz's house and was named after him. He was close also to his uncle's sister, Rebecca Gratz, who visited Kentucky in 1843, and he visited her in Philadelphia during his student days at Yale (1845-1847).

In 1872, B. Gratz Brown, as he was often called, was a candidate for U. S. president at the Liberal Republican party convention in Cincinnati.

Brown turned his support to Horace Greeley, and the convention named Greeley as its candidate for president and Brown for vice-president. The Democrats also accepted the Greeley-Brown ticket. However, they were defeated by Republican Ulysses S. Grant in the election.

Ardently pro-union and anti-slavery, Brown had replaced secessionist Waldo P. Johnson as U.S. senator from Missouri in 1863, and Brown consistently supported ultra-liberal (for those days) ideas like universal suffrage, an eight hour work day for government employees, merit system in the Civil Service, and government ownership of telegraph lines. From 1871–1873, Brown served as governor of Missouri.

General Joseph Shelby, one of the great Confederate cavalry leaders, was another nephew of Benjamin Gratz and was raised very devotedly by Gratz as his own son.

For Further Reading:

Norma L. Peterson. *Freedom and Franchise: The Political Career of Benjamin Gratz Brown,* Columbia. University of Missouri Press, 1968.
Daniel O'Flaherty, *General Jo Shelby: Undefeated Rebel,* Chapel Hill, University of North Carolina Press, 1954.

Q. Where any Jews involved in the founding of the American Medical Association?

A. Dr. Isaac Hays (1796–1879) came from a large and prominent Jewish family of colonial days. Taking his M.D. from the University of Pennsylvania in 1820, Hays went on to a distinguished career as an ophthalmologist, occupying himself with research and writing, and the invention of surgical instruments. He was one of the founders of the American Medical Association and wrote its Code of Ethics.

His son, Isaac Minis Hays (1847- 1925), was also a well known ophthalmologist and was for many years secretary of the American Philological Society. In that capacity he published two books on Benjamin Franklin, the Society's founder.

For Further Reading:

UJE, 5:257.

Q. Who was "Curly-haired white chief with one tongue"?

A. Julius Meyer came to Iowa from Germany in 1866 and joined his brothers in trading with the Indians. He became very close to Chief Standing

Bear and his Pawnees. Learning six Indian dialects, Meyer served as a government interpreter. The Pawnees adopted him and named him Box-ka re-sha-hash-ta-ka, curly-haired white chief with one tongue, i.e., honest white man. Meyer later opened a curio shop in Omaha which became a headquarters for visiting Indians. Interested in music, he helped found Omaha's first opera house in 1885. He was an active member of Temple Israel of Omaha.

For Further Reading:

"Trail Blazers of the Trans-Mississippi West," *AJA,* VIII, 1956, 119–120.

Q. How was Benjamin Nathan murdered?

A. Benjamin Nathan, one of New York's worthiest and wealthiest citizens, was murdered July 29, 1870 in his own home on W. 23 Street. Member of the 9th Street Synagogue and vice president of the New York Stock Exchange, Nathan had been staying in his Morristown, Pennsylvania estate, but came to New York to be at the synagogue for his mother's yahrzeit. His sister was married to Rabbi J.J. Lyons.

Nathan was beaten to death with an iron rod, apparently by a burglar. The crime was never solved although a $10,000 reward was offered by the Stock Exchange for apprehension of the murderer. The crime shocked the city and made front page news for two weeks.

For Further Reading:

Rowland Thomas. "The Unsolved Murder of Benjamin Nathan," *AJA,* VIII. 1956, 14–21.

Q. What were the political repercussions of General Grant's famous Order Number 11, and was General Grant an anti-Semite?

A. In 1863, while commanding Union forces in Tennessee, General Ulysses S. Grant issued an order designed to end illegal trade with the Confederacy in his army's sector. The Order specifically singled out "Jew peddlers." Protests immediately went to President Lincoln, who countermanded the order.

When Grant ran on the Republican ticket for president in 1868, opponents attacked Order 11 as a sign of Grant's anti-Semitism. R. Isaac Mayer Wise of Cincinnati often repeated the charge in his journal, "The Israelite," while Jewish supporters of Grant defended him. Some anti-Jewish articles appeared in the press. Grant claimed, probably in truth, that he had issued the order without reflection, on the prompting of advisors during a tense military situation and that he had not been thinking of the Jews as a race, but rather of the few that were involved in the illegal trade.

As president, Grant was always friendly to Jews, appointing a number to government posts and offering a position in the cabinet to his friend, Joseph Seligman. He opposed efforts to ban kosher slaughtering of animals on ground of its supposed cruelty. Grant never mentioned Order #11 in his memoirs. Years later he became the first American president, albeit out of office, to visit Jerusalem.

For Further Reading:

Joakim Isaacs. "Candidate Grant and the Jews," *AJA*, XVII, 1965, 3–15.
Sarna, Jonathan, *General Grant Expelled the Jews*, 2012

Q. Who invented the popular pants called Levis?

A. Legend attributes their invention to Levi Strauss, a prospering San Francisco Jewish merchant in gold rush days. However, another account is probably more accurate. In 1872, Jacob Davis, a Russian Jewish tailor in Reno, Nevada. wrote to Strauss describing work pants that he had been making out of denim and blue cloth with rivets to strengthen the pockets. Strauss went into partnership with Davis, who moved to San Francisco to supervise the production of the pants.

For Further Reading:

Harriet and Fred Rochlin, *A New Life in the Far West,* Boston; Houghton Mifflin Co. 1984

Q. What father and son served simultaneously as chief justice and governor of South Carolina?

A. Franklin Moses Sr. and Franklin Moses Jr. served respectively as chief justice of the state supreme court (1868–77) and as governor (1872–74) of South Carolina . The elder Moses came out of a distinguished Jewish family, married the well-connected Jane McClellan and served with distinction in a number of public offices both before and after the Civil War. Franklin Jr. was also an able man, but his checkered career has earned him the description by one notable historian, R.H. Woody, as "a shrewd scoundrel."

The younger Moses liked to talk of his devotion to the Confederacy, and he boasted of having raised the Confederate and Palmetto (South Carolina) flags over Fort Sumter when it fell in 1861. However, after the war he aligned himself with the Scalawags who tried to gain political advancement

1850-1881: CIVIL WAR AND EXPANSION 107

by posing as defenders of the newly freed slaves. As speaker of the state house (1868-1872) and then governor of South Carolina, Moses Jr began to involve himself more and more openly in graft and bribery, drawing widespread indignation and some critical cartoons by Thomas Nast in *Harper's Weekly*. When political opponents tried to arrest him he called out four Black companies of militia to defend him. Moses did not gain renomination as governor. However, he did win election to a circuit judge position and was prevented from taking it only on legal technicalities.

Bankrupt, disgraced, and rejected by his family, Moses went north in 1877. Over the next three decades, he became addicted to drugs and was jailed several times in several cities on charges of petty swindling. He died in Winthrop, Mass., in 1906, a probable suicide.

For Further Reading:

R.H. Woody, "Franklin J. Moses, Jr.: Scalawag Governor of South Carolina, 1872-1874," *North Carolina Historical Review*, X, 1933, 111-132.

Q. What was the Alaskan Commercial Co.?

A. In 1870, the U.S. government granted to a group of San Francisco businessmen a 20 year exclusive lease to administer the vast new territory of Alaska, (which had been purchased from Russia in 1867), and to catch seals on the Pribilof Islands.

The new company was an outgrowth of the Hutchinson-Kohl company led by Lewis Gerstle and Louis Sloss, two Jewish immigrants. The company bought out the entire stock of the previous Russian company. Sloss became the first president of the new Alaska Commercial Company.

A most efficient organization, the ACC had both the resources and the know-how to bring men and supplies through the vast territory. The ACC also played an important social and political role, providing schools and medical services, and maintaining law and order in the interior. They treated the natives far better than the petty traders did and were helpful to explorers and scientists, particularly to the Smithsonian Institute.

The company was criticized for not encouraging the opening of Alaska to more settlement and for maintaining a strong lobby in Washington. However, there were never any serious charges of wrongdoing. Opponents could resent their power and success, but could not malign their ethics.

The ACC persuaded the U.S. government to outlaw pelagic (open sea) sealing, instead taking a controlled harvest of seal skins yearly on the Pribilof Islands. Nevertheless, other merchants sent ships to attack the seals on their migration north through the Pacific. Many seals sank beneath the waves after being shot and their skins were not recovered. Both the slaughter and the waste were dreadful. The ACC lease was not renewed in 1890 and Alaska was made a U.S. Territory. Today, Alaska contains a Gerstle River which flows from Gerstle Glacier and a village, Gerstle Point, which sits on the shore of Gerstle Bay.

Sloss and Gerstle married sisters, Hannah and Sarah Greenbaum, and were both active in Jewish society in San Francisco. A curious sequel: in the 1970's a descendant of Sloss and Gerstle married a young man who had won medals in the javelin throw at the Maccabiah Games. The wedding canopy was held up by four javelins. After the ceremony the newlyweds changed into jogging suits labeled "Just Married" and jogged around the Stanford University campus together.

For Further Reading:

Claus Noske and Herman Slotnick, *Alaska: A History of the 49th State,* Norman, University of Oklahoma Press, 1987.
Rudolf Glanz, *Jews in American Alaska 1867–80,* New York, 1953.
Ernst Gruening, *The State of Alaska,* New York, Random House, 1968.

Q. What Jewish conductor successfully introduced Richard Wagner's music to American audiences?

A. Born in Posen, Prussia, Leopold Damrosch (1832–1885) gave up the practice of medicine to devote himself entirely to music. He had secretly studied violin as a child despite his parents disapproval. Earning a reputation as a fine violinist and conductor, he was invited to New York in 1871 to become conductor for the Arion Society.

In 1884, he went to Germany and in five weeks brought back the singers who helped him to introduce German opera in the U.S. Richard Wagner, perhaps the greatest of German opera composers, was a bitter Jew-hater whose works are rarely played in Israel today. It is ironic that it was a Jewish conductor, Damrosch, who introduced Wagner to American audiences.

For Further Reading:

JE. IV, 421–422.
Walter Damrosch, *My Musical Life,* 1923.

Q. When did Jews first become involved in college football?

A. As early as 1870, in the very infancy of American football, Moses Henry Epstein played for Columbia University. Emil Hirsch, later a prominent

1850–1881: CIVIL WAR AND EXPANSION   109

rabbi, played for the University of Pennsylvania in 1871. Henry Joseph, of McGill University in Montreal, appeared in three games against Harvard in 1874. The first Jewish All-American was Phil King of Princeton in the early 1890's.

Jake Rosenthal, later a physician in Detroit, won letters on the Notre Dame squad (1894–1896), and Nathan Silver was a Fighting Irish quarterback (1902–1905). Benjamin Rosenbloom played tackle for West Virginia University (1900–1901) and went on to become a U.S. congressman and mayor of Wheeling.

The earliest known Jewish professional player was Samuel Jacobson, who organized and played for the Syracuse Athletic Association in the late 1880's.

Paul "Twister" Steinberg apparently did not play college football. However, he was a catcher on Connie Mack's Philadelphia Athletics major league baseball team, 1902–1904, and played halfback on the Philadelphia Athletics professional football team, also managed by Mack.

For Further Reading:

Bernard Postal, Jesse Silver and Roy Silver. *Encyclopedia of Jews in Sports*, NY; Bloch Publ. Co., 1965.

Q. What distinction did Lucius N. Littauer hold in the world of sports?

A. Littauer was Harvard's first football coach. After having played football for Harvard in 1875 and 1877, Littauer was invited back in 1880 to coach the team. Football was in its infancy and coaching was nothing like the full time high profile job it is today. Littauer functioned as an unpaid advisor to the players. The team's record was 5–1–2.

For Further Reading:

Bernard Postal, Jesse Silver and Roy Silver, *Encyclopedia of Jews in Sports*, NY; Bloch Publ. Co., 1965.

Q. What was the effect of the great Chicago fire of 1871 on the city's Jewish community?

A. The great Chicago fire began, it is said, when Mrs. O'Leary's cow kicked over a lantern. It was the evening of the Shemini Atzeret holiday, but the city had little to celebrate as hundreds of buildings were destroyed. The Jewish community suffered among the rest. 500 of the city's 10,000 Jews were left homeless. Five synagogues and many Torah scrolls burned. Four B'nai B'rith lodges were destroyed. The Jewish hospital was completely razed, but the patients were saved.

Only two synagogues were untouched — the Zion Congregation and the Kehilath Anshe Mayriv. The latter, ironically, was destroyed in another fire three years later.

For Further Reading:

Morris A. Gutstein, *Our Priceless Heritage: The Epic Growth of Nineteenth Century Chicago Jewry*, NY: Bloch Publ. Co., 1953.

Q. What did Mark Twain refer to as the "only really large and handsome witticism that was ever born" in his Hannibal, Missouri hometown district?

A. In his autobiography, Mark Twain talks of two Jewish boys who went to school with him in Hannibal in the 1840's. They were the first Jews he ever met, and he felt awed by a sense of their musty, remote antiquity. The boys were named Levin and their schoolmates called them twenty-two always following it with the explanation that "Twice Levin twenty-two." Most southerners in those days, if they lived outside the main cities, had little contact with Jews and Twain's experience was fairly typical.

Twain's daughter Suzy, at age 13, wrote a biography of him in which she told of a conversation between him and novelist William Dean Howells. Howells said that in his *Silas Lapham* he had written a sentence about a Jew which was true and which had no ill intent. But after the story was published, several Jews wrote him saying they wished he had not written that way about them. Now, his conscience was bothering him as the Jews had been persecuted enough, and he was going to remove the sentence from the next printing. Twain responded that a certain Jew who read his books avidly wondered why Twain seemed the only humorist who had never said anything against the Jews. After thinking it over, Twain decided that the reasons were that the Jews were, in his mind, a race much to be respected. Also they had suffered much and to make fun of them would be like attacking a man who was already down, so that there was nothing funny in ridiculing a Jew. In addition, he felt, the Jews should be particularly respected for taking care of their poor.

Daughter Clara Clemens wrote that, "Father had always been a great admirer of the Jewish race and spoke eloquently in defense of them so often that it was rumored that he himself was Jewish." When the Clemens family visited Vienna, Twain invited many of its "talented and celebrated Hebrews" to visit him.

Mark Twain wrote in his Notebook, "The Jews have the best average brain in the world. The Jews are the only race who work wholly with their brains and never with their hands. There are no Jew beggars, no Jew tramps, no Jew ditchers, hod carriers, day laborers or followers of toilsome mechanical trade. They are peculiarly and conspicuously the world's intellectual aristocracy."

Howells himself, already a famous novelist in the 1880's, warmly encouraged Abraham Cahan, then a fledgling writer for Yiddish newspapers, to try his hand at fiction. Howells had been impressed with Cahan's insight into the condition of workingmen's lives in New York. He must have felt flattered too, when he learned that Cahan had read all his works.

When soon afterward, Cahan wrote his own first novel, *Yeki*, Howells saw it through several rejections to its publication by D. Appleton and Co., and he wrote a laudatory review of it for the *New York World*. In 1917, Cahan published *The Rise of David Levinsky*, which has taken its place as one of the best American Jewish novels.

For Further Reading:

Rudolf and Clara Kirk, "Abraham Cahan and William Dean Howells," *AJHQ*, Lll, 1962, p.27-57.
Clara Clemens, *My Father Mark Twain*, New York; AMS Press, 1976, p, 203f.

Q. Who was the first Lubavitcher to visit an American president in the White House?

A. One of the largest and most active Hasidic groups of the 21st century is the Lubavitcher, first organized under R. Shneur Zalman of Liadi in the late 18th century. R. Yosef Yitzhak Schneersohn was one of the most important Hasidic leaders to escape the Holocaust, and his visit to President Franklin Roosevelt in the White House in 1941 was well covered in the Jewish press of the time.

Almost forgotten today is the White House visit in 1870 of Haim Zvi Schneersohn, a great-grandson of the founder of Lubavitch. Born in Russia, Haim Zvi Schneersohn had emigrated as a small child to Palestine. By 1860, he was traveling widely to Australia, India, and the Far East to raise funds for the impoverished Palestinian Jews and to rebuild the old city of Jerusalem. In the late 1860's he journeyed to France and England and reached New York in 1869. He met with Secretary of State Hamilton Fish to protest that the American consul in Jerusalem was doing missionary work among the Jews, and Schneersohn was invited by President Ulysses Grant to a reception at the White House. Schneersohn described to Grant the conditions of poverty and of political disenfranchisement of the Palestinian Jews under Turkish rule. Their only shelter was through their coreligionists who worked in foreign consulates. Perhaps, the President could see to appointing a Jew to some position in the American consulate. Both Grant and the other guests seemed visibly moved by Rabbi Schneersohn's speech.

From New York in 1870, Schneersohn wrote to the President thanking him for removing the offending consul in Jerusalem. He went on to lecture all across the United States. At Wilson's Hall in Los Angeles he was introduced to the audience by California Governor John F. Downey and at Cooper Institute in New York by Dr. Howard Crosby, a prominent Christian clergyman. By the time of his return home later that year, Rabbi Schneersohn had been granted American citizenship.

For Further Reading:

Harold Sharfman, *The First Rabbi: A Biography of the Origins of Orthodox and Reform Polemic in America*, J. Simm., 1988.

Q. What European Jewish composer made a concert tour of the U.S. in 1876?

A. Son of a German Jewish cantor, Jacques Offenbach (1819–1880) became one of Europe's most popular composers with his light operettas and their gaudy chorus lines. In 1876, Offenbach visited the U.S., conducting 30 concerts at the huge fee of $1,000 apiece. The concertmaster at his first performance, at the Hippodrome in New York, was John Philip Sousa. Offenbach wrote a witty and entertaining memoir of his American visit, *Orpheus in America*. On the ship back to Paris, he began work on "The Tales of Hoffman," probably his best known opera.

For Further Reading:

Jacques Offenbach, *Orpheus in America: Offenbach's Diary of His Journey to the New World*, Bloomington, University of Indiana Press, 1957.

Q. What prominent non-Jewish North Carolina politician used to lecture on Jewish History?

A. Zebulon Baird Vance (1830- 1894) was a leading figure in both North Carolina and national politics for over thirty years. Born and raised in the western part of the state, when it was still in a frontier condition, Vance was elected to Congress in 1858, became North Carolina's governor during the Civil War, and went on to serve in the U.S. Senate from 1879–1894. He was widely known for his humanity and his warm and often lowbrow wit. There were few Jews in North Carolina in those times, but Vance became friendly with several. Knowledgeable in the Bible and in world history, Vance developed an admiration for the Jews and a sense of the challenges of Jewish life through the centuries. A popular speaker, he delivered a lecture on Jewish History, "The Scattered Nation," hundreds of times all around the U.S. beginning about 1870, and it was considered one of his best. In it, Vance praised the Jews not only for having introduced monotheism and the Bible to mankind, but also for their continuing social and economic contributions.

Vance's friendship with Samuel Wittkowsky, a Polish Jewish immigrant prospering as a hat manufacturer, may well have helped to arouse his interest in Jews. In May, 1865, Vance, as North Carolina governor, was arrested in Statesville by Federal cavalry, and he was to be taken north for possible trial as a rebel leader. In the wake of the war's destruction, there were no good horses available and Vance, a large built man, faced the prospect of a long arduous journey to the railroad at Salisbury on an army mule. Wittkowsky showed up with a buggy for his friend Vance and drove him the whole distance under the guard of Federal cavalry. Vance never forgot Wittkowsky's kindness.

Once, years later, after he delivered "The Scattered Nation" address in Chapel Hill, a number of local Jews presented Vance with a gift of a gold headed cane. When the cane was stolen, a Jew in New York was able to locate it and return it to Vance.

Every year, Vance's birthday (May 13) is remembered by the Asheville chapter of B'nai B'rith and the United Daughters of the Confederacy, who hold a joint program and place a wreath at his monument.

For Further Reading:

Robert Dowd, *Life of Zebulon Vance*, Charlotte, 1897.
Franklin Ray Shirley, *Zebulon Vance: Tarheel Spokesman* , Charlotte, McNally and Lofton, 1962
Glenn Tucker, *Zeb Vance:Champion of Personal Freedom,* Bobbs Merrill, 1965 .

Q. Who first baked Passover matzos by machine in the U.S.?

A. As is well known, matzo, unleavened bread, is an important item for the Passover holiday. For many centuries matzo had been baked only by hand. In early America, where Jewish facilities were limited, matzos were sometimes baked by Gentiles who might or might not be supervised by synagogue officials. When machine-made matzos were introduced in New York in the early 1850's, a letter was sent to Chief Rabbi Nathan Adler of London inquiring as to whether the Jewish law sanctioned their use. Rabbi Adler answered that they were permissible as long as the correct procedures were carefully followed in the baking. However, a group led by Judah Middleman continued to use only the hand-made.

The first matzo baking machine in the U.S. was owned by Moses S. Cohen of 288 Front Street. His ad in *The Asmonean* included a drawing of his machine. Of companies that bake matzo today, the oldest is the Goodman Co. which began in Philadelphia in 1865 and moved to New York in 1875.

Rabbi Dov Ber Manischewitz began baking matzo in 1888 in Cincinnati and he was the first to use gas ovens instead of iron coal stoves. The Manischewitz Company received some unusual publicity in July, 1969, when astronaut Buzz Aldren setting foot on the moon in the first lunar landing exclaimed in his excitement, 'Man-o-Manischewitz,'" the company's famous slogan.

For Further Reading:

Tina Levitan, *The First of American Jewish History,* Brooklyn, the Charuth Press, 1957, 115–117.

Q. Which state of the Union was the last to accord full political rights to Jews?

A. The Constitution of the United States, formulated by brilliant and original minds like James Madison and Benjamin Franklin, had assured full political rights for all citizens regardless of creed. However, many individual state governments continued long standing religious practices by favoring Protestants over Catholics, Unitarians, dissenters, freethinkers, and Jews. The separation of church and state was not as widely accepted nor as natural in the eighteenth century as it would become later. The new states never restricted the practice of religions nor did they refuse any citizen the right to vote due to religion. However, the right to hold office was sometimes limited.

New Hampshire, one of the original thirteen states, did not allow non-Protestants to hold high office until 1876. In practicality, the prejudice was directed against Catholics more than Jews, of whom there were never more than a handful. However, well into the twentieth century, a clause in the New Hampshire constitution still ordered that "every denomination of *Christians*... (our italics) shall be equally under protection of the law." In 1980, Warren Rudman, a Jewish Republican, was elected to the Senate from New Hampshire. He co-authored the Gramm-Rudman Act.

For Further Reading:

Marcus, *USJ*, I, 509.

Q. Who was Francis Cardozo Sr.?

A. Born in Charleston in 1837, to a free mulatto and a member of the Jewish Cardozo family, Francis Cardozo won prizes in Greek and Latin at the University of Glasgow and later attended the London School of Theology. He went on to hold a number of distinguished positions in post-bellum South Carolina. His brother, Thomas Y. Cardozo, was state Superintendent of Education in Mississippi. It is rumored that Francis L. Cardozo, a brilliant Black politician of the Reconstruction Era, was a distant cousin.

For Further Reading:

Jacob Marcus, *EAJ*, II, 218.

Q. What sign of growing anti-Semitism occurred at the Grand Union Hotel in Saratoga, New York in 1876?

A. Near Saratoga, New York in 1777, Generals Horatio Gates and Benedict Arnold defeated General John Burgoyne's British invaders in one of the decisive battles of the American Revolution. Ninety-nine years later there occurred in the same spot what many view as the first significant anti-Jewish incident in American history.

Joseph Seligman, who had developed a major finance business, had been in Washington D.C. working with Secretary of the Treasury John Sherman on a plan to straighten out some serious financial issues facing the U.S. government, including repayment of the national debt from the Civil War. The work completed, Seligman decided to go up to Saratoga, then a major vacation spot, for a brief rest. However, when he arrived at the Grand Union Hotel, where he had stayed before, he was denied admission by Judge Henry Hilton, who represented the owners, the reason being Seligman's Jewishness. This incident seemed to herald an increase in the number of hotels, clubs, and neighborhoods that would exclude Jews. Hotel owners would excuse themselves by arguing that Christians would not lodge at accommodations where Jews were also allowed to stay. (Grosse Pointe, Michigan, for example, used a point system into the middle 1950's. If one was Jewish, dark-complexioned and the like he piled up a stated number of points against him and after a certain score one was not permitted to live in Grosse Pointe. One Christian minister quipped that Jesus would have been denied residence in Grosse Pointe inasmuch as he was Jewish, swarthy, of mideastern birth, and a carpenter by profession.)

The restrictions continued in many places until the Civil Rights movement of the 1960's. As to Saratoga, within a few years after the Seligman incident, Jews had bought many of Saratoga's hotels and the city became a favorite vacation spot for them.

One further note on the Seligmans. Henry Seligman, Joseph's brother who ran the family business branch in Frankfort, Germany, advanced money to Mary Todd Lincoln, the president's widow when she lived there in 1870, to pay for her son Tad's schooling and her household expenses. It was largely through the efforts of the Seligmans that Congress finally decided to provide her with a pension. As to Judge Hilton, his law firm lost business from both Jewish and Christian clients after the Grand Union incident

For Further Reading:

Ross Muir and Carl White, *Over The Long Term: The Story of J. and W. Seligman and Co.1864–1964.* 1964
EJ, XV: 1649.

Q. Was Rabbi Jacob Meyer a Christian?

A. After serving as a cantor in Cincinnati and as rabbi of Tifereth Israel in Cleveland, Jacob Meyer accepted a position as rabbi of Temple Har Sinai in Baltimore in 1874. A fine orator with a rich baritone voice, Meyer became very popular not only among his parishioners, but also in the Christian community.

Spurred by some strange stories about Meyer's past, his fellow Rabbis Henry Hochheimer and Benjamin Szold investigated Meyer's background and publicly accused him of having engaged in Christian missionary work among the Jews of North Africa. Meyer vigorously denied the charges, saying that the missionary was actually his twin brother, Jesias, while Hochheimer and Szold claimed that Meyer never had a twin. Meyer's supporters urged him to go to court to seek redress against his accusers. After some months of charges and countercharges. Meyer resigned his pulpit and went to Philadelphia, where he founded a new congregation, the Freie Gemeinde (Free Congregation) whose members were largely non-Jewish religious radicals.

For Further Reading:

I. Harold Sharfman, *The first Rabbi*, J. Simon, 1988, p. 475–478.

Q. Who was the first American born ordained rabbi?

A. Henry W. Schneeburger (1848–1916) was born in New York where he received a B.A. from Columbia College in 1866 and an M.A. in 1867. He studied Talmud under two private tutors, a Mr. Sachs and Professor Selig Newman. Determined to continue his Jewish studies, Schneeburger went to Europe where he studied first in Mainz under Rabbi Marcus Lehman, who was well known also as a novelist and journalist. Schneeburger was ordained in 1870 by Rabbi Azriel Hildesheimer, head of the great Orthodox seminary in Berlin. In the same year he also completed a Ph.D. at the University of Jena with a dissertation on Rabbi Judah Hanasi, the second century Patriarch of Judea. This work strongly criticized the writings of liberal scholars like Nachman Krochmal and Zachariah Frankel and especially the historian Heinrich Graetz whose views, said Schneeburger, were presented with their "accustomed superficiality."

Returning to the U.S., Schneeburger served as rabbi of the Chizuk Amuno synagogue from 1876. Orthodox in practice, he became involved with the early leaders of the Conservative movement at a time when it was hardly distinguishable from Orthodoxy.

For Further Reading:

Israel Goldman, "Henry W. Schneeburger: His Role in American Judaism," *AJHSQ*, LVI, 1967, 153–190.

Q. Who was America's first internationally known Jewish sportsman?

A. Philo Jacoby (1838–1922) of San Francisco made his reputation as a sharpshooter, winning medals and prizes all over the U.S. and Europe. He returned from one tour to Europe in the early 1870's with what was described as "a bushel full of prizes." One of his favorites was a gold medal presented by the Austrian Emperor Franz Joseph. A journalist by profession, Jacoby founded a Jewish newspaper, *The Hebrew,* in San Francisco in 1863 and served as its editor for four decades. In his travels, he often wrote articles for American papers about European Jewry. One article described a visit in Mainz, Germany to Rabbi Marcus Lehman, editor of the *Israelite* and author of Jewish historical novels. In 1910 Jacoby wrote a book, *The Rifle in California.*

For Further Reading:

William M. Kramer and Reva Clar, "Philo Jacoby: California's First International Sportsman," *WSHJ*, XXII, 1989–1990, 3–7, 122–136, 243–257.

Q. In what four major inventions did Emile Berliner (1851–1929) play a major role?

A. Without formal training in science, Emile Berliner used a brilliant mind and a lot of hard work to make important contributions to the invention of the telephone, record player, helicopter and acoustic tile. In 1877 while working full time in a dry goods store in Washington D.C., Berliner invented a microphone that greatly improved the usefulness of the original telephone produced by Alexander Graham Bell only two years before. Soon Berliner joined Bell to continue his research into reproducing sounds.

Ten years later he created a horizontal record player far more useful than Thomas Edison's earlier model. The record players of the 20th century are based on Berliner's work. It now became possible to duplicate records in mass numbers, making the record player useful and available to every home.

In the early 1900's Berliner began to experiment with building a workable helicopter, an accomplishment that had eluded generations of earlier inventors. Finally in 1907, Paul Cornu, a Frenchman, constructed a helicopter that got off the ground momentarily. A year later Berliner built one that managed to get off the ground three times. He continued to experiment with other aviation devices, often aided by his son Henry.

Berliner's longtime interest in music and sound led him to the invention of acoustic tile in 1926. He also wrote music and sang in conductor Leopold Damrosch's New York Oratorio Society.

After almost losing an infant daughter to an intestinal illness, Berliner devoted himself to reducing the appalling infant mortality rate. Careful study brought him to realize that many serious diseases including typhoid and tuberculosis were being spread by infected milk. The solution was to pasteurize the milk, a process developed some years earlier by Louis Pasteur, but opposed by many doctors and by the prestigious American Pediatric Association, who argued that heating milk only took the nourishment out of it. Berliner and his colleagues pressed for years until pasteurization and proper cool storage became standard and infant mortality greatly decreased.

Although his father had been a Talmudic scholar back in Hanover, Berliner was himself inclined toward agnosticism. Nevertheless, he actively interested himself in the Jewish settlement in Palestine and especially in Hebrew University.

For Further Reading:

Frederic C. Wile, *Emile Berliner: Maker of the Microphone*, Indianapolis, Bobbs-Merrill Co.. 1926.

1881–1924

Eastern European Immigration

1881 BEGAN A BUSY and active period for American Jewry. Eastern European Jews had been immigrating to the U.S. for some years, but the numbers accelerated in the 1880's largely because of intensified anti-semitism in Czarist Russia. The new immigrants tended to concentrate in the large cities, but some settled in smaller towns. New York became the largest Jewish community in the world with well over a million Jewish residents. The settled German Jews, in one sense, looked down on the Eastern European immigrants, but they also built communal organizations which helped provide them with schools, medical care, and recreation. The new immigrants developed their own social, labor, and cultural organizations and built their own smaller synagogues, far less imposing than the magnificent Reform temples of the German Jews.

Reform Judaism made great strides primarily among Germans and the American born. Its very liberal doctrines were expressed in the Pittsburgh Platform of 1885. Conservatism can be said to have begun officially in the U.S. with the opening of the Jewish Theological Seminary in 1887. Orthodoxy declined as the children of Orthodox immigrants devoted themselves to succeeding in their new world, and they turned to the more liberal branches of Judaism or simply abandoned formal Jewish attachments. Many continued to be active in Jewish affairs even as their piety declined. Reconstructionist Judaism was founded by Mordecai Kaplan at the end of this period.

There were few day schools or advanced yeshivot, and while some afternoon Hebrew schools taught well, most did not. Sunday schools had little serious educational success. Most Jewish children thus received minimal or no Jewish education.

Social mores and economic necessity helped hold families together, and divorce was not common. Women were busy in the home, although many joined social movements like the Suffragettes. Intermarriage and conversion were also rare.

Public schools were open to Jewish children and education seemed a good path to success. Jewish students did well. Yiddish speaking youngsters learned English quickly and were soon entering universities and heading into a variety of professions and businesses. The contributions of Jews in many areas were hardly less than astonishing. Jews held public office at many levels from local municipal governments to the U.S. Senate; and Louis Brandeis was appointed to the U.S. Supreme Court.

Some Jewish leaders feared that the rise of Jewish immigration would provoke anti-Semitic reactions. Indeed some social clubs and hotels excluded Jews, and by the early 1920's some universities set quotas for admitting Jewish students. Organized opposition to immigration arose, which although not aimed only at Jews, threatened to shut America's doors. Jews and other immigrant leaders battled the threat of restriction for years. But isolationism and restrictionism gained strength in Congress so that in the early 1920's a series of laws reduced the heavy immigration wave to a trickle.

Q. What event in Europe prompted the huge wave of immigration to the U.S. in the late 19th century?

A. On March 1, 1881, Czar Alexander II, who seemed the most liberal and benevolent of Russia's rulers, was assassinated by revolutionaries. They were boarding with a Jewess, Hessia Helfman, who may have known of their plan.

In the nervous atmosphere following the assassination, an anti-Semitic pogrom broke out in the town of Yelizavetgrad on April 11. Young strangers from the countryside had begun to appear in the town, and a rumor spread that the new Czar Alexander III had ordered Orthodox Russians to attack Jews. A few days later a Jewish tavern owner demanded payment from a gentile customer for a glass he had broken. An argument began and spread until rioters attacked the Jewish quarter. Hundreds of homes and shops were destroyed by the time a downpour stopped the violence the next evening. The rioting spread to Odessa, Kiev, and other cities with little opposition from the government.

In the wake of the intensifying anti-Semitism, many Jews began to flee their homes, even Jews who had turned away from their Jewish roots and thought of themselves as modern, enlightened Russians. Thousands were soon streaming across the Austrian border at Brody.

The French based Alliance Israelite Universelle, represented in Brody by Dr. H. Schafier, decided to start sending large numbers of the refugees across the Atlantic to the U.S., where most of the refugees wanted to go. Thus began the great wave of Eastern European Jewish immigration to the United States.

For Further Reading:

Ronald Sanders, *Shores of Refuge. A Hundred Years of Jewish Immigration,* New York, Henry Holt and Co., 1988.
Zoza Szajkowski, "The European Attitude to Eastern European Jewish Immigration (1881–1893)." PAJHS, XLI. 1951, 127–162.

Q. Why did Adolphus Solomons turn down an appointment as governor of Washington D.C.?

A. A devout Jew, Adolphus Solomons (1826–1910) turned down President Ulysses Grant's offer to appoint him governor of Washington D.C. (1871) because he would not work on Saturdays. Solomons' most notable accomplishments were in the area of public health work to which he turned his efforts after visiting a Jewish ward in a hospital in Frankfurt-am-Main. He was one of the founders and later a vice-president of the American Red Cross, whose first meeting took place in his house in 1881, and he ran the organization during President Clara Barton's extensive absences. Active in both D.C. politics and in the Jewish community, Solomons was treasurer for the U.S. branch of the Alliance Israelite Universelle, and served as director of the Baron De Hirsch Fund for America, and as acting president of the Jewish Theological Seminary Association.

For Further Reading:

Abraham Voorsen, "Adolphus Solomons and Clara Barton," *AJHQ,* LIX, 1970, 331–356.
Cyrus Adler, "Adolphus S. Solomons and the Red Cross," *PAJHS,* XXXIII, 1934, 211–230.

Q. What favor did General Lew Wallace, author of *Ben Hur,* do for the Jews?

A. General Wallace, author of the famous novel *Ben Hur* and an important figure at the Civil War battles of Shiloh and the Monocacy, was U.S. minister to Turkey in 1882. Russian Jews, fleeing the new wave of pogroms, were coming into Turkey penniless and starving. Wallace's compassion was aroused and, with the backing of Secretary of State Frelinghuysen, he sought to help them. Although the Turks did not want more Jews settling in their province of Palestine, some of the Russian refugees in Jerusalem were given American citizenship by the American consul and thus enabled to stay there.

For Further Reading:

Cyrus Adler, "Jews in the Diplomatic Correspondence of the U.S.," PAJHS, XV, 1906, 7–9.

Q. Who was Josephine Earp?

A. The gunfight at the OK Corral in Tombstone, Arizona, 1881, has made Wyatt Earp and Doc Holliday a part of American legend. To whom did Wyatt go home after his big day's work? Undoubtedly, he returned home to his Brooklyn born Jewish wife Josephine Marcus Earp. She later wrote a highly admiring book about their years together — *I Married Wyatt Earp: The Recollections of Josephine Sarah Marcus Earp*. In fact, Wyatt led an active career as a lawman, gunfighter, gambler, and entrepreneur, and historians are divided as to whether he should be classified as a Western hero or a gangster.

For Further Reading:

Josephine Marcus Earp, (Glen Boyer, ed.). *I Married Wyatt Earp: The Recollections of Josephine Sarah Marcus Earp*, Tucson, University of Arizona Press, 1976.

Q. What is the first recorded instance of a question of agunah in American History?

A. Agunah is the Hebrew term for a woman whose husband has disappeared without witnesses. Is she still considered married to him or can she be considered a widow and therefore eligible to remarry? Each case has its own complexities.

On January 19, 1883, the liner Cimbria sank en route from Hamburg to New York. The husbands of seven Jewish women were thought to have been on board. What could be done for their wives? The question went to Rabbi Yitzchak Elchonon Spektor of Kovno, the leading rabbinical respondent of that day, who accepted the passenger list as adequate evidence that the husbands had gone down with the Cimbria. The women were thus free to remarry.

For Further Reading:

J.D. Eisenstein, "The Development of Jewish Casuistry in America," *PAJHS*, XII, 1904, 139–148.

Q. What was the famous "terefah banquet?"

A. In 1883, at an emotional ceremony, the first four graduates of the new Hebrew Union College in Cincinnati were ordained as rabbis by Rabbi Isaac Meyer Wise. The four were Israel Aaron, Henry Berkowitz, Joseph Krauskopf, and David Philipson. An ecstatic crowd wept and hugged each other joyfully. The proceedings continued with a banquet at the Highland House, a well-known resort. Philipson, in his account of the incident (*My Life as an American Jew*), claims that many of the guests at the banquet kept kosher and thus a Jewish caterer had been engaged. However, when the first course began to come out, it was greeted with tumult, and several people bolted for the door. Shrimp, a non-kosher food, was being placed on the tables. Philipson blamed the bungling on the caterer. In any case, the incident provoked a storm of criticism, particularly in the Orthodox press, and soon became known as the "terefah (non-kosher) banquet."

Perhaps it is just as well that the departing guests did not wait for the rest of the menu for it included more shellfish and frog-legs, both non kosher, and an ice cream dessert to follow the meat meal.

For Further Reading:

David Philipson, *My Life As An American Jew*, Cincinnati, John G. Kidd and Sons, 1941.

Q. Why was famous newspaperman Joseph Pulitzer referred to as "Hungry Joe"?

A. Competition among newspapers in New York in the 1880's was very lively, led by Charles Dana's *Sun* and James Gordon Bennett's *Herald*. In 1883, Joseph Pulitzer, son of a Hungarian Jewish father from St. Louis, purchased the *World* from Jay Gould, the famous financier, and entered the journalistic wars with his own brand of sensational reporting.

Exasperated by Pulitzer's growing success, Dana often attacked him as poisoning journalism. As it would have been indecent to call Pulitzer Jew or sheeny, Dana instead called him "Hungry Joe" which actually meant "Hungarian Jew." Pulitzer is best remembered today as the founder of the Pulitzer Prize. He also was elected to Congress from New York in 1885.

Pulitzer left no written description of his early life and the widespread view was that his father was a Hungarian Jew and his mother was an Austro German Catholic. However, documents brought to light in Hungary in recent years reveal that in fact both his father, Phillip, and his mother, Elize Berger Pulitzer, were Hungarian born Jews.

For Further Reading:

Abraham Cahan, *The Education of Abraham Cahan*, Philadelphia, Jewish Publication Society, 1969, p. 357–359.

Andras Csillag, "Joseph Pulitzer's Roots in Europe: A Genealogical History," *AJA*, XXXIX, 1987, 49–68.

Q. Why was Edward Israel, an American Jew, in Greenland in the 1880's?

A. Born in Kalamazoo, Michigan in 1859, Edward Israel attended the University of Michigan and then served in the U.S. army signal corps. In 1881 he joined the Lady Franklin Bay Expedition to northern Greenland as an astronomer. The youngest member of the party, Israel was amiable, well-liked and devoted to his work.

The expedition reached a point farther north than any previous explorers. However, supplies began to dwindle and on May 27, 1884, Israel died of starvation, one of 16 deaths in the camp at Cape Saline that winter. A rescue party arrived with supplies three weeks later. The expedition leader Greely was a man of no more than mediocre ability, but the heavy loss of life was to be blamed more on the failure of relief efforts than on Greely's leadership.

Another avid polar explorer of those days was Dr. Isaac Israel Hayes (1832–1881), an M.D. from the University of Pennsylvania, who served as the physician on a number of Arctic expeditions. He wrote several books about his adventures and lectured widely. However, although Hayes is listed both in the *Encyclopedia Judaica* and in the *Universal Jewish Encyclopedia*, contemporary reports refer to him as being born of Quaker parents in Chester County, Pennsylvania. It is possible that later historians assumed that Hayes was Jewish because there was an important Jewish family named Hayes in America since colonial times and also because Hayes was a physician.

For Further Reading:

Barry Lopez, *Arctic Dreams: Imagination and Desire in a Northern Landscape*, NY: Scribner, 1986, p. 368–370.

George W. Callum, "Doctor Isaac I. Hayes," *Journal of the American Geographic Society*, XIII, 1881, 110-124.

Q. Were there any Jewish cowboys in the Old West?

A. The matter involves some dispute among historians. According to Professor Jacob Marcus, most Jews who went out west in the second half of the 19th century tended toward supply businesses and almost none worked as cowboys. We do have record of two Jewish cowboys, Samuel Lazarus of Texas and Alexander Rittermaster in Colorado. Some Jews went into cattle raising, and a few gained notable success in that risky pursuit. Jews sometimes became cattle owners because someone paid them a debt in animals rather than cash.

Isaac Gransky owned herds of over 50,000 sheep in Texas and New Mexico, but they were wiped out, largely by cholera, and Gransky died a pauper in 1911. Charles Pepper, a wholesale butcher in Utah in the 1860's, branched out into ranching in order to fulfill his supply contracts with the army. The Halff brothers operated the 50,000 acre Circle Dot Ranch in southern Texas. Levi Strauss, the famous clothing manufacturer, owned a large ranch in California. Despite the notable success of a few individuals, Jews rarely entered the cattle business and those who did rarely found much success.

On the other hand, Harriet and Fred Rochlin, in their *Pioneer Jews*, claim that numerous Jews did enter the livestock business at every level from cowpoke to tycoon. Their book depicts cattle brands used by 24 Jewish owned ranches.

For Further Reading:

Marcus, USJ, II. 132–137.
Harriet and Fred Rochlin, *Pioneer Jews: A Whole New Life in the Far West*, Boston, Houghton Mifflin, 1984.

Q. Why in the late 19th century did a number of Jewish congregations transfer their Sabbath services from Saturday to Sunday mornings?

A. The idea of moving the Jewish Sabbath from Saturday to Sunday was proposed in Germany as early as about 1812, by David Friedlander, one of the first leaders of Reform. Friedlander argued that Judaism must undergo great changes in the light of the emancipation he thought was taking place in European society in those days. In the 1840's a temple in Berlin did substitute Sunday for Saturday as their Sabbath day. In Baltimore in 1854, a small radical group broke away for a short time from the Reform Har Sinai Verein and conducted its Sabbath services on Sunday.

Rabbi Kaufmann Kohler began Sunday services at Sinai Congregation in Chicago in 1874, and about 35 American temples tried them at one time or another, often in addition to the Saturday service rather than in place of it. Most Reform temples continued to meet Saturday mornings and added a late Friday evening service as well.

In 1903, Dr. Jacob Voorsanger, of San Francisco, wrote a report for the Central Conference of American Rabbis, the Reform rabbinical organization. He argued against changing the Sabbath from Saturday despite the widespread neglect in its observance. It was doubtful too, whether any rabbinical body could assume the authority for such a change. A dissenting report by Dr. Hyman Enelow of Louisville argued the merits of the change to Sunday and ended with a long quotation from Dr. Samuel Holdheim, the great proponent of the Sunday Sabbath in Germany two generations earlier.

The CCAR (Central Council of American Rabbis) published a study headed by Enelow in its 1906 Yearbook. Eighteen rabbis responding to questionnaires reported that their Sunday services were well attended, drawing many non-Jews as well as Jews. In some temples, interest in Saturday services also was said to have increased. Still, most rabbis preferred Saturday to Sunday as a Sabbath, and saw the Sunday Sabbath as an expedient. Rabbi Kohler himself eventually became an opponent of the Sunday Sabbath.

The reasons widely offered in those years were that all other Americans held their Sabbath on Sunday so that the whole atmosphere of the nation was more conducive to a day of rest. Also, it was exceedingly difficult for a Jew living in America to take Saturday off from work, even if they had been very observant in Europe. Synagogues and temples had a difficult time attracting people on Saturdays, and it was hoped that more people would come to a Sabbath service on Sunday. Of course the change was strongly opposed by more traditional Jews. In the long run, in fact, the Sunday services did not produce sufficient results, and most temples switched back to Saturdays by the mid-twentieth century.

For Further Reading:

Michael A. Meyer, *Response to Modernity: A History of the Reform Movement in Judaism*, New York, Oxford University Press, 1988.

Q. What was the Jewish background of famed news correspondent Walter Winchell?

A. The famed and controversial radio commentator of the mid-20th century not only was Jewish but was a grandson of the first cantor imported into the U.S. from Europe. Sometime around 1885, Chaim Weinshel was hired by the Anshe Suvalk congregation of New York in order to attract new members. Although successful as a cantor, the learned and sophisticated Weinshel was not impressed by the Jewish atmosphere in America, and he wrote a poem mocking the low-class people who had become wealthy communal leaders.

For Further Reading:

Mark Slobin, *Chosen Voices*. University of Illinois Press, 1989.

Q. What was the relationship between Reform Judaism and Unitarianism in the U.S. in the nineteenth century?

A. Both were very liberal, emphasizing universal moral principles over religious dogma and ritual. Rabbis often exchanged pulpits with liberal non--Jewish clergymen and cooperated in various activities. Not infrequently, Jews would express interest in a merger between Unitarianism and Judaism. However, most Reform rabbis, even the most liberal, opposed any serious merging with a three pronged argument. First, they said that Jews have a passionate allegiance to their own unique history and their own special mission. Second, Unitarianism, although rejecting the godhood of Jesus, still placed great emphasis on his teachings, while Judaism did not. Third, Jews' sense of kinship and of responsibility for each other has been intensified by anti-semitism, an experience in which Unitarians could not have shared.

For Further Reading:

Benny Kraut, "Reform Judaism — The Unitarian Challenge," *Journal of Ecumenical Studies*, XX.III, 1986.

Q. What American rabbi sought a position as a Unitarian minister?

A. In the late nineteenth century, there was some feeling among radically liberal Jews that there could be a rapprochement with Unitarianism or with other liberal universalist religions. Rabbi Solomon Hirsch Sonneschein (1839- 1908), spiritual leader of the Reform Shaare Emeth Congregation in St. Louis, went secretly to Boston in 1886 to meet with Unitarian leaders like Edward Everett Hale and Minot J. Savage to apply for a Unitarian pulpit. Sonneschein had studied in European yeshivot and had held several rabbinical positions, but he was always too radical in his beliefs and too volatile in his manner for his congregations' tastes. Called to St. Louis in 1869, he continued his controversial career, often quarreling with members of his temple. His marriage too was stormy, and he occasionally sought refuge in drink.

By 1886, having alienated a good part of his membership and threatened with the loss of his job, he went to Boston. The Unitarian leaders, unsure of Sonneschein's state of mind, put him off and he never submitted a formal application. We can only guess as to whether Sonneschein's action was opportunistic or based on sincere religious conviction. It is well documented that he was interested in the universalist view of religion that Unitarianism preached and that he had corresponded for some years with leaders of that church.

Sonneschein's trip to Boston became public knowledge and stirred a furor in St. Louis, but the matter soon calmed down and Sonneschein continued in his rabbinical career, holding several positions around the United States. A new marriage seems to have finally brought some peace into his life. He died with the Shema on his lips.

For Further Reading:

Todd Endelman. ed. *Jewish Apostasy in the Modern World*.
Benny Kraut, *A Unitarian Rabbi: The case of Solomon Sonneschein*, New York, Holmes and Meier Co., 272–308.

Q. One of the first great publishers of popular music was the Witmark brothers of New York. What hit song got their new business off to a strong start?

A. Isidore (age 17), Julius (13), and Jay (11) Witmark opened a printing business in New York in 1886 with a printing machine won as a prize in school. Their father had been a prosperous businessman in the south, but he had lost everything in the Civil War and moved north.

Hearing a rumor that President Grover Cleveland was about to get married, Isidore Witmark quickly wrote a wedding song and printed several thousand copies. Three days later the engagement was officially announced, and the brothers were first on the market with a suitable song.

The Witmarks were the first of a growing number of Jews who would make it big in popular music in the late 19th century, in what would become known as Tin Pan Alley. Many of the famous songs of that era were written by Jews — "After the Ball", "My Merry Oldsmobile," "By the Light of the Silvery Moon," "A Bird in a Gilded Cage", "Hello, My Baby" and others.

For Further Reading:

Kenneth Kanter, *The Jews in Tin Pan Alley: The Jewish Contribution to American Popular Music*, 1830–1940, New York, Ktav, 1982, p .14f.

Q. What religious approach did the Jewish Theological Seminary offer at its founding?

A. Today, JTS is the school which trains students for ordination as Conservative rabbis. However, it was founded in 1887 as a traditional institution to counter the new Reform Hebrew Union College in Cincinnati. Sabato Morais suggested calling it the Orthodox Seminary, and its early administration freely described the school as Orthodox.

The ten rabbis of the original faculty included five who were comfortably Orthodox, like Sabato Morais and Bernard Drachman, and five others who were friendly to Reform, like Marcus Jastrow and Alexander Kohut.

The term Conservative was apparently first used by Solomon Schechter, who became JTS chancellor in 1907. Schechter, who questioned the traditional belief in the divine origin of the Bible, helped to broaden the differences in belief and practice between Orthodoxy and early Conservatism. The growing immigrant Orthodox community never felt at home with JTS and formed its own institutions. The founding of JTS helped set the pattern of tripartite Judaism in the U.S. — Orthodox/Conservative/Reform.

For Further Reading:

Abraham Karp, *Haven and Home: A History of the Jews in America*, New York, Schocken, 1985.
Marc Lee Raphael, *Profiles in American Judaism: The Reform, Conservative, Orthodox, and Reconstructionist Traditions in Historical Perspective*, San Francisco, Harper & Row, 1984.
Moshe Davis, *The Emergence of Conservative Judaism: The Historical School in Nineteenth Century America*. Philadelphia, JPS, 1963.

Q. How did the royal family of Hawaii come into possession of a Torah Scroll in the 1880's?

A. In 1887, Elias Rosenberg, a con-man who claimed to have occult powers, gained great influence over Hawaiian King David Kalakaua. Within months a revolution limited the king's authority, and Rosenberg returned to California, leaving with King David a Torah Scroll with a silver *yad* or pointer, which he had brought with him. The Torah remained in possession of the Hawaiian royal family through several generations and was lent to the Jews of Honolulu yearly for High Holiday services until 1945.

The scroll then disappeared until 1972 when Homer Hayes, a family member, offered a Torah Scroll, apparently the same one although much damaged, to the Temple Emanu-el. The *yad* had been presented to the temple several years earlier by another relative.

For Further Reading:

Bernard Postal and Lionel Koppman, *American Jewish Landmarks*, New York, Fleet Press Corporation, 1977, IV, 170–172.

Q. What American Jewish physician performed the first successful operation on a ruptured appendix?

A. Surgery in the 19th century was primitive compared to the vastly developed medical techniques of the 21st century. By the time of the U.S. Civil War, doctors had developed a procedure for opening and cleaning the abdominal cavity to treat what they called "inflammation of the bowels."

Dr. Simon Baruch, father of long time presidential advisor Bernard Baruch, insisted that the real cause of this problem was the appendix, which should be removed to save the patient's life. Baruch is generally credited with being the first doctor to diagnose, preoperatively, a case of ruptured appendix in which a successful operation was performed saving the patient's life, 1887.

As a surgeon in the Confederate army, Dr. Baruch had written an important text on the treatment of bayonet wounds. Around the turn of the century, he was instrumental in pushing the building of public bath facilities. Family tradition traced the Baruchs' ancestry to Baruch ben Neriah, disciple of the biblical prophet Jeremiah.

For Further Reading:

Margaret L. Coit, *Mr Baruch*, Boston: Houghton Mifflin Co., 1957, p. 52–54.

Q. What nineteenth century American wrote an Aramaic-English Dictionary?

A. Born in Poland and holder of a doctorate from the University of Halle, Marcus Jastrow (1825–1903) came to America as rabbi of Congregation Rodeph Shalom in Philadelphia in 1866. Originally Orthodox, Rodeph Shalom was now veering toward Reform. Jastrow saw his main task as modifying this trend by emphasizing Jewish education and introducing certain modifications in the ritual. His changes included mixed pews, late Friday night services, discontinuing the established schedule of Torah readings, and removing references in the prayer book to the restoration of the sacrificial services. However, his program failed and finally, in 1892, Jastrow was bumped up to rabbi emeritus and William Berkowitz, a Reform rabbi from HUC, was hired in his place.

Jastrow's many scholarly activities brought him greater satisfaction. His *Dictionary of the Targum, the Talmud Bavli, and the Midrashic Literature* is still widely used. Over seventeen hundred pages in its one volume reprint in 1971, it gives English translations and explanations of Aramaic words in rabbinic literature and also identifies words borrowed from other languages like Greek, Latin, or Persian.

A parallel work was R. Alexander Kohut's *Arukh Hashalem*, an eight volume lexicon in Hebrew of Talmudic terms, written in the form of a commentary on the Medieval *Arukh* of R. Nathan ben Yehiel of Rome. Kohut published the first four volumes in his native Hungary and the last four after coming to New York in 1885 to serve as rabbi of Congregation Ahabath Chesed. The lexicon occupied him heavily for almost 20 years. On one occasion, Kohut had to rewrite a large part of the manuscript that was lost in a ship-sinking in the North Sea. Kohut was one of the founders of the Jewish Theological Seminary and served as its first Talmud professor.

For Further Reading:

Moshe Davis, *The Emergence of Conservative Judaism: The Historical School in Nineteenth Century America*, Philadelphia, JPS, 1963.
Rebekah Kohut, *His Father's House*, New Haven; Yale University Press, 1938.

Q. What was Chicago's Jewish Training School?

A. Conceived by philanthropic German Jews of Chicago, the Jewish Training School was to serve the Children of East European immigrants. Its board consisted largely of members of the Reform Sinai Congregation, and its financial base was supplied by the Mandel brothers and Henry Frank in 1888.

Although officially non-sectarian, the school had almost all Jewish students. In addition to academic subjects, the curriculum emphasized manual training like metal work, weaving, etching, sewing, and mechanical drawing .Enrollment averaged about 600 students. By 1893 a second branch opened on the city's south side. Many German Jews, well established and Americanized by the early 1900's, felt a sense of noblesse oblige toward their

Eastern European brethren and provided schools, public medical services, and the like, to help ease their process of derussification and of assimilation into American life.

For Further Reading:

Morris Gutstein, *A Priceless Heritage,* New York, Bloch Publishing Co., 1953.
Hyman Meites. *History of the Jews of Chicago,* Chicago, 1924.

Q. Who was America's only chief rabbi?

A. For over a century, the chief rabbinate in England had been an important position filled by highly distinguished men, but the institution has never taken hold in the U.S. The only chief rabbi here was Rabbi Jacob Joseph, who served from 1888–1902.

The increase in immigration of Eastern European Jews in the 1880's raised a new need for religious leadership in the U.S. Abraham Joseph Ash served as a sort of chief rabbi in the 1870's and 1880's in between attempts to set himself up in business. In 1879 the position was offered to R. Meir Leibush Malbim, a distinguished European scholar, and author of a noted commentary on the Bible. In 1887, the leading congregation in New York, after much deliberation, offered the position to R. Jacob Joseph of Vilna, a highly respected scholar and preacher. A disciple of R. Israel Salanter and of R. Naftali T.Y. Berlin of Volozhin, he was popularly known as Reb Yankele Charif (the brilliant). R. Jacob was not anxious to leave Vilna, but he was deep in debt and needed to improve his income,

He arrived in New York July 7, 1888, and his opening sermon, on Sabbath Nahamu, was widely praised. But the honeymoon was soon over. The rabbi's efforts to bring some order into areas like kosher meat production met with strong opposition. Also, Conservative rabbis like H. Pereira Mendes feared that R. Jacob's projects would divert much needed funds from the new struggling Jewish Theological Seminary. Sabato Morais harshly accused him of lacking modern western culture and literary attainments. Socialists, anarchists and other assorted leftists, who saw religion as the opiate of the masses, penned particularly nasty attacks in the newspapers.

Rabbi Joshua Segal set himself up as a rival chief rabbi. Supporters were found among the Galician Jews, who resented R. Jacob's Lithuanian origin, and among kosher butchers, and various small time religious functionaries, who resented having to give account of themselves to any authority.

A scholarly and respectable man, R. Jacob Joseph acted with dignity despite the constant harassment and accusations by all the self-seekers. A final trouble was yet to come. When he passed away in 1902 after a long illness, 100,000 Jews turned out to march in his funeral procession. But the procession was attacked by hooligans who benefited from the support of anti-Semitic policemen. A near riot ensued. The Jews fought back earning praise from local newspapers. The incident led to a greater effort toward eliminating Jew-haters from the New York police force.

For Further Reading:

Abraham Karp. "New York Chooses a Chief Rabbi," *PAJHS*, XLIV, 1955, 129- 198.

Q. Who founded Barnard College?

A. In the mid-nineteenth century, few American women went to school beyond the elementary level. Higher education, rare enough even for men, was seen as useless for girls, if not indeed harmful. President Bartlett of Dartmouth College was quoted in 1877 as saying that, "Girls cannot endure the hard unintermitting and long continued strain to which boys are subjected ... I rather fear their success with its penalty of shortened lives or permanently deranged constitutions."

Nevertheless, as the U.S. grew, interest in college education increased, and women began to feel a desire for educational opportunities. In the 1870's, several girls were quietly sitting in on classes at Columbia College in New York. A few years later, the college introduced a program called Collegiate Course for Women, in which women could attend regular classes with the men. About two dozen girls came, and a few graduated. One of these young ladies was Annie Nathan (1867–1951), a descendant of Jewish families that had been in America since colonial times. She dropped out after a year to marry Dr. Alfred Meyer. However, her desire for learning remained strong. Feeling that the Collegiate Course for Women was too restrictive, she sought some other means. Melvil Dewey, then head of Columbia's library, persuaded her to start a women's college herself.

Mrs. Meyer, then only 20 years old, stirred up support among a number of New York's social and political leaders. The result of her efforts was Barnard College, which opened in 1889 as a women's branch of Columbia. It was named for Frederick Barnard, former president of Columbia, who had been a strong supporter of higher education for women. The school's first treasurer was Jacob Schiff, who gave so much of his time and money to the public benefit and who had served on the state Board of Education. The first year's budget was $7,500.

Mrs. Meyer went on to some fame as a novelist, writing about issues like careers for women and artificial insemination long before the Feminism of the 1960's. She also wrote a play about the faculty of a great Black school.

In her eighties, she published her entertaining autobiography, *It's Been Fun*. She claims to have been the first woman in the U.S. to ride a bicycle.

Despite her liberal leanings, Meyer opposed women's suffrage even after it was made law, on the grounds that no good would come of it. In contrast, her sister Maud Nathan was a leading and militant suffragette and feminist, active in a variety of both general and Jewish affairs. She too wrote an autobiography.

For Further Reading:

Annie Nathan Meyer, *It's Been Fun,* NY: Henry Schuman, 1951.
Maud Nathan, *Once Upon A Time and Today,* New York, G. Putnam's Sons, 1933.

Q. Who first attempted to translate the entire Babylonian Talmud into English?

A. Michael Rodkinson (1845–1904) wrote several ·books and edited Hebrew periodicals in his native Russia before emigrating to the U.S. in 1889. In his last years, he busied himself with preparing an English translation of the Babylonian Talmud. Although an important pioneering effort, Rodkinson's translation is far less useful to the student of Talmud than the later Soncino edition or the Steinsaltz and Art-Scroll editions which began to appear in the late 1980's.

For Further Reading:

EJ, XIV, 218.

Q. What sort of column on the weekly Torah reading did Abraham Cahan write for the Yiddish Socialist journal, *Arbayter Tsaytung*, in the late 19th century?

A. A devoted socialist, but disturbed by the hatred of Jews within international Socialism, Cahan began his journalistic career with the radical *Arbayter Tsaytung* in 1890, writing a series of columns which used the weekly Torah reading as a base for a socialist sermon. This seemed to Cahan a more genuine expression of Jewish Socialism in a time when many Jewish Socialists had no use at all for Jewish tradition.

Cahan's first column dealt with Moses' method of collecting materials for the construction of the Tabernacle in the Wilderness and went on to deride Capitalism and modern taxation as exploiting the workers and to explain the new ideas offered by Socialism. Cahan signed his name as Der *Proletarishker Maggid* (the proletarian preacher).

The Jewish workers of that era were strongly drawn to Socialism and other workers' movements that promised improvement of the immigrants' hard life in their tenements and sweatshops. Also, Jews typically felt an idealistic sense of moral obligation to make the world a better place for all.

Cahan went on to a long and productive career as a journalist and spokesman for the secularist-socialist wing of the Jewish immigrants. His novel, *The Rise of David Levinsky*, provides an important picture of immigrant life.

For Further Reading:

Nora Levin, *While the Messiah Tarried: Jewish Socialist Movements 1881- 1917*, New York, Schocken Books, 1977.

Q. How did the Jews of St. Louis try to determine the correct Hebrew spelling of the name of their city?

A. In the late nineteenth century, two St. Louis rabbis differed over the Hebrew transliteration of the name St. Louis. Rabbi Joseph Rosenfeld spelled it with a *samekh*, while Rabbi Shalom Elchanan Jaffe spelled it with a *zayin*. The matter arose in regard to the wording of a Jewish divorce document. The question was appealed to R. Shmuel Salant of Jerusalem, but he refused to interfere saying that the people of St. Louis knew better than he how to pronounce the name.

For Further Reading:

J.D. Eisenstein , "The Development of Jewish Casuistic Literature in America," *PAJHS*. XLI, 1904, 119–147.

Q. When did American Christians become interested in Zionism?

A. As early as the 1820's, President John Quincy Adams had written to Mordecai Noah, "I really wish again in Judaea an independent nation." In 1891, Americans reacted with outrage to new persecutions of Jews in Czarist Russia. Rev. William C. Blackstone of Chicago presented a petition to President Benjamin Harrison asking the U.S. government to call an international conference "to consider the claims of the Jews to Palestine and their ancient home, and to promote the alleviation of their suffering condition ..." Palestine was the "inalienable possession (of the Jews) from which they were expelled by force." Many leading personalities signed the petition including Chief Justice Melville Fuller, Cyrus McCormick, J. Pierpont Morgan, Speaker of the House Thomas B. Reed, William McKinley, John

D. Rockefeller and Cyrus Field. Blackstone argued that if the world powers could take Bulgaria, Serbia and other provinces from the Turkish Empire and give them to their natural owners, the Bulgars, Serbs, etc., as they did at the Treaty of Berlin in 1878, then Palestine should also be rightfully restored to the Jews. The petition reflected the rising tide of nationalism all over the world and the sympathy of certain Christian groups or Biblical ideals. Blackstone was a forerunner of the Zionist Christians of the next century.

A leading opponent of Blackstone's petition was Dr. Emil Hirsch of Chicago's Sinai Congregation. A radical Reform rabbi, he was wholeheartedly opposed to any sort of nationalist or Zionist tendencies in Judaism. Zionism was strong among Eastern European immigrants, who had already organized Hovevei Zion groups in Chicago in the 1880's.

For Further Reading:

Morris Gutstein, *A Priceless Heritage: The Epic Growth of Nineteenth Century Chicago*, New York, Bloch Publ. Co. 1953

Q. What were the Whitecaps?

A. In the 1890's, agricultural depression brought hard times to the farmers of southern Mississippi. Rising costs and falling prices pushed them into debt so deeply that they often had to accept liens on crops they had not yet grown. As debts rose, many lost their lands to their creditors. White farmers blamed the merchants, some of whom were Jewish, and also the Blacks, who usually preferred to rent land from Jews rather than work for poor Whites.

In 1891, mistakenly feeling themselves to be victims of a Jewish conspiracy, poor white farmers began to arrange secret societies, which they called Whitecaps, to terrorize Blacks and Jews. Homes were burned, and people were beaten or killed. One major target was H. Hiller, a Jew who lived in Summit Pike County and who owned about 400 small farms. Late in 1892, night riders burned about 27 houses on his lands. The state government reacted weakly, and Governor John Stone's proclamation in January, 1893 banning Whitecapping had little permanent effect. Finally, a strong minded Judge J.B. Chrisman in Copiah County began to crack down on the Whitecappers, and by the end of the year Whitecapping was finished.

For Further Reading:

William F. Holmes, "Whitecapping; Anti-Semitism in the Populist Era," *AJHQ*, LXlll, 1974, 244–261.

Q. Who were the first Jewish American feminists?

A. The term feminist was being applied to liberated, activist women, at least as early as the 1890's. In the U.S., Jewish women were forming groups to campaign for women's suffrage and all sorts of social reforms. More and more women attended universities and entered professions.

It seemed typical that American Jewish women interested in careers outside the home would devote themselves deeply to public service. For example, Dr. Love Rosa Hirschmann Gantt (1875-1935) was a medical doctor who specialized in the treatment of eye, ear, nose and throat in Spartanburg, SC. She also devoted herself to public health work, like medical inspection of school children, educating the public about sanitation, interesting the American Medical Women's Association in the problems of rural Appalachia, providing healthmobiles, pushing health legislation through the state government and much more. Social projects also drew her interest - like a girls' reform school and women's suffrage - and she organized the ladies auxiliary of the Congregation B'nai Israel in Spartanburg.

However, these women often gave up domestic security and an unusual number went through divorces or married non-Jews at a time when these percentages were still very small in the general population. Newspaper articles of the early years of the twentieth century, often written by women, would bemoan the increasing divorce rate and complain of women who neglected their children to devote themselves to activities outside the home whether social reforms or mah jong at their clubs.

For Further Reading:
NAW, II, 10-11.

Q. Who wrote the famous poem, "Hatikvah"?

A. "Hatikvah," the famous Zionist poem and anthem of the State of Israel was written by Naftali Herz Imber (1856-1909). Born in Galicia, Imber showed precocity in Talmud as a child, but left home at an early age to live as a vagabond. After traveling as far as India, Imber settled for some years in Palestine, where he became secretary to Laurence Oliphant, a famous English Christian Zionist. It was rumored that Imber may at one point have accepted Christianity simply to get food from missionaries.

Through the years he wrote Hebrew poetry, producing "Hatikvah" either in Europe in 1878 or in Jerusalem in 1884. Set to a Rumanian folk tune, "Hatikvah" soon became a popular song among Zionists, although it was not formally adopted as their anthem until 1933.

In 1892 Imber came to the U.S. and resumed his poor artist lifestyle, writing poems and essays with the patronage of Judge Meyer Sulzberger of Philadelphia. In his last years, he frequented New York's cafes where he would improvise poems for the price of a drink. Ten thousand people attended his funeral.

For Further Reading:

Eisig Silberschlag, "Naftali Herz Imber," *Judaism*, V. 1956, 147–159.

Q. What prominent American Jewish statesman wrote a biography of Rhode Island founder, Roger Williams?

A. Oscar Straus, of the famous Straus brothers who owned Macy's, was U.S. ambassador to Turkey and later Secretary of Labor and Commerce. A devoted student of early American History, he wrote the *Origin of the Republican Form of Government in the USA, in* 1885, which emphasized the religious bases of the American Revolution and the colonists' understanding of the government of the ancient Hebrew commonwealth.

The biography of Roger Williams, written in 1894, praised Williams as a hero of the concept of religious liberty. Straus named one of his own sons Roger Williams Straus. Jews of Straus' generation were anxious to reconcile their twin loyalties to Judaism and to the American way of life.

Straus sponsored a book by Maier Kayserling on the Jewish background of Columbus' discovery of America and served as the first president of the American Jewish Historical Society founded in 1892.

For Further Reading:

Naomi Cohen, *A Dual Heritage: The Public Career of Oscar S. Straus*, Philadelphia; JPS. 1969.

Q. Why was a Jew, Oscar Straus, sent as ambassador to Moslem Turkey?

A. Oscar Straus, one of several U.S. Jewish diplomats to Turkey, was sent three times by three different presidents. His main function was to protect American citizens in Turkey, many of whom were Christian missionaries. There was some rumble of opposition to sending a Jew to such a post; however, a letter from the Reverend Henry Ward Beecher to President Grover Cleveland turned the scales definitely in favor of Straus' appointment.

In Turkey, Straus worked not only for American missionaries, but also for the Jewish community in Palestine, then under Turkish rule. He tried especially to help the refugees fleeing the new wave of pogroms in Russia and Romania, as in fact previous American consuls had. Straus received a fully embossed memorial of thanks from the Jews of Jerusalem, bearing the signatures of Ashkenazic chief rabbi Samuel Salant and Sephardic Chacham Bashi Rafael Meir Panisel.

Straus was sent back to Turkey in 1898 by President William McKinley, as relations between Turkey and the U.S. deteriorated over the issue of Turkey's treatment of Americans. The problem was cleared up and Straus was further able to induce the Sultan Abdul Hamid to issue a statement to the Moslems of the Philippines that they should not join the rebellion of Emilio Aguinaldo against American rule.

In 1909, President William Howard Taft sent Straus out to Turkey for a third tour of duty, the job having in the meantime been invested with full ambassadorial status. During these years Straus also had served as Secretary of Labor and Commerce in Theodore Roosevelt's cabinet and had sat on the Permanent Court of Arbitration at the Hague. In 1912, he ran with Roosevelt's Progressive (Bull Moose) Party for governor of New York.

For Further Reading:
Oscar Straus, *Under Four Administrations*, NY; Houghton Mifflin Co., 1922.

Q. How was the National Council of Jewish Women founded?

A. The NCJW has been an important Jewish philanthropic organization since its founding at the Chicago World Fair of 1893. Hannah Greenebaum Solomon (1856-1942), daughter of one of Chicago's earliest Jewish families, helped organize the Jewish Women's Section of the Parliament of Religions at the Fair. Notable Jewish women led the proceedings. One featured speaker was Henrietta Szold, who stirred her listeners with a talk on "What has Judaism Done for Women." The delegates decided to organize a permanent group, the NCJW, to unite the efforts of Jewish women interested in religion, philanthropy and education.

Mrs. Solomon was named as first president and remained active in the Council into her eighties. There was some criticism of her in the early years for observing the Sabbath on Sunday, as a loyal member of Dr. Emil Hirsch's Sinai Temple.

Mrs. Solomon actively advocated increased rights for women both in the U.S. and Europe, and she was a friend and admirer of Susan B. Anthony. She believed that greater women's influence could act as a check on the unrestrained lust for power in what seemed to her very much a man's world of the early 20th century.

For Further Reading:

Hannah G. Solomon, *Fabric of My Life,* NY; Bloch Publ. Co., 1946.

Q. What was the Immigration Restriction League?

A. Disconcerted by the increasing flow of immigration to the U.S., three Harvard students, Prescott Hall, Charles Warren and Robert Ward, founded the Immigration Restriction League in 1894, with the aim of saving Anglo-Saxon America from degrading foreign influences. The three young men were strongly affected by the ideas of Teutonic superiority taught at Harvard and by the fear that the new immigrants would corrupt the Anglo-Saxon virtues of traditional New England society.

The main political sponsor for the League was Massachusetts Senator Henry Cabot Lodge, an Anglophile who wrote a Ph.D. history thesis that extolled the virtues of Medieval Anglo-Saxon law and who was fascinated with the achievements of his own ancestors in old New England. The way, he felt, to limit degrading outside influences on the American spirit was to restrict foreign immigration. The League strongly advocated tough literacy tests for prospective immigrants, and several such laws were cut down only by presidential vetoes. Although condemning religious and racial bias in its first years, the League soon turned to rabble-rousing propaganda and pseudo-scientific racist doctrines. The League's ideals were fulfilled more or less by the immigration restriction laws of the 1920's and resurfaced in the isolationism of the 1930's.

For Further Reading:

Barbara Solomon, *Ancestors and Immigrants,* Cambridge; Harvard University Press, 1956.

Q. Are the Jews a race or a religion?

A. This question took on a direct practical importance in terms of Jewish efforts to oppose restrictions on immigration to the U.S. in the early 1900's. Jewish leader Simon Wolf put the question to a number of prominent Jews in 1903 and was disappointed that some felt that Jewish immigrants should be registered as Jewish in race as well as religion. Louis Dembitz, a lawyer, and Rabbi Bernhard Felsenthal, a leading Reform rabbi, told Wolf that the racial classification would provide the U.S. government with much useful information about immigrants. For example, had Benjamin Disraeli immigrated, he would have been registered as an Episcopalian by religion, a Jew by race, and Englishman politically. Dr. Solomon Schechter, dean of JTS, argued that the Jews are a race by virtue of "common origin" and "common blood." This view, he said, could be easily misunderstood and misused politically; however, the contrary viewpoint could lead to assimilation which is more dangerous to Judaism than anti-Semitism. Other Jewish leaders, including Judge Meyer Sulzberger, Rabbi Marcus Jastrow, Leo Levi and Rabbi Emil Hirsch, felt that to classify Jews as a race was neither correct nor helpful.

For Further Reading:
Esther Panitz. "In Defense of Jewish Immigration," *AJHQ*, LV, 1965, 57–97.

Q. What is the JWV?

A. The Jewish War Veterans consists of Jewish veterans of U.S. wars and involves itself in a number of Jewish causes both at home and around the world. The first Jewish veterans' group was the Hebrew Union Veterans formed in 1896 by 78 former soldiers of the Union army. Their primary aim was to combat aspersions against the military and patriotic records of American Jews. Hebrew Veterans of the Spanish American War formed a few years later. The two groups merged in the Hebrew Veterans of the Wars of the Republic, changing the name in 1929 to Jewish War Veterans.

For Further Reading:
Gloria Mosesson, *The Jewish War Veterans Story*, Washington, DC, 1971.

Q. What 19th century American rabbi had once converted to Eastern Orthodox Christianity?

A. Henry Gersoni (1844–1897) had studied in yeshivot in his native Vilna and later at the University of St. Petersburg. In 1866, he went to England and two years later published an account of his conversion to the Russian Orthodox Church, his marriage to a Christian, and his subsequent flight from Russia and return to Judaism.

In 1869, Gersoni came to the U.S., where he taught in Temple Emanu-el Sabbath school in New York and later occupied pulpits in Atlanta and Chicago. He wrote books and journal articles and translated some of Ivan Turgenev's short stories from Russian to English. In 1871, he published a Hebrew translation of Longfellow's poem "Excelsior" for which he received a letter of thanks from the poet. His *Sketches of Jewish Life and History* is still of value as a source of historical information.

For Further Reading:

JE. V, 641.

Q. Who was the first professor of pediatrics in the U.S.?

A. A fugitive from the revolution of 1848 in Germany, Dr. Abraham Jacobi (1830–1919) came to the U.S. in 1852 at a time when leeching and bloodletting were still standard practices among physicians. In 1860, he joined New York Medical College as the nation's first professor of pediatrics. Over the years, he wrote prolifically, gaining a reputation as a leader of the American medical profession. His wife Mary Putnam Jacobi attained wide recognition in her own right as an M.D.

For Further Reading:

New York Times July 12, 1919.
DAB, V:1, p.563 .

Q. What was the relationship between the *Chattanooga Times* and the *New York Times*?

A. In 1878 Adolph Ochs, already at age twenty a veteran newspaperman, joined with Colonel John McGowan to buy the *Chattanooga Times,* a failing newspaper with only 250 readers. Within a few years, Ochs had built the *Times* into a reputable and profitable enterprise.

Ochs invested a great deal of money in a land boom, a common practice in frontier days, but the boom collapsed and he was left with some worthless properties and no money. In order to save his newspaper, he decided to buy a second newspaper, a risky step which would require heavy borrowing.

In 1896, after a deal for the *Nashville Courier* fell through, Ochs bought the *New York Times*. A very reputable paper, the *New York Times* had fallen into deep financial trouble in the 1890's through some foolish expenditures. By 1896, its circulation was down to 9,000 and it was losing advertisers. Ochs' family opposed the deal, arguing that the *New York Times* would fail and drag the *Chattanooga Times* with it, but Ochs went ahead. He rebuilt the *New York Times* into one of the U.S.'s leading newspapers. Ochs lived to celebrate the 50th anniversary of the *Chattanooga Times* in 1929 and to see his son-in-law, Arthur Sulzberger succeed him as head of the *New York Times*.

For Further Reading:

Iphigene Ochs Sulzberger, *Iphigene:Memoirs*, New York, Dodd, Mead, 1981.

Q. Who was the first prominent Jewish woman pianist in the U.S.?

A. Fannie Bloomfield-Zeisler (1863–1927) grew up in Chicago and made her debut at age 12. After studying under Theodor Leschetizky in Vienna, she returned home in 1883 and gained widespread recognition as one of the foremost woman pianists of her day in the U.S. She appeared on many successful concert tours through Europe and at home. Critics praised her energy and her well developed technique. Her repertoire was unusually large. During a tour in California in 1912, she played eight recitals in 18 days with no repetitions. She particularly liked to play the music of women composers, and she delivered a lecture on women in music at the 1890 convention of the Music Teachers' National Association, an almost entirely male organization. Zeisler was also an influential and devoted teacher.

Her husband, Sigmund Zeisler (1860–1931), who came from the same small town, Bielitz in Silesia, was a prominent lawyer who wrote and lectured on a variety of cultural topics. Maurice Bloomfield, her older brother, was professor of Sanskrit at Johns Hopkins University and president of the American Oriental Society (1910–1911).

For Further Reading:

DAB, X, 2, 647–648.

Q. Who was the first American woman to function (at least almost) as a rabbi?

A. Born in San Francisco in 1865, Ray (Rachel) Frank a descendant of the Gaon of Vilna developed quite a reputation on the west coast in the 1890's as a gifted preacher and teacher of Judaism. Newspapers praised her as a female messiah and a modern Deborah, and she was offered rabbinical positions, as in Stockton in 1896. Both bemused and irritated when people referred to her as rabbi, Ray Frank was in some ways very traditional, and women rabbis were as yet unheard of. The suffragettes of her day also appeared to her too radical and too hostile to men, and she reproached women for neglecting homes and motherhood.

Ray Frank did study briefly at Hebrew Union College in 1893, but did not take a degree. Main themes in her teaching were the importance of unity and peace among the discordant branches of Judaism and the work of Jewish women in history. In 1901, she married Dr. Simon Litman, an economist, and lived most of the rest of her life in Urbana, Illinois where her husband taught at the University of Illinois. Dynamic intellectual women have certainly made their mark in Jewish history from the earliest times.

For Further Reading:

Marcus, *AJW*, p. 380–384.

Q. What unique Jewish institution was located in Doylestown, Pennsylvania?

A. The National Farm School, to train young Jewish men in modern farming, opened in 1897 in Doylestown under the impetus of a Reform rabbi, Dr. Joseph Krauskopf. He believed that returning Jews to farming would offer a practical solution to the crowding of Jewish immigrants into American cities. Krauskopf had met Leo Tolstoy, the famed writer, during a trip to Russia and at his suggestion had visited the Jewish Agricultural School at Odessa. Within a few years, the National Farm School housed over 40 students learning the use of farm machinery, soil treatment, caring for livestock, operating dairies, raising poultry, fruit growing and the like.

For Further Reading:

Jewish Encyclopedia, VIII, 119.

Q. Who was the first president of the American Association for Thoracic Surgery?

A. Dr. Samuel James Meltzer (1851–1920) grew up in Ponevez, Lithuania and showed early precocity in the study of Talmud. However, after his marriage at the age of 19, he went to the University of Berlin to study philosophy, later transferring to medicine. Upon completing his studies in 1882, he was offered several positions, but on the condition that he be baptized into Christianity. Instead, he emigrated to New York.

Interested primarily in research, Meltzer was respected as an authority in several areas of medical knowledge. He developed a method of "intratracheal insuffliation anesthesia," which greatly advanced the possibilities for successful thoracic surgery. He made important contributions to the study of asthma, diabetes and kidney disease.

For Further Reading:

Adolph Meltzer, "Dr. Samuel James Meltzer: Physiologist of the Rockefeller Institute," *AJA*, XLII, 1990, 49–65.

Q. What Yiddish poet was known as the People's Bard?

A. Eliakum Zunser (1836- 1913) became famous in Russia during the 1860's for his wedding (badchen) performances in which he would sing poems specially improvised by himself for the occasion. Apprenticed at age six to a weaver of gold lace, he was kicked out by his employer six years later without the wages due him. At age thirteen, he tutored the children of an innkeeper, who after a year had him drafted into the czar's army rather than pay him. Zunser wrote his first poems about the life of the Jewish child army conscripts (cantonists). Wit and humor were much the essence of Zunser's poetry. However, in a truer sense, his poems were very serious, reflecting on deeper human feelings, on sanctity, justice, on good and evil, and on life and death. Lyrical adoration of nature so common in Western literature plays a much smaller part in Jewish writing.

Showing an occasional political interest, Zunser wrote a poem sympathetic to Czar Alexander's suppression of the Polish Revolution of 1863 and sang it at weddings. A book of poems published in 1870 included some social satire.

While in the U.S. on a performance tour in 1889, Zunser received a cable from his family telling him that they would join him. His wife, Feigel, had been called in for questioning by Czarist authorities. Fearing that Eliakum would be in danger if he returned to Russia, Feigel instead took the family to him.

Settling in New York where one could not make a living as a badchen, Zunser opened a printing shop and began to write songs which reflected the immigrants' experience. Among his most popular American songs were "The Peddler," "The Golden Land," and "The Greenhorn". Most of his works are hopeful, ending in an upbeat note. In 1905, on the 50th anniversary of his beginnings as a poet, Zunser was honored at a mass meeting at Cooper Union in New York. Zunser can be considered, in his last years, a patriarch among the American Yiddish writers who were creating Modern Yiddish literature.

For Further Reading:

Sol Liptzin, *Eliakum Zunser,* New York: Behrman House Inc., 1950.

Q. What 1890's group can be viewed as a sort of precursor of Young Israel?

A. In the late 1890's, Bernard Drachman, an American born Orthodox rabbi teaching at the Jewish Theological Seminary, organized the Jewish Endeavor

Society to try to win American Jewish adolescents back to their religion. The first workers were JTS students like Herman Abramowitz and Gabriel Davidson. The society placed great stress on prayer services conducted in a refined and wholly Orthodox manner.

The society met with considerable success at first, but began to decline, as its chief workers graduated from JTS and moved on to other places and other fields of work. The Young Israel movement, founded several years later, worked toward similar goals although it supporters came from other circles.

Rabbi Drachman also served as the first president of Tomche Sabbath, a group which sought to encourage Jews to observe the Sabbath. Emphasizing practical methods, they set up an employment bureau for Sabbath observers, interceded directly with Jewish employers to close their businesses on Saturday, and kept up a difficult battle against the Sunday closing laws, which existed in most states. Tomche Sabbath actively supported the adoption of a five day work week long before it became standard in the U.S.

For Further Reading:

Bernard Drachman, *The Unfailing Light*, New York: RCA, 1946.

Q. Two world famous Jews grew up in the small town of Appleton, Wisconsin in the late 19th century. Who were they?

A. The two were escape artist Houdini (Erich Weiss) and novelist Edna Ferber. Houdini's father was Rabbi Meyer Samuel Weiss, a scholarly man who eked out a livelihood as rabbi of a small Orthodox synagogue in Appleton. Often short of funds, Rabbi Weiss once had to sell some of his beloved books. Years later when Houdini was already world famous, he learned that Rabbi Bernard Drachman's synagogue in New York was in possession of Rabbi Weiss' set of Maimonides' *Mishneh Torah*. Houdini bought it back from the synagogue at a generous price.

Edna Ferber wrote a number of famous novels including *Show Boat*, *Cimarron*, and *So Big*. Her two volumes of autobiography depict the pleasant life of Jews in Appleton. Ferber herself sang in the temple choir and developed a strong feeling for her Jewishness, although she was never very observant ritually. For many years the mayor of Appleton was a Jew named David Hammel. The Jews were able to prosper and participated in community life with no great fear of anti-Semitic prejudice. This contrasted strongly with Ferber's earlier years in Ottumwa, Iowa, where she often faced anti-Semitic harassment both from children her age and from older people.

As an adult, she was both deeply proud of being Jewish and highly sensitive to anti-Semitism. In her autobiography, *A Peculiar Treasure,* she wrote, "I should like, in this book, to write about being a Jew ... I have felt that to be a Jew was, in some way at least, to be especially privileged. Two thousand years of persecution have made the Jew quick to sympathy, quick witted (he'd better be), tolerant, humanly understanding. The highest compliment we can pay a Christian is to say of him that he has a Jewish heart.'

For Further Reading:

Edna Ferber, *A Peculiar Treasure: Autobiography,* Garden City, New York, Doubleday and Co., 1960.

Q. During which war did the American army first employ Jewish chaplains on a regular basis?

A. In the Spanish American War, a number of Jewish chaplains served in the armed forces. The first to volunteer was Edward Benjamin Morris Browne, a controversial rabbi from Columbus, Georgia. However, he was already in his mid-fifties, too old for the army. We have no record of the army's reply to R. Browne, if there ever was one, but he was lampooned in several Jewish periodicals. R. Isaac Meyer Wise's editorial in the "American Israelite" was thoroughly sarcastic.

Paul Wollenberger had a taste of army bureaucracy when stationed in Managuete in the Philippines. An order came from Washington to let all Jewish soldiers go to Manila for the High Holidays. The order arrived long after the holidays were over, but Wollenberger was told that since the order was issued he had to go to Manila anyway, a four day trip by boat, and attend religious services. Wallenberger went to Manila, had a good time and reported back to his post without once entering a synagogue.

For Further Reading:

Bertram Korn, "Jewish Welfare During The Spanish-American War," *PAJHS,* XLI, 1952, 357–380.

Q. How many Jews served in the Spanish-American War?

A. The list covers 94 pages in the American Jewish Yearbook of 1900–1901. There were, for example, five Jewish volunteers in a state regiment from Tampa, Florida, 37 from San Francisco, and 18 from Kansas. Seventeen Jews are listed in Company B of the 12th New York State Volunteer Infantry. Eight were among Colonel Theodore Roosevelt's Rough Riders, including

Samuel Greenwald of Prescott, Arizona, who was promoted to lieutenant for gallantry.

For Further Reading:

Bertram Korn. "Jewish Welfare During the Spanish-American War," *PAJHS*, XLI, 1952, 357–380.

Q. How did Jewish Socialists in the U.S. react to the Spanish-American War and the Dreyfus Case, two important issues of the late 1890's?

A. The Jewish Socialists divided into two parties. A doctrinaire wing led by Daniel De Leon took a straight Marxist line. They claimed the U.S. was interested only in territorial expansion and power. Socialists ought to support the fight against Capitalism at home and not support foreign wars. The unjust imprisonment of Captain Alfred Dreyfus in Devil's Island was important only in that Dreyfus was a victim of Capitalist oppression. The second group was mainstream Socialists, represented by their newspaper, *The Forward*. They were more responsive to popular Jewish feelings. They supported the U.S. in the war against Spain, a nation which they associated both with the Inquisition and with the harsh colonial rule of Cuba. *The Forward* also gave expression to the Jews' intense concern and empathy with Dreyfus.

Angered over De Leon's stand, Jews turned their support away from him. His newspaper, *Das Abendblatt*, was out of business by 1902. Indeed, Socialism at the turn of the century was distinctly disunified, fragmenting into bitterly quarreling factions on almost every important matter. Nevertheless, the workers' movements were important in fostering political ideas that would later become part of American life, especially during the New Deal, and also in creating a Yiddish socialist culture that influenced Jewish-American life for some decades.

For Further Reading:

Nora Levin, *While Messiah Tarried: Jewish Social Movements. 1881–1917*, New York. Schocken Books. 1977, p. 159 and 214.

Q. How did the Jewish agricultural settlements get their start?

A. The typical Eastern European immigrant of the period around 1900 settled in noisy poor neighborhoods in big cities along the eastern seaboard. A few tried their luck at farming, an unusual occupation for Jews, since land ownership in Europe had generally been forbidden to them by law. Nevertheless, there was a movement to settle immigrants on farm co-ops. One reason was that such settlements might help to draw people away from the crowded city conditions. Also, in intellectual circles in those days, there was a utopian idealization of the simple harmony of rural life — town mouse vs. country mouse. The attempts to create utopias form an important chapter of 19th century American history, long before the Jewish immigration waves.

The Jewish farm communities were on the whole unsuccessful, as the settlers were not experienced in agriculture, and their outside support was not adequate. Ideological differences among the early settlers heightened internal dissensions. The heyday of these colonies was about 1885–1905, although the dream continued to stir in liberal minds into the 1930's.

Two Jewish farm settlements in Michigan were fairly typical. In 1891, twelve Jewish peddlers, eleven from Bay City, Michigan and one from Detroit, bought land at Bad Axe in the thumb area to build the Palestine farm colony. None of the settlers knew anything about farming and the first winter was a terrible struggle. With the help of Detroit philanthropists, Emanuel Wodic and Martin Butzel and the Baron De Hirsch Fund, the colonists stuck it out and began attracting new members. A small synagogue and school were built, and the Sabbath was observed as a day of rest. However, the financial pressures proved too much. By 1899, settlers began to move out and in 1900 the land reverted to the Hubbard Co. from which it had been rented.

One of the latest farm experiments, the Sunrise Colony near Bay City, Michigan, was notable for its main crop, peppermint, which was used in medicines in those days. Founded in the early years of the Great Depression, it attracted people of leftist leanings, who associated Judaism with leftist social theories and not traditional religion. Most Sunrise settlers came from the Detroit area, while Joseph Cohen, the leader, was a well known New York newspaper editor. Despite some outside support, Sunrise Colony soon ran into trouble because of infighting over ideologies. Also, because buyers hesitated to do business with leftists, at first the colony could not sell its produce. Finally with the help of a University of Michigan professor, they were able to sell the first year's peppermint to Parke-Davis. However, peppermint proved to be an especially difficult crop for the inexperienced settlers, and yields in the following years were poor. Soon, the colony was empty. Cohen and a few others surfaced again in a short lived colony in Virginia several years later.

For Further Reading:

Uri D. Herscher, *Jewish Agricultural Utopias in America.* 1880–1910, Detroit, Wayne State University Press, 1981.

Robert Rockaway. *The Jews of Detroit.* 1762–1914, Detroit, Wayne State University Press, 1986.

Q. Why did Hebrew Union College withdraw its offer of a professorship to Louis Ginzberg?

A. In 1899, Isaac Mayer Wise invited Louis Ginzberg from Europe to teach at HUC. Ginzberg had a brilliant record as a talmudist trained in Lithuanian yeshivot and also the highest credentials from the universities of Heideberg and Strassbourg. Ginzberg was already en route from his home in Amsterdam to Cincinnati when he received a message notifying him that the offer had been withdrawn. Instead, he assumed a position at New York's Jewish Theological Seminary, where he entered into a long and highly distinguished career as a scholar and teacher.

The HUC position was given to Dr. Henry Malter of Berlin. The reason for the withdrawal of the offer to Ginzberg seems to have been Dr. Wise's mistaken belief that Ginzberg accepted the Higher Criticism of the Bible as taught by the Wellhausen school. This was too radical a break from the Jewish religious view for Wise to tolerate in a school which prepared young men for the rabbinate.

For Further Reading:

Hebrew Union College — Jewish Institute of Religion: A Centennial Documentary. AJA, XXVI. 1974.

Q. Who was the first RIETS student to take secular courses and what became of him?

A. The Rabbi Isaac Elchonen Theological Seminary, which later developed into Yeshiva University, was founded in New York as a small school for advanced students of Talmud in 1897. Almost all the early students were young men of Eastern European background. Some of the students wanted to take secular courses also, but the Board of Directors would not allow it. The mashgiach (supervisor), Rabbi Nahum Dan Baron, although an old style Talmudic scholar, sympathized with the students. Finally, he defied the Board by allowing one student, Hillel Rogoff, to attend high school and then college, as well as RIETS.

The experiment did not work. Rogoff abandoned Orthodox Judaism and eventually became editor of the *Jewish Daily Forward,* a leftist newspaper. When other students asked to be allowed to take secular courses, the Board's ready response was, "Look what happened to Rogoff."

Secular courses were first offered at RIETS several years later, in 1904, but were terminated after a few months. In 1908, the students went on strike primarily over the issue of secular courses. Under increasing pressure, the directors surrendered to the inevitable and agreed that RIETS would offer both rabbinical and secular courses so as to help prepare students to serve in the American rabbinate. Thus, the beginning of Yeshiva University.

For Further Reading:

Gilbert Klaperman, *The Story of Yeshiva University,* New York, MacMillan Co., 1969, pp. 80–110.

Q. Who was the first woman to receive a Ph.D. from the University of Heidelberg?

A. In the late 19th century, college educated American men often went on to the great German universities for graduate training. However, the German universities were less hospitable to women students. The first woman to earn a Ph.D. at the prestigious University of Heidelberg was Ida Hyde (Heidenheimer) (1857–1945), a Jew from Davenport, Iowa.

After taking a degree from Cornell in 1891, Hyde went on to the University of Strassburg, where because of her sex she was eventually not permitted to take the Ph.D. exams despite a good academic record. She then turned to Heidelberg, where she received the Ph.D. in physiology in 1896, over the hostility of some faculty members.

In 1898 she began teaching at the University of Kansas and was promoted to full professor in 1905. Her main professional interest was in the problems of both vertebrate and invertebrate animals.

For Further Reading:

NAW, II, 247–249.
Marcus, *AJW,* 40f.

Q. Who was the Jewish J.R.?

A. Julius Rosenwald, or J.R. as he was generally known, failed in two businesses in New York, moved to Chicago, and within a few years was head of a booming Sears and Roebuck Company. Exceptional generosity vied in him with great stinginess. He built hundreds of schools in the South for underprivileged Black children. Ambassador Ralph Bunche and opera diva Marian Anderson attended those schools. At the same time, he refused to buy tennis balls for his children to play on the courts of his own estate and made them set up a lemonade stand to earn spending money.

Rosenwald attended Sinai Congregation in Chicago regularly and was its vice-president. He was very active in local Jewish charities and in supporting both HUC and JTS.

For Further Reading:

M.R. Werner. *Julius Rosenwald: The Life of a Practical Humanitarian*, New York, Harper and Bros. Publishers, 1939.

Q. What two Jewish brothers from Louisville headed research institutes of international importance?

A. Moritz and Esther Flexner migrated from Central Europe to Louisville before the Civil War and produced a large family of brilliant offspring. Their children included Simon (1863–1946), organizer and first head of the Rockefeller Institute, and Abraham (1866–1959), founder and first head of the Princeton Institute for Advanced Study.

A brilliant medical researcher, Simon was invited in 1901 to be first head of the newly formed Rockefeller Institute for Medical Research in New York, and he remained there until 1935. He planned the Institute to concentrate on laboratory research in medicine, and he employed some of the nation's best medical minds. Simon's own contributions to medical knowledge were important and prolific. He discovered a widespread strain of dysentery bacillus, since known as the Flexner Type. In 1905, Simon helped slow down an outbreak of meningitis in New York by discovering that the serum was far more effective when injected into the spinal canal. An administrator of unusual ability, Flexner was admired by his workers both for his helpfulness and his scrupulous honesty.

As a child, Simon seemed to show little promise. He failed the fifth grade, dropped out of school before finishing the sixth and went through a series of jobs, none of which lasted more than a short time. Finally, he took a job in a drugstore where he became fascinated with the microscope. He went on to pharmacy school in Louisville and was admitted to a postgraduate program to study bacteriology and pathology at Johns Hopkins, although he had never attended either college or high school.

Abraham Flexner took a degree from Johns Hopkins where he was deeply influenced by the personality and the high-minded educational views of its president, Daniel Coit Gilman. After 19 years of high school teaching, Flexner decided to devote himself to the study of higher education, and he wrote several books which helped bring about important reforms in American medical schools and graduate schools in general.

In 1930, he was approached by Louis Bamberger and his sister Carrie Bamberger Fuld, who had just sold their dry goods business, L. Bamberger and Co., to Macy's for $25,000,000. They wanted to donate $5,000,000 to an important university project. Concerned about the decline of the great German universities after World War I, Flexner came up with a plan to found a research institute which would devote itself to post-graduate research and study for its own sake. Leading scholars would be able to pursue their work in close contact with colleagues and with a minimum of distraction.

The Princeton Institute for Advanced Study opened in 1933 with Abraham Flexner as its first head, just in time to attract leading scientists and scholars, many of them Jews, in flight from Nazism. Among the first were Albert Einstein and John Von Neumann in Physics and Mathematics, and Erwin Panofsky, Ernst Herzfeld, and Hetty Goldman in Humanistic Studies. The Institute more than fulfilled the early hopes of Abraham Flexner, becoming one of the world's major centers of scholarship. Louis Bamberger and Carrie Fuld kept up their support, donating about $18,000,000 over the years.

A third able Flexner brother was Bernard (1865–1945), an attorney who became a devoted Zionist after visiting Jewish communities in Romania in 1917 and seeing the dreadful conditions there. At the Paris Peace Conference following World War I, Bernard was a counsel for the Zionist delegation. He served as chairman of the medical and sanitary committee of the American Jewish Joint Distribution Committee and as president of the Palestine Economic Corporation. He was instrumental in bringing in Jewish leaders like Louis Marshall, Herbert Lehman, and Felix Warburg to help develop the economy of Palestine.

Simon's son James Thomas Flexner is well known for his four volume biography of George Washington. He also wrote a biography of his parents.

For Further Reading:

Abraham Flexner, *I Remember*, New York, Simon and Schuster, 1960.
James Thomas Flexner, *American Saga: The Story of Helen Thomas and Simon Flexner*, Boston: Little, Brown and Co., 1984.

Q. How did Theodore Roosevelt as New York Police Commissioner handle an anti-Semitic rally?

A. In 1901, President Theodore Roosevelt answered a letter inquiring about his relationship with American Jews. He wrote that he encouraged Jews to develop their "Maccabee" or "fighting" side as well as their other abilities. For this reason, he had encouraged Jews to join the New York police force, when he was commissioner. "When Rector Alward came over here to preach an anti-Jewish crusade, after some thought I decided that the best thing to do was to have him protected by forty Jewish policemen. Of course, it was my duty to see that he was not molested, and it struck me to have him protected by the very members of the race he was denouncing was the most effective answer to that denunciation." TR went on to speak of several Jews who won medals with his Rough Riders, and of several others whom he had appointed to judgeships or other government positions.

Q. Who invented the teddy bear?

A. In 1902, Morris Michtom, owner of a Brooklyn toy store, was inspired by a cartoon of President Theodore Roosevelt's bear hunt in Mississippi to make a stuffed bear for children and to call it Teddy. Supposedly, Michtom wrote to Mr. Roosevelt to ask for permission to use his name. The president is reported to have responded, "I don't think my name will mean much to the bear business, but you're welcome to use it."

For Further Reading:

Nathan Miller, *Theodore Roosevelt*, New York, Morrow, 1992.

Q. Did the Jewish Theological Seminary once seek to merge with Dropsie College?

A. Moses Aaron Dropsie (1821–1905), a prominent Philadelphia lawyer, left a large bequest for the founding of a Jewish Studies college in his city. Dr. Solomon Schechter and Louis Marshall, leaders of JTS, were joined to the Board of Governors at Dropsie College with the idea of having a sort of interlocking directorate and close co-operation between the two schools. JTS leaders, concerned that Dropsie with its large endowment might injure other Jewish schools, proposed that JTS and Dropsie should merge and were even willing to move JTS to Philadelphia. Dr. Cyrus Adler, head of Dropsie College, and Judge Meyer Sulzberger dissuaded them, feeling that it would be a great mistake to leave New York, the largest Jewish community in the world, without a Jewish College. Moses Dropsie had originally designated his bequest for a college in Philadelphia, not New York, because he was angry over the failure of Jewish leaders in New York to support Isaac Leeser's Maimonides College in the 1870's. Dr. Cyrus Adler (1863–1940), a noted Judaica scholar and formerly librarian of the Smithsonian Institute in Washington D.C., served as president of Dropsie College from its founding in 1908. In 1915, he succeeded Dr. Schechter as president of JTS, holding both posts simultaneously until his death in 1940, but the two schools remained separate.

For Further Reading:

Cyrus Adler, *I Have Considered the Days.* Philadelphia; Jewish Publication Society, 1941. p. 273–277.

Q. Thousands of Jewish women rioted in New York in June 1906. Why?

A. The women, perhaps nervous over large government-sponsored pogroms in Bialystok, Poland at that time, went into a panic over a story that physicians in East Side schools were cutting children's throats. Thousands of women swept down on the school buildings smashing doors and windows, intent on rescuing their children. They did not realize that the youngsters were merely being vaccinated and in some cases having adenoids removed.

When the teachers realized why the women were rioting they began to march the youngsters out of the buildings. The disturbances quickly ended as the women caught hold of their offspring and hurried them safely home.

For Further Reading:

Jacob Marcus, *The American Jewish Women,* New York: Ktav, 1981, p. 545- 549.

Q. What Jewish husband and wife held a Congressional seat for 36 years between them?

A. After eleven years as a successful actor, Julius Kahn (1861–1924) became an attorney. He then served as Congressman from San Francisco's fifth district from 1899 to 1903 and again from 1905 to 1924. A strong advocate of military preparedness as chairman of the Military Affairs Committee, he helped push the Selective Service Act through Congress in 1917, when the U.S. entered World War I. Kahn was the first member of Congress to call attention to the necessity of publishing statistics on campaign contributions and expenditures. He helped arrange a program to exterminate the

Mediterranean fruit fly in Hawaii and to prevent it from being introduced into California.

When Kahn died in 1924, his wife Florence Prag Kahn (1866–1948) was elected to fill his seat, which she held until 1936. Known for her wit and candor on the House floor, Florence Kahn continued her husband's strong interest in military affairs and in veterans' benefits. She also was a supporter of the FBI and an advocate of highway construction and of radio and aviation development.

For Further Reading:

San Francisco Chronicle, December 19, 1924.
Irena Narell, *Our City: The Jews of San Francisco,* San Diego, Howell-North, 1980.
    Marcus, *AJW,* 749–755.

Q. What difference of opinion caused the resignation of three professors from the Hebrew Union College faculty in 1907?

A. Professors of Bible, Max Margolis and Max Schloessinger, and Henry Malter, who taught philosophy and Talmud, resigned from the HUC faculty in 1907. The main matter of dispute was that the three professors were Zionists and could not get along with the college president, Dr. Kaufmann Kohler, an outspoken anti-Zionist. There were charges that academic freedom in the classroom was being repressed by the anti-Zionist faction. Shortly before the resignations, Margolis had delivered a pro-Zionist sermon in the HUC chapel which was followed by a public argument with Kohler. Supporters of Kohler charged that the firings were prompted by the professors' insubordination, but this seems hardly likely. In two separate incidents, Judah Magnes, 1903, and Caspar Levias, 1905, had also left the HUC faculty, at least partly because of their Zionist sympathies. This was still the early period of the political Zionist movement, when Zionism was not yet acceptable to most American Reform Jews.

For Further Reading:

Samuel S. Cohon, "The History of Hebrew Union College," *PAJHS,* XL, 1950, 17–56.
Naomi Cohen, "The Reaction of Reform Judaism to Zionism, 1897–1922," *PAJHS,* XL, 1950, 361–394.

Q. What was unusual about the art collecting of Etta and Claribel Cone?

A. Etta (1870–1949) and Claribel (1864–1929) Cone were among the early supporters of modern art in the opening years of the 20th century. The sisters were raised in Baltimore by immigrant German Jewish parents who had made a fortune in southern textile mills.

Claribel graduated first in her class from Women's Medical College and worked as a professor and researcher until 1920. She never opened a private practice. Etta became interested in the art world, spending time in Paris and befriending Pablo Picasso and Henri Matisse, about 1905. Matisse painted portraits of both sisters and Picasso painted Claribel. The sisters built a sizable art collection in their residence in Baltimore.

They were considered eccentric in high society both for their Victorian dress and for their modern taste in art. Their collection of Matisse paintings and sculptures became perhaps the world's best. The art works were bequeathed to the Baltimore Museum of Art.

For Further Reading:

Barbara Pollack, *The Collectors: Dr. Claribel and Miss Etta Cone*. Indianapolis, Bobbs-Merrill, 1962.

Q. What prompted David Lubin to found the International Institute of Agriculture?

A. David Lubin came to the U.S. in 1855 fleeing a pogrom in his native Russia. After several years of prospecting and other laborious jobs with nothing to show for it, Lubin opened a successful dry goods store in Sacramento. In 1884 he fulfilled a promise to take his mother to visit Eretz Israel. Impressed by the Jewish pioneers and their sense of historical fulfillment, and by the promise of economic growth of the ancient homeland, Lubin returned to the U.S. imbued with a new vivid sense of mission. Over the next years he devoted himself to helping farmers. In 1896, he proposed an International Institute of Agriculture which would provide statistical, technical and economic information to farmers.

Snubbed by the governments of the U.S., England, and France, Lubin was finally able to win the support of King Victor Emanuel of Italy. In 1905 the International Institute of Agriculture was founded with the endorsement of 46 countries. The IIA carried on its work right through the First World War. Lubin had always hoped that the IIA would be the first step toward forming a world government, and it did help set a pattern for the founding of the League of Nations.

For Further Reading:

Olivia Rosetti Agresti, *David Lubin*, Berkeley, University of California Press, 1941.

Q. What world renowned Wagnerian contralto was, at least partly, Jewish?

A. The name of composer Richard Wagner is associated with the most rabid sort of anti-Semitism. It is therefore somewhat ironic that perhaps the greatest Wagnerian contralto of the twentieth century was of partly Jewish ancestry. Born near Prague, Ernestine Schumann-Heink (1861- 1936) was raised as a Catholic by her parents Hans Roessler, an officer in the Austrian army and Charlotte (Goldman) Roessler. Her musical talent was first recognized by her Jewish maternal grandmother, Leah Kohn, whom she adored.

After many years of minimal sucess, she emerged in the 1890's as perhaps the greatest Wagnerian singer of her day.

Schumann-Heink continued to perform into the 1930's making her last operatic appearance in 1932 at the Metropolitan in New York. She had become an American citizen in 1905.

When Hitler came to power, she declared a self-imposed exile from Germany on herself and proudly proclaimed her Jewish ancestry. A warm and generous personality as well as a great singer, Schumann-Heink was very popular with American audiences.

For Further Reading:

Mary Lawton, *Schumann-Heink: Last of the Titans,* New York; MacMillan & Co., 1940.

Q. What dentist became a major translator of English poetry into Yiddish?

A. Abraham Asen came from Brest-Litovsk (Brisk), Russia to the U.S. in 1903. A practicing dentist, he devoted his spare time to translating poetry from English to Yiddish. His translations include Lord Byron's "Hebrew Melodies," the "Rubaiyat of Omar Khayyam," Shakespeare's sonnets, and poems of Longfellow and Whitman.

The new eastern European immigrants were taking full advantage of the greater opportunities for culture in the New World, and many great works of world literature from Homer's epics and on were being rendered into Yiddish.

For Further Reading:

UJE, I, 536.

Q. Who wrote the famous poem about Tinker to Evers to Chance?

A. The great Chicago Cubs infield of the early 1900's turned many a dazzling double play. However, it was the poem of a Jewish writer, Franklin Pierce Adams that truly immortalized them:

These are the saddest of possible words
"Tinker to Evers to Chance."
Trio of bear cubs and fleeter than birds "Tinker to Evers to Chance."

Ruthlessly pricking our gonfalon bubble Making a Giant hit into a double

Words that are heavy with nothing by trouble "Tinker to Evers to Chance."

Despite his name, Franklin Pierce Adams was indeed Jewish. Starting out as a teen-aged insurance salesman, he went early one February morning to sell a policy to humorist George Ade and found him eating strawberries for breakfast. Adams decided that any profession which enabled a man to afford strawberries for breakfast in the winter was the right line of work for him.

Adams managed to get a job at the Chicago Journal and in 1903 went on to New York and to fame as a columnist with his "Always in Good Humor" and "The Conning Tower." An excellent judge of literary talent, he helped launch the careers of a number of talented young writers including Sinclair Lewis, Dorothy Parker, Edna Ferber, George Kaufman, and Ring Lardner.

For Further Reading:

Scott Meredith, *George S. Kaufman and His Friends*, Garden City, New York, Doubleday and Co., 1974.

Q. Who invented Ex-Lax?

A. One of the world's most popular laxatives was invented by Max Kiss (1882–1967), a Hungarian Jew, who came penniless to the U.S. after finishing high school in 1897. Earning a pharmacist's degree in 1904, he worked hard and saved enough money to return to Hungary for a visit in 1906. There he learned of the work of Zoltan von Vamossy, a chemist, who had discovered that phenolphthalein, a simple chemical used to test wine for impurities, also worked as a laxative. Kiss added phenolphthalein to a chocolate tablet to produce an effective laxative that, unlike castor oil, also had a pleasant taste.

Kiss named his new product after a Hungarian legal term for legislation blocked in parliament. It could also stand for "excellent laxative." The Ex Lax Pharmaceutical Co. was incorporated in 1908. Kiss was very active in philanthropy, feeling that this was his way of repaying the U.S. for the opportunities it had given him.

For Further Reading:

DAB, Suppl. VIII, 338.

Q. What western state has had two Jewish senators and a Jewish governor?

A. Oregon. Joseph Meier (1874–1937) practiced law, then became a partner in Meier and Frank, a major department store. Although involved in public affairs and president of Portland's Temple Beth Israel, he had never mixed in politics. Then George Joseph, his former law partner, died suddenly while running for governor in 1930. Joseph's followers nominated Meier in his stead. Running as an independent, Meier won against three opponents. As governor, he injected sound business practices into state government and was especially interested in conservation.

Joseph Simon (1851–1935) served as head of the Oregon state senate in the 1890's and went on to the U.S. Senate (1898–1903) where he sat on the Committee on Irrigation and Reclamation of Arid Lands. He returned home and served as Mayor of Portland (1909–1911).

Richard L. Neuberger, a journalist and author with a special interest in the Pacific Northwest, served as Oregon state senator. At the same time, his wife, Maurine Brown Neuberger (she was not Jewish} served in the state legislature. In 1954, he was elected to the U.S. Senate as Oregon's first Democratic senator in 40 years. Maurine succeeded him upon his death in 1960 and remained in the Senate until 1967.

For Further Reading:

Duane Nystrom, ed.. *Biographical Dictionary of the United States Congress. 1774- 1989,* 1989.

Q. Why did Lucius Littauer not run for reelection to Congress in 1906?

A. Wealthy glove manufacturer Lucius Littauer (1859–1944) served his New York district in the House of Representatives from 1896–1906. A strong supporter of Theodore Roosevelt, he was also actively concerned with the problems of Jews in Russia and Romania during a time of pogroms and political unrest in those lands.

In 1906 it was learned that gloves produced in Littauer's factories were being sold to the U.S. Army. A law of that time held that no Congressman was allowed to enter into a contract with the government. Littauer was only the manufacturer, not the distributor, and he had not broken the law. Nevertheless, soured by politically motivated criticism, he did not run for reelection.

Involving himself in charitable works, he set up the Lucius N Littauer Foundation in New York, plus the Littauer School of Business Administration and the Littauer professorship in Jewish Literature and Philosophy at Harvard, his alma mater. The latter chair was held first by Professor Harry A. Wolfson, well known for his work on Philo of Alexandria and medieval Jewish philosophy, and later by Professor Isadore Twersky, author of *Introduction to the Code of Maimonides* and other distinguished works.

For Further Reading:

Burton Boxerman , "Lucius Nathan Littauer," *AJHQ*, LXVI, 1977, 498–572.

Q. What South American country was seriously considered for large scale Jewish settlement in 1907?

A. Joseph Fels, Jewish head of Fels Naptha Company, became interested in writer Israel Zangwill's Jewish Territorial Organization which was seeking a place that could absorb thousands of Eastern European Jewish refugees. Long occupied with a variety of economic reform plans, especially Henry George's single tax doctrine, Fels wrote to Zangwill in 1906 suggesting that Paraguay might be of interest. He was impressed with the possibilities for Jewish farm settlements and he urged the Paraguayan government to offer attractive incentives. Ultimately nothing came of the plan, although Fels bought some Paraguayan land for himself, planning to employ Jewish laborers to grow products for his soap enterprise.

This was one of a number of plans in the early years of the Zionist movement to seek alternatives to Jewish settlement in Palestine, beginning with Theodore Herzl's suggestion of Uganda in 1897, and later eastern Libya, Baja de California, Brazil, Angola, Rhodesia, Iraq and others. Of course, none of these ideas were carried through, as many Jews continued to fulfill their age old yearning to return to Palestine.

One curious by-product of this Zangwill-Fels connection was a series of three line poems that Zangwill, already famous as a poet, playwright, and translator of Hebrew literature, wrote about Fels-Naptha. One sample:

Who rubs the clothes to make them clean With groans and grumbles in between

The wretch who never yet has seen Fels Naptha.

For Further Reading:

Arthur P. Dudden, *Joseph Fels and the Single Tax Movement,* Philadelphia; Temple University Press, 1971

Mary Fels, *The Life of Joseph Fels,* New York, Doubleday, Doran & Co. 1940.

Q. Three presidents of temples presided over by Rabbi Stephen S. Wise served as U.S. ministers to Turkey. Who were they?

A. Solomon Hirsch, later president of Rabbi Wise's Beth Israel congregation in Portland, Oregon, was sent to Turkey by President Benjamin Harrison. Henry Morgenthau, who played an important role as minister to Turkey in the early years of World War I, was later president of Rabbi Wise's Free Synagogue in New York. Woodrow Wilson told Morgenthau that he was being sent to Turkey because of the interest of American Jews in the welfare of the Jews in Turkey's province of Palestine. Ironically, Morgenthau's law partner, Samson Lachman, was Solomon Hirsch's nephew. While in Istanbul, Morgenthau made a point of publicly cultivating the acquaintance of Chief Rabbi Nahoun, and he openly frequented the local B'nai Brith to give it greater dignity in the eyes of the Turkish government.

Abraham Elkus followed Morgenthau into both positions. In 1920, Elkus also served as a commissioner of the League of Nations to settle a border dispute between Finland and Sweden, for which he received high honors from the governments of both England and France.

Two other Jews also served as minister to Turkey. Laurence Steinhardt was sent to Istanbul in the early 1940's and helped prevent Turkey from entering World War II on the side of the Axis. Oscar Straus, as noted before, holds the record with three terms of service to the Turks. On one occasion. President Taft offered the post to Judge Meyer Sulzberger of Philadelphia. but he turned it down.

For Further Reading:

Stephen S. Wise. *Challenging Years,* New York; Putnam, 1949.

Henry Morgenthau, *All In A Lifetime,* Doubleday and Co., 1949.

Q. Why did some Jews oppose the immigration of Eastern European Jews to America in the early 20th century?

A. Despite the hardships of Jewish life in Eastern Europe, with its pogroms, poverty, and lack of opportunity, there were Jews who spoke out against Jewish immigration to the U.S. Three main views can be delineated. First, some established American Jews feared that a great tide of immigrants might arouse an anti-Semitic reaction among American gentiles. Also, since the immigrants would typically be poor and unaccustomed to American life, they might become a burden and an embarrassment to the established U.S. Jewish community.

Second, some leading European rabbis feared that Jews who came to America would give up religious observances and ultimately lose their Jewishness. The famous Chafetz Chaim, R. Israel Meir Hacohen of Radin, published a letter opposing immigration to the U.S.

A third view was expressed by liberals like writer Israel Zangwill, who wrote that the Russian Jews had achieved an unusual level of idealism and intellect and that this would be swallowed up in Americanism. Only America's anti-Semitism might help to keep it alive. "If I had my way, not a single Russian Jew should enter America."

History has by now rendered its verdict on these three approaches. The first was entirely mistaken. The Jews have a record of great accomplishment in America. The second and third were more accurate in that Jewish religious observance and the study of Torah did decline through several generations, and some Jews did indeed assimilate into American society to the extent of losing their Jewish identity.

For Further Reading:

Ronald Sanders, *The Shores of Refuge. A Hundred Years of Jewish Emigration*, New York, Henry Holt and Co., 1988

Q. Why was Melvil Dewey, founder of the Dewey library classification system, fired from his position as head of the New York Library system?

A. Melvil Dewey (1851-1931) was the originator of the Dewey decimal system for the classification of books that is widely used in libraries today. Appointed State Librarian for New York in 1889, he resigned in 1905 after the State Board of Regents formally censured him for openly anti-Semitic remarks. He also headed the Lake Placid Company, a hotel business which excluded Jewish guests. Although the exclusion of Jews was not strictly illegal in those days, it was considered unsuitable for a man in a public position, as Dewey was, in a state like New York in which 750,000 Jews then resided.

A strong protest to the state government against Dewey's remarks was led by a letter from Louis Marshall and other Jewish leaders. The incident reflected the exclusion of the Jews from various social institutions, especially clubs and resorts in those years, following the famous case of Jesse Seligman in Saratoga in 1876.

For Further Reading:

Charles Resnikoff, ed., *Louis Marshall: Champion of Liberty*, Philadelphia, JPS, 1957.

Q. How did Jacob Gordin become a playwright?

A. In Russia, Jacob Gordin (1853–1908) had founded the Duchovno *Bibleiskoye Bratsvo*, a radical Jewish biblical sect modeled after the Russian Shundists, which preached simplicity, hard work and pacifism. He attracted several hundred followers but the group collapsed during the pogroms of 1881. Gordin wrote a self-hating article arguing that the Jews had brought on the pogroms by their own greed. As can be imagined, the article was received with anger among Jews. Gordin left for New York in 1891 after a police raid on his house. He had a wife and eight children, and desperate for money he took the advice of Philip Krantz, editor of the monthly "Zukunft," and began to write Yiddish plays. These were the fledgling days of the Yiddish theater and Gordin found talented actors like Jacob Adler, Boris Thomashefsky, and Bertha Kalish and a ready audience of Yiddish speaking immigrants.

Gordin would attend performances and bang with his silver cane if an actor ad-libbed any lines. When actor Sigmund Feinman persisted in his ad-libbing, Gordin slapped his face. In all, he published over 60 plays in Yiddish including *Der Yiddishe Kenig Lear* (King Lear), and *Der Yiddishe Kenigen Lear* (Queen Lear), also called *Mirele Efros*. It is told that on the Monday following the opening of *Der Yiddishe Kenig Lear*, a play dealing with children neglecting aging parents, long lines of young people formed in front of Lower East Side banks to send money to their parents in Europe.

Some of Gordin's plays dealt with current social issues and provoked bitter controversies, including a personal vendetta from journalist Abraham Cahan which ultimately ruined Gordin's career. His plays returned to popularity in the great years of the Yiddish theater in the U.S. between the World Wars.

For Further Reading:

Melech Epstein, *Profiles of Eleven*, Detroit, Wayne State University Press, 1965

Q. What name did Reuben Ewing, Phil Cooney, and Harry Kane, three major league baseball players, have in common?

A. All changed their names from the original Cohen. Harry Kane pitched fifteen games for several big league teams (1902-06). Cooney played one game for the New York Highlanders (today's Yankees) in 1905. Ewing, born in Odessa, Russia, played three games for the St. Louis Cardinals in 1921. It was not unusual for Jews in those days to Americanize their names either merely to simplify the pronunciation or to cover their Jewishness.

For Further Reading:

Joe Reichler ed., *Baseball Encyclopedia*, New York; MacMillan, 1988, 7th edition.

Q. Did American Jewry influence the victory of Japanese arms during the Russo-Japanese War of 1904-1905?

A. Indeed yes. American financier and Jewish leader Jacob Schiff arranged for five million pounds sterling to be loaned from American banks to Japan early in the war. This matched a similar loan to Japan from British banks. Schiff felt that the Japanese cause was the more just. Also, he bore a grudge against the czarist government because of its persecution of its Jews. The loan was given early in the war before the important Japanese victory at the Yalu River. Schiff was instrumental in raising additional large funds during the Port Arthur campaign. This was all the more striking in view of the fact that Americans of that day rarely showed interest in foreign investment.

When Schiff toured Japan in 1906, he was granted the signal honor of a private audience with the emperor. At the time of the Portsmouth Conference that ended the war, Schiff pressed Russian minister Count Sergei Witte to improve the conditions of Russian Jews.

Although much interested in the thinking of Reform Judaism and attending Reform services, Schiff could never follow a party line in religion or anything else. He observed the Sabbath and never hesitated to make it known. Once when invited on an important railroad tour, he replied that he would be happy to come, as long as arrangements could be made not to travel on the two Saturdays included in the schedule. Schiff prayed daily, recited grace after meals and refrained from eating forbidden foods.

He respected both Orthodox and Reform Judaism and would frequently quote Moses' wish, "Would that all the Lord's people were prophets." And he actively supported Hebrew Union College, the Jewish Theological Seminary and Orthodox schools as well.

For Further Reading:

Cyrus Adler, *Jacob Schiff: His Life and Letters,* Garden City, Doubleday Doran, 1928.

Q. Who was Boss Ruef?

A. Abraham Ruef's (1864–1936) Jewish background and high intellect set him off sharply from the usual turn of the century political bosses like Marc Tweed of Tammany Hall in New York. Born in San Francisco, Ruef graduated from the University of California with honors at age 18, having mastered several languages, ancient and modern. Entering San Francisco politics as an idealistic reformer, Ruef soon became disillusioned and drifted into the corrupt city political machine. He led a Union Labor party which secured the election of Eugene E. Schmitz as mayor in 1901, 1903 and 1905, and owned the city board of supervisors in a vast network of government graft and corruption. Usually operating his puppets from offstage in the manner typical of big city bosses of those days, Ruef was angling toward appointment for himself to a Senate seat for 1909. (In those days, U.S. senators were elected by state legislatures, not by popular vote).

Then with federal help, Fremont Older, editor of the *San Francisco Bulletin,* organized an investigation which revealed the corruption of the city administration. Ruef and his associates were indicted on 383 counts of graft. In a very messy sequence of events, Ruef thought prosecutor Francis Henne had assured him of immunity if he turned state's evidence and pleaded guilty. However, when Ruef offered the guilty plea and supplied the information, he was brought to trial and sentenced to jail. Two local rabbis Jacob Nieto and Bernard Kaplan tried to help Ruef, publicly accusing Henne of reneging on his promise. The whole matter was further complicated by an explosion in the home of a city councilman and by the shooting of Henne by Morris Hass, a juror who had been ejected from the jury when it was learned that he was an ex-con. It was never clear if these two incidents were directly connected with Ruef.

Ruef was sent to San Quentin in 1911. However, help now came from an unexpected source. Ruef's former accuser, Fremont Older, felt guilty about Ruef's fate and visited Ruef in San Quentin to ask for forgiveness. Ruef then wrote a sort of confessional autobiography which Older's paper published in serial form, "The Road I Have Traveled . . .", in the hope of arousing public sympathy. In 1915, Ruef was released from prison and he went on to build a new fortune in real estate and then lose it in the Great Depression.

For Further Reading:

Walton Bean, *Boss Ruef's San Francisco: The Story of the Union Labor Party. Big Business and the Graft Prosecution,* Berkeley, University of California Press, 1952

Q. What was the relationship between Henrietta Szold (1860-1945), the founder of Hadassah, and Professor Louis Ginzberg (1873-1953), of the Jewish Theological Seminary?

A. Miss Szold's biographer, Joan Dash, devoted 30 pages to the story of the not-quite romance between these two brilliant and dynamic people. In 1903 Henrietta Szold, daughter of a Baltimore rabbi and in her forties, was a student at the Jewish Theological Seminary in New York at a time when the thought of a woman rabbi would have shocked even most very liberal minds. Ginzberg was a 30 year old professor, a sharp thinking former student of Lithuanian yeshivas, and holder of a Ph.D. from the University of Heidelberg.

According to a biography by Ginzberg's son Eli, Miss Szold had apparently fallen in love with Ginzberg but, well aware of the discrepancy in their ages, had kept rein on her feelings. This grew increasingly difficult for her as time went on. For Ginzberg, the relationship meant a close working friendship, as Szold assisted him in some of his scholarly projects. Ginzberg in those years was writing his *Geonica, Yerushalmi Fragments From The Geniza,* and *Legends of the Jews,* important scholarly works. When Ginzberg went to Europe in 1907 to be with his ill father, he and Szold carried on an emotional correspondence. The relationship was already a matter of discussion in Ginzberg's family, who were concerned about Szold's age. A year later Ginzberg, again, visited Europe and this time met and married Adele Katzenstein after a brief courtship. She was an attractive young lady, but Ginzberg was probably by now feeling pressured too by the relationship with an older woman that was growing too serious.

Ginzberg went on to a pleasant married life. Szold remained single all her days and devoted herself with great success to public causes. She helped settle many European children in Israel and led the Hadassah organization. It is a curious turn of history that Eli Ginzberg, the son of Louis and Adele, married Ruth Szold, a cousin of Henrietta. Eli Ginzberg became a professor of economics and wrote both in his chosen field and on Jewish issues.

For Further Reading:

Eli Ginzberg, *Keeper of the Law*, Philadelphia, JPS, 1966.
Joan Dash, *Summoned to Jerusalem: The Life of Henrietta Szold,* New York; Harper and Row Puhl., 1979.
Irving Fineman, *Woman of Valor: The Life of Henrietta Szold* , 1860–1945, New York; Simon and Schuster, 1961.

Q. Who was Sam Dreben, The Fighting Jew?

A. In the early 1900's at the height of the great immigration wave, American Jews looked for heroes in the world of physical prowess and courage to show that Jews could be as brave and strong as anyone. Damon Runyon's 1922 poem about the brave Jewish soldier Sam Dreben well suited this need. Dreben had fought in the Spanish American War, the Boxer Rebellion, several small wars in Latin America, General Pershing's expedition against Mexican bandit chief Pancho Villa, and finally in World War I. He had even ridden with Pancho Villa at one time but left him after Villa conducted a raid on the American town of Columbus, New Mexico.

There's a story in that paper I just tossed upon the floor ,
That speaks of prejudice against the Jews. There's a photo on the table
That's a memory of the war
And a man who never figured in the news. There's a cross upon his breast
That's the D.S.C.
The Croix de Guerre, the Militaire, These too.
And there's a heart beneath the medals, That beats loyal brave and true,
A Jew.
He is short and fat and funny And the nose upon his face,
Is about the size of bugler Dugan's horn. But the grin that plays behind it,
Is wide and soft *and sunny*
And he wore it from the day that he was born.
There's *a cross upon his chest -*
That's the D.S. C.
The Croix de Guerre, the Militaire, Mon Dieu!
He's a He-man out of Texas
And he's all man through and through That's Dreben,
A Jew.

Now whenever I read articles That breathe of racial hate,
Or hear arguments that hold his kind to scorn,
I always see that photo With the cap upon the pate
And the nose the size of bugler Dugan's horn

I see upon his breast The D.S.C..
The Croix de Guerre, The Militaire These too.
And I think, thank God Almighty , We will always have a few,
Like Dreben,
A Jew.

For Further Reading:

Sydney G. Gumpertz, *Jewish Legion of Valor,* New York, 1934, p. 211–234.

Q. How did the *Porotergus Gimbeli,* a species of electric fish, get its name?

A. In 1910, the Carnegie Museum of Pittsburgh sent an expedition to South America under Dr. Max Ellis to find specimens of a species of electric fish which attacked larger enemies after first stunning them with electric shocks from its own body. The fish had been thought mythical until Ellis's findings proved it was for real.

The fish was named for a cousin of the famous Jewish department store family, Jake Gimbel (1876–1943) philanthropist from Vincennes, Indiana, who had financed the expedition.

For Further Reading:

J. Solis-Cohen, "Jake Gimbel: Hoosier Philanthropist," *PAJHS,* XLVIII, 1959, p. 256–261.

Q. What prominent 20th century San Francisco born Jew served as rabbi in both Reform and Conservative synagogues and was associated with the founding of Young Israel, the New York Kehillah, and Hebrew University?

A. Judah Leon Magnes (1877–1948) was the first graduate of Hebrew Union College to come from west of the Mississippi. Magnes was articulate, decisive, straight-forward, and independent. As editor of the school newspaper at HUC, he refused to obey an administration directive limiting his editorial freedom. His first positions were in large Reform temples in New York. However, he soon became critical of Reform's distance from tradition, and he openly preached the need for a counter-reformation of Reform. He found himself in close agreement with Drs. Solomon Schechter and Mordecai Kaplan, two leaders of Conservative Judaism, and in 1911 he left the Temple and accepted the pulpit of a Conservative synagogue, Bnai Jeshurun, in New York. Magnes was also involved in the founding of Young

Israel, an Orthodox group in 1912. However, Young Israel soon proved itself too Orthodox for him.

In 1908, New York Police Commissioner Theodore Bingham published an article in the *North American Review* asserting that half the criminals in the city were Jews. A storm of protest rose, and a conference of Jewish groups met at Clinton Hall to plan a unifying central organization for New York Jewry. This became the Kehillah or "Jewish Community of New York," which Magnes led until its termination in 1922. It achieved some success in addressing a wide variety of needs — social, economic, religious, educational and political.

An ardent Zionist, Magnes emigrated to Palestine in 1922, where he became chancellor and later president of the new Hebrew University.

For Further Reading:

Arthur A. Goren, *New York Jews and the Quest for Community: The Kehilla Experiment. 1908–1922*, New York; Columbia University Press, 1970.

Arthur A. Goren, *Dissenter in Zion. From the Writing of Judah Magnes*, Cambridge, Harvard University Press, 1982.

Q. What was Harry Fischel's significant contribution to the real estate business?

A. Harry Fischel (1865–1948) migrated from Meretz, a small town in Russia, to New York in 1885, and after various tribulations made a large fortune in the real estate business. All through his life, Fischel remained a very pious Jew and devoted his time and money to Jewish causes.

His biographer, Herbert Goldstein, writes that in 1915 New York's real estate market was still struggling to recover from the Panic of 1907. Fischel studied the problem carefully and came to realize that the difficulty was to be found in the fact that lenders were calling in mortgages as soon as they were due. When real estate owners were unable to meet the demands, the mortgage would be foreclosed and the owner would lose everything. Fischel advanced a plan in which mortgages would be amortized gradually over a long period instead of the quick calls for full payment. Investors would feel safer and the mortgagee would not end up taking a property that he really did not want.

Fischel's proposal was favorably received by leaders of business and finance and was widely discussed in print. Many businesses began to follow this idea. The New York real estate market did soon improve and perhaps some of the credit should go to Fischel. This sort of mortgage is, of course, in widespread use in the real estate business a century later.

Fischel was careful in his observance of the Sabbath all his life, even under trying circumstances in his early years. Goldstein recounts that in 1915, Fischel, his wife, and two daughters were travelling to San Francisco by train, expecting to arrive at noon Friday, in plenty of time for the Sabbath. On Thursday evening, the train had just entered the Great Desert when the conductor informed Fischel that they would arrive in San Francisco 12 hours late, long after the beginning of the Sabbath. Further, there was no place to leave the train before Sacramento, which would also not be reached until past sundown.

Beside himself at the thought of travelling on the Sabbath, Fischel told the train crew that he had an important appointment in San Francisco and would pay them any amount of money if they could get him there on time. Money can sometimes move mountains. The train zoomed along at high speed, and Fischel arrived in San Francisco in plenty of time for his Day of Rest.

For Further Reading:

Herbert Goldstein, *Forty Years of Struggle for a Principle,* New York; Bloch Publishing Co., 1928, p. 169–180.

Q. What resident of Chicago, Illinois was the author of a major rabbinical commentary on the Jerusalem Talmud?

A. Rabbi Jacob David ben Zeev Willowski, whose initials formed the acronym Ridbaz, gained a prodigious knowledge of Talmud at an early age without any formal schooling. As rabbi of Izballin, Russia he produced a series of scholarly works. In 1899, while head of the yeshivah in Slutsk, (R. Isser Zalman Meltzer, later head of the Eitz Hayyim Yeshiva in Jerusalem, was one of his students) he began the publication of two commentaries on the Jerusalem Talmud, Hidushei Haridbaz and Tosafot Ha-Rid. The Babylonian Talmud, compiled in the fifth century C.E., has been the central work in traditional Jewish life ever since and has invited multitudes of commentaries. The Jerusalem Talmud, compiled by Judean scholars a century earlier, has remained relatively inaccesible. The Ridbaz's commentaries fill an important hiatus and are now printed as glosses in all standard editions. The subscription fund was exhausted with only four of the six volumes completed, so in 1900 the Ridbaz visited the U.S. to raise the necessary funds to complete the remaining volumes.

Ridbaz was shocked by the deterioration in religious interest among American Jews, the neglect of Torah study and of Sabbath observance, and he criticized the decline strongly both in public lectures and in his writings.

Nevertheless, after five months, he had raised the necessary funds, and he returned home.

From there he decided to fulfill a long time dream and settle in Palestine. Hoping to gain financial independence first, he went again to the U.S. in 1903 and took a position as chief rabbi of Chicago. Ridbaz remained in Chicago only a year, during which he was constantly harassed by jealous colleagues and by butchers who did not want anyone to supervise their kashrut. Ridbaz resigned his position and refunded his salary, feeling that he had accomplished nothing worthwhile for his congregants.

For some months, he traveled extensively through the U.S. lecturing and selling the remaining sets of his Talmud commentaries. Late in 1905, the Ridbaz departed for Safed where he enjoyed another eight years of study and writing.

The U.S. in the early 20th century was not yet ready for rabbis like Ridbaz or Rabbi Jacob Joseph, who was still living in New York, but in poor health and neglected, when Ridbaz came to America. Like many European immigrants, Ridbaz found life in America not entirely to his taste. He was able to accomplish his aims here and go on to what was for him the more congenial lifestyle of the old religious community of Safed.

For Further Reading:

Aaron Rothkoff , "The American Sojourns of Ridbaz: Religious Problems Within the Immigrant Community," *AJHQ*, LVII, 1968, 557–572.

Q. Who wrote the first sports story to appear in any foreign language newspaper in the United States?

A. According to journalist Harry Golden, his father Leib Goldhurst, a freelance writer and journalist, wrote an account of the boxing match between Jim Jeffries and Jack Johnson in Reno in 1910 for the *Jewish Daily Forward*. He referred to the Black man, Johnson, as the *schvartzer*, although not in a disrespectful manner. Goldhurst was attempting to illustrate how sports in America had become democratized.

For Further Reading:

Harry Golden, *The Right Time: An Autobiography*, New York, G.P. Putnam's Sons, 1969.

Q. What was the Galveston Plan?

A. Mention of Galveston, Texas will arouse for many Americans memories of the mighty hurricanes that have battered that port town and also of Glen

Campbell's popular song of the 1970's "Galveston o Galveston, I have heard your sea waves breaking ..."

Galveston is also the center of a curious chapter in the history of the Jewish immigration to the U.S. in the early twentieth century. The great wave of Jewish immigration beginning in 1881 caused crowded and unpleasant tenement conditions in New York. Most Jews tended to remain there, feeling comfortable with their own brethren, rather than moving into regions where there were fewer Jews. Jewish leaders began to seek ways to settle them elsewhere in the United States. As early as 1904, Galveston was being mentioned as one of a number of possibilities, along with Savannah, Baltimore, Boston, New Orleans, and others. In the 1890's there had been talk of Minnesota or Mexico. A Jewish Territorial Organization, founded by writer Israel Zangwill in 1905, wanted the refugees to form their own state. However, this idea was widely viewed as impractical. By 1907, a plan was formed, largely by Jacob Schiff, to arrange for the immigrants to go straight from Europe to Galveston. Both President Theodore Roosevelt and Secretary of Commerce and Labor Oscar Straus supported the plan. By July, 1907, the first shiploads were arriving in Galveston. After a few weeks of training in English, the new arrivals were sent on according to their professions — furniture workers to Grand Rapids and Topeka, butchers to stockyard towns like Kansas City and Omaha and the like.

The financial panic of 1907 made it difficult to place workers, and immigration through Galveston slowed to a trickle for a couple of years. However, by 1912, 5000 people had come through at a cost of about $30 each, paid by the JTO. The project ended in 1914 as organizational problems developed on the European end and difficulties were raised by U.S. officials who feared that immigration laws were being broken.

For Further Reading:

Cyrus Adler, *Jacob H. Schiff: His Life and Letters,* Garden City, Doubleday Doran, 1928.

Q. Who opened America's first drive-in gas station?

A. Stephen Birmingham, in *The Rest Of Us,* claims that the first drive-in gas station was opened by Louis Blaustein (1869–1937), a pioneer magnate in the U.S. oil industry. Before that, drivers would pull up to curbside machines which could not measure accurately the amount of fuel they dispensed. Blaustein was at first associated with Standard Oil of New Jersey (1892–1910), then went on to found the American Oil Co., in Baltimore, and finally to head Pan-American Refining Co.

For Further Reading:

Stephen Birmingham. *The Rest Of Us*, Boston, Little Brown and Co., 1984.

Q. What Jew was the first major movie cowboy?

A. Actor Gilbert M. Anderson (1883–1971), born Max Aronson, appeared in his first film, "The Messenger Boy's Mistake," in 1902. He played three roles in 'The Great Train Robbery," (1903) considered a classic among early silent films. Raised in Little Rock, Arkansas, Anderson learned how to ride a horse only after his acting debut, but he was instrumental in launching the American cowboy movie. In 1908, he starred in "The Bandit Makes Good," the first of many films about Bronco Billy, a Robin Hood type bandit of the wild west, and he later played Alkali Ike in another series of westerns.

Anderson's last film was made in 1918. By then new cowboy heroes like William S. Hart had moved into the market. Forty-seven years later, "Bronco Billy" returned to play in the "Bounty Killer"with Clint Eastwood. In 1957, Anderson received an Oscar for his pioneer work in the film industry.

For Further Reading:

New York Times. January 21, 1971, p. 38.

Q. For what important social legislation was Sophie Loeb largely responsible?

A. Born in Rovno, Russia and raised in McKeesport, Pennsylvania, Sophie Irene Simon Loeb (1876–1929) came to New York in 1910 and almost single-handedly launched a crusade for legislation to provide aid to mothers of dependent children, arguing that it was better for them to be raised by their own families than to be moved to orphanages, in the usual practice. As a reporter for the *Evening World*, Loeb publicized the problems of widows with small children in the slums. In 1915 she was named president of a newly formed New York Child Welfare Board. She continued to press both in the papers and through legislation for social improvements.

In the 1920's she extended her campaign to legislatures of other states. In 1925, she went to Palestine to study the conditions there. A year later she brought her crusade to the League of Nations.

For Further Reading:

DAB. VI, 1, 345–355. *NAW*.li. 416–417.

Q. Why did the U.S. abrogate its 1832 commercial treaty with Russia in 1913?

A. Anti-Semitism intensified in Russia in the late 19th century, and the czarist government cruelly harassed not only its own Jewish citizens but American Jewish visitors as well. This led to several protests from the U.S. State Department, and President Theodore Roosevelt too spoke out at the urging of Oscar Straus and Jacob Schiff.

However, in 1907 the State Department announced that it would no longer give passports to Jews going to Russia unless the Russian government consented. The newly formed American Jewish Committee protested and called for the abrogation of the 1832 U.S.-Russia trade treaty as a sign of America's displeasure with the czarist government.

During the election campaign of 1908, Republican William Howard Taft promised his support, but once he reached the White House, he would take no decisive step. Taft was generally well disposed toward Jewish interests, but he may have felt that putting too much pressure on Russia would benefit neither the U.S. nor the Jews. In any case, AJC leaders like Schiff, Straus and Louis Marshall were disappointed.

The State Department continued to oppose the abrogation strongly, and after an angry meeting at the White House between the AJC leaders and Taft, Schiff refused to shake the president's hand. In 1911, the AJC began to take their campaign for abrogation to the American public and to Congress. Both houses of Congress were favorably inclined toward abrogation, and Taft finally agreed to support it. Late in 1913 the House voted 301-1 to abrogate the treaty, and in the Senate the vote was unanimous.

Historian Naomi Cohen has argued that perhaps time proved the president right. The Russians were bitter about the abrogation of the treaty and both anti-Semitic and anti-American feeling increased there. Also, trade between Russia and the U.S. declined, and other European governments did nothing to support the U.S. stand.

For the American Jewish Committee this was the first major public activity. Their success was more apparent than real, and they typically assumed a less aggressive approach in their later dealings with the U.S. government.

For Further Reading:

Naomi Cohen, *Not Free To Desist: The American Jewish Committee. 1906–1966.* Philadelphia, JPS, 1972.

Q. What Oklahoma oil baron became head of a great Jewish institution of learning?

A. Bernard Revel came to the U.S. in 1906 as an accomplished Talmudist and by 1912 had earned a Ph.D. from Dropsie College in Philadelphia, the first granted by the school. In 1911 he married Sarah Travis, whose family had struck it rich in Oklahoma oil. Revel worked with his in-laws in the oil business for several years, but his heart was in the world of scholarship. Returning to academia, he became the first president of the young Yeshivah University in New York in 1915 and helped develop the school into a major center, both of Jewish and general studies.

For Further Reading:

Aaron Rakeffet-Rothkoff, *Bernard Revel: Builder of American Jewish Orthodoxy*, New York. Feldheim, 1981.

Q. A young ophthalmologist gave up a promising career in medicine to develop an American Hebrew school system. Who was he?

A. Samson Benderly (1876–1944) was instrumental in adapting modern methods of education to Jewish schools and also in developing the pattern of the American afternoon Hebrew school of the 20th century. His own career took many strange turns.

Born and raised in a pious family in old Safed, Benderly was befriended by two American sisters named Ford, both Christian missionaries, who worked in a medical clinic near his home. He also became close to a Mr. Friedman, an American Jew who had converted to Christianity and who had come to Palestine to do missionary work. It was under Friedman's influence that Benderly decided, much against his family's wishes, to leave Safed and its ways and to attend the Syrian Protestant College in Beirut. It was probably also from these American Christians that Benderly absorbed his deep feeling for the United States.

In 1898, Benderly migrated to Baltimore and by 1900 completed his M.D. in opthalmology. He began his medical residency, but soon resigned and decided to devote his life to teaching both Judaism and his own brand of Americanism to American Jewish youth.

Because Benderly believed that only attendance in public school would properly integrate youngsters into American life, he preferred the afternoon Hebrew school for a few hours a week to a full day parochial school. He kept apace with modern techniques in education and greatly influenced a new generation of Jewish educators. However, adherents of traditional Jewish education argued that Benderly was merely secularizing Jewish learning and was emphasizing Hebrew conversation, higher Bible criticism, and Zionism at the expense of serious study of Bible and Talmud. Benderly directed the Bureau of Jewish Education in New York and pioneered Jewish summer camps, like Camp Achvah, and correspondence courses for adults.

For Further Reading:

Nathan Winter, *Jewish Education in a Pluralist Society: Samson Benderly and Jewish Education in the United States*, New York, New York University Press, 1966.

Q. How did Oscar Straus become the Bullmoose candidate for governor of New York in 1912?

A. Unhappy with William Howard Taft's performance as president of the U.S., his former mentor Theodore Roosevelt launched the Progressive or Bullmoose party in 1912 and ran for president against Republican Taft and Democrat Woodrow Wilson.

Oscar Straus, a long time diplomat and formerly Secretary of Commerce and Labor under Theodore Roosevelt, was presiding over the Progressive party's convention in New York where William Prendergast, William Hotchkiss, and Bainbridge Colby were locked in a heated battle for the New York gubernatorial nomination. Chairman Straus was trying to call a recess, but a colorful figure, John "Suspender Jack" McGee, dressed in a mustard-colored suit, a neckerchief, and a brown sombrero that had seen better days, demanded the floor. McGee, a former Indian fighter, policeman, and rider in Buffalo Bill Cody's Wild West Show, had never met Straus, but now he strode to the platform and to everyone's surprise nominated Straus himself for governor. The convention broke into loud cheering and the singing of "Onward Christian Soldiers," as Straus accepted. The election was won by Democrat William Sulzer, a Protestant who attracted many Jewish votes because of his long record of support on issues of Jewish interest during his years as a congressman.

For Further Reading:

Naomi Cohen, *A Dual Heritage: The Public Career of Oscar S. Straus*, Philadelphia, JPS, 1969, p. 205–223.

Q. After what notable American was the city of Netanya named?

A. Netanya, Israel's lovely coastal city, is named after Nathan Straus (1848-1931), brother of Isidor and Oscar, in recognition of his massive philanthropic contributions to the Jews of Eretz Israel. On his second visit to Palestine, in 1912, Straus founded a health department, and in 1913 he launched a Pasteur Institute which helped in controlling diseases like malaria. In 1916, he sold his magnificent yacht and gave the money to aid orphans in Palestine. In the 1920's he founded Hadassah Child Welfare Stations and major health care centers in Jerusalem and Tel-Aviv.

As park commissioner and health commissioner in New York in the 1890's, Straus organized, at his own expense, a system for pasteurizing and distributing milk to poor children in New York City and another system for distributing coal and food to the poor. By 1920, 297 such milk stations operated in 36 American cities, saving the lives of thousands of infants. During the harsh winter of 1914-1915, he maintained stations in New York that served good breakfasts to the needy for a penny. In 1909, Straus built a "preventorium" in Lakewood, NJ to combat tuberculosis among children. This pioneer effort became the model for many others throughout the U.S. In 1917, he opened the Jewish War Relief Fund with a gift of $100,000.

Nathan Straus and his brother Isidor became partners in R.H. Macy's in 1874 and sole owners in 1889. Isidor too was deeply devoted to a variety of community services, including a term in Congress. He and his wife were lost in the sinking of the Titanic in 1912.

For Further Reading:

David De Sola Pool, *AJYB*, 1931-1932, 135-154.

Q. What is the Spingarn Award?

A. The Spingarn Award, presented by the NAACP yearly since 1913 for outstanding achievement, was originated by a Jewish professor, Joel E. Spingarn (1875-1934). One of the leading spirits of the founding of the NAACP, Spingarn served the NAACP as treasurer and later as president. He was instrumental in securing a camp for the training of Black officers at Fort Des Moines in World War I. His brother, Arthur, was the first head of the NAACP's legal committee and succeeded Joel as president.

A brilliant and original scholar and writer, Spingarn was dismissed from his professorship at Columbia University in 1911 because of his political activism and personal tactlessness. Lewis Mumford described him as a "Renaissance gentleman equally at home in garden, library, office or battlefield."

Spingarn's liberalism exemplified a strong trend among early twentieth century Jews of scientific, secular learning who, while surrendering much of

Jewish traditions and ritual trappings, retained a strong sense of moral and social obligation to make the world a better place for the underprivileged.

For Further Reading:

Moses Rischin, "The Jews and Liberal Tradition in America," *AJHQ,* LI, 1961, 4–29.
Marshall van Deusen, *J.E. Spingarn,* New York, Twayne, 1971.
B. Joyce Ross, *J.E. Spingarn and the Rise of the NAACP,* 1911–1939, New York Atheneum, 1972.

Q. Whose recording of "Carry Me Back to Old Virginny" sold well over a million copies?

A. Romanian born Reba Fiersohn (1884–1938) started out as a secretary. Pursuing her love of music, she attracted the attention of Conductor Arturo Toscanini and in 1909 made her debut at the Metropolitan Opera using the name Alma Gluck. Although very successful in opera, Gluck preferred lieder and concert singing, and she made numerous gramophone records including "Carry Me Back to Old Virginny" which sold well over a million copies, a fantastic number in those early days of recording. The great violinist, Efrem Zimbalist, pursued her like a stage struck admirer for several years until she married him.

For Further Reading:

Jacob Marcus, *AJW,* 556–559

Q. Why did famed Yiddish writer Sholom Aleichem immigrate to the U.S.?

A. Perhaps the greatest of Yiddish fiction writers, Sholom Aleichem (Shalom Rabinowitz 1859–1916) is today as well known as ever because of the musical, *Fiddler on the Roof,* which was based on his stories. In August, 1914, the author and his family were vacationing at Albeck, a resort on the Baltic in Germany, when news came of the outbreak of World War I. As Russian citizens and thus enemy aliens, the family was in great danger of being incarcerated for the duration of the fighting. All Germany's borders were closed except Denmark. The Rabinowitzes, with some difficulty, reached Copenhagen. The Yiddish press in Russia was already closed down and America seemed the only hope. After four months in Copenhagen, Shalom Aleichem and his family headed on to America, where he continued to write until his death two years later.

For Further Reading:

Marie Waife-Goldberg, *My Father. Shalom Aleichem,* New York, Simon and Schuster, 1968.

Q. How did American Jews react to President Woodrow Wilson's appointment of Louis Brandeis as the first Supreme Court Justice of Jewish background?

A. Many Jewish leaders, like Jacob Schiff and Louis Marshall, felt that Brandeis' attachment to Judaism was not adequate for him to serve as a representative Jew in the higher echelons of the U.S. government, inasmuch as he had never really practiced Judaism and had never been involved in Jewish issues. His new support for Zionism was seen by some as a political move. Republicans and big business vigorously opposed the nomination in the Senate as Brandeis had long been a strong supporter of the Labor movement and other causes of social justice.

Former president William Howard Taft greatly coveted a seat on the Court, although he knew that the Democratic President Wilson would never appoint him. No anti-Semite, Taft nonetheless saw Brandeis as a hypocrite and conniver who changed his public Jewish image for political gain. Of course, most Jews were proud to have a coreligionist in so high a position. Brandeis went on to become one of the Court's most distinguished members.

For Further Reading:

Ben Halperin, "Brandeis' Way to Zionism," *Midstream,* XVII, 1972, 10–71.

Q. Who was the first non-Mormon governor of Utah?

A. Campaign anecdotes tell of how Simon Bamberger picked up votes in his race for governor of Utah in 1916 when voters realized that he was not a "gentile." Bamberger, a German Jewish immigrant, had settled in Utah in 1869, only 22 years after the Mormons themselves had arrived. Honest and hard-working, Bamberger succeeded in several business enterprises, including the Bamberger Electric Railway, and a resort named Lagoon. His excellent business reputation and his support of a prohibition law against alcohol helped propel Bamberger to the Democratic nomination for governor in 1916. To elect a non-Mormon to high office was a difficult prospect in Utah. However, tensions between Mormons and non-Mormons had been easing, and Bamberger was personally popular. His campaign emphasized his honesty and generosity in business to counteract the standard anti-Semitic cliche of the miserly Jew, and Bamberger defeated Republican Nephi L. Morris.

His administration enacted many reform measures including laws on workmen's compensation, fair election practices, child labor, food storage, and public utilities. An extensive road-building program would be paid for by an automobile license tax.

In 1922, Earnest Bamberger, Simon's nephew, ran for the U.S Senate on the Republican ticket. A capable man with a good record in business, Earnest Bamberger was defeated by Democrat William King on a very close vote — 58,749 to 58,188.

For Further Reading:

Brad E. Hainsworth, *Utah State Elections*. 1916–1924. Ph.D. diss.. University of Utah, 1968.

Q. Who locked himself in his mansion for fear that Nathan Straus might murder him?

A. Born in rural Georgia, Tom Watson (1856–1922) began as a progressive populist friendly to farmers, workers, and Blacks, one of the bright young leaders of the New South. Elected to Congress as a Democrat in 1890, Watson joined the Populist Party and ran for vice president on the Populist and Democratic tickets in 1896 with William Jennings Bryan. Several years later, embittered by political setbacks, Watson retired from politics and devoted himself to writing. His political views began to shift and he turned into a demagogue, crusading against big business, Catholics, liberals, foreigners, Blacks, and Jews.

His weekly publication, *The Jeffersonian*, typically carried vituperative personal attacks on individuals like Bryan, President Woodrow Wilson, and the Pope. As to the Black man, "In the South, we have to lynch him occasionally and flog him, now and then, to keep him from blaspheming the Almighty by his conduct and on account of his smell and color."

Watson remained silent for some time when the Leo Frank case first came to trial in Atlanta in 1913. Frank was a northern Jew, wrongly accused of the brutal murder of 14 year old Mary Phagan. Watson turned down an offer of $5,000 to serve as Frank's attorney and also refused to assist the prosecution. The Frank case was soon arousing intense national interest, and early in 1914 Watson leaped into the turmoil with a series of lurid, vicious anti-Semitic attacks on Frank in his paper. Watson loudly defended the Atlanta mob which attacked Governor John Slaton's mansion after he commuted Frank's death sentence on June 21, 1915. Watson may have helped to plan the lynching of Frank six weeks later. In the next issue of his *Jeffersonian*, he devoted eight pages to expressing his approval of the lynching.

According to Nathaniel Weyl in his *The Jew In American Politics*, Watson locked himself in his home, at one point, paranoid with fear that Nathan Straus, of the famous Straus brothers of Macy's, was trying to kill him because of his role in the Frank case. Watson's mind, perhaps always unstable, was hit hard by misfortunes in his family. Nevertheless, the people of Georgia elected him to the U.S. Senate in 1920.

For Further Reading:

C. Vann Woodward, *Tom Watson: Agrarian Rebel*. New York; Rinehard and Co., 1938.
Nathaniel Weyl, *The Jew In American Politics*; New Rochelle Arlington House, 1968

Q. Did the U.S. Congress ever keep a Jewish Sabath?

A. Adolph Joachim Sabath (1866–1952) served Chicago's 5th district in Congress for 45 years, 1907–1952. Popular with the district's predominantly immigrant population, Sabath was a consistent advocate of liberal legislation like workmen's compensation, old age pensions, and wages and hours laws, and he fought for years against the growing drive to restrict immigration. In the 1930's and 1940's he strongly supported the New Deal and Fair Deal programs of Presidents Roosevelt and Truman.

Never losing his heavy European accent, Sabath was not a good speaker, and he would often lapse into his native Czech when under stress. Still, he gained the respect of both colleagues and constituents as a dedicated and fair minded legislator, and he chaired the powerful House Steering and Rules Committees. From the late 1930's, Sabath strongly supported the founding of a Jewish state in Palestine and opposed British restrictions on Jewish immigration.

For Further Reading:

Burton A. Boxerman, "Adolph Joachim Sabath in Congress," *Journal of the Illinois State Historical Society*. 66, 1973, 327–346 and 428–443.

Q. Which were the first advanced yeshivot in the United States?

A. Advanced yeshivot, institutions devoted primarily to the study of Talmud, did not exist in the U.S. until the late 19th century. The first were Rabbi Isaac Elhanan Theological Seminary in New York in 1896, Orthodox

Rabbinical Seminary in New Haven under Rabbi Judah Levenberg in 1917, and Hebrew Theological College in Chicago founded by Rabbi Saul Silber and others in 1922. Mesivta Torah Vodaas added a high school to its elementary department in 1926 led by Rabbi Shraga Feivel Mendlowitz, and Mesivta Tifereth Jerusalem opened an advanced division under Rabbi Joseph Adler in the early 1930's. The Ner Israel Rabbinical College was founded in 1933 by Rabbi Jacob Ruderman.

These schools opened at a time when Orthodox practice was in decline, and they all struggled constantly both to attract students and to provide the basic physical needs of a school. Nevertheless, the students they produced became leaders of Orthodoxy in the next generations and helped sow the seeds of the great expansion of yeshivot decades later.

For Further Reading:

William Helmreich, "Old Wine in New Bottles, Advanced Yeshivot in the United States," *AJH*, LXIX, 1979, 234–275.

Q. How many Jews fought in the U.S. armed forces in World War I?

A. Jews fought in the armies of every European country involved in World War I. When the war broke out in 1914, some American Jews of German or Austrian background sympathized with the Triple Alliance - Germany, Austria-Hungary, and Turkey. However, by the time the U.S. joined the war on the side of England and France in April, 1917, American Jews were fully behind the U.S. war effort. 250,000 Jews served in the American armed forces. About 3,500 were killed in action. The 77th division from New York was 40% Jewish and was in the thick of the Meuse-Argonne fighting in France.

About 10,000 Jews became commissioned officers including several generals, such as Milton Foreman of the 33rd division and Abel Davis of the 132nd Illinois infantry. Rear Admiral Joseph Strauss commanded the mine force of the Atlantic fleet. 2,500 Jews served in the marines and over 3,000 in the Air Force. Six Jews won the Congressional Medal of Honor.

People back home joined in the usual activities to support the war effort — everything from buying government bonds to joining knitting circles that made stockings for soldiers, to entertainers that raised money in benefit performances.

For Further Reading:

UJE, 9, 625–629.

Q. What beloved cantor was offered the huge sum of $1,000 a performance to sing opera?

A. The great Yossele Rosenblatt (1882–1933) was offered $1,000 a performance by the Chicago Opera Association Director Cleofonte Campanini to sing Elazar in Halevy's opera "La Juive". Campanini, the discoverer of many great operatic stars, assured Yossele that he would not have to trim his beard or perform on Sabbaths or holidays, and that kosher food would always be available. After due deliberation, Rosenblatt concluded that the world of opera was no place for a pious Jew, and he refused the offer.

A short time later, Rosenblatt appeared on the steps of the New York Public Library as part of a World War I government savings stamp benefit concert. At the completion of his number, he was warmly embraced and kissed by none other than the great Enrico Caruso himself.

On another occasion Yossele was introduced to Thomas Edison, who was working at Victor Co. laboratories in Camden, New Jersey. He pronounced a blessing that is said upon meeting a great genius. Edison, very moved, took a graph of Rosenblatt's voice and proclaimed it as having the largest range of any ever recorded.

The prima donna with whom Rosenblatt was to have appeared in "La Juive" was contralto Rosa Raisa, (Rose Burnstein) originally from Bialystok. Curious to hear him lead a service. she attended the Lubavitch Synagogue on Watkins Street in Brooklyn's Brownsville section. Her presence in the ladies balcony caused quite a stir. She was deeply moved by his singing of the musaf service. As they both left the synagogue there was a great shouting and cheering in the streets.

On a ship from Cherbourg to Paris in 1928, Yossele shared a compartment with Boston Symphony conductor Sergei Koussevitsky, who was born a Russian Jew, but had been baptized into Greek Orthodoxy. Rosenblatt influenced Koussevitsky's return to Judaism, and the conductor became active in Jewish Theological Seminary and also helped organize the music department at Brandeis University.

For Further Reading:

Samuel Rosenblatt, *The Days of My Years,* New York, Ktav Publ., 1976.
Samuel Rosenblatt, *Yossele Rosenblatt,* New York, Farrar Strauss and Young, 1954.

Q. Two foreign Jews who later made their mark as notable world leaders spent part of World War I in exile in New York. Who were they?

A. The two were Leon Trotsky, future organizer of the Soviet army and rival of Joseph Stalin, and David Ben-Gurion, future Prime Minister of the State of Israel.

Unwelcome in the czar's Russia because of his revolutionary activities, Leon Trotsky escaped from Russia and wandered for some years, eventually reaching New York in January, 1917. During a stay of several months, Trotsky supported himself and his family by lecturing to audiences composed largely of Jewish radicals and writing for several journals including the *Jewish Daily For*ward. After the Kerensky revolt deposed Czar Nicholas in March, 1917, Trotsky decided to return to Russia and was feted at a gathering of 800 people at the Harlem River Casino on 127th Street.

In his autobiography, Trotsky would later ridicule American leftists as dull commercial "philistines" and "Babbits." Only Socialist leader Eugene Debs was sincerely idealistic. Although Jewish by birth, Trotsky was raised on a farm outside the Jewish Pale of Settlement. He was enrolled briefly in a cheder (Hebrew school) at age seven, but he had no interest in religion and his association with Jews through his life, including during his stay in New York, was only in terms of his political interests.

David Ben-Gurion (1886–1973) came to New York in 1915 with Yitzchak Ben-Tzvi, a future president of Israel, after being deported by the Turks from Palestine because of their work for Poalei Zion. Like Trotsky, Ben-Gurion used his time in the U.S. for political activity. He traveled widely, speaking to Zionist groups in many cities and urging the formation of a Jewish army to help wrest Palestine from the Turks. Ben-Gurion was not considered a great speaker, and Zionist branches showed no interest in receiving him. In 1918, when the British organized a Jewish Legion, Ben Gurion joined it and returned to Palestine.

There is no record that Ben-Gurion and Trotsky ever met in New York. However, Ben-Gurion certainly knew of Trotsky inasmuch as Ben Gurion's wife, Paula, whom he married in 1917, claimed that Trotsky had been attracted to her when she attended one of his lectures.

For Further Reading:

Isaac Deutscher, *The Prophet Armed* , New York, Oxford University Press, 1954.
Leon Trotsky, *My Life,* New York; Pathfinder Press. 1970.
Shabtai Teveth, *Ben-Gurion: The Burning Ground* 1886–1948, Boston; Houghton-Mifflin Co., 1987.

Q. What noted Jewish conductor married Mark Twain's daughter, the soprano Clara Clemens?

A. Raised in an assimilated Jewish family in Russia, Ossip Gabrilowitsch (1878-1936) gained repute as a pianist, and in 1918 was brought to Detroit as the conductor of its new symphony orchestra. At his insistence, the city built Orchestra Hall, an excellent musical facility. Gabrilowitsch married Clara Clemens in 1905 after meeting her in Europe.

Despite the lack of Jewish connection in his childhood, Gabrilowitsch visited Palestine in the 1920's and was much taken with its beauty, both ancient and new. He wrote his wife glowing accounts of the accomplishments of the Jewish settlers, gave a benefit concert in Tel Aviv, and helped found the Hebrew University music department. He continued to interest himself in Jewish and Zionist activities, once bringing his orchestra into Detroit's Temple Beth El for a concert. In 1926 he organized a highly successful benefit performance for Yeshiva University in New York's Madison Square Garden.

It was Gabrilowitsch who persuaded the great maestro Arturo Toscanini to join a musicians' protest against Adolph Hitler in 1933. When Gabrilowitsch felt that the musicians' letter to the Nazi leader was not strong enough, he added his own personal note "I am not enchanted over the idea of addressing as 'your excellency' a man for whom I have not the slightest respect. Neither do I think it quite truthful to say 'We are convinced that such persecutions were not based on your instructions whereas I am convinced that Hitler is personally responsible for all that is going on in Germany at the present time. I also want to make it clear that I am not in the least afraid to add my signature."

For Further Reading:

Clara Clemens, *My Husband Gabrilowitsch,* New York, Harper and Bros., 1938.

Q. Why did Bernard Baruch try to have Josephus Daniels (1862-1948) removed from his post as Secretary of the Navy?

A. Colonel Edward M. House, close confidant of President Woodrow Wilson, asserts in his *Diaries* that Bernard Baruch, well known Jewish financier and advisor to many presidents, approached Wilson in 1916 and urged him to remove Daniels. In fact, Baruch and Daniels were and remained close friends, and there seems to be no truth in House's statement. Press reports of the time indicate that it was probably House himself who sought Daniels' removal.

Daniels, a North Carolina Methodist well known as a philo-Semite, had experienced kindness from local Jews in Wilson, North Carolina where he spent his boyhood. He became an early supporter of Zionism, delivering pro-Zionist speeches as early as 1918. His writings contain favorable references to Jews, particularly the public spirit of people like Julius Rosenwald and the Schiff family. Daniels helped remove a quota on Jewish students at the University of North Carolina Medical School in 1937. In the 1940's he helped Harry Golden, then a struggling young journalist, to launch his writing career. As U.S. ambassador to Mexico in the 1930's, he took special interest in the needs of Mexican Jews. His last public appearance was delivering a pro-Zionist speech, yarmulke on his head, in the House of Jacob Synagogue in Raleigh.

For Further Reading:

Joseph Morrison, "A Southern Philo-Semite: Josephus Daniels of North Carolina," *Judaism*, XII, 1963, 78–91.

Q. **What Jewish businessman was a mayor in one state and later mayor and governor in a second?**

A. Raised in abject poverty in Bavaria, Moses Alexander (1853–1932) came to America in 1867 and went to work at a cousin's store in Chillicothe, Missouri. Successful in business and interested in public affairs, Alexander was elected mayor in 1887. Two years later he moved to Montana hoping to improve his health and better his fortunes. Montana was a frontier area of a few small towns and large wide open spaces. About a hundred Jews lived in Boise, where Alexander settled. They soon organized a temple, Beth Israel, with Alexander as its vice-president.

By 1897, Alexander was elected mayor of Boise. In 1916 he became governor of Montana after losing an election for that post in 1908. The state government expenditures, long criticized as too high, had soared since 1912 under Republican governor John Haines, and the GOP had been further damaged when the state treasurer, a Republican, was jailed shortly before the election for a large defalcation in his accounts. As governor, Alexander helped restrain government spending by judicious use of the veto. Interested in reform of the conditions of workers, he led the passage of laws on worker's compensation and state insurance. However, he was a strong opponent of radical worker organizations like the International Workers of the World, which advocated the violent overthrow of government. Threats by radical groups to burn Idaho forests led to a police crack-down. A fresh young state, Montana's infrastructure was not yet well developed. Governor

Alexander built the Dallas Ceilo Canal, Arrowrock Dam, and the state highway system.

In 1915, while attending the governor's conference in Boston, he was honored by HIAS (Hebrew Immigrant Aid Society) at a dinner in Faneuil Hall attended by several thousand Jews who came to see one of America's foremost Jewish politicians.

For Further Reading:

Merrill D Beal and Merle W. Wells, *History of Idaho*, New York, Lewis Publishing Co., 1959.

F. Ross Peterson, *Idaho*, New York, W.W. Norton, 1976.

Arthur Weyne, "The First Jewish Governor: Moses Alexander of Idaho," *Western States Jewish Historical Quarterly,* IX, 1976, 21–42.

Q. What was the mission of Samuel Mason for HIAS (Hebrew Immigrant Aid Society) in Yokohama, Japan in 1918?

A. Living conditions for Jews in Russia grew worse than ever during World War I, and the route of emigration through Western Europe was blocked by the war. Thousands of Jews sought to escape eastward through Asiatic Russia, Japan, and across the Pacific to the U.S. In 1915, HIAS established branches in San Francisco and Seattle to help the refugees who made it across, but many were stranded all through China and Japan, with no means for even food and shelter.

In 1917, the 14 Jewish resident families of Yokohama, Japan organized an emigrant aid society to help as many refugees as they could. Samuel Mason was sent from the American HIAS to Yokohama to help set up the Royal Hotel, which the Yokohama Jews had already bought, into a residence for the immigrants providing them kosher food, medical care, and classes in English. Official ceremonies opening the facility on February, 1918 were attended by Mayor K. Ando of Yokohama, the American Consul George Scidmore, and other dignitaries.

For Further Reading:

Ronald Sanders, *Shores of Refuge. A Hundred Years of Jewish Emigration,* New York, Henry Holt and Co., 1988.

Q. How did the U.S. Congress react to the Balfour Declaration?

A. In its famous Balfour Declaration of 1917, the British Government recognized the Jews' right to a homeland in the land of Israel, which the British had recently conquered from the Turks. Neither very liberal Reform, nor many Orthodox rabbis, were strongly pro-Zionist in those days. Yet, President Woodrow Wilson declared his support of the Balfour Declaration and was asked what he would do if any of those rabbis protested. The president pointed to a large wastebasket near his desk and said, "Is not that basket capacious enough for all their protests?" The State Department was antagonistic, being hardly willing to acknowledge that the U.S. had endorsed the Balfour document.

Congress was generally favorable. In June, 1918, the Zionist Organization of America (ZOA) sent letters to members of Congress asking for their views. Sixty-nine Senators and 231 Representatives replied, preponderantly in approval. The reasons they gave were historic justice for the Jewish people, fulfillment of the Biblical prophecies and a sense of romance and idealism that gripped the imagination. One respondent compared the Balfour Declaration to the decree of the ancient Persian Emperor Cyrus which allowed Jews to resettle in Judea in the 530's BCE after the Babylonian exile.

For Further Reading:

Stephen S. Wise, *Challenging Years: The Autobiography of Stephen Wise*, New York, G.P. Putnam's Sons, 1949, p. 191
Reuben Fink, *The American War Congress and Zionism,* New York, 1919.
Naomi Cohen, *American Jews and the Zionist Idea,* New York, Ktav Publ. House, 1975.

Q. What nine holidays were recommended for Jewish observance in the secularist Woman's Circle schools at their 1920 convention?

A. Rejecting the traditional practice of Judaism as a religion, the secularists of that day saw Judaism instead in terms of such ideas as social justice, support of the oppressed, and love of freedom, and they centered the curriculum in their schools around Yiddish language and literature and Jewish history. A curriculum plan offered in 1920 called for Jews to observe nine holidays which, in the secularist view, reflected those ideals.

1. *Passover - as the Jewish holiday of freedom.*

2. *Lag ba-Omer - in memory of the struggle of Bar Kokhba and Rabbi Akiva.*

3. *The First of May - as the holiday of labor brotherhood and an expression of* world *peace.*

4. *Hanukkah - as the holiday of emancipation from the Greek yoke.*

5. *March 18 - the holiday of labor's struggle for freedom.*

6. *Purim - as a children's holiday (for costuming, exchange of gifts and other amusements).*

7. *July 4 - American freedom.*

8. *February 12 (Lincoln's Birthday) - emancipation of the Negroes (sic.).*

9. *Russian Revolution (The Conference leaves to each school the choice of the day).*

For Further Reading:

Lloyd Gartner, *Jewish Education in the United States*, New York, Teachers College Press, 1969.

Q. What major event in Henry Ford's life was associated with the launching of his anti-Semitic newspaper, *The Dearborn Independent*?

A. A son of poor farmers, auto industrialist Henry Ford retained all his life a Populist's distrust of big cities, civilization, and intellect. Although he hated bankers, he borrowed $75,000,000 in 1919 to buy out his partners: however, declining sales during the economic slump of 1920 left him with large debts and a lot of unsold cars. It was at this point that Ford launched his attacks in *The Dearborn Independent*, charging that the Jews manipulated the American economy through an international conspiracy of Jewish bankers. Disappointed too, that the victorious allies did not produce a better world after World War I, Ford placed the blame again on Jewish bankers who, he said, arrange wars to make money. Ford became so obsessed with his fears that Jews controlled everything from the League of Nations to professional baseball, that some of his business associates wondered if he had become mentally unbalanced.

For Further Reading:

John Higham, *Strangers in the Land*. New Brunswick; Rutgers University Press. 1988, p. 283–285.

Q. How was the menace of pellagra ended?

A. Pellagra, a disease which can cause dermatitis, digestive problems and mental disturbance, was a terrible scourge in the southern U.S. into the early twentieth century. For years scientists were unable to find the bacteria that caused pellagra. Then in 1913, Dr. Joseph Goldberger (1874–1929), a son of Austrian Jewish immigrants, was appointed director of the field pellagra investigation in the south.

Feeling that field research was not less important than laboratory work, Goldberger soon realized that pellagra was not contagious, and he proved it conclusively by injecting himself and several others with blood of a pellagra victim and remaining healthy. The problem was diet, primarily a lack of niacin in a region where corn mush and sweet potatoes were the poor people's daily fare. The addition of milk, meat, and certain green vegetables like kale and collard greens to the diet, prevented pellagra. Yeast was also found to be a good preventative. A public information campaign pretty well eradicated pellagra by the mid-1920's.

For Further Reading:

New York Times, January 18 and 19, 1929.
DAB, IV:1, 363.

Q. Otto Kahn was a longtime director and later president of the Metropolitan Opera. Why was he not allowed to own one of the Opera Company's 35 boxes?

A. Otto Kahn (1867–1934), a German born Jew, made a huge fortune in his work at Kuhn, Loeb and Co., one of the U.S.'s most powerful finance houses. This enabled him to pursue a lifelong love of music by joining the board of directors of New York's Metropolitan Opera in 1903. In those golden days at the Met, New York's wealthiest aristocrats owned 35 lavish private boxes. It was understood that no box could ever be sold to a Jew. Kahn served the Met board with a full heart and pocketbook for 17 years before he was finally allowed to buy Box 14. Over the years he bought up the Met's stock until he practically owned the company. He did all this, not to make money but to raise the American cultural level. In fact he poured huge sums of his own fortune into a large number of cultural projects. Among Kahn's many unique achievements were the bringing of famed Maestro Arturo Toscanini from Italy to the Met, bringing in Giulio Gatti-Casazza from La Scala of Milan as the Met's director, and paying hundreds of thousands of dollars out of his own pocket to sponsor the Ballet Russe on a U.S. tour in 1916. He intervened with the Emperor Franz Joseph of Austria to release the great dancer Nijinsky from incarceration in Budapest during World War I. Kahn was instrumental in helping the careers of Paul Robeson, Feodor Chaliapin, Kirsten Flagstead, Grace Moore, and other great performers (and had affairs with several leading divas).

Although born Jewish, Kahn felt little attachment to Judaism through most of his life and was more drawn by the great aesthetic expression of Catholicism. His children were all baptized. He felt limited in the world of art too, because of his Jewishness. In 1931, he resigned from his presidency at the Met saying that other leaders had always been cool and uncooperative to him because he was a Jew. By 1933 he decided to convert to Catholicism. However, the horrors had already begun for Jews in Germany, and Kahn did not go through with the conversion, feeling that he should not appear to be deserting his own people at such a time.

Popular entertainer Fanny Brice, in her first talking movie, sang a number called "Is Something The Matter With Otto Kahn."

For Further Reading:

John Kobler, *Otto the Magnificent: The Life of Otto Kahn,* New York, Chas Scribner's Sons, 1988.
Mary Jane Matz, *The Many Lives of Otto Kahn,* New York, The MacMillan Co., 1963.

Q. In 1919, Ambassador Henry Morgenthau (1856–1946) met with the Hasidic rabbi of Gora-Kalavaria (Ger) and despite the vast differences in their ways of life found themselves in agreement on one major point. What was it?

A. Morgenthau, a German born Jew who had risen to the highest levels of American business and political life, was sent to Poland by President Wilson after World War I with two other Americans to investigate reports of anti-Semitic violence. The commission spent two months in Poland visiting many areas and talking to people, both great and small. One of the most interesting interviews was with Rabbi Pinchas Alter, leader of the large Gerer Hasidic movement.

Morgenthau, a liberal Reform Jew and president of a Reform temple, found himself very much in agreement with the rabbi's opposition to Zionism. Morgenthau described the meeting in his autobiography, *All in a Lifetime.* "Our principal conflict," the rabbi told him, "is with Jews: our chief opponents at every step are the Zionists. The Orthodox are satisfied to live side by side with people of different religions. The Zionists sidetrack religion." The Hasidim of that time generally opposed Zionism as being a political rather than a religious form of Judaism.

American Reform Judaism too, was in those days opposed to Zionism, arguing that America was the true homeland for American Jews and that Judaism should be purely a religious philosophy with no nationalist interest in a Jewish homeland. Only a handful of Reform leaders like Stephen S. Wise and Richard Gottheil were as yet Zionists. Ironically, today, Reform Jews are generally supportive to the State of Israel, the successors to the Gerer Rebbe live in Israel, and many Gerer Hasidim serve in the Israeli army.

For Further Reading:

Henry Morgenthau, *All in a Lifetime*, Doubleday and Co., 1949.

Q. How many American cities have had Jewish mayors?

A. It is hard to imagine that we will ever have a full and exact list of all the Jewish mayors in American history, but Bernard Postal and Lionel Koppman have listed many hundreds in every nook and corner of the U.S., in their book, *American Jewish Landmarks*. Almost all served after 1870, and the list from 1880-1920 is strikingly large. Jews were often among the first important business and civic leaders in new developing towns as the population of the U.S. moved west. Sometimes when towns did not attract many Jews, the Jewish leaders gave up their political positions and moved to larger settlements; for example, William Saulson, mayor of St. Ignace, Michigan in 1911, later moved his family to Detroit. Several Jews gained repute as mayors of cowboy towns, like Adolph Gluck in Dodge City, Kansas in 1891, and Solomon Star in Deadwood, South Dakota in 1884.

The variety of towns, large and small, which sported Jewish mayors is indeed surprising. The list includes:

New Haven, CT
Gary, IN
Nome, AL
Pittsfield ,MA
Natchez, MS
Shreveport, LA
Colfax, WA
Harrisonburg, VA
Denver, CO
Montgomery , AL
Minneapolis , MN
Omaha, NB
San Francisco, CA
Santa Fe, NM
New York, NY
Wichita, KS
Somerset. KY
Dublin, TX
Jacksonville, FL

The record holder is undoubtedly Miami Beach, with seven Jewish mayors as of the early 1980's. The runner up is Cincinnati with six.

Q. Who founded Maidenform Inc.?

A. Maidenform, the first company to manufacture modern brassieres, was founded by Ida Rosenthal (1889–1973) in 1923, with an initial outlay of $4,000. Before this, ladies dresses had always been made for individuals, but in the early 20th century, for the first time, they were being mass-produced in standard sizes in factories. Rosenthal, in her small dress shop, began to make undergarments that would accommodate differences in individual body shapes. At first, she gave them for free to customers who bought dresses. Her husband William developed a mass production method under which brassieres were assembled from parts. With Ida as the "front man" and William managing production, Maidenform grew into a major corporation. Their daughter Beatrice Coleman took over management in 1973.

Ida Rosenthal was active in Jewish philanthropies, contributing significantly to the Judaica collection of New York University Library and to Yeshiva University's Albert Einstein College of Medicine.

For Further Reading:

Caroline Bird, *Enterprising Women*, New York; W.W. Norton and Co., Inc. 1976.

Q. In 1922, two scions of old American families helped push bills favoring the establishment of a national Jewish homeland in Palestine through the American Congress. Who were they?

A. Senator Henry Cabot Lodge and Representative Hamilton Fish. "The Lowells speak only to Cabots and the Cabots speak only to God," says the old verse. But in March, 1922, Senator Lodge received a Zionist delegation accompanied by Speaker of the House Francis Gillett. They sought his support for a Jewish homeland in Palestine. By April 12, Lodge introduced a resolution of U.S. support for the Jewish National Home in accordance with Great Britain's Balfour Declaration of 1917. Coincidentally, Hamilton Fish, Jr. of New York had, on his own initiative, offered a similar resolution in the House. Both were adopted despite opposition from Arab delegations and from prominent Reform rabbis like David Philipson of Cincinnati.

Some of the most vigorous and vitriolic criticism came from the *New York Times* and its editor, Adolph Ochs, who accused Congress of catering to Jewish votes. Fish would later write that his support of the resolution was on humanitarian grounds - the Jews had suffered much, and it seemed only just and fair to give them a place to settle.

For Further Reading:

Irwin Adler, "American Zionism and the Congressional Resolution of 1922," *PAJHS*, XLV, 1955, 35–47.

Q. What was the connection between Rabbi Mordecai Kaplan and poet Matthew Arnold?

A. Mordecai Kaplan (1882-1983) was one of the Jewish Theological Seminary's first graduates and first professors. Growing restless with traditional Jewish thinking, Kaplan began to study non-Jewish works including the writings of Matthew Arnold, a well known British poet and scholar, who had a particular interest in both Hellenism and Judaism. Arnold knew little of actual Jewish thought through the ages but, like many 19th century Britons, he knew his Bible well. In his autobiography, Kaplan wrote that Arnold's "was the first frank attempt to free the Bible from the need of regarding it as supernatural and infallible as a prerequisite to appreciating its high worth ... it is not the purpose of the Bible to teach a metaphysically correct conception of God ... but to inculcate that God is a power that makes for righteousness." Also, "Arnold extricated me from the morass of doubt and questioning, but led me up to a mount of vision where new vistas were opened to me."

Kaplan's new radical views led to his removal from the faculty of JTS amidst the sharp rebukes of his former teachers. His Sabbath prayer book was met with a cherem (ban) from the Orthodox rabbinical organization, Agudas Harabbonim. Kaplan went on to found the Reconstructionist branch of Judaism and its Reconstructionist College (1968) for the training of rabbis.

For Further Reading:

Mordecai M. Kaplan, "The Way I Have Come," in Ira Eisenstein and Eugene Kohn eds. *Mordecai M. Kaplan: An Evaluation*, New York; Jewish Reconstructionist Foundation, Inc., 1952.

Q. Why did the Chrysler Corporation once use a star as a symbol on its automobiles?

A. Rabbi Judah Levin (1861-1926), dean of Orthodox rabbis in Detroit, received a phone call from an executive of the Chrysler Corporation asking about the meaning of the Star of David. R. Levin answered that the star stood for honesty, morality, patriotism, and so forth. The executive thanked him. Shortly afterward a star began to appear as the symbol on Chrysler automobiles.

Rabbi Levin, an accomplished Talmudic scholar, and an alumnus of the great yeshiva of Volozhin, was also a talented mathematician. He invented a machine that could both add and subtract at a time when the Burroughs machine could only add. R. Levin's machine is today in the Smithsonian Museum in Washington D.C.

For Further Reading:

Robert Rockaway, *The Jews of Detroit: From the Beginning, 1762–1914*, Detroit, Wayne State University Press, 1986.

Q. Which great American Jewish composer could not read music?

A. The son of a cantor, Irving Berlin (1888–1990) published well over 1000 songs during his long career, but he never learned either how to read music or to play a piano properly. He played his songs only on the black keys and used a sort of piano common in the early 1900's on which the performer could change the keys by moving a lever under the keyboard. Berlin's formal school education ended at age eight when he quit the second grade to sell newspapers.

While working as a singing waiter in 1907, he wrote the lyrics of his first song, "Marie From Sunny Italy." The printer mistakenly printed his name on the cover as I. Berlin instead of Israel Baline, his name from birth, and the name stuck.

"Marie From Sunny Italy" earned its writer 75 cents, of which half went to Nick Nicholson, Berlin's collaborator. Berlin's first well-known song was "Alexander's Ragtime Band" (1910), although it was some time before the song became popular. By 1912, he was earning $100,000 a year, enough to move his mother from a poor tenement to a large house in a fashionable neighborhood in the Bronx.

Strangely, it was this Russian born Jew, Irving Berlin, who reshaped American Christians' conception of their holidays with his songs "White Christmas" and "Easter Parade" and who gave "God Bless America" to his adopted country, the USA.

Berlin's mediocrity as a pianist appears in a story recounted by Moss Hart, the well known playwright. Berlin once rushed into Hart's apartment in a state of excitement and played him "Easter Parade," which he had just written, to serve as the grand finale for their new review, "As Thousands Cheer." It sounded awful and Hart didn't know what to do. Then he had an idea. "Irving," he said , "play 'Blue Skies' for me." Berlin did, and it too sounded terrible. "Okay," said Hart, "I think Easter Parade must be a terrific song." And it was.

For Further Reading:

Laurence Bergreen, *As Thousands Cheer: The Life of Irving Berlin*, New York. Viking Press, 1990.
Michael Freedland, *Irving Berlin*, New York, Stein and Day, 1978.
Rex Harrison, *A Damned Serious Business*, New York, Bantam Books, 1991.

Q. What was the first sporting event ever broadcast on radio?

A. David Sarnoff (1891-1971) devoted long hours to the study of Bible and Talmud in his native Uzlian, Russia before coming to the United States at the age of nine. He first gained fame when, as a young radio operator, he received the distress signal from the sinking Titanic, in 1912. Going on in the infant radio business, Sarnoff helped to found the RCA Company. Constantly seeking new uses for radio, Sarnoff arranged for a broadcast of the championship boxing match between Jack Dempsey and Louis Charpentier in 1921. As there were no radios in homes, the broadcast was carried to over 100 receivers all across the eastern United States, in halls where charity affairs were being held to raise money for the rehabilitation of France from the devastation of World War I. The ringside account was handled by Andrew J. White, editor of RCA's internal magazine. White's description came to a transmission shed where technician J. D. Smith repeated White's account from his headset into another microphone and on to the world.

No one was more instrumental than Sarnoff in the development of radio, and later television. In 1939, at the New York World's Fair, his speech announcing the opening of regular TV service in America was the first news event ever recorded on public television.

During World War II, Sarnoff devoted the resources of RCA to the American war effort. Appointed as General Eisenhower's chief of radio communications, with the title of brigadier general, Sarnoff organized and coordinated all radio communication for the Western front.

Sarnoff's work on radio and television has revolutionized twentieth century living, perhaps as much as Thomas Edison's or Henry Ford's. In his last years, Sarnoff returned to the study of Jewish religious literature for the first time since his childhood.

For Further Reading:

Kenneth Bilby, *The General David Sarnoff and the Rise of the Communication Industry*, New York. Harper and Row, 1966.

Q. What 20th century Jew was dubbed "the modern Samson?"

A. Sigmund (Zisha) Breitbart (1883–1925) astounded audiences in the early 1920's with such feats of strength as bending iron bars, out-pulling teams of horses and drawing a truckload of people down a street by means of a rope held in his teeth. In visits from Europe to the U.S., he was feted by sportswriters and local dignitaries in kosher restaurants and was hailed as living proof that Jews could be as strong and athletic as anyone else. Not merely a boorish jock, Breitbart owned a large library, pursued a special interest in Ancient Roman History and wrote an autobiography.

For Further Reading:

Zisha Breitbart, *Zisha Breitbart.* (Yiddish), New York, 1925.

Q. After years of mass immigration, the U.S. passed the Immigration Restriction Act of 1924. Why?

A. In the late nineteenth century, in the early years of the immigration wave, there were already Americans who wanted to restrict immigration on various grounds. Immigrants might take jobs away from American workers or might pollute the supposed Anglo-Saxon quality of American life and spirit. Immigrants might even be criminals or political radicals.

Bills requiring immigrants to take a literary test passed through Congress five times between 1895 and 1917, but each was blocked by a presidential veto until the 1918 bill was passed by Congress over President Wilson's veto. A series of laws placed various minor restrictions on immigration, but none of this had sufficient effect to please the nativists.

Finally, the Quota Act of 1921 limited the number of immigrants allowed from each country to 3% of the foreign born from that country living in the U.S. in 1910. This law was known as the Johnson Act after Senator Albert Johnson of Washington. In 1924, Johnson led the passage of a new Immigration Act which further toughened the quotas to admit only 2% of a nationality already in the U.S. in 1890. This plan was aimed largely at blocking immigration from eastern and southern Europe and had comparatively little effect on people from western or northern Europe, i.e., of "Anglo-Saxon" racial background. Asiatics were almost totally excluded.

For Further Reading:

Stephen Thernstrom ed., *Harvard Encyclopedia of American Ethnic Groups.* Cambridge, Harvard University Press, 1980, pp. 492–493.

1924–1945
Americanizing

BY THE MIDDLE 1920's, new laws cut off most of the flow of immigration from Europe. At the same time, the Americanization of the Jewish immigrants moved ahead quickly as they continued to enter more and more into the mainstream of American life — into the workforce, academia, entertainment, politics, and even major league sports. Jewish communal organizations were active and strong. Old neighborhoods altered as Jews moved onward and upward to new neighborhoods.

Jews suffered with other Americans in the Depression of the 1930's, as many lost jobs or homes or saw their businesses fail. Nazism and anti-Semitism grew strong in Europe, and many Americans sought refuge in isolationism and anti-Semitic nativism.

Reform Judaism flourished, and Eastern Europeans were joining the established German Jews in the temples. At first strongly opposed to Zionism, Reform increased its attachment under the leadership of rabbis like Stephen S. Wise and Abba Hillel Silver. There were signs too, that the drift away from tradition was slowing, as was expressed in the Columbus Platform of 1937. By the 1930's, temples were moving their Sabbath services from Sunday back to Friday night and Saturday morning. More temples were reciting the kiddush and increasing the use of Hebrew in their prayers.

Orthodoxy reached a nadir as the children of the immigrants, inadequately educated in Judaism, turned away from observance of traditions. It seemed that only old people still went to *shul*. Day schools were few. Orthodox youth movements like Young Israel had some success but could hardly compete with the attractions of Conservatism and Reform.

Conservatism was making the largest gains, drawing much of its following from the children of observant immigrants. In the 1920's, many synagogues that allied themselves with Conservatism were still Orthodox in practice, with men and women sitting separately.

Jews loved Franklin Delano Roosevelt and strongly supported his New Deal. They enthusiastically joined the U.S. effort in World War II, and many fought in Europe or the Pacific, some even rising to high rank. However, American Jews could do little to prevent the destruction of their brethren in Europe at the hands of the Nazis.

Among Jewish intellectuals, there was great soul searching in an attempt to reconcile their Jewishness with the ideas and mores of the general society. Their internal conflict was expressed in their writings and in their lives. Their efforts were often not successful, resulting, in some cases, in giving up Judaism or even in suicide. Alfred Kazin's *New York Jew* offers a perceptive account of some of these people.

The end of the war would begin a very new time for America's Jews.

Q. Was there ever a quota on Jewish students at Harvard?

A. Bright, ambitious Jewish students began to attend American universities in increasing numbers in the early 20th century. Between 1900 and 1922, the percentage of Jews in the student body at Harvard rose from 7% to 21.5%. This roused fears in some quarters that the old ideal of the sociable, clean-cut college man would be altered by the serious, scholarly, and ambitious Jewish youngsters.

In the early 1920's, several ivy-league schools, including Harvard, Yale, Columbia, Princeton, and Dartmouth, enacted informal, but effective, quotas on Jews. "Psychological" tests and personal interviews were used to exclude students with Jewish sounding names and Jewish looking faces.

Jews faced strong discrimination when seeking professorships as well. At Harvard, Harry Wolfson was *the* Jewish presence for many years. Paul Weiss broke the ice at Yale, when he joined the philosophy department in 1946, and Lionel Trilling was a pioneer when he joined Columbia in 1939 to teach American literature, one of the most difficult areas for Jews to enter.

Graduate students generally had less trouble, except for medical students, who faced restrictions both in entering medical school and later in securing internships. Only a handful of wealthy ones were admitted. In the 1920's, word got out that the excellent Scottish colleges in Edinburgh, Glasgow, St. Andrews, and Aberdeen were admitting Jews to their medical schools. When the Depression hit, these institutions became desperate in their search for scholars. Many students went over and later became leaders and pioneers in medicine back in the U.S. Other American Jews went to

Latin American schools. The discrimination against Jews was strongest in the northeast. Western and southern schools offered Jews more or less equal opportunities.

For Further Reading:

Dan Oren, *Joining the Club*, New Haven, Yale University Press, 1985.
James Michener, *The World is My Home*, New York, Random House, 1991.

Q. How did the Purple Gang get its name?

A. Prohibition spawned a number of criminal organizations which took in large profits from the illegal trade in alcoholic beverages. One of the most vicious of these groups was the Purple Gang in Detroit. Composed almost entirely of Jews, the Purple Gang was involved in a variety of illegal activities, including shipping liquor across the Detroit River from Windsor, Ontario, where it was legal, to Detroit, MI. From Detroit, it was sent on to the Capone mob in Chicago. The Purples are credited by some sources with introducing the tommy-gun to gang warfare.

There are several versions of how they got their name. In one story, their name came from Sammy Purple, a tough with whom they associated in their early days. Another story tells that when the gangsters were still teenagers, some of them stole fruit from a market and the owner, unable to stop them, sputtered angrily, "They're, they're, they're purple." A third tale associates the name with some loud bathing suits in which they were once seen.

The Purples prospered in the 1920's partly because of the weakness of Detroit's Mafia. However, when the Mafia regrouped in the early 1930's, and with Prohibition coming to an end, the Purple Gang went out of business. Many members were already in prison or had met violent ends.

It is told that in 1945, several old Purple Gangsters were let out of a Michigan state prison and sent to murder Warren Hooper, a state senator who was investigating political corruption. The killers returned to jail and received special privileges after accomplishing their mission. It is also claimed that in their heyday, a carload of Purples drove up to Toronto and gunned down some members of an anti-Semitic gang.

For Further Reading:

Files of Burton Collection, Detroit Public Library
Bruce Rubenstein, *Three Bullets Sealed His Lips*, E. Lansing, Michigan State University Press, 1987.
Robert Rockaway, *The Were Good to Their Mothers*.

Q. Of what major league baseball player was it said that, "He knew 12 languages, but couldn't hit in any one of them?"

A. Moe Berg, a catcher for 4 major league teams over a 17 year career, was also a genuine scholar, graduating with honors from Princeton and the Sorbonne and earning a law degree from Columbia in 1929. Far beyond his athletic skills, Berg mastered a number of languages, including Japanese, and did important espionage work for the U.S. government. As part of a team of major leaguers touring Japan in 1934, Berg gathered information and took photographs which helped American bombers later during World War II. He also spied behind German lines posing as a nuclear scientist.

For Further Reading:

Ira Berkow, *NY Times*. 12-4-89

Lewis Kaufman, Barbara Fitzgerald and Tom Sewell, *Moe Berg: Athlete, Scholar, Spy*. Boston, Little Brown and Co., 1974.

Q. Were Yeshiva University and the Jewish Theological Seminary once one institution?

A. They never were, although there were efforts to unite the two schools, the most serious in the late 1920's. Many leaders and teachers at JTS were observant, but there were some major differences of philosophy and of educational aims. JTS's program was designed largely to train rabbis and teachers, while YU was also committed to producing educated laymen. Also, the presence of Dr. Mordecai Kaplan, later the founder of Reconstructionist Judaism, on the JTS faculty was unacceptable to the YU people. The Seminary was becoming increasingly identified with Conservative Judaism, whereas YU was solidly Orthodox.

For Further Reading:

Aaron Rakeffet Rothkoff, *Bernard Revel, Builder of American Orthodox*. NY, Feldheim, 1981, p. 94-114

Gilbert Klaperman, *The Story of Yeshiva University: The First Jewish University in America*. NY, MacMillan and Co, 1969

Q. What is the Hart Trophy?

A. Professional hockey's most valuable player award is the Hart Trophy named for a Jew, Cecil Hart 1883-1940. Descended from Aaron Hart, a prominent Jewish settler in 18th century Canada, Cecil Hart managed both the Montreal Canadiens and the old Montreal Maroons. Every Canadien team Hart led made it to the Stanley Cup playoffs. The original trophy was donated by Cecil's father, Dr. David Hart. The first winner was Frank Neighbor of Ottawa.

For Further Reading:

Bernard Postal, Jesse Silver, and Roy Silver, *Encyclopedia of Jews in Sports*. New York. Block Publ. Co., 1965.

Zander Hollander, *The Complete Encyclopedia Of Ice Hockey*, Englewood Cliffs. NJ, Prentice Hall Inc., 1974

Q. When did Boro Park become predominantly Jewish?

A. Located in the south part of Brooklyn within the area of the old Dutch settlement of Utrecht, Boro Park became a stronghold of Orthodox Jewry in the late 20th century. When Jews first moved into the area in the 1890's, much of it was still farmland.

About 20,000 Jews lived there by 1900, and two Conservative synagogues were soon built — Temple Emanu-El in 1904, and Temple Beth El in 1906. As of 1918, there were 150 Orthodox congregations, along with 7 Conservative and 5 Reform. By 1930, the Jewish population had reached about 60,000, forming an Americanized Jewish community. It remained stable in both size and character until the 1950's. At that time, large numbers of Orthodox Jews, often Hasidic, began to move into Boro Park, forming a large, strong, politically conscious Orthodox entity with its own communal institutions, schools, stores and styles of dress.

For Further Reading:

Egon Mayer, *From Suburbia To Shtetl: The Jews of Boro Park*, Philadelphia; Temple U. Press, 1979.

Q. How were Dr. Bernard Revel, head of Yeshiva University, and Dr. Nelson Glueck, head of Hebrew Union College related?

A. Bernard Revel was the uncle of Nelson Glueck. Glueck's father was a son of Revel's brother, Moshe Yitzchak Revel, who changed his name to Morris Glueck upon immigrating to the U.S. YU is, of course, a leading Orthodox school, while HUC is the home base for the training of Reform rabbis.

For Further Reading:

Aaron Rakeffet-Rothkoff, *Bernard Revel: Builder of American Orthodoxy*, NY, Feldheim 1981.

Q. Who was the "Meitscheter Genius?"

A. R. Solomon Polachek (1871–1929) was known as the Meitscheter *Ilui*, because he was born in Meitschet, Russia and was considered a genius in Talmud. A disciple of the greatest rabbinic scholars of Eastern Europe, especially Rabbi Naftali Tzvi Yehuda Berlin of Volozhin and of R. Chaim Soloveitchik of Brisk, Rabbi Polachek was also known for his good character and his mastery of secular knowledge. As such, he was a highly suitable choice to teach the highest Talmud class at Yeshiva University, which he did from 1922 until his death. He was succeeded in his position by very distinguished scholars, R. Moshe Soloveitchik and R. Joseph B. Soloveitchik.

For Further Reading:

Gilbert Klaperman. *The Story of Yeshiva University: The First Jewish University in America*. New York, MacMillan and Co., 1969

Q. How did Sidney Franklin become interested in bullfighting?

A. In 1922, Brooklyn born Sidney Franklin ran away to Mexico after an argument with his father, and took a job in a poster business with a specialty in advertising bullfights, although he had never seen one. Finally, after attending a fight, he got into an argument with someone over whether Americans could be good bullfighters. He decided to try it himself and was soon on his way to a great career.

For Further Reading:

Sidney Franklin, *Bullfighter From Brooklyn,* Prentice-Hall Inc.. 1952.

Q. Was there ever an accusation of ritual murder against Jews in America?

A. The charge that Jews have murdered Christian children in order to use their blood for religious rituals has provoked many pogroms over the centuries in Europe and has been popularized in famous books like Chaucer's *Canterbury Tales*. The charge was, of course, always totally false. Nevertheless, even in twentieth century United States, this old lie would occasionally resurface, the most notorious incident occurring in the town of Massena, New York in 1928. A young Christian girl was missing on the day before Yom Kippur. A rumor spread that the Jews had kidnapped and murdered her in order to use her blood for a holiday ritual. Jewish leaders were called in by the police for questioning, and the mood in the town began to grow threatening. About 4:00 p.m. shortly before the start of the holiday, searchers found the girl in the nearby woods. She had simply gotten lost. Mention of ritual murder is found too, in several old ballads that have been passed on in rural areas of the southern United States.

For Further Reading:

Saul S. Friedman, *The Incident at Massena*, NY, Stein and Day 1978.

Q. What prominent American rabbi and teacher started his career with jobs such as working in a candy store and selling ice cream?

A. Rabbi Shraga Feivel Mendlowitz (1886–1948) was born in Vilag on the border between Poland and Hungary and studied in Eastern European yeshivas. An avid student, he delved not only into Talmud, the main interest of the yeshivas, but also into Hasidism, Kabbalah, philosophy, and Jewish History. He learned German so that he could read the great non-Jewish philosophers, and he studied deeply in the works of the German Orthodox thinker Rabbi Samson Raphael Hirsch. Although an ordained rabbi, Mendlowitz at first sought other types of employment like working in a candy story in Humenne, Hungary and as an ice cream man in Scranton, Pennsylvania, after coming to America in 1913.

All through his life he preferred to be called Mr. and not Rabbi Mendlowitz. However, the desire to study and teach consumed him and, in 1921, he accepted a position as head of a 4 year old day school, Torah Vodaas, in New York. "Mr." Mendlowitz proved to be an effective and dedicated administrator and teacher. He developed close personal relationships with his students both in and out of the classroom, thus creating the style of the Orthodox day school of the 1940's and 1950's, and encouraged the founding of day schools all over the United States. In 1944, "Mr." Mendlowitz was the guiding light in the founding of Torah Umesorah, a national organization for Jewish day schools.

For Further Reading:

Leo Jung, ed., *Men of the Spirit*, New York, Kymson Publishing Co., 1964. ch. 26.

Q. What disrupted the first Kol Nidre service in Miami Beach's new Congregation Beth Jacob in 1926?

A. One of the first recorded organized high holiday services in the history of Miami Beach was the Kol Nidre service on September 18, 1926. The service was disrupted by a fearsome hurricane, which the New York Times described as the worst hurricane in the history of the U.S. Hundred mile an hour winds smashed into south Florida, leaving over 1000 dead, and near 40,000 homeless, destroying thousands of buildings and sinking every ship in Miami's harbor. Martial law was declared, and the National Guard moved in to prevent looting.

For Further Reading:

Bernard Postal and Lionel Koppman, *American Jewish Landmarks*, New York. Fleet Press Inc.. 1977.

Q. What famous American company began in the Australian outback?

A. At age 18, Helena Rubenstein (1870–1965) left her native Cracow, Poland to join an uncle in the small town of Coleraine in the outback of Australia. The women of Coleraine admired Rubenstein's soft skin compared with their own, which was dried by steady exposure to sun and wind. Rubenstein had brought twelve jars of her mother's special facial cream with her. The cream had been developed by Dr. Lykusky, a chemist in Cracow.

The women of Coleraine were all anxious to buy it. Soon Rubenstein had to send back to Cracow for more, and her beauty business had begun. She opened a shop in Melbourne and brought Dr. Lykusky to Australia to teach her how to make what she now began to call Creme Valaze.

Over the coming years, Rubenstein expanded to London, Paris, and the U.S., building a complete line of beauty products and treatments in one of the world's giant corporations. Many branches of the business were run by Rubenstein's relatives. Energetic in mind and body into a ripe old age, she wrote her autobiography at 94. The Helena Rubenstein Art Pavilion in Tel Aviv was founded as an expression of her admiration for Israel.

For Further Reading:

Helena Rubenstein, *My Life for Beauty*, New York. Simon and Schuster Inc., 1964.

Q. What were the unusual research specialties of 2 prominent Jewish bacteriologists named Kahn?

A. After earning his Ph.D. from Cornell in 1924, Charles Morton Kahn devoted himself to research on bacteria and led a number of scientific expeditions to Latin America, primarily Dutch Guiana, where he studied tropical diseases.

Another American bacteriologist, Reuben Leon Kahn, taught for many years at the University of Michigan where he was faculty advisor to the Hillel Foundation. In 1923, he developed the Kahn Test to detect syphilis.

For Further Reading:
UJE, VI, 289-290.

Q. Who was the founding director of the Child Study Association of America?

A. Sidonie Matsner Gruenberg (1881-1974), a nationally known authority on child raising, developed an interest in issues involving women and children and became active in the innovative Federation Child Study in New York. Her first book, *Your Child Today and Tomorrow,* written in 1912, was based on the idea that child raising requires skills and knowledge that can be taught, and she explained scientific research on family issues in a down to earth manner.

In 1924, Gruenberg expanded the Federation into the Child Study Association of America, which she directed until 1950. She edited *The Encyclopedia of Child Care and Guidance* in 1954 and wrote a number of important books and articles in her field. One of her favorite themes was the importance of babysitting for gaining experience on how to handle younger children, especially in modern small families where such experience was less available.

For Further Reading:
NAW, The Modern Period, p. 295-296

Q. What calendar reform, proposed in the decades between the World Wars, posed a serious threat to Jewish practice?

A. A movement led by George Eastman, of Kodak Co. sought to change the calendar so that it would consist of 13 months of 28 days each, with every year beginning on a Sunday. This would have meant that the Jewish Sabbath would occur on a different day every year, i.e., sometimes Sunday, sometimes Monday, and so on. The effect on Jewish Sabbath observance would have been devastating. Rabbi Moses Hyamson of New York led the League for Safeguarding the Fixity of the Sabbath, and worked against the calendar change, in particular opposing efforts to adopt it in the League of Nations and in the U.S. Congress.

For Further Reading:

Bernard Drachman, *The Unfailing Light:* New York; RCA 1948.

Q. Who was known as the "Banana King"?

A. Migrating from Kishinev to Selma, Alabama in 1892, Samuel Zemurray (1877–1961) made himself the head of United Fruit Co., a major tropical fruit business. The company was to become the biggest landowner and corporate employer in Costa Rica, Guatemala, and Honduras.

Beginning as a banana peddler about 1898, Zemurray built up his business, and in 1910 he bought five thousand acres on the Cuyamel River in Honduras. When new government policies threatened his business, Zemurray helped organize a revolution led by former president Manuel Bonilla.

Zemurray continued to acquire land and his business prospered. Paternalistically generous with workers at a time when most Central American employers were not, Zemurray endowed medical clinics, housing projects, recreational facilities, and schools on his plantations. He gave important support to efforts to control tropical diseases like malaria and yellow fever. He also restored ancient Mayan ruins and presented them to the Guatemalan government.

Zemurray donated to Jewish and Zionist causes and headed the Palestine Economic Corp., which was founded in 1926 to promote the export of commodities from Palestine. In 1947, he helped send ships from Central America to bring Jewish refugees from Europe to Palestine, and he lobbied for Central American support for the U.N. vote on the partition of Palestine which made possible the founding of the State of Israel.

A less favorable picture comes from Pablo Neruda, famed Chilean poet of Communist leanings, who expressed his bitterness toward American big business and particularly United Fruit Company, in "La United Fruit Co.":

"The United Fruit Co., Incorporated reserved for itself: the heartland and coasts of my country, The delectable waist of America. They rechristened their properties: The Banana Republics and over the languishing dead . . . They established an opera bouffe. They ravished all enterprise. (transl. B. Belitt"

For Further Reading:

Stephen Whitfield, "Strange Fruit: The Career of Samuel Zemurray." *AJH*, LXIII, 1984, 307–323.

Q. Why was Rosika Schwimmer denied U.S. Citizenship?

A. Born in Budapest to a prosperous Jewish family, Rosika Schwimmer (1877–1948) became an active advocate of both feminism and pacifism. Through the first decade of the 20th century, she developed a reputation as a fine writer and a stirring orator at women's meetings all over Europe.

When World War One began, she tried to rally pacifist support to stop the fighting. She met with U.S. Secretary of State William Jennings Bryan to present a petition signed by a million European women urging the American government to mediate an end to the war. In 1915, she persuaded Henry Ford to charter a "peace ship" to travel to Europe and encourage the cause of peace. The scheme was ridiculed by the press and, when the ship reached Norway, Ford gave up and went home. Schwimmer was later accused of spying for the Germans and also of duping an idealistic but gullible Ford. Both charges were false.

In 1924, when she applied for U.S. citizenship, groups like the American Legion loudly demanded that she be refused. Her case went to the Supreme Court, which denied her petition in a 6–3 vote on the grounds that as a pacifist, she had stated that she would not bear arms in defense of the U.S. The three justices who voted in her favor were Oliver Wendell Holmes Jr., Louis D. Brandeis, and Edward T Sanford. Holmes was quoted as saying that all Schwimmer had done wrong was to agree with the Sermon on the Mount.

Schwimmer stayed on in the U.S. as an alien, continuing her political activities and devoting herself to a variety of idealized plans for a world government. Like many women of that era she sacrificed domestic stability for activities outside the home. She was married briefly to a Hungarian journalist and had no children.

For Further Reading:

NWA II, 246–249.

Q. How did Jews obtain wine for Kiddush during Prohibition?

A. The Eighteenth Amendment, passed in 1919, forbade the sale of alcoholic beverages. However, every family was allowed to purchase 10 gallons yearly for sacramental purposes. The wine was to be purchased from the local clergyman, to whom the government granted special allotments.

A number of congregations, whose sole purpose was to sell wine, soon came into existence. The members often carried very gentile sounding names. Several rabbis were indicted under the Volstead Act, to the great embarrassment of the Jewish community.

For Further Reading:

Howard M. Sachar, *A History of the Jews in America,* New York, Alfred A. Knopf, 1992.

Q. Was Belle Moskowitz the most important woman in American politics in the 1920's?

A. At least her biographer, Elizabeth Perry, thinks that she was. Belle Moskowitz played a unique role in the inner circle of Governor Alfred Smith of New York, beginning with his first election in 1918. Women in those days were active in political and social movements, but they began to play a highly visible role in government only in the 1930's. They had been first allowed to vote under the 19th amendment in 1920.

Moskowitz was deeply loyal to Governor Smith. She showed no self-interest and never held a high level position. But she wielded great power in Smith's administration, albeit quietly, and she knew it. Early on, she brought excellent people like Robert Moses, Abraham Elkus, and Henry Dwight Chapin into Smith's service, and she handled publicity and liaison work very effectively.

Smith's campaign for president in 1928 had little chance of success. A Democrat, a Catholic, and an opponent of Prohibition, Smith faced a Republican party that had presided over eight years of prosperity. It was more than Moskowitz's publicity skills could deal with, and Smith was soundly defeated, losing even in his home state of New York.

Smith would have liked the Democrat nomination again in 1932, and Moskowitz supported him. However, the party nominated Franklin Roosevelt, who had succeeded Smith as Governor of New York.

Moskowitz had been active since the 1890's in social work on the Lower East Side. One major project was the clean up of dance halls which had become dens of iniquity. For some time she was involved with the National Council of Jewish Women, which was in those days very progressive and politically active.

For Further Reading:

Elizabeth Israels Perry. *Belle Moskowitz: Feminine Politics and the Exercise of Power in the Age of Alfred E. Smith.* New York; Oxford University Press, 1977

Q. A daughter of a leading American Jew studied psychoanalysis under Sigmund Freud. Who was she?

A. Ruth Mack Brunswick (1897-1946) was the daughter of Judge Julian Mack, a leader of both Reform Judaism and Zionism. After earning an M.D. from Tufts Medical School in 1922, Brunswick went to Vienna to be psychoanalyzed by Sigmund Freud, and she joined his intimate circle of psychoanalysts. Freud often referred patients to her, including the famous "wolf-man" case, and she developed a special interest in severe mental disorders.

After sixteen years in Austria, Brunswick was forced to flee when the Nazis marched in. She returned to the U.S. and taught at the New York Psychoanalytic Institute.

For Further Reading:

NAW, l. 262-263.

Q. There have been 2 U.S. senators named Cohen. What did they have in common besides their names?

A. Cohen is the Hebrew word for priest, and anyone bearing that name is likely to be descended from the priests of the ancient temple in Jerusalem. It is remarkable then, that Senators John Stanford Cohen of Georgia, 1932-33, and William Sebastian Cohen of Maine, 1979-1997, were not Jewish. Both Senators Cohen were non-Jews born of Jewish fathers and non-Jewish mothers.

John Sanford Cohen's father was descended from Portuguese Jews who were among the first settlers in Georgia. His mother was the daughter of Confederate General Ambrose Robinson Wright and Mary Hubbell Savage, whose ancestors had immigrated to Virginia in 1607. A newspaperman by profession, Cohen had worked for several major papers and was for many years owner and editor of the *Atlanta Journal*. He was one of the sponsors behind the building of the first great international highway, from New York through Virginia and Atlanta to Jacksonville, Florida.

John Cohen was appointed to the Senate in 1932 to complete the term of Senator William J. Harris. He did not run for reelection.

William Sebastian Cohen's father was an Eastern European Jewish immigrant, who ran a bagel business, but his mother was a Christian and Cohen was not raised Jewish. Senator Cohen has been supportive to Jewish and Israel needs, but he himself is Unitarian. He has published poetry and several books, including, *The Double Man,* a novel of international intrigue co-authored with Senator Gary Hart of Colorado.

For Further reading:

DAB p. 805.
Biographical Dictionary of the United States Congress. 1774–1989, Washington D.C., 1989.

Q. Who was New Mexico's Jewish governor?

A. Arthur Seligman (1871–1933) was born in Santa Fe, New Mexico, to German Jewish immigrants. Involved early in politics, Seligman served in many public positions including Mayor of Santa Fe (1910–1912) and Democratic governor of New Mexico (1930–1933). Seligman's election as governor ended a period of Republican dominance in New Mexico and launched a period of Democratic success. Nevertheless, Seligman included capable Republicans in his administration. He worked hard to balance the budget, but finally had to admit that it could not be done without cutting important services. He developed the state highway system and improved scenic areas like Carlsbad Caverns. From early childhood, Seligman had been interested in local history, and he collected Indian relics.

The first Eastern European Jew known in New Mexico was Solomon Spiegelberg, who arrived in 1846 when it was still Mexican territory. Other early Jews included Jacob Nussbaum, who became postmaster in Santa Fe, Sam Dittenhoefer, called "Navajo Sam," Nathan Jaffa, territorial secretary, and Henry Jaffa, who served as mayor of Albuquerque.

For Further Reading:

Paul A. F. Winter, "Arthur Seligman," *New Mexico Historical Review,*" VIII, 1933.
Oliver Lafarge, *Santa Fe:The Autobiography of a Southwestern Town,* Norman; U. of Oklahoma Press, 1959.

Q. When did the Hasidic Rebbe of Lubavitch first come to the United States?

A. When Rabbi Joseph Isaac Schneerson of Lubavitch escaped the Nazis and came to the U.S. in 1940, he was invited by President Roosevelt to visit the White House in a much publicized event. However, it is often forgotten that this was in fact not the rebbe's first visit to the U.S. He had come in 1930 to raise funds for his school in Europe. As a major Jewish leader, he was received by President Hoover at the White House. He was greeted everywhere by throngs of people who gathered at train depots to accompany him to his hotel and to listen to his lectures at local synagogues. The rebbe told interviewers that the Jewish soul was strong enough to survive any threat. What was more troubling to him was the lack of Torah study in America. People had become too involved in mundane matters. He hoped that Jewish youth would revolt against this condition and turn back to Torah with their full hearts.

For Further Reading:

Joseph I. Schneersohn, *Some Aspects of Chabad Chassidism,* introduction by Nissan Mindel, New York, Machne Israel, 1957.

Q. What do the songs "Happy Days Are Here Again" and "My Yiddishe Momme" have in common?

A. The lyrics for both were written by Polish born Jack Yellen (1893- 1991). "Happy Days are Here Again" become famous as the Democratic Party theme song during the New Deal era. Ironically, Yellen considered himself a Republican. "My Yiddishe Momma" which he wrote in 1925 for Sophie Tucker, became a worldwide favorite. Among Yellen's other hit songs were "Down By The Ohio," "What's Become of Sally," "Ain't She Sweet," "Hard Hearted Hanna," and "Are You Havin' Fun."

For Further Reading:

New York Times, April 19, 1991

Q. Why did Professor Lionel Trilling's father come to the U.S.?

A. Professor Lionel Trilling (1905–1975) was a leading scholar of literature and one of the first Jews to teach it at an Ivy League school, joining the faculty of Columbia University in the 1930's. In those days of Jewish quotas, President Nicholas Murray Butler of Columbia had to twist a lot of arms to get appointments for Jews like Trilling and also for Dr. Salo Baron, in Jewish History. Trilling's father David was descended from Talmudic scholars in Bialystok, and he showed early signs of precocity in his yeshiva studies. However, at his bar mitzvah, he broke down during the reading of the haftarah. His parents, deeply embarrassed, sent him off to the U.S. against his will. Author Alan Wald has argued that both David and Lionel Trilling were troubled with deep fears of failure. This was perhaps why it took Lionel Trilling almost 12 years to write his doctoral dissertation, on poet Matthew Arnold.

For Further Reading:

Alan Wald, *The New York Intellectuals,* University of North Carolina Press, Chapel Hill, 1987.

Suzanne Klingsenstein, *Jews in the American Academy. 1900 1940,* New Haven, Yale University Press, 1991.

Q. What fellow Jew swore in Herbert Lehman when he became governor of NY?

A. On Dec. 31, 1932, the newly elected Governor Lehman succeeded President-elect Franklin Roosevelt to the governorship of the Empire state. The oath of office was administered by the new governor's brother, Judge Irving Lehman of the Court of Appeals, at Herbert's Manhattan apartment. Unfortunately, the occasion was tinged with sadness. A sister, Clara, had just died and her funeral was pending. A public inaugural ceremony was held on January 2 at the State assembly in Albany.

For Further Reading:

Alan Nevins, *Herbert Lehman and His Era,* New York; Charles Scribner's Sons, 1963, p. 13lf.

Q. Who were the two Weisses who played important roles in the story of Louisiana Senator Huey Long, the Kingfish?

A. Louisiana Senator Huey Long's promising career as a populist demagogue was cut short by an assassin's bullet in 1935. Outspoken in his criticism of FDR, Huey Long had become famous for his Share the Wealth program. Unlike many populists, he does not seem to have been hostile to Jews, two of whom, Seymour Weiss and Abe Shushan, were devoted aides and friends of his. Huey had a New Orleans airport named after Shushan. Both Weiss and Shushan were indicted on charges of graft and income tax fraud shortly after the Kingfish's death. Strangely, the man who shot Huey Long was a Dr. Carl Austin Weiss, a bitter political foe of Huey's. Carl Weiss was not Jewish.

For Further Reading:

T. Harry Williams, *Huey Long,* New York, Alfred A. Knopf, 1969.

Q. What Jewish man's wife left him to marry a king?

A. Earnest Aldrich Simpson gave up his wife to marry divorcee Wallis Warfield. Wallis was an American born woman whose many lovers had included

Galeazzo Ciano, later son-in-law of Mussolini and foreign minister of Italy, by whom she had become pregnant. It was a well kept secret, probably even from Wallis, but the name Simpson had been changed from Solomons, and her husband's family was Jewish. Wallis left Simpson in 1937 and married King Edward VIII of England, whom she had been eyeing for a long time. Edward abdicated his throne to marry Wallis, and the pair lived out their lives as the Duke and Duchess of Windsor.

For Further Reading:

Charles Higham, *The Duchess of Windsor,* NY: McGraw-Hill, 1988.

Q. What role did Jews play in the administration of FDR's New Deal?

A. American Jews admired the New Deal both for its aim of helping people and because intellectuals played an important role in setting it up. Although no Jew initially held a cabinet post (Henry Morgenthau came in a bit later), Felix Frankfurter was appointed by FDR to the U.S. Supreme Court and Benjamin Cohen, Samuel Rosenbaum, and David Niles were close advisors to the president. The 1930's witnessed the most intense anti-semitism of any decade in U.S. history. Many highly qualified young Jewish lawyers, who could not find jobs in law firms because of anti-Semitism, worked for the federal government, especially in the Department of Labor under Frances Perkins and in the Department of the Interior under Secretary Harold Ickes. FDR's friendships with Jews and his care for the poor were comforting to Jews, who voted for him in increasing numbers each time he ran.

For Further Reading:

Samuel Hand, *Counsel and Advice: A Political Biography of Samuel I. Rosenman,* New York, Garland Puhl. Co., 1979.
Leonard Dinnerstein, "Jews and the New Deal,"*AJH*, LXII, 1983, 461–476.

Q. What was the great intellectual immigration of the 1930's?

A. The Eastern European Jews of the great immigration waves of the 1880's through 1920's had received most of their education in a Jewish milieu, whether cheders, advanced yeshivot, or secular Jewish schools. However, the refugees from Hitler's Europe in the 1930's included a large number of university educated Jewish scholars and scientists. Laura Fermi, wife of famed physicist Enrico Fermi, wrote *Illustrious Immigrants,* a fascinating study of the European intellectuals who escaped to the U.S. in that period. She compares them to the intellectuals who fled to Italy when the Turks conquered Constantinople in 1453 and who helped spark the Italian Renaissance.

The European exodus of the 1930's included many Jews who made major contributions to American science and culture. The importance of the Manhattan Project is noted elsewhere in these pages. Just to drop a few of the leading Jewish names in other fields:

Psychology	Max Wertheimer, Frieda Fromm-Reichmann, Erich Fromm, Helene Deutsch, Bruno Bettelheim, Theodor Reik
Novelists	Ferenc Molnar, Franz Werfel, Lion Feuchtwanger
Symphony conductors	Bruno Walter, George Szell, Antal Dorati, Maurice Abravanel,
Mathematics	Samuel Eilenberg, Salomon Bochner, Abraham Wald
History	Ernst Kantorowicz, Bernard Weinryb, Erwin Panofsky (Art History)

Two Italian Jewish immigrants won Nobel Prizes, Emilio Segre in Physics, 1959, and Salvador Luria in medicine, 1969. Theodore Von Karman won a Nobel Prize for his important research in aerodynamics.

For Further Reading:

Laura Fermi, *Illustrious Immigrants: The Intellectual Migration From Europe. 1930–1941*, Chicago, University of Chicago Press. 1971.

Q. How did the rise of Nazism in Germany affect composer Arnold Schoenberg?

A. Mostly self-taught in music, Arnold Schoenberg (1874–1951) developed radical new techniques in tonality and became one of Europe's major composers. In 1921, he had converted to Catholicism. Nevertheless in 1933, because of his Jewish birth, the Nazis dismissed him from his position at the Prussian Academy of Arts in Berlin. He then emigrated to the United States. Formally returning to Judaism, he composed a number of works on Jewish themes, including *Kol Nidre* (1938), A *Survivor from Warsaw* (1947), and *Jakobsleiter*, and an opera, *Moses and Aaron*. Schoenberg left his books and manuscripts to the National Library in Jerusalem.

For Further Reading:

EJ, XIV 988–989

Q. Why did the Young Jewish Lawyers' Association not support a fellow Jew, Henry Horner, in his bid for re-election as governor of Illinois in 1936?

A. One important reason cited in their statement was that Horner refused to grant a delay in the execution of Morris Cohen, a Jewish convict scheduled to go to the electric chair on Yom Kippur, 1933. Horner had postponed the execution of a non-Jew scheduled for the same day. In fact, 4 years later Horner did allow a delay of execution because of a Jewish holiday, for a Jew convicted of murder.

Governor Horner nevertheless did not do much in his public capacity as governor on Jewish issues. It was perhaps for this reason that many Jews did not support his re-election campaign in 1936, including Chicago Democratic leaders like Jacob Arvey and Barnett Hodes. However, local infighting between the Chicago Democratic organization and the state party was probably the main factor. Despite all this, Homer won re-election by a comfortable margin. Another story about Horner was related by Rabbi Louis Mann of Temple Sinai in Chicago. One day in April, 1933, Mann was told that Horner had decided to veto a bill which would require the placing of drops of silver nitrate in the eyes of newborn babies as a preventative against gonorrheal blindness. The bill had already been vetoed once by Horner's predecessor, Governor Louis Emmerson, on the ground that it infringed on personal liberties. Rabbi Mann hurried by train to the governor's office in Springfield to argue his case in favor of the law. Horner pointed to a pile of telegrams opposing the bill, but Rabbi Mann remonstrated with him until he agreed to let the bill go through. The last train to Chicago was delayed at the station while the governor's car hurried the rabbi there for his trip home.

Governor Horner was a grandson of Hannah and Henry Horner, who had married in Chicago in 1849 and who were among the first members of congregation Anshe Maayriv.

For Further Reading:

Thomas Littlewood, *Horner Of Illinois,* Evanston, Northwestern U . Press 1967.

Q. When did Jews begin to vote heavily Democratic in presidential elections?

A. Through the late nineteenth and into the early twentieth century, Jews tended to vote Republican, which seemed the more progressive party. The Democrats were identified with Populism and the Old South, and big city political machines were often dominated by the Irish. This voting pattern began to change when Jews turned to Woodrow Wilson, whom they liked as a liberal intellectual.

In 1928, 72% of the Jewish vote went to Al Smith who openly sought Jewish support and who had Jewish campaign managers, Joseph Proskauer and Belle Moskowitz. The Jews gave FDR 82% of their vote in 1932, and were up to 90% in 1940 and 1944, even as other ethnic groups were reducing their support for him. Roosevelt denoted the liberalism of the New Deal, and he had close Jewish associates like Samuel Rosenman, Benjamin Cohen and Felix Frankfurter. Even in 1952, Republican candidate Dwight Eisenhower could win only 36% of the Jewish vote, despite his record as a popular war hero and his helpfulness on Jewish issues during the war. However, for Jews, he still represented the conservative party of big business against the liberal idealism of Democrat Adlai E. Stevenson.

For Further Reading:

Lawrence Fuchs, *The Political Behavior of American Jews*, Glencoe, Ill., Free Press. 1956.

Q. Why were so few German Jewish refugees admitted to the U.S., even after Hitler's accession to power in 1933?

A. A series of restrictions on immigration were entered into American law by the middle 1920's, slowing the vast immigration wave to a trickle. In 1930, under pressure of the great economic Depression, President Hoover ordered very strict enforcement of the laws. FDR continued the practice; for example, only 2732 German Jews were admitted in 1933 and 11,352 in 1937. The Jews of America protested but feebly, many fearing that helping new refugees under the existing social and economic conditions would be too great a burden. Indeed, Jews were already meeting increased discrimination in the job market, sometimes from Jewish employers. All this despite economists' arguments that immigration actually increased, not decreased employment.

Even after Germany's takeover of Austria in 1938, American public feeling was still heavily opposed to relaxing the immigration restrictions. Bills by Jewish congressmen Emanuel Celler and Samuel Dickstein that aimed at easing the restrictions had to be tabled. Jewish organizations generally remained inactive, their spokesmen continuing to defend themselves uncomfortably against anticipated accusations that they wished to loosen the restrictions. Jews feared that they would be seen by other Americans as trying to push the U.S. into war to save European Jews and that immigration would evoke a strong anti-Semitic reaction. Even the landsmanschaften groups, which had maintained close ties through the years with their home towns in the old country, said little now about Jewish immigration to America. There was occasional mention of placing a few colonies of Jewish immigrants in Australia, Baja de California, Alaska, and other places. Rabbi Stephen S. Wise once suggested the Dominican Republic, which in fact did admit 500 families.

By the late 1930's, many Jews feared that more Jewish immigration would stir up anti-Semitism at a time when it was growing in any case. In fact, American opposition to immigration was probably rooted more in traditional isolationism than in anti-Semitism per se. American Jews did not want to be identified with refugees. The B'nai B'rith had suggested in 1937 that many refugees be moved out of the New York City area so that they would be less visible.

For Further Reading:

David Brody "American Jewry, the Refugees and the Immigration Restriction (1932–1942)" *PAJHS*, XLV, 1956. 219–247.
John Higham, "Social Discrimination Against Jews in America," *PAJHS*, XLVII, 1957, 1–33.

Q. What was the relationship between gangster Dutch Schultz and Arthur Flegenheimer?

A. Arthur Flegenheimer was the birth name of Dutch Schultz, the notorious mobster (1902–35). Schultz was raised in a Jewish family in Manhattan but would later say that his parents were not at all religious and had never taken him to a synagogue. Apparently, Schultz's father deserted the family early.

Though Schultz started with petty crimes, by the late 1920's he developed a large criminal organization that thrived in the numbers rackets, Prohibition liquor, and gang violence in New York. Schultz was not without intellectual interests, supposedly having read Shakespeare and Plato, but he could also personally shoot a man in cold blood.

Although accused of a number of crimes and referred to as Public Enemy # 1 by FBI head J. Edgar Hoover, Schultz managed to stay out of jail. However, in October, 1935, he was seriously wounded in a Newark restaurant by gunmen from the Syndicate. Three of Schultz's henchmen died, riddled with bullets. Schultz's wound, though less serious, became infected. Beginning to fail quickly, he called for Father McInerny. The priest baptized him into the Catholic faith and administered the last rites of the church.

Several articles in Catholic publications debated whether a man like Schultz should have been admitted to the church. "If a guy like that can go to Heaven," remarked one writer, "there won' t be anyone in Hell."

For Further Reading:

Paul Sann, *Kill the Dutchman*, New Rochelle, NY; Arlington House, 1971.

Q. Why did the United States participate in the 1936 Olympics in Nazi Germany despite strong protests at home?

A. The 1936 Olympics are remembered today, primarily, for the heroics of track star Jesse Owens and the embarrassment he brought to Hitler as an Afro-American winning out over Aryan "superman" athletes. In fact, many people opposed sending any American team to Germany at all, as this would have implied acceptance of Hitler's racial policies. The one most responsible for pushing U.S. participation was Avery Brundage, a man for whom sports and personal ego were far more important than morality and humanity.

A former Olympic runner himself (Stockholm, 1912), and president of the American Olympic Committee in 1935, Brundage had visited Hitler's Germany and fooled himself into believing Hitler's promises that Germany's Jews would be allowed to participate freely in the games. The AOC's failure to take an anti-Nazi stand led to an increasing swell of protest from many sides, but Brundage stood firm. In late 1935, Germany announced that there would be two Jews on its team. One was Gretel Bergmann, a high jumper from Stuttgart, by then living in England. The second was Helene Meyer, a fencer living in Oakland, California, whose mother was not Jewish. Brundage's associate, General Charles Sherill, proclaimed this a major concession by the Nazis. Many important people and organizations including the NAACP, Mayor LaGuardia of New York, and even Father Charles Coughlin went on record against U.S. participation in the games. But Brundage ruled the Olympic Committee with an iron hand, accusing his opponents of using the Games as a weapon in their opposition to Nazism.

The U.S. ultimately did send a team to the 1936 Olympics — to a stadium which was only half an hour's drive from the Oranienburg Concentration

Camp. Hitler and Nazi Germany gained great prestige, having perpetrated a major con job on the world with the help of Mr. Brundage.

Brundage went on to bigger and better things, becoming president of the International Olympic Committee in 1952, where his insensitivity and inhumanity continued to alienate well meaning people. In Munich, at the 1972 Olympics, Brundage pushed the continuation of the games. despite the murder of 11 Israeli athletes by terrorists. At the memorial service, he tactlessly and publicly criticized African countries that were disturbed about the presence of a team from White- ruled Rhodesia.

Two other disturbing incidents occurred at the 1936 Olympics. At the 400 meter relay, the two Jewish runners on the American team, Martin Glickman and Sam Stoller, were replaced at almost the last minute by Coach Dan Cromwell, who explained only that he expected some sort of surprise from the German team. If Cromwell's act was not anti-Semitic, it was certainly at least highly insensitive in the atmosphere of the times.

In a second perturbing incident, Helene Mayer, the half Jewish California fencer who represented Germany, won a silver medal after a classic match with Austrian Ellen Preis. When Mayer was presented her medal she stood proud and tall and saluted her Fuhrer and his citizens with a Heil Hitler salute.

For Further Reading:

Richard Mandell, *The Nazi Olympics,* Urbana; University of Illinois Press, 1987.
Duff Hart-Davis, *Hitler's Games: The 1936 Olympics,* NY; Harper & Row 1976.

Q. Who was FDR's first ambassador to France?

A. Jesse Straus, son of Isidor Straus of Macy's, had managed the Temporary Emergency Relief Administration in New York for Governor Franklin D. Roosevelt in 1931. He was one of the few major businessmen to support Roosevelt's first presidential campaign in 1932. This entitled Straus to a reward, but there were already 3 New Yorkers in the new cabinet. FDR thought of naming him ambassador to Germany, where Hitler had just come to power. Instead, he sent Straus to France. Anti-Semitism was rising all over Europe in the 1930's, and France, like other countries was rent by social and political unrest. Straus relished his duties as ambassador, mixing with the high society of all the world. However, he was criticized for showing no public reaction to Hitler's growing atrocities in Germany or other outbreaks of anti-Semitism in Europe. He complained privately that activists like R. Stephen S. Wise were causing trouble for the Jews, that they made the Jews seem a separate race which could never be a part of any country in which they lived.

For Further Reading:

Naomi Cohen, *A Dual Heritage: The Public Career of Oscar S. Straus,* Philadelphia, JPS, 1964.

Reginald Kauffman, "Jesse Isidor Straus: A Biographical Portrait," New York, privately printed, 1973.

Q. Did American Jews fight in the Spanish Civil War of 1936–39?

A. The Spanish Civil War, fought between Loyalist supporters of the new democratic government and Francisco Franco's Fascist oriented rebels, helped set the stage for the Second World War, which began shortly afterward. Young Americans were drawn by the Loyalist fight for freedom, and they formed the Abraham Lincoln Brigade which served in Spain on the Loyalist side.

About 6300 American Jews joined up and fought in many battles, suffering 217 killed and many wounded. Jews from Eastern Europe, France, and Palestine also fought in the Loyalist armies, in one case forming a Yiddish speaking unit. Ironically, Franco himself probably had Jewish ancestry on both sides of his family, and he was helpful to Jews on several occasions, especially during World War II.

For Further Reading:

UJE. IX. 612.

Q. Who was the founder of the House Committee on UnAmerican Activities?

A. The roster of the House Committee on UnAmerican Activities has featured the names of leading anti-Communist, anti-New Deal, racist head hunters, like John Rankin, Karl Mundt, and J. Parnell Thomas, who usually included lots of uninhibited Jew baiting in their repertoires.

Congressman Samuel Dickstein, who represented a largely Jewish district in New York City, was concerned about both communist and Nazi subversive activities in the U.S. In January, 1934, after Hitler's rise to power in Germany, Dickstein founded the congressional committee to investigate Nazis in the U.S. The Dickstein Committee, as it was often called, formed with Representative John McCormack (Dem. Massachusetts) as its chairman and Dickstein as vice-chairman.

In 1937, Dickstein introduced a resolution to widen the scope of the committee to probe all "un-American activities." The proposal failed to pass, partially because some congressmen felt that Dickstein was too interested in personal publicity. Some months later, after the Austrian *anschluss*, the Sudeten crisis, and the growth of Nazi organizations in the U.S., a comparable resolution proposed by Martin Dies (Dem-Texas) passed with the support of the House leadership.

The Dies Committee, which began its work in August, 1938, was populist and reactionary, and Dickstein was not on it. The Committee went on to a long career of investigating suspected Communists, and harassing highly liberal intellectuals, writers, artists, and show people, a far cry from Dickstein's original intentions. Dickstein served in Congress from 1923–1945 and then sat on the Supreme Court of the State of New York.

For Further Reading
Walter Goodman. *The Committee*. NY: Farrar, Strauss and Giroux, 1968.

Q. Why did Rabbi Abba Hillel Silver become a Republican?

A. Reform Rabbi Abba Hillel Silver (1893–1963) was an ardent and outspoken Zionist and a devotee of Hebrew language and literature in an era when Reform Judaism was, as yet, neither Zionist nor Hebraist. A dominating orator, Silver started out as a Democrat in politics, and he supported Franklin Roosevelt, although quietly, in 1932 and 1936. However, by 1940, Silver felt that the country needed a change, and he endorsed Republican Wendell Wilkie against FDR's bid for a third term. Again, Silver was moving against the current of increasing Jewish support for FDR. By 1942, Silver openly challenged the sincerity of Roosevelt's assurances to the Jews about both Palestine and the atrocities in Europe. In 1944, the Republicans invited Rabbi Silver to give the benediction at their convention.

For Further Reading;
Marc L. Raphael, *Abba Hillel Silver*, New York; Holmes and Meier Publishers, 1989.

Q. How did the big Jewish American gangsters of the 1930's feel about Nazis?

A. At least two of them, Meyer Lansky and Benjamin "Bugsy" Siegel, loathed the Nazis. Lansky was once quoted as saying, "I was a Jew and I felt for those Jews in Europe who were suffering. They were my brothers." Lansky organized attacks against Nazi Bund meetings in the United States.

In 1938, on a visit to Rome, Bugsy Siegel found out that Joseph Goebbels and Hermann Goering were his fellow guests at the villa of one of Siegel's lovers, Countess Dorothy Di Frasso. He fully intended to 'rub them out' but was dissuaded by the countess. It is told that he always regretted not doing so. Both Lansky and Siegel were suspected by FBI leader J. Edgar Hoover of being involved in a plot to assassinate Adolph Hitler, but investigations turned up nothing.

For Further Reading:

Robert Rockaway, *But — He Was Good To His Mother: The Lives and Crimes of Jewish Gangsters.* Jerusalem, Geffen Publ., 1993.

Q. How Jewish was Fiorello LaGuardia?

A. The former Manhattan Congressman (1917–21, 1923–33), mayor of New York (1934–1945), and fighter for the rights of the underdog and the underprivileged, never thought of himself as a Jew. However, he was of highly distinguished Jewish ancestry. His mother, Irene Coen, born in Trieste in 1859, was the daughter of Fiorina Luzzatto, scion of a Sephardic Jewish family that produced luminaries like Rabbi Moshe Chaim Luzzatto, Shmuel David Luzzatto, and Italian Prime Minister, Luigi Luzzatti.

Irene Coen and her husband, Achilles Luigi Carlo LaGuardia, a non-practicing Italian Catholic, came to America in 1880. Although Irene identified herself as Jewish, she was very Italian in culture and ran her home as an Italian. Strangely, Luigi taught the children Hebrew prayers out of respect for his wife.

Fiorello's sister, Gemma, became a practicing Protestant. Yet, she married a Hungarian Jew with whom she moved to Budapest. She kept a kosher home and raised her children as Jewish even while continuing to attend a Protestant church. She and her husband ultimately shared the fate of millions of European Jews of the 1930's and 40's. They were imprisoned in a concentration camp where he perished. Gemma was liberated by her illustrious brother Fiorello.

"Little Flower," as the five foot mayor was known, had a facility for languages. He spoke about seven of them well, including Yiddish, and was always popular with the voters, especially the Jews.

For Further Reading:

Arthur Mann, *LaGuardia: A Fighter Against His Times,* New York, J.B. Lippincott and Co., 1959

Q. What was the Barnwell Ring?

A. The name was given to a group of several politicians out of Barnwell, South Carolina, who became leaders in the state government in the late 1930's. Perhaps the most prominent of these was Solomon Blatt, son of poor Russian immigrants who settled in Blackville, SC in 1893.

Sol Blatt was elected to the SC House of Representatives in 1933 and served as its Speaker from 1937-1973, (except for 1947-1951, during Strom Thurmond's governorship). A great believer in sound fiscal policy, Blatt opposed the excessive patronage that often characterized Southern state governments of that era. In the 1930's, the Barnwell Ring led a tough fight to keep the state Highway Department fair and honest. This was extremely important inasmuch as the designation of new highway routes could mean prosperity or stagnation for a town.

Blatt gained the deep respect of his colleagues in the House and was honored by them several times. Once, when the Anderson Independent made a sneering reference to Blatt's Judaism, the House voted a resolution of confidence in their Speaker. Blatt's first run for a seat in the legislature failed, and there may have been some anti-Semitism involved but, in general, Blatt's religion posed no hindrance to him even in the early days when he was the only Jew in the legislature.

Like many southerners of his time, Blatt held a rather paternalistic attitude toward Blacks, but South Carolina accepted integration when it came, more easily than most parts of the South, for which Blatt's admirers give him much of the credit.

For Further Reading:

John Cauthen, *Speaker Blatt,* Columbia, University of South Carolina Press, 1976.
Eli Evans, *The Provincials. A Personal History of Jews in the South,* New York, Athenaeum,1973

Q. Edgar A. Guest wrote a poem to honor a great Jewish baseball player who did not play on Yom Kippur, although his team was involved in a hot pennant race. Who was the player?

A. Hank Greenberg, a nice Jewish boy from New York, became one of major league baseball's greatest sluggers, once hitting 58 home runs in a season. In 1934, his Detroit Tigers were in a close race for the pennant as the High Holidays approached. Although not especially observant, Greenberg hesitated about playing on Rosh Hashana. After some soul searching, he decided to play and hit two home runs in a 2–1 victory over the Boston Red Sox. When he mentioned his guilt feelings to teammate Marv Owen after the game, Owen replied that he would be glad to suffer some guilt any time he could hit two home runs.

The next week, on the afternoon before Yom Kippur, Greenberg hit another home run and as he rounded the bases. the fans called out to him, "It's okay Hank. You can take the day off tomorrow." Greenberg did not play on Yom Kippur, spending the day in the synagogue instead. This story, along with Edgar Guest's poem honoring Greenberg, have became part of baseball lore.

SPEAKING OF GREENBERG
by Edgar A. Guest

The Irish didn't like it when they heard of Greenberg's fame
For they thought a good first baseman should possess
an Irish name;
And the Murphys and Mulrooneys said they never dreamed they'd see
A Jewish boy from Bronxville out where Casey used to be.
In the early days of April not a Dugan tipped his hat
Or prayed to see a "double" when Hank *Greenberg came to bat.*
In .July the Irish wondered where he'd ever learned to play.
"He makes me think of Casey!" Old Man Murphy dared
to say;
And with fifty -seven doubles and a score of homers made
The respect they had for Greenberg was being openly displayed.
But on the Jewish New Year when Hank Greenberg came to bat
And made two home runs off Pitcher Rhodes they cheered like mad for
that.
Came Yom Kippur holy fast day world wide over to the Jew.
And Hank Greenberg to his teaching and *the old tradition true*
Spent the day among his people and he didn't come To play.
Said Murphy to Mulrooney , "We shall lose *the game today !*
We shall miss him on the infield and shall miss *him At the bat,*
But he's true to his religion
and I honor him for that!"

Perhaps no ballplayer ever made the impact on Detroiters, both Jewish and Gentile, that Greenberg did, both as a great ballplayer and as a fine human being.

For Further Reading:

Ira Berkow. ed. Hank Greenberg, *The Story of My Life*, New York, Times Books, 1989.

Q. What unusual change did writer Samuel Hoffenstein make on the script of a Tarzan movie?

A. Samuel Hoffenstein, a poet who did some Hollywood screenwriting in the 1930's and 1940's was asked to rework the script for a new Tarzan movie and to give it a more original twist. Finding little to improve in the text, he fulfilled his orders by returning some weeks later with the entire script translated into Yiddish.

For Further Reading:

Peter Hay, *Movie Anecdotes*, New York, Oxford University Press, 1990.

Q. Did American Jews contribute money to Hitler?

A. Unfortunately, a few Jews, including one prominent manufacturer who shall here remain nameless, were fooled into believing, at least in the early 1930's, that Hitler would bring stability to Germany and that he would leave the Jews alone. In Germany itself, Jews had a long tradition of patriotism, and many were decorated for valor in World War I. A Jewish organization in Germany called the Schwarz Fahne (Black Flag) foolishly supported the Nazi regime for some time.

Q. Were the Roosevelts really Jews?

A. It was great sport in the 1930's and 40's for enemies of FDR, if they were also Jew-haters, to proclaim that the Roosevelts were actually Jews named Rosenberg or Rosenfeld. Reasonable people always laughed off the charge as ridiculous. Strangely enough, it is quite possible that the Roosevelts were, in fact, descended from Dutch or Sephardic Jews, who migrated to these shores in the 17th century.

Jewish journalist, Philip Slomowitz wrote that a New Jersey congressman and a senator from Michigan both claimed that they had heard from Theodore Roosevelt that his ancestors were Jewish. A friend of Eleanor Roosevelt told Slomowitz that, according to Eleanor Roosevelt, nothing irked Franklin's mother as much as being reminded of her Jewish antecedents.

For Further Reading:

Philip Slomowitz. *Purely Commentary,* Detroit; Wayne State University Press. 1981.

Q. Was Eleanor Roosevelt anti-Semitic?

A. As a young woman growing up in the gentile aristocracy of New York, Eleanor Roosevelt shared, some of the anti-Jewish prejudices of her class. In 1918, when her husband Franklin first brought home Felix Frankfurter, the distinguished Jewish legal scholar, she sensed his brilliance, but was bothered by what she considered his Jewish mannerisms. She was appalled as well by the "Jew party" given for Bernard Baruch that she had to attend that same year. Her biographer, Joseph Lash, noted that her letters of that period contain a number of anti-Semitic remarks.

However, as years went on, Mrs. Roosevelt grew to be one of the kindest and most truly compassionate people in American political life, a great benefactor and ardent worker both for the Jewish refugees of World War II and for the State of Israel.

For Further Reading:

Joseph P. Lash, *Eleanor and Franklin*, New York, W.W. Norton and Co., 1971, and *Eleanor:The Years Alone*, NY, W.W. Norton, 1972.

Q. Who was Irving Lahrheim?

A. Lahrheim was the given name of famed comedian Bert Lahr. Lahr's father Jacob was one of those German American Jews who hated all religions. Devoted to his wonderful new country, the U.S.A., he was still very German in culture and thought. Young Irving spoke German with his parents as a young child, but his father stopped using German in the house when the U.S. entered World War I.

Lahr began his show business career with a few friends, as a black face street singer, on Wilkins Street in the Bronx. Among his most famous roles were the Cowardly Lion in Wizard of Oz and one of the fathers in The Fantastiks. He acted with most of the great comic actors of his day - Beatrice Lillie, Ed Wynn and Claudette Colbert.

For Further Reading:

John Lahr. *Notes on the Cowardly Lion,* NY: Knopf, 1969.

Q. Who built the Golden Gate Bridge?

A. Joseph Strauss (1870-1938), head of the Strauss Engineering Corporation, is best known for constructing San Francisco's Golden Gate Bridge. Opened in 1937, it was the longest single span suspension bridge in the world until 1964. In all, Strauss participated in the building of over 500 bridges in North America and Europe, including the George Washington Bridge across the Hudson River in New York City and the Arlington Memorial Bridge, which crosses the Potomac at Washington D.C.

Another well-known American Jew, Admiral Joseph Strauss (1861-1948), fought in the navy during the Spanish-American War and in the First World War commanded the mine force of the Atlantic Fleet. In 1921, he was named head of the United States' Asiatic Fleet. He was noted for his scientific brilliance and was one of the navy's foremost ordnance experts.

For Further Reading:

UJE, X, 82-83.
DAB, suppl. II, 636-637.
NYT Dec. 31, 1948, p.15.
Newsweek, Jan. 10, 1949, XXXIII, 54.

Q. How did the modern U.S. Jewish day school movement develop?

A. There were Jewish day schools in a number of American cities in the 1840's and 50's, but they all closed within a few years as public schools became widespread. The modern Jewish day school movement began when Eastern European immigrants poured into New York in the 1880's. The first day school, Eitz Chaim, opened in New York in 1886. However, progress was slow and by 1920, there were still only a few schools. Most Jewish leaders, including some prominent Reform rabbis, preferred public schools, arguing that afternoon or Sunday schools were adequate for Jewish learning. And parents generally agreed.

In the 1930's, the number of day schools began to increase significantly. By 1940, there were 7,700 students in 35 schools. In 1950, 23,000 students attended 139 schools. By 1976, 4600 schools taught 85,000 students. The number continues to grow. All the day schools were Orthodox, until Conservative oriented schools, some under the name Solomon Schechter, began to open in the late 1950's.

Studies have made clear that the double curriculum of the day schools produced graduates who were on the whole strong both academically and in their commitment to Judaism. Professor Alvin Schiff, in his book, *The Jewish Day School in America,* offers several reasons for the spurt of day schools which began in the 1940's; dedicated and able leaders like Rabbi Shraga Feivel Mendlowitz and Zev Gold, and a number of rabbinic scholars fleeing the Nazis; Orthodox refugees who wanted Jewish education for their children. Decline of the 3 day a week afternoon schools: increased concern about conditions in the public schools; recognition of the accomplishments of day schools by Jewish leaders of all sorts all had their effect.

For Further Reading:

Alvin I. Schiff, *The Jewish Day School In America,* NY: Jewish Educational Committee Press, 1966.

Q. What famous Viennese-Jewish conductor was rescued from the Nazis by LBJ?

A. In 1938, a young Erich Leinsdorf had completed an engagement as conductor with the Metropolitan Opera in New York and was staying on in the U.S. with some friends. One day it dawned upon him that his temporary visa had almost expired and that his application for an extension had not yet been answered.

His hosts decided to approach an aggressive young congressman from Texas with whom they were acquainted, Lyndon Baines Johnson. Johnson immediately began work in the same effective, thorough style that he would employ in running the U.S. Senate and the White House years later.

First, he found out that Leinsdorf's application had, indeed, been rejected. But, for some reason, the rejection slip had not been mailed. LBJ took advantage of the clerical oversight by replacing "You have seven days to leave the U.S." in the letter with "You have six months."

The congressman then proceeded to have Leinsdorf's status changed to "permanent resident." This was done by the device of having the conductor go abroad, in this case to Cuba, and then return to the U.S. as a regular immigrant. Of course, Johnson meticulously checked to make sure that Leinsdorf had all the necessary documentation. Leinsdorf went on to a distinguished career as conductor of the New York City Opera, the Boston Symphony and other major American orchestras.

For Further Reading:

Robert A. Caro. *The Path to Power: The Years of Lyndon Johnson.* New York, Alfred A. Knopf. 1982.

Q. What U.S. Congressman was literally killed by an anti-Semitic diatribe in the House of Representatives?

A. In June, 1941, Congressman Michael Edelstein (D-NY) died of a heart attack in the lobby of the House of Representatives after trying to refute an anti-Semitic harangue by John Rankin (D-Miss) on the House floor. Rankin was the most anti-Semitic member of Congress at that time, and he did nothing to hold back his venom. In 1944, also in the House, he referred to a Jewish columnist as "that little kike."

For Further Reading:
New York Times June 4, 1941.

Q. What was Charles Lindbergh's controversial Des Moines speech?

A. Charles A. Lindbergh flew to international adoration when he became the first to solo pilot a plane across the Atlantic Ocean, New York to Paris, on May 21, 1927. A brilliant pilot with a good practical knowledge of aviation science, Lindbergh was less able in his politics, and through the 1930's he managed to lend his name into some unpleasant associations.

Visiting Nazi Germany several times in the late 1930's, Lindbergh became convinced that Germany had the military ability to destroy France and Great Britain, and he hoped that the U.S. would stay out of any European war. A general war, he said, might entirely destroy White European civilization. In 1938, two weeks after the Munich Pact, he naively accepted a medal from Luftwaffe chief Hermann Goering and planned to spend the winter of 1938–39 in Berlin.

Although not usually a pacifist, Lindbergh became a leader of the isolationists in the U.S., often speaking at rallies of the America First party. He was criticized sharply by prominent Americans like Secretary of the Interior Harold Ickes, who called him a "Number one Nazi fellow traveler."

Three months before the attack on Pearl Harbor, at an America First rally in Des Moines, Iowa, Lindbergh charged that "the three most important groups who have been pressing this country toward war are the British, the Jewish, and the Roosevelt administration. He discussed these groups in some detail, concluding that they were trying to create a series of incidents which would force the U.S. into the war.

The Des Moines speech touched off an explosion of criticism at Lindbergh and probably did more harm than good to the isolationist cause. Lindbergh's own mother-in-law, Constance Morrow, spoke out strongly and publicly against Lindbergh and her daughter, authoress Anne Morrow.

At Des Moines, Lindbergh also stated that "No person with a sense of the dignity of mankind can condone the persecution of the Jewish race in Germany. But no person of honesty and vision can look on their pro-war policy here today without seeing the dangers involved in such a policy, both for them and for us." Lindbergh was undoubtedly sincere in deploring the Nazi persecution of the Jews but, at the same time, he admired the German accomplishments and sense of order, and he could not understand why they had to be so "unreasonable" (Lindbergh's diary for November, 1938) about the Jews.

The Des Moines speech also aroused some of the anti-Semites in the U.S., and letters came into newspapers and public organizations for some days praising Lindbergh's courage in speaking up against the Jews. Radical isolationist Senator Gerald P. Nye of North Dakota publicly defended him. In 1944, at age 42, Lindbergh went to the Pacific as a civilian technical representative for United Aircraft Co. and, in that capacity, flew fifty combat missions. He also made some important technical suggestions which the Air Force used to good effect in its tactics against Japan.

For Further Reading:

Wayne S. Cole, *Charles A. Lindbergh and the Battle Against American Intervention in World War II*, NY; Harcourt, Brace & Jovanovich, 1974.
Walter S. Ross, *The Last Hero: Charles A.Lindbergh* NY: Harper & Row Publishers, 1968.

Q. What happened to famous author Emil Ludwig's history of B'nai B'rith?

A. In his day, Emil Ludwig was well known for biographies of Napoleon Bonaparte, Cleopatra, and other famous historical figures. B'nai B'rith hired him to write a history of the organization in honor of its centennial in 1943. However, Ludwig's first 3 chapters were deemed unsatisfactory by President Henry Monsky and his associates. They claimed that Ludwig did not seem to know much about B'nai B'rith or about Judaism, and they canceled the contract. A number of attempts over the years to write a history of B'nai B'rith failed until Edward Grusd published his volume in 1966.

For Further Reading:

Edward Grusd, *Bnai Brith: Story of A Covenant,* New York, Appleton Century, 1960.

Q. Why did a group of Jews approach Felix Frankfurter to persuade him to refuse his appointment to the U.S. Supreme Court?

A. President Franklin Roosevelt nominated Felix Frankfurter to replace Benjamin Cardozo on the U.S. Supreme Court in 1939. A Harvard law professor and an important presidential advisor, Frankfurter nevertheless faced some nasty questioning from Senator Pat McCarran of Nevada in the Senate hearings. McCarran even claimed that Frankfurter was not a U.S. citizen.

Many Jews felt that with the pressures inside the U.S. and the growing threat of war from Europe, this was not an opportune time to appoint a Jew to a high office. A number of Jewish leaders, headed by Arthur Hays Sulzberger, publisher of the New York Times, urged FDR not to appoint Frankfurter. A delegation went to Frankfurter personally to ask him to refuse the nomination. "So you would create your own ghetto," he told them. Within the Roosevelt administration, Harry Hopkins, Robert Jackson, and Harold Ickes strongly supported Frankfurter's nomination, as did Senator George Norris of Nebraska and Justice Harlan Fiske Stone. Ickes told Roosevelt that Frankfurter's "ability and learning are such that he will dominate the Supreme Court for 15 to 20 years to come."

For Further Reading:

Joseph P. Lash, *From the Diaries of Felix Frankfurter,* New York, W.W. Norton, 1975.
Liva Baker, *Felix Frankfurter,* New York, Coward Mccann, 1969.

Q. What problem did actor Danny Kaye encounter at his first screen test?

A. In 1942, movie mogul Sam Goldwyn saw a young Danny Kaye in a stage play in New York and signed him to a movie contract without even giving him a screen test. When Kaye came to Hollywood and took his first screen test, Goldwyn was horrified. From every camera angle, Kaye's nose seemed as long as Pinocchio's. And though Goldwyn did not want to say it, Kaye looked too Jewish.

A proud man, Goldwyn would not admit that he had made a mistake in signing Kaye. He spent an entire night arguing with himself and with his wife trying to solve the problem of Kaye's nose. The next morning at the studio, Goldwyn suddenly jumped up yelling, "I've got it." He had Kaye's hair dyed blond instead of its natural dark reddish-brown. The blond hair indeed seemed to draw attention away from the nose and gave Kaye a Scandinavian look. Kaye went on to a successful career as a very popular entertainer.

The story typifies the mood of a Hollywood in which there were many Jews who could be and were known as Jews, but where Jewishness still had to be soft keyed and sanitized.

For Further Reading:

Stephen Birmingham, *The Rest of Us*, Boston, Little, Brown and Co. 1984, p. 258 f.

Q. There is an inspiring story of the bravery of four chaplains during World War II. Were any of them Jewish?

A. Alexander D. Goode was the first of several Jewish chaplains who died in the line of duty during World War II. In February, 1943, Goode sailed aboard the troopship Dorchester along with three Christian chaplains. When the ship was torpedoed in the North Atlantic, four chaplains gave their lifebelts to soldiers who did not have them. Soldiers reported seeing the chaplains praying arm in arm as the ship sank. The story became a symbol of the devotion of American chaplains to their men. In all, 262 Jewish chaplains served in the army, and 43 in the navy during the war. Two were at Pearl Harbor when it was bombed, six landed with the soldiers at the Normandy beaches on D-Day, and three served in the fighting at Iwo Jima. Alexander Goode was posthumously awarded the Distinguished Service Cross.

For Further Reading:

Louis Barish, ed., *Rabbis in Uniform*, NY: Jonathan David Publ., 1962.

Q. What American poet broadcast anti-American and anti-Semitic messages during World War II?

A. A descendant of early New England settlers, Ezra Pound (1885–1972) was one of America's best known poets by the 1910's. However, despite his poetic brilliance, his thinking in other areas was disturbed and murky. Settling in Italy in 1924, he began to read a great deal of anti-Semitic literature, and by the late 1930's was convinced that Jews were responsible for many of the world's problems. His writings contain a number of anti-Semitic attacks. From 1941–1943, he presented regular broadcasts over Italian radio in which he praised Hitler and Mussolini, abused Franklin Roosevelt and viciously and wildly attacked the Jews who, he claimed, controlled and degraded both the U.S. and Great Britain.

Pound was indicted for treason and arrested by the U.S. in 1945, but he was declared insane and not brought to trial. Instead, he spent 12 years in St. Elizabeth's, a mental institution in Washington D.C. While there, he was awarded the prestigious Bollingen Prize for his *Pisan Cantos*. The award touched off a furious protest from those who believed that Pound's behavior made him unworthy of honor. In 1972, he was denied the Emerson Thoreau Medal of the American Academy of Arts and Sciences.

For Further Reading:

Clemens D. Heymann, *Ezra Pound: The Last Rower A Political Profile*, NY: Viking Press. 1976.
Noel Stack, *The Life of Ezra Pound*, NY: Pantheon Books, 1976.

Q. For which Chinese leaders did Moshe Avraham Cohen serve as bodyguard?

A. Morris "Two Gun" Cohen had a most unusual career. Born in London, England, to an Orthodox family, he moved to Canada, where some Chinese friends recommended him to Chinese leader Sun Yat Sen as a bodyguard. Blessed with a sharp mind as well as a strong physique, Cohen soon became one of Sun's leading financial advisors. He went on to serve Sun's successor, Chiang Kai Shek, who named Cohen a general in the Chinese army. Cohen began calling himself General Ma, an acronym of his Hebrew name, Moshe Avraham. General Ma was captured by the Japanese, but escaped to Canada. After the war he went to San Francisco as part of the Chinese delegation to the opening conference of the new United Nations. There he helped arouse the Chinese delegates' interest in the Zionist cause.

For Further Reading:

Melvin Urofsky, *We Are One: American Jewry and Israel*, Garden City, New York; Anchor Press/ Doubleday, 1978, p. 99–100.
Charles Drage, *The Life and Times of General Two-Gun Cohen*, New York; Funk and Wagnall, 1954.

Q. Who was the Jewish chaplain on the the River Kwai?

A. The Hollywood movie, *Bridge on the River Kwai,* starring William Holden and Sir Alec Guiness, has its Jewish parallel in the book, *Chaplain On the River Kwai.* The book is Rabbi Chaim Nussbaum's memoir of his captivity in the Japanese prisoner of war camp on the River Kwai in Thailand.

Nussbaum, a Dutch citizen, had been ordained as rabbi in the Telshe Yeshiva in Lithuania and had earned an M.A. in Theoretical Physics at the University of Leiden. When World War II broke out, Nussbaum fled Lithuania, where he was teaching. With his family, he made his way to Java, where he enlisted in the Dutch army as a chaplain. He was taken prisoner there in 1942 when Singapore fell to the Japanese.

During three years in captivity, most of it on the River Kwai, Nussbaum faced the daily experience of life and death in the camp with a unique and sensitive faith formed both in his rabbinic scholarship and in his love of science. Reunited with his family after the war, he lived in Canada and the U.S., where he pursued a fruitful career as an educator and writer.

For Further Reading:

Chaim Nussbaum, *Chaplain on the River Kwai*. N Y : Shapolsky Publishers, 1988.

Q. When General George Patton slapped an American soldier during the Italian campaign in World War II, what anti-Semitic remark did he make?

A. One of the great battle commanders in American military history, General George Patton nevertheless often found himself in trouble of his own making off the battlefield. In 1943, while visiting wounded GI's in a military hospital in Italy, Patton came across a man who had been sent back from the front lines suffering from shell shock, as it was then called. When Patton learned that the soldier's wounds were psychological, not physical, he loudly accused him of cowardice, slapped him with his gloves in the face and kicked him. As the soldier hurried away, Patton said, 'There is no such thing as shell shock. It's an invention of the Jews."

About 20 news correspondents witnessed the incident and agreed not to report the story until General Eisenhower had a chance to respond. Furious with Patton over his treatment of the soldier, Eisenhower forced him to apologize and then asked the reporters as a personal favor, to keep the incident under wraps, which they did. However, 3 months later, columnist Drew Pearson got wind of the story and made it public. Patton survived that and several other instances of personal misbehavior to play an important role in the Allies' ultimate victory in Europe.

There is no doubt that Patton had strong anti-Semitic feelings related, some think, to an incident in his childhood when a bank owed by a Jew foreclosed a mortgage on his father's winery. When he saw Jewish DP's just out of the concentration camps after the war, he openly referred to them as sub-human, and he ignored orders from Washington to remove Nazis from public offices.

For Further Reading:

Martin Blumenson, *Patton*, NY Berkley Books, 1987.
Philip Knightley, *The First Casualty: From The Crimea to Vietnam. The War Correspondent as Hero. Propagandist and Mythmaker*, New York, Harcourt, Brace, Jovanovich, 1975, p.320.

Q. What was the Gillette-Rogers Resolution?

A. In November, 1943, with evidence growing of the destruction of European Jewry, Senator Guy Gillette (D-Iowa) and Rep. Will Rogers Jr. (D Cal) introduced resolutions in Congress urging the creation of a presidential commission to formulate a plan for immediate action to save the surviving Jewish people of Europe. The resolution was prompted and applauded by the Emergency Committee to Save the Jewish People of Europe, the activist group led by Peter Bergson (real name Hillel Kook). It was opposed by established Jewish leaders like Congressman Sol Bloom, who preferred to keep a lower profile and to work through regular channels like the American Jewish Committee.

The resolution quickly and unanimously passed the Senate Foreign Relations Committee and was scheduled for debate in the Senate. However, Congressman Bloom, Chairman of the House Foreign Relations Committee, held up the debate.

Meanwhile, Secretary of the Treasury Henry Morgenthau Jr., won over by a visit from Rabbis Aron Kotler and Avraham Kalmanovitch and perturbed over the indifference of the State Department toward the refugees, went straight to President Roosevelt. FDR created the War Refugee Board by executive order. John Pehle, a trusted assistant of Morgenthau at the Treasury Department, was named the Board's director. This fulfilled the aims of Gillette and Rogers, who then withdrew their bill.

For Further Reading:

Rafael Medoff, *The Deafening Silence*, NY: Shapolsky Publishers, 1987, 131–141.

Q. How much money did the U.S. government allot for opening the famous Manhattan Project?

A. The next time your congressman asks for a multi-million dollar grant for some insignificant idea, remind him that the Atomic Age was launched by a mere $6,000. Late in 1939, famed physicists Edward Teller, Leo Szilard, and Eugene Wigner (all Jewish and all future Nobel or Fermi Prize winners) met with military officials to discuss the formation of a project to develop an atom bomb. Scientific research in that area had progressed in the late 1930's, and American scientists were fearful lest the Nazis build the bomb first.

Teller asked the government for $6,000, which was granted only after months of bickering. This small sum led to the Manhattan Project, which developed the atom bomb in time to force Japan to surrender without a high casualty U.S. invasion. The top-secret project involved about 1000 people, centered mostly in Los Alamos, New Mexico.

The Manhattan Project holds a unique place in Jewish history as well as American history. The group included a number of Jewish scientific geniuses, with a long list of accomplishments.

The project head was J. Robert Oppenheimer (1904–1967), a New York born Jew, who was highly respected as a physicist and equally able as a director of people. Oppenheimer got to know hundreds of the Los Alamos personnel closely and seemed able to get a high level of work out of each one. Knowledgeable in languages, Oppenheimer relaxed by reading Sanskrit literature. Albert Einstein, dean of American scientists, was not included in the Manhattan Project and never set foot in Los Alamos. However, his earlier work contributed mightily to the project's success.

Interestingly, most of the major contributors, Johann "Johnny" Von Neumann, Edward Teller, Leo Szilard, and Eugene Wigner were all born in Hungary. Von Neumann, one of the great mathematical minds of the century, applied his scientific concepts to economics also, and some of his ideas were important in the beginning of computer science.

Author Steve Heims, in his *John Von Neumann and Norbert Wiener*, writes that Hungarian Jews had to deal with an ever present threat of anti-semitism. They felt that they could best protect themselves by achieving as much as they could in their professions. What they stored in their minds would still be useful if they ever had to flee to another country. Laura Fermi, in her book *Illustrious Immigrants* supports this general line of thinking.

Of this group of Manhattan Project physicists, Teller took the strongest interest in Jewish affairs, participating in scientific projects in Israel and lecturing in Israeli universities. Von Neumann, although reputedly of rabbinic ancestry, converted to Catholicism.

For Further Reading:

Stanley A. Blumberg and Gwinn Owens, *Energy and Conflict: The Life and Times of Edward Teller,* New York, G.P. Putnam's Sons, 1976.

Laura Fermi, *Illustrious Immigrants: The Intellectual Migration from Europe, 1930–1941*, Chicago University Press, 1971.
Ronald Clar, *Einstein: The Life and Times*, New York, Avon Books, 1984.
Leslie Groves, *Now It Can Be Told: The Story of the Manhattan Project*, New York, Da Capo Press, Inc., 1983.
Steve Heims, *John Von Neumann and Norbert Weiner: From Mathematics to the Technologies of Life and Death*, MIT Press, 1980.

Q. What was the Fort Ontario camp?

A. The War Refugee Board presented a plan to open up some refugee camps in the U.S., Europe, and North Africa. By the time the restrictionists and anti-Semites in the U.S. State Department were finished with the plan, the U.S. would agree to open only one camp on its own soil, for 1000 people at Fort Ontario, near Oswego, New York.

A group of 982 refugees arrived from southern Italy in August, 1944, in an army troopship. Nine hundred eighteen were Jews, and of that number, about 100 had survived Dachau or Buchenwald. Even this minimal show of interest in war refugees met with sharp criticism and aroused fears that after the war, the refugees would end up staying in the U.S. Columnist Westbrook Pegler warned that these were only the first of a great mass of people that President Roosevelt was planning to bring in.

Living conditions in Fort Ontario were not easy, either physically or emotionally, and internees were allowed out only for short trips into Oswego or for hospital care. The refugees could not work outside the camp. By March, 1945, four internees had been removed to mental institutions, and one had committed suicide. Their widespread depression worsened after Germany surrendered in May 1945, and the inmates began to worry about what would become of them with the arrival of peace. For some inmates, peace might well mean separation from spouses, children, brothers or sisters already living in the US.

In December, 1945, President Truman decided that the Fort Ontario inmates would be allowed to settle in the U.S. as regular immigrants. This was part of a larger plan for the admission of displaced persons into the U.S. Congressman Samuel Dickstein of New York and Secretary of the Interior Harold Ickes had led the effort to win Truman over to this plan. The Fort Ontario camp was empty by early 1946.

For Further Reading:

David Wyman, *The Abandonment of the Jews: America and the Holocaust, 1941–1945*, New York, Pantheon Books, 1984.

Q. How many Jews served in the American armed forces during World War II?

A. Almost 600,000 Jews served. Over 60,000 awards or citations, including the Congressional Medal of Honor, were awarded to Jewish soldiers. There were nineteen Jewish generals, three admirals, and one commodore. One example: Sergeant Abraham Todres from Brooklyn left college to join the Air Force in 1941. In the next four years, he fought on several fronts in the Pacific and Europe, was shot down several times, was taken prisoner by the Germans and escaped, and won 30 medals.

A most poignant story is that of Lieutenant Raymond Zussman, who was serving in the U.S. army in the Rhine Valley in September, 1944. Handling a carbine and later a submachine gun, he killed eighteen German soldiers and captured another ninety-two. He was awarded a Congressional Medal of Honor. The medal was awarded posthumously; Lieutenant Zussman was killed in battle only days after his extraordinary exploit. Zussman's father, a World War I veteran, accepted the award from President Truman.

For Further Reading:

I. Kaufman, *American Jews in World War II*, The Dial Press, 1947.
Eugene Applebaum, *Michigan Jewish History*, March, 1961, p.2–9.

Q. Why did the Nazis not treat captured American Jewish soldiers as they did the Jews of Europe?

A. Late in 1944, a message came through to Rabbi Aron Kotler, a leading Orthodox rabbi and scholar, in his capacity as head of the Vaad Hatzala, saying that the Nazis were going to start separating Jewish prisoners of war from the other Allied POW's, an almost certain death sentence. Having received little help from President Roosevelt in earlier requests to help the Jews of Europe, the Vaad leaders instead approached David Niles, a Jewish assistant to the president.

Niles wisely passed the information on, not to Roosevelt, but to General Dwight Eisenhower, the Allied Commander in Europe. Incensed, Eisenhower prepared a strongly worded message warning the Germans that the Allies knew of their plan and would hold them accountable if it were carried through. The message worked and the Jewish POW's were not separated.

For Further Reading:

Amos Bunim, *Fire In His Soul: Irving M. Bunim*, New York, Feldheim, 1989, p. 122–123.

Q. Who took the famous photograph of the U.S. Marines raising the Stars and Stripes at Iwo Jima?

A. Joseph Rosenthal, (1911–1959), born in Washington DC to Russian Jewish parents, was a combat photographer for the Associated Press. In February, 1945, U.S. Marines took the island of Iwo Jima from the Japanese after bloody fighting, and the Marines raised the stars and stripes on Mt. Suribachi. Rosenthal was on the spot to take the famous photo. It is said that the event was actually restaged shortly after its first actual occurrence, and that Rosenthal's photo is of the restaging.

For Further Reading:

John H. Richter, *Judaica on Postage Stamps*. Ann Arbor; Lithocrafters Inc., 1974.

Q. Who was the commanding officer of the Prisoners of War Interrogation Unit in the American army in World War II?

A. Colonel Eric Warburg, German born American citizen, won a Croix De Guerre from France, the Order of the British Empire, and the American Legion of Merit for his brilliant work in interrogating German prisoners. Eric was the son of Max Warburg whose German family was among the leading bankers in both Germany and the U.S.A. Born in Germany in 1900, Eric Warburg showed little interest in the family bank. In his early twenties he wanted to break free from his roots and he tried to move to Oregon. His New York uncles persuaded him to return to the business world, and he settled in New York.

When the war broke out he discovered in himself a previously untapped skill in interrogation. On one occasion he was faced with a German officer who Warburg was sure had important information. Thirty-five letters from the prisoner's mistress had been found with him. Eric told the man that he would get one letter back every time he gave over some useful information. Otherwise, the letters would be sent to his wife. The German turned pale, "It is not enough,' he cried, "that we will probably lose the war and that I will lose my job as a professional officer. Now you will destroy the last thing that I have — my family life." Warburg was also the first to interrogate Reichsmarshall Hermann Goering after his capture in April, 1945.

With the war ended, the U.S. government asked Warburg to move back to Hamburg and resume his banking career there, hoping that a man of his experience, background, and ability could help bring about smoother relations between former enemies in a difficult post-war world.

A distinguished family of Jewish bankers, the Warburgs traced their roots to Moritz Warburg (1838–1920). Eric's father Max had remained in Germany, when many other Warburgs had moved to New York.

For Further Reading:

David Farrer, *The Warburgs*, New York; Stein and Day, 1975, pp. 186–194.

Q. How did Henry Ford react to the news of the concentration camps of Nazi Germany?

A. When Henry Ford first viewed the uncut just-released films of Majdanek in 1945, it suddenly dawned upon him that it might have some connection to the anti-Semitism spawned by his *Dearborn Independent* newspaper. The shock seemed to disorient him to such an extent that he never really seemed the same afterward.

For Further Reading:

Carol Gelderman, *Henry Ford: The Wayward Capitalist*, New York, St. Martin's Press, 1989.

Q. Which two famous Nazi criminals did Major Henry Plitt capture?

A. Late in May, 1945, several weeks after the war in Europe had ended, U.S. Major Henry Plitt heard that a high ranking Nazi was hiding in a nearby Austrian town. Plitt came to the house and saw a man painting outside. The man's ID card had the initials J.S. "Julius Streicher?" asked Plitt. "Yes, this is me," he answered. Julius Streicher had been the publisher of the *Der Stuermer*, a newspaper vicious and lurid in its anti-Semitism. It was all Plitt could do to refrain from killing him on the spot and instead brought him back for trial. Streicher was later tried at Nuremburg and executed.

On a second occasion, Plitt, following a tip, led a few soldiers to the hiding place of Robert Ley, head of the German Labor Front and likewise a vile anti-Semite. As the Americans burst into his room, Ley reached for a poison pill on the nightstand, but a soldier knocked it out of his hand. Ley claimed to be a schoolteacher, but his true identity was soon revealed. He committed suicide in his cell at Nuremburg.

For Further Reading:

U.S. Holocaust Memorial Council Newsletter, March, 1992, p.6.

1945–1980

Cross-Currents

A NEW ERA BEGAN with the end of World War II. Jewish life in the U.S. in those years can perhaps be best understood in terms of a pattern of cross currents, as people moved from one form of Judaism to another, or into or out of Judaism altogether. Jews were in the forefront of all the great social movements—civil rights, feminism, and the protest against the Vietnam War.

Large numbers of GI's returning from the Second World War prompted a growth of new housing, and Jews moved en masse to the suburbs. Many major cities were empty of Jews by the 1970's. Jews who remained in mixed urban neighborhoods, especially in New York, were occasionally victims of the eruptions of urban tensions involving both individual violence and mob incidents in which synagogues and Jewish buildings were attacked.

Jewish families were caught up with everyone else in the great change in family structure. Family units typically were small, except among the yeshiva oriented. By the 1970's growing numbers of young Jews were not marrying at all, or were marrying out of the faith, and divorce rates grew.

American Jews paid close attention to developments in Israel, visiting and contributing huge sums of money. They watched anxiously as Israel defended itself in a series of wars against intransigent Arab neighbors. For some Jews, Zionism became almost a substitute for religion.

On the religious front, Conservative Judaism reached a peak in the 1950's and 60's, building large synagogues in the growing suburbs. Congregations became increasingly liberal, adopting innovations like bat mitzvah celebration, the triennial Torah reading cycle, and women rabbis. A generation of new young rabbis had fewer links with Orthodox Eastern European antecedents. The old guard at the Jewish Theological Seminary, men like

Louis Ginzberg, Louis Finkelstein, Abraham Joshua Heschel and Saul Lieberman were aging and passing from the scene.

Reform congregations grew both in size and in scope of activity. Reform embraced Zionism by 1948 and began to reintroduce bar mitzvah and to introduce bat mitzvah celebrations to the temples. The rabbi and cantor were more likely to wear a talit, prayer services used more Hebrew, and more congregants prayed with their heads covered. Old German families were still prominent, but the Eastern European families also joined the leadership. The new Reform prayer book, adopted in 1976, reflected both the diversity within Reform and the growing interest in tradition.

Orthodox refugees, who had survived Nazi Europe, brought a new dose of yeshiva educated Jews to the U.S. after World War II, and helped spark the resurgence of day schools and advanced yeshivot. By the 1960's, a new self-confident Orthodoxy began to show itself. Large Hasidic enclaves developed, notably the Lubavitch community in Crown Heights and Satmar in Williamsburg, New York. In the 1950's many traditional synagogues were turning Conservative, but this trend slowed greatly as Orthodoxy reasserted itself.

Jews continued to make important contributions, far out of proportion to their numbers, in many fields. They served in government and, at one point in the 1980's, seven Jews sat in the U.S. Senate.

Q. How did the U.S. government deal with immigration after World War II?

A. After World War II, Europe was filled with people whose lives were totally uprooted. Congress passed a Displaced Persons Act in 1948, as a temporary measure, to allow almost 500,000 refugees to enter the U.S. over the next several years. Sixteen percent of the refugees were Jews. In 1952, the McCarran-Walter Act passed through Congress over President Truman's veto. This long and complicated bill restricted immigration even beyond the laws of the 1920's. Quotas were still based on national origins, and deportations became easier.

A more liberal law proposed by Senators Hubert Humphrey (D-Minn) and Herbert Lehman (D-NY) was rejected, and a proposal by Representative Emanuel Celler (D-NY) to set up a three year emergency program to allow immigration beyond the established quotas was kept in committee. The McCarran-Walter law was strongly supported by anti-alien organizations, by the AFL, which feared competition from new potential workers. The McCarran-Walter Act became an issue in the presidential election campaign of 1952, and both Adlai Stevenson and Dwight Eisenhower spoke out against it. With Eisenhower's support, an emergency law providing for a temporary increase in immigration passed through Congress in July 1953, but the McCarran-Walter Act was not overturned.

For Further Reading:
AJYB, 55. 1954, p. 63-72.

Q. Who nominated a segregationist, Senator Richard Russell, as candidate for president at the Democratic Convention of 1948?

A. Southern Jews, in earlier generations, often shared the segregationist views of their neighbors. Charles J. Bloch (1893-1974), a strong advocate of state's rights, delivered the nominating speech for Georgia Senator Richard Russell at the tense Democratic convention of 1948 in Philadelphia. The Southerners later bolted to form a new party in disagreement with the Democrats' support for Civil Rights. During the racial agitation in Georgia in the 1950's and 1960's, Bloch was often retained as counsel by local governments fighting in the law courts against integration. Long active in politics, Bloch had served in the Georgia legislature in the 1920's where he formed his close friendship with Richard Russell. In 1958 he wrote *State's Rights: the Law of the L*and.

For Further Reading:
Atlanta Constitution, August 27, 1974,
Harry Golden. *Our Southern Landsman.* NY; F.P. Putnam's. 1974.

Q. Did American Jewish gangsters help in the founding of the State of Israel in 1948?

A. Judaism has certainly never glorified criminality. Yet, it is clear that at least on occasion, Jewish gangsters have stuck up for their people. In 1948, the Jews of Israel were desperate to acquire funds and military supplies to help defend themselves against the treacherous attacks by their Arab neighbors. Historian Robert Rockaway wrote in an article for the Jerusalem Post that some of these men did in fact help out. One night, an Israeli emissary was brought to a clandestine meeting in a basement in Baltimore. A sinister group of men were cajoled by the host until within a few minutes the emissary walked out of the house with $90,000 in a paper bag. Meyer Lansky prevailed on his associates who controlled the docks in New York and New

Jersey to smuggle shipments of illegal arms through to Israel, no questions asked.

In 1946, Bugsy Siegel, notorious crime boss of Las Vegas, sent a suitcase filled with small bills every week to a Haganah representative to a total of about $50,000. Rockaway argues that perhaps these criminals still felt some need to be accepted by the Jewish community.

There were exceptions. Two Detroit Jews were convicted in a conspiracy to sell American airplanes to Egypt during the 1948 War.

For Further Reading:

Robert Rockaway, *But they Were Good to their Mothers*, Jerusalem, Geffen, 1993

Q. How is it that there is a Torah scroll in the Truman presidential library in Independence, Missouri?

A. Shortly after the founding of the State of Israel, its first president, Chaim Weizmann, came to the U.S. and visited President Harry Truman in Washington D.C. In line with a very old custom and in gratitude for Truman's quick recognition of the new state, Weizmann presented him with a Scroll of the Torah. Truman was taken by surprise, not having been previously informed about the gift. Very pleased nevertheless, Truman accepted the scroll with a smile, not knowing which way was right side up, and he said to Weizmann, "Gee. I've always wanted to have one of these." This is the Scroll that now rests in a fine Holy Ark in the Truman Library.

Bernard Postal, in his *American Jewish Landmarks,* tells that the Torah Scroll had originally been given as a bar-mitzvah present to Ezra Finkelstein, son of Dr. Louis Finkelstein, of the Jewish Theological Seminary, who suggested to Weizmann to present it to President Truman. On other occasions, David Ben Gurion sent Truman an 18th century menorah, and Israel Chief Rabbi Isaac Herzog sent three ancient glass vessels bearing symbols of the twelve tribes of Israel.

For Further Reading:

Bernard Postal. *American Jewish Landmarks*. NY Fleet Press Corp. 1977, III, 87.

Q. Did Congressman John F. Kennedy support the establishment of the State of Israel in 1947–1948?

A. Boston lawyer Lew Weinstein had worked for the young John F. Kennedy in his first campaign for a Congressional seat in 1946. In June 1947, with the United Nations getting ready to make a decision on the future of British ruled Palestine, Weinstein invited Kennedy to speak at the New England Zionist Regional convention. Kennedy turned down the offer explaining that in his view Great Britain had no authority to issue the Balfour Declaration and the Arabs had also been given certain assurances. Besides, a Jewish homeland could hardly maintain itself in the midst of a huge Arab sea. Weinstein and Kennedy agreed to meet for lunch to discuss the issues in detail. Taking the matter seriously, JFK showed up with several pages of detailed written questions. He had obviously been doing his homework.

After five hours of discussion, Kennedy told Weinstein that he was now convinced that he had been wrong. A Democratic Jewish state would be just what was needed in the Middle East, both for the Jews and the United States. Kennedy spoke at the Zionist convention on June 14, at the Bradford Hotel in Boston, arguing clearly his support for the establishment of the Jewish state and receiving thunderous applause from the audience.

For Further Reading:

Lewis H. Weinstein, "John F. Kennedy: A Personal Memoir, 1946–1963" *AJH*, LXXV, 1985, pp. 5–30.

Q. What was the policy of the U.S. government toward the fledgling State of Israel after 1948?

A. President Harry Truman granted de facto recognition to The State of Israel only 11 minutes after its birth on May 14, 1948. Sympathetic to the plight of Jewish survivors in Europe after World War II, he had strongly supported their immigration to Palestine despite British opposition. However, through the Truman and Eisenhower administrations, the U.S. attitude toward Israel was inconsistent, shaped by a number of considerations.

The U.S. was deeply concerned about the Soviet expansion into the Middle East and also about the potential cut-off of Arab oil supplies. Thus, it felt a need to maintain good relations with the Arab states, all of whom were deeply hostile to Israel. Further, the U.S. State Department housed many civil servants who were pro-Arab and anti-Semitic and who consistently supported Arab interests. At the same time, the American public and many congressmen were sympathetic to Israel, both as the Mid-East's only democracy and because of the Jewish suffering during World War II.

While offering helpful economic aid to Israel (all the loans were repaid on time), the U.S. would do nothing about the Arab boycott or terrorism and gave no significant military aid to Israel. Yet, the U.S. did send arms to several Arab nations and would not recognize Jerusalem as Israel's capital.

When Israeli troops crossed the borders to retaliate against terrorist raids by its neighbors, the U.S. usually expressed disapproval of Israel alone.

Finally, under increasing Arab pressure, Israel invaded Egypt in the Sinai Campaign of 1956. Britain and France joined with Israel in response to Egypt's nationalizing of the Suez Canal. However, President Eisenhower, fearing Russian intervention, exerted heavy pressure on the Israelis and forced them to withdraw.

While the State Department was cold toward Israel, many congressional leaders like Senators Hubert Humphrey (D-Minn), Lyndon Johnson (D-Tex), Herbert Lehman (D-NY), Robert Taft, (R-Ohio), Estes Kefauver (D-Tenn), William Knowland (R-Cal), and Congressmen Sam Rayburn (D-Tex) and John McCormick (D-Mass) were friendly to Israel. Vice President Alben Barkley was one of a number of prominent active Christian Zionists. The American people too were, on the whole, sympathetic to Israel. However, there were those who preferred the Arabs, whether on religious or political grounds. They accused American Jews of dual loyalties and claimed that Israel mistreated Arab refugees.

A small group of Anti-Zionist Jews like Lessing Rosenwald and Alfred Lilienthal organized the Holy Land Emergency Liaison Program to help Arab refugees. At one point, John Foster Dulles and Christian Herter, both later Secretaries of State in the Eisenhower administration, were members. However, the group disbanded by 1951, Dulles stating that he was satisfied that Israel was doing its best on the refugee problem. Writer Dorothy Thompson and archaeologist Millar Burrows were among those sharply critical of Israel in regard to its handling of the Arab refugee problem.

For Further Reading:

Herbert S. Parmet, *Eisenhower and the American Crusade*, New York, The MacMillan Co., 1972.
Dwight Eisenhower, *Waging Peace* 1956–1961, Garden City, NY, Doubleday, 1965.
Lucy Dawidowicz, "The United States, Israel and the Middle East," *AJYB*, LIX, 1958, pp. 200–221.

Q. Who are the German Jews of Washington Heights?

A. Jewish refugees from Nazi Germany began to settle in the Washington Heights area of Upper Manhattan in the 1930's. Rabbi Dr. Joseph Breuer, the head of the Jewish community of Frankfort, escaped Germany after Kristallnacht and became the *rov* (rabbi) of the Washington Heights group in 1939. A grandson of Rabbi Samson Raphael Hirsch, highly educated and capable, Rabbi Breuer set out to build a Jewish community that would carry on the traditions of the German Orthodox Kehillah. The new central synagogue was named K'hal Adath Jeshurun after the Frankfurt Kehillah.

Schools and communal institutions soon developed. The synagogues continued to use German liturgical customs and melodies. The central location at Bennett Avenue was occupied in 1952. Rabbi Shimon Schwab was named as Rabbi Breuer's second in 1958 and headed the community after Rabbi Breuer's passing at age 98 in 1981. The community continued to uphold Rabbi Hirsch's principle of *"Torah im Derech Eretz,"* i.e., that knowledge of Torah and general knowledge enhance each other. Nevertheless, some younger people began to incline more toward the view which emphasizes only Torah, and not secular knowledge for its own sake.

The kehillah reached its peak by the mid-1960's with about 25,000 members. Its influence was strong enough to help induce a local Conservative synagogue to accept the practice of separate seating of men and women during services and to merge with an Orthodox congregation.

For Further Reading:

M. Lowenstein, *Frankfurt on the Hudson. The German Jewish Community of Washington Heights. Its Structure and Culture,* Detroit; Wayne State University Press, 1989.

Q. What did Ambassador James McDonald predict in 1951 for Israel's future?

A. James McDonald, an able and intelligent career diplomat with a lot of experience in refugee problems, served as the U.S.'s first ambassador to Israel, 1948–1950. Dealing with questions arising from the Arab-Israeli War and the multitudes of Arab refugees, he generally found President Truman sympathetic to Israel and the State Department pro-Arab. McDonald got to know the Israeli leaders and spoke highly of David Ben-Gurion, Moshe Sharrett, and particularly of Golda Myerson (Meir), then ambassador to Russia. He understood well the forces that went into the making of modern Israel. Yet, in 1951, he recorded at least one prediction that turned out to be very inaccurate. Within 10 years, he wrote, Israel would have a formal peace with all its Arab neighbors, except possibly Iraq and Saudi Arabia.

For Further Reading:

James G. McDonald, *My Mission to Israel. 1948–1951,* New York, Simon and Schuster, 1951.

Q. What are the Jewish origins of Cybernetics?

A. The vast information revolution of the late 20th century is rooted in the growth of computer science, a whole new way of processing and storing information. The theoretic basis of computer science is cybernetics, a very original field which has brought into an entirely new plain the way that both human beings and machines process information.

Norbert Wiener (1894–1964), who founded and named the field of cybernetics, was a great-grandson of Rabbi Akiba Eiger (1761–1837), one of the towering Talmudic geniuses of his day. Wiener wrote two fascinating autobiographies which depict his work in his chosen field and his growing up as a child prodigy.

His father, Leon Wiener, a professor of languages at Harvard, tutored Norbert intensely so that his high native intellect developed quickly. He entered high school at age 9 and graduated Tufts University with honors at age 15. He was denied Phi Beta Kappa only because of his youth. He went on to earn a Harvard Ph.D. in philosophy at age 19.

Norbert Wiener brought his many years of work together in his book *Cybernetics,* 1948. He took the term from the Greek word kubernetos, steersman. It is curious that, although Wiener probably did not know it, the same word was borrowed by ancient Hebrew.

Wiener's connection to Judaism is a remarkable story in itself. Although both his parents were Jews, Wiener did not know it until age 15, when he overheard his father mention idly to a fellow professor that some very old documents traced the family's ancestry back to Maimonides. Young Norbert looked up Maimonides in the encyclopedia and learned that he was a great Jewish scholar and physician. Norbert's mother, though Jewish, was a thorough racist, quite unrestrained in her constant attacks against Jews and other racial or religious groups. The father saw himself as a universalist and never mentioned his Jewish background.

As Wiener describes in his autobiographies, there were certain tell-tale signs of Jewishness. His grandmother read Yiddish papers, his father wrote articles and a full length book on Yiddish literature, and a cousin had told him that the family was Jewish. However, his mother insisted emphatically that they were not, and Norbert never thought to question her authority until he overheard the conversation about Maimonides. Wiener took his discovery seriously, but hardly knew what to do about it. He could not live the lie of a self-hating Jew nor would he turn to a religious life totally unfamiliar to him. Instead, he found an uneasy peace by developing a strong antipathy to prejudice of all kinds. A remarkable passage describing Wiener's psychoanalysis from his *I Am A Mathematician* reveals well both the nature of his deep creative impulse and his sense of identity.

"I performed the usual analytical reporting on the psychiatric couch and tried to supplement it by all that my insight could furnish concerning my own motivations and my internal set of values. I let the analyst know how deep I found the impulse to creative work and how much the satisfaction of success in this work was of an aesthetic nature. I also told him what my tastes in literature were, particularly in poetry. There are passages from Heine, especially in his Disputation *and his* Prinzessin Sabbath, *that relate and express the religious exaltation of the Jew, which I cannot recite without tears. I told him, moreover, how the sudden shift in Heine's attitude between awareness of the degradation and baseness in daily life and the exaltation of declaring the glory of God and the dignity of the despised Jew, create (sic.) in me a deep sense of awe."*

For Further Reading:

Norbert Weiner, *I Am A Mathematician*, MIT Press, 1956.
Norbert Weiner, *Ex Prodigy*. MIT Press, 1953.

Q. Was actor Cary Grant Jewish?

A. One of the most appealing actors of the 20th century, Cary Grant was born in Bristol, England to poor working class people, Elias and Elsie Leach, according to local records. His given name was Archibald Alec Leach. However, Grant's biographers, Charles Higham and Roy Moseley, believe that Grant was actually the illegitimate son of a Jewish woman named Lilian, who either died in childbirth or deserted her infant son. It is possible that Grant met with Lilian during a visit to England in 1938.

Grant appears himself to have been undecided as to his possible Jewishness. He would tell some people that he was Jewish, others that he was not. In 1939, he gave actor Sam Jaffe, with whom he had starred in *Gunga Din*, $25,000 for the United Jewish Appeal, and later sent money to Israel saying that it was in memory of his Jewish mother. Grant declined the lead role in *Gentleman's Agreement,* a movie about a Gentile posing as a Jew in order to study anti-Semitism, because he felt that no Jew could play that role well. The part went to Gregory Peck.

For Further Reading:

Charles Higham and Roy Moseley, *Cary Grant: The Lonely Heart,* San Diego, Harcourt, Brace and Jovanovich, 1989.

Q. What was Paula Ackerman's unusual function at Temple Beth Israel in Meridian, Mississippi?

A. When Rabbi William Ackerman died in 1951 after 25 years in the pulpit of Temple Beth Israel, his wife Paula succeeded him as the congregation's spiritual leader. This was long before women were being ordained, and Mrs. Ackerman never used the title "Rabbi." However, she did preach from the pulpit, conduct marriage ceremonies and participate in interfaith meetings for several years until a new rabbi was brought in. Mrs. Ackerman had grown up in Pensacola, Florida, and she served as rabbi there too, for a time, after her experience in Meridian. Women rabbis of later decades could look to Paula Ackerman as an important precursor.

Based on information from Dr. William Ackerman.

Q. How did "The Goldbergs," the 1950's TV show, get its start?

A. Gertrude Edelstein Berg (1899-1966) gained her place in the history of American television with her portrayal of Molly Goldberg, a warm-hearted, nurturing Jewish mother on "The Goldbergs" in the early 1950's. In 1928, she wrote a series for CBS radio, which was cancelled after one show, about a Jewish family, the Goldbergs. When she submitted her first script to NBC, she wrote it illegibly so that they would have to hear her read it aloud. Thus auditioned, Berg was given the role of Molly Goldberg. A month later, when she had to take a few days off because of laryngitis and a stand-in took the role of Molly, NBC was flooded with complaints.

The idea for the Molly Goldberg character began in skits Berg used to write as a teenager for her family's summer hotel.

The character's original name had been Maltke Talnitzky. "The Goldbergs" continued on radio through most of the 1930's and 40's. Berg also starred in a stage version, "Me and Molly," in a movie, "Molly" (1951) and finally in the popular TV series.

Berg wrote that her autobiography, *Molly and Me*, was aimed at portraying a happy life, not offering a psychoanalytic confession. As a child, she felt great warmth from very kind parents and grandparents. Passover was always a special time, but one year the young Gertrude had diphtheria and was despondent at being unable to attend the seder at her grandparents. However, their apartment was right across a courtyard from her bedroom. So her grandmother moved the dining room table next to her window and had Gertrude's mother move Gertrude's sick bed next to Gertrude's window. Grandpa Harris read the seder service loud enough for Gertrude to hear in her bed.

"That was a small but wonderful thing that they did for me. It was the first time, I think, that I really knew what it meant to be thankful... and I remember it came to me that I wasn't just a child, a daughter, a granddaughter, a relative — I belonged to people... That feeling of being loved and loving will always be a part of the Seder memory for me."

For Further Reading:

Gertrude Berg with Cherney Berg, *Molly and Me*, NY; McGraw-Hill Book Co., 1961
DAB, Supplement, VIII, 32–34.

Q. What famous American was offered the presidency of the State of Israel?

A. The presidency of the State of Israel, largely a symbolic and ceremonial office, was first held by the distinguished scientist and Zionist leader Chaim Weizmann from 1948 until his passing in November, 1952. A few days later, an article in the Israeli newspaper, *Maariv*, mentioned Albert Einstein as his possible successor. The world's most illustrious scientist, the 73 year old Einstein, had for many years been an active supporter of Zionism. At first, he refused to take seriously the press reports of the offer. However, on November 16, Abba Eban, Israeli ambassador to the United States, telephoned Einstein's home near Princeton University to sound him out informally. Although deeply moved, Einstein rejected the offer saying that his physical strength was suffering the inroads of advancing age. In a letter to the editor of *Maariv*, Einstein also expressed the concern that as a government leader he might at times feel compelled to go along with policies with which he could not agree.

For Further Reading:

Ronald Clark, *Einstein: The Life and Times*. NY: World Publishing Co., 1971, p. 617–619.
Jamie Sayen, *Einstein in America*, NY, Crown Publishing Co., 1985.

Q. How did the Sinykin family, living on a farm near the Badlands of South Dakota, obtain a Jewish education for their children?

A. In 1908, twenty-five Russian Jews founded a farm settlement just north of the Badlands of South Dakota. After three years, only the Sinykin family, who had moved from Sioux Falls, remained. The latter went too, leaving behind one son, Louis, who had been a bronco buster in his youth, on a 5,500 acre farm. In the early 1950's, desiring to obtain some Jewish learning for their four growing children, Louis and his wife wrote to Yeshiva University, which sent out as tutor Michael Zuckerman, a 16 year old who planned to become a veterinarian. The last of the Badlands Sinykins moved on to Rapid City in 1957.

For Further Reading:

Bernard Postal and Lionel Koppman, *American Jewish Landmarks*, NY, Fleet Press Corp., 1977, IV, p. 238.

Q. What two facts are true about the following people: Milton Berle, Fanny Brice, Mel Brooks, Don Adams, Shelly Berman, Pinky Lee, Rodney Dangerfield , Sid Caesar, Eddie Cantor, the Marx Brothers, Elaine May, Marty Feldman, Joan Rivers, Jack Benny, Jackie Mason, Carl Reiner, Henny Youngman, Soupy Sales, Red Buttons, Gene Wilder, Myron Cohen, Phil Silvers, George Burns, Alan King, Buddy Hackett, Mort Sahl, Joey Bishop, Sammy Levinson, the Three Stooges, Joan Rivers, Gilda Radner, Don Rickles, Ed Wynn, Jerry Lewis, Allen Sherman. Neil Simon, Madeleine Kahn, Bert Lahr, Danny Kaye?

A. They are all American Jews, and they all gained considerable repute in the field of comedy. There is, of course, no one simple explanation for Jews' success in this area, but several important factors are perhaps typical of the Jewish experience.

Mel Brooks, a very bright and well read man, has explained two basic motivations of the comic: Comedians have a need to be accepted by other people, and they seem to gain attention and acceptance through comedy. And, "Another could have been pure hate — for the whole world. For being short. For not being born Franklin Roosevelt or Johnny Weismuller — just a bit of hatred. Getting even in an oblique way through comedy instead of just yelling insults and taunts and getting my head smashed in."

In a similar vein, Carl Reiner has said that "a certain amount of suffering is necessary to hone a comedy mind." [The comedian is] "still thrashing out at society, making fun of society, saying terrible things about society. It's a kick in the pants no matter how you look at it." It's the only way that a lowly court jester can ever tell the king he's full of it without getting a whipping.

What Brooks and Reiner said fits well the historical experience of the Jews, who were typically suppressed by the peoples among whom they lived, and who developed an often sardonic and introspective sense of humor as a way of lightening their burdens.

May we suggest a second historical cause. The Jews have, for centuries, been devoted to the intense study of their sacred books. Schools aimed not merely at producing graduates but at accustoming people to devote themselves to the study of the sacred books as the central goal and activity of their lives. Study was more important than work, sleep, or entertainment. Such intense concentration on books produced a great awareness of words and of their polyphony of meanings and implications. The same appreciation for words filtered out into the general Jewish society, and the Yiddish language is filled with Biblical and Talmudic quotes and quips, which became like part of the air the people breathed. Turns of phrase, words, even single letters were precious. Yiddish speaking Jews brought all this with them to the U.S., and it seemed to make comedy a natural road to success.

For Further Reading:

Larry Wilde, *How the Great Comedy Writers Create Laughter*, Chicago: Nelson-Hall, 1976.

Q. Who has been the leading Talmudic scholar in Conservative Judaism?

A. Professor Saul Lieberman, (1898–1983) of the Jewish Theological Seminary, was a Talmudist of magnitude as well as an expert on Greek and Latin Studies. His *Tosefta Kifshuta* is a multi-volume study of the Tosefta, an important work of rabbinic law that first appeared in the third century as an adjunct to the Mishnah. Thoroughly knowledgeable in the great rabbinic commentaries, Lieberman also used modern techniques of philology, history, and related sciences. Two other books, *Greek in Jewish Palestine* (1942), and *Hellenism in Jewish Palestine* (1950), study the effect of Greek language and culture on Jewish life and thought of the Talmudic era.

A very dedicated scholar, Lieberman devoted long hours and years to his work. The author heard the following story from a young rabbi who happened to be staying in a hotel room next to Lieberman at a rabbis' conference. The younger rabbi woke up in the middle of the night and noticed a light on in his distinguished neighbor's room. Fearing that the elderly Lieberman may have taken ill, the young rabbi knocked on his door. Upon entering he found Professor Lieberman poring over several volumes of the Talmud, as he often did in the wee hours.

Saul Lieberman's wife was a daughter of Rabbi Meir Bar-Ilan and granddaughter of Rabbi Naftali Z.Y. Berlin, long-time head of the yeshiva of Volozhin. A fine scholar in her own right, Judith Lieberman wrote a book, *Robert Browning and Hebraism*, on Jewish themes in the works of Robert Browning, the great English poet. Browning had some interest in Hebrew and touched on Jewish ideas in his poems, particularly "Rabbi Ben Ezra."

For Further Reading:

Louis Finkelstein, ed. *Thirteen Americans: Their Spiritual Autobiographies,* New York. Institute for Religious and Social Studies, 1953.

Q. When did Conservative Judaism introduce its own version of the Jewish marriage contract or ketubah?

A. After many years of discussion, the (Conservative) Rabbinical Assembly of America introduced a new form of the ketubah at its 1954 convention. Under the new document, prepared by Professor Saul Lieberman of JTS, the bride and groom would give over their rights to a rabbinic court, which would have the authority to compel a recalcitrant husband to agree to a Jewish divorce and could deal with cases in which a husband had disappeared, leaving his wife an *agunah* (grass widow). The new ketubah was attacked by Orthodox leaders as not acceptable within Jewish Law.

For Further Reading:

AJYB, 1954, 55, pp. 193–194.
EJ: ketubbah.

Q. What popular American non-Jewish movie actor of the mid-twentieth century was descended from the famous Jewish Mendelsohn family?

A. Popular actor William Bendix (1906–1964) was a direct descendant of both Moses Mendelsohn, the philosopher, and his grandson, composer Felix Mendelsohn. Bendix never sought to conceal his Jewish ancestry, but it was distant for him, as he was born and raised a Christian. In fact, not one of Moses Mendelsohn's numerous progeny was still Jewish a century after his death.

Bendix starred in many movies, including *Guadalcanal Diary* (1943), and *The Babe Ruth Story* (1948), and later played in *The Life Of Riley* series on radio (1944- 1953) and television (1953- 1959).

Q. Henry Lascau represented the U.S.A. in the Olympics three times in an unusual sport. What was it?

A. Lascau escaped from a Nazi concentration camp in 1938 and immigrated to the U.S. He represented his new country in three Olympics, 1948, 1952, and 1956, as a racewalker. He set a world record for an indoor mile at Madison Square Garden in 1951, and won, in all, 42 U.S. championships.

For Further Reading:

Bernard Postal, "He Walks His Way to Fame," *Jewish Digest*, 2, 1956, pp. 59-62.

Q. What role did author James Michener play in the Hungarian Revolution of 1956?

A. One of Michener's lesser known works, *The Bridge at Andau*, describes the Hungarian Revolution of 1956. Michener was deeply involved in rescuing refugees, many of them Jews, from the Communists. He was very helpful in getting Jews to pass themselves off as Catholics or Presbyterians, whose U.S. quotas had vacancies.

For Further Reading:

James Michener, *The Bridge at Andau*, New York, Random House, 1957.
Ibid., *The World is My Home*, New York. Random House, 1992, p. 388.

Q. Let's name a Jewish, all time, all star, basketball team.

A.

1. Dolph Schayes, one of the NBA's greats, was named to the all star team 12 times between 1949-1963 and is a member of basketball's Hall of Fame.
2. Barry Kramer won the Haggerty Award and was named All American while starring for New York University in 1963. He went on to an outstanding NBA career with the New York Knicks and the San Francisco Warriors.
3. Rudy LaRusso played college basketball at Dartmouth and later distinguished himself on the great Los Angeles Lakers teams of the 1960's.
4. Max Zaslofsky played between 1947 and 1956 and led the league in scoring in 1948.
5. Nat Holman was one of the original Boston Celtics in the 1920's and one of the greatest professionals of his day.

   Substitute: Hall of Famer, Marty Friedman, who starred for the old New York Whirlwinds.

For Further Reading:

Martin Greenberg, *The Jewish Lists*, New York; Schocken, 1979.

Q. How about an all-star, Jewish, Major League baseball team?

A. Infield.
- o   Hank Greenberg. 1930, 1933–1940,1945–1947. 1628 hits, 379 home runs, 1276 rbi's, 313 b.a.
- o   Buddy Meyer. 1925–1941. 2131 hits. 38 home runs. 850 rbi's. 303 b.a.
- o   Al Rosen. 1947–1956. 1063 hits. 192 home runs. 717 rbi's. 288 b.a.
- o   Billy Nash. 1884–1898. 1606 hits. 61 home runs. 977 rbi's. 275 b.a.

Outfield.
- o   Sid Gordon 1941–1955. 1415 hits. 202 home runs. 805 rbi's. 283 b.a.
- o   George Stone. 1902, 1905–1910. 984 hits. 23 home runs. 268 rbi's. 301 b.a.
- o   Lipman Pike. 1876–1881,1887. 223 hits. 5 home runs. 88 rbi's. 304 b.a.

Catcher.
- o   Johnny Kling. 1900–1913. 1152 hits. 20 home runs. 513 rbi's. 272 b.a.

Pitcher
- o   Sandy Koufax. w-l 165–87. SO 2396. ERA 276.

Greenberg and Koufax are members of the Baseball Hall of Fame. Lipman Pike was the first professional baseball player.

For Further Reading;

The Baseball Encyclopedia. New York; MacMillanPublishing Co., 1990

Q. When did discrimination against Jews at resorts and hotels in the U.S. truly come to an end?

A. Exclusion of Jews from lodgings and social clubs began in the last decades of the 19th century and greatly declined with the liberalizing trend of the 1960's and the social gains of Afro Americans.

Surveys conducted by the Anti-Defamation League of B'nai Brith in 1957 and 1963 highlight this trend. In 1957, 23% of hotels and resorts in the U.S., Canada and the Caribbean excluded Jews. By 1963, it was less that 10%. Florida was down from 23% to 10% and Arizona from 45% to 22%;

from 34% in Michigan, Minnesota and Wisconsin to 14%; from 56% to 15% in Maine, Vermont and New Hampshire. Only one hotel in New York discriminated against Jews. Besides the social and political changes, hotels began to find that anti-Jewish policies hurt them financially, because they were losing convention business.

For Further Reading:

C. Bezalel Sherman, "Discrimination at American Resorts," *The Jewish Frontier*, 31, April, 1964, pp.19–22.

Q. Why have Jews been so prominent in writing musical plays?

A. Jewish names dominated the 20th century American musical theater - Irving Berlin, Jerome Kern, Sigmund Romberg, George and Ira Gershwin, Harold Arlen, Lorenz Hart, Richard Rodgers, Oscar Hammerstein (his father was Jewish, his mother was not), Steven Sondheim, Alan Lerner, Frederick Loewe, Burt Bacharach, and Neil Diamond.

Yip Harburg, lyricist for "The Wizard of Oz," "Finian's Rainbow," "Brother Can You Spare A Dime," "Lydia the Tattooed Lady, " and many more, offered his own explanation of the Jewish contribution. In whatever country Jews have lived, he said, they absorbed something of the native music, whether the flamenco in Spain or the Tchaikovsky romantic element in Russia, into their own Jewish styles. American Jewish composers expressed this combination of old Jewish music with newly learned Black tunes. In Harburg's view, songs like Harold Arlen's "Stormy Weather" and "Get Happy" could have been written only by a person steeped in Jewish liturgical music, and Arlen's father was a cantor. Gershwin's "Summertime" also is in this tradition. Harburg himself, went regularly to both synagogue and Yiddish theater as a child. Even an American patrician like Cole Porter was fascinated with Jewish music, adapting it in songs like "Begin the Beguine" and "What is this Thing Called Love."

For Further Reading:

Bernard Rosenberg and Ernest Goldstein, *Creators and Disturbers*, New York, Columbia University Press, 1982, ch. 8.

Q. What leading American anti-Semite purchased Israel bonds?

A. On January 6, 1955 "radio priest" Father Charles Coughlin, of the Shrine of the Little Flower in Royal Oak, Michigan, purchased $500 worth of State of Israel bonds, proclaiming the Jewish state a bulwark against Communism.

Coughlin had achieved national notoriety for his impassioned radio broadcasts during the 1930's and 40's. He held millions mesmerized as he railed against Bolsheviks, socialists, Roosevelt, the Jews, and the moneyed powers. Coughlin also published a newspaper, "Social Justice," which espoused his views.

For Further Reading:

Sheldon Marcus, *Father Coughlin: The Tumultuous Life of the Priest of the Little Flower*, Boston, Little, Brown and Co., 1973.

Q. Who wrote the first great "rock and roll" song?

A. Rock and roll can be said to have been born the moment a swivelly hipped young Elvis Presley sang "Hound Dawg" on the Ed Sullivan Show in 1956. This and a number of other early rock hits like "Jailhouse Rock," "Spanish Harlem," and "Yakety Yak" were written by Jeremy Leiber and Mike Stoller. Both were born on the east coast and transplanted to California, and both were strongly interested in Afro-American music.

Jews have not influenced rock and roll as they have the world of Broadway musicals, although many have been involved on the business side. Bob Dylan is probably the best known Jewish rock figure, although his active connection with religion has varied from fundamentalist Christianity to Orthodox Judaism. Phil Specter and Mamma Cass Elliot were also Jewish rock stars in the early years.

For Further Reading:

E. Anthony Rotundo, "Jews in Rock and Roll: A Study in Cultural Contrast," *AJH*, LXXll, 1982, 82–107.

Q. What famous operatic tenor wore *tsitsit* (ritual fringes) even when performing in costume?

A. Richard Tucker, born Reuben Ticker, was one of the great operatic tenors of the 20th century. Brother-in-law of the equally famous Jan Peerce (with whom he did not get along), Tucker started out as a cantor in a small synagogue and retained a strong religious orientation. He donned tefillin (phylacteries) regularly and wore tsitsit all day, every day, even when performing. In fact, he always kept a spare pair ready in case one got sweated up during a performance.

Once when recording in Rome, Tucker received a phone call from New York notifying him of the birth and imminent circumcision of his first grandson. He flew home and returned two days later, exhausted and several thousand dollars poorer. The recording company deducted the cost of his absence from his royalties.

Richard Tucker's cantorial recordings found at least one unusual fan. In the early 1950's, a teenage boy in Memphis, Tennessee, liked to go visit Rabbi Alfred Fruchter, his upstairs neighbor, and listen to the rabbi's cantorial records of Tucker and Cantor Moshe Kussevitsky. The boy was Elvis Presley.

For Further Reading:

James A. Drake, *Richard Tucker: A Biography*, New York, E.P. Dutton, Inc. 1984.
Robert Merrill, *Between Acts: An Irreverent Look At Opera and Other Madness*, New York, McGraw Hill, 1976.

Q. When did Governor Adlai Stevenson have a Passover seder?

A. Adlai Stevenson served as the governor of Illinois from 1949 - 1953, was Democratic candidate for president twice, and later the U.S. ambassador to the United Nations. One spring night in the late 1950's, author Harry Golden, a good friend of Stevenson, was staying at the Sheraton in Chicago. Adlai called to invite him over for dinner. Golden also had an invitation from a well-known lawyer to participate in a Passover seder. But Golden chose to visit Stevenson instead. When told of this, Stevenson exclaimed "Let's have a Passover right here." Golden proceeded to tell the story of the Egyptian exodus and asked his host "Why is tonight different from all other nights?" Later, they proclaimed together, "Next year in Jerusalem."

For Further Reading:

Harry Golden, *The Right Time*, New York, G.P. Putnam's Sons, 1969.

Q. How accurate have predictions been about the future of American Judaism?

A. One could write a very interesting book on predictions, right and wrong, about American Judaism. In the spring of 1957, several leading scholars became embroiled in a public controversy over such prognostications. Professors Jacob Marcus of HUC and Oscar Handlin of Harvard argued in a B'nai Brith publication that the Jewish intellectual tradition would decline. Also, the uniformities of suburban life, the apparent decline of anti-Semitism, and the increase of intermarriage would make Jews more and more like their Christian neighbors. Rabbi Wolfe Kelman, addressing the Rabbinic

Association (Conservative), accepted the Marcus-Handlin position and urged Conservative synagogues to develop more education programs and summer camps as a way of strengthening Judaism.

Two optimistic dissenting opinions soon appeared. Professor Louis Finkelstein of the Jewish Theological Seminary stated that Americans, both Jewish and Christian, were in the process of a spiritual revival and were rediscovering their faiths. Rabbi Solomon Scharfman, president of the Rabbinical Council of America (Orthodox) and rabbi of a Young Israel synagogue in Brooklyn, argued that Orthodoxy was assuming a new vigor on American soil and was capturing the minds of American Jewish youth.

Q. Was Conductor Herbert Von Karajan a Nazi?

A. Herbert Von Karajan (1908–1989) gained world renown as conductor of the Berlin Philharmonic, 1954–1989. However, his performances in the U.S. after World War II were often greeted by protests and complaints regarding his supposed Nazi affiliations. Music lovers would boycott his concerts, and well known Jewish musicians and singers refused to appear on stage with him.

Although Von Karajan would later play down his Nazi connection, documents brought to light in 1957 show that he did join the Nazi Party in Salzburg, Austria as early as April, 1933, mere weeks after Hitler came to power in Germany. In 1935, in Aachen, Von Karajan directed 100 musicians and 750 singers in a performance of Nazi music. including the notorious "Horst Wessel Song." The text for the performance was written by Baldur Von Schirach, later head of the Hitler Youth. Von Karajan first conducted in Berlin in 1938, where Hermann Goering used him as a weapon in his rivalry with Joseph Goebbels, who preferred Wilhelm Furtwangler, the Berlin Philharmonic's regular conductor. Furtwangler was unpopular with many Nazis because of his work on behalf of Jewish musicians.

It has been alleged, but not proven, that Von Karajan joined the DS or Security Service, a branch of the SS. Hitler himself disliked Von Karajan's conducting and the Nazi leadership further disapproved of the conductor's 1942 marriage to Anita Guterman, who had some Jewish ancestry. Despite Von Karajan's accomplishments as a conductor, his connections with Nazism seem clear.

For Further Reading:
Roger Vaughn, *Herbert Von Karajan*, New York, W.W. Norton. 1986.

Q. What single person was the greatest influence on the growth of advanced yeshivot in the U.S. after World War II?

A. Most would agree that it was Rabbi Aron Kotler (1891–1962). Head of the yeshivah of Kletzk in Poland before World War II and recognized as a Talmudic genius, Rabbi Kotler escaped to the U.S. and founded an advanced yeshiva in Lakewood, New Jersey, the Beth Medrash Gevoha, which by 2015 would have over 6,000 students.

Rabbi Kotler devoted his years in the U.S. to helping Jews all over the world and particularly to fostering the study of Torah. His greatest influence, however, came not through any specific institutions that he founded or position that he held, but mainly through the effect of the constant and passionate love of Torah that constituted his entire being. For Rabbi Kotler, Torah was the breath of life, the source of all good, the meaning of Creation. One of his students wrote of him that he "ignited others with his excitement for learning."

While he always stood strong in matters of principle, he was deeply considerate of other people, whether great scholars and leaders or workaday people. He would often speak to his students of the importance of good character — consideration for others, respectful speech, neatness and punctuality. His students often repeat the story that whenever he was traveling on a highway. he would shun the automatic toll booth in favor of a manned booth saying that it was "disrespectful of humanity to pass up a man for a machine." Many of Rabbi Kotler's students became the next generation's leaders of yeshiva Jewry.

For Further Reading:

Shaul Kagan, "Rabbi Ahron Kotler," *The Jewish Observer,* IX, 1973 pp. 3–13.

Q. What was the Haifa Clause?

A. In 1958, the U.S. Navy included a clause in each contract it signed involving oil cargo ships. The Haifa Clause, as it became known, warned that the U.S. government retained an option to cancel the contract if Arab governments would refuse to accommodate a contractor's ships. Because of the Arab economic boycott against Israel, once a ship docked in Haifa, Israel, the Egyptians would not let it pass through the Suez Canal, nor would any Arab country let it enter its ports. The effect of the Haifa Clause was that U.S. shipowners doing business with Israel would not be able to ship oil cargoes for the U.S. Navy. The Department of Agriculture maintained a similar practice. This aroused strong protest when it became public knowledge in

1960. In response, the Navy announced that it would eliminate the Haifa Clause from its contracts. The Department of Agriculture continued to include the clause.

For Further Reading:

AJYB, 62, 1961, pp. 188–189.

Q. Who bombed the Hebrew Benevolent Congregation in Atlanta, Georgia on October 12, 1958?

A. The old strict segregation between whites and blacks in the southern U.S. was beginning to ease in the middle 1950's, but not without great agitation and even violence. Some racists turned against Jews as well as blacks, and in 1958 several synagogues through the south were bombed. The Hebrew Benevolent Congregation, on Peachtree Street in Atlanta, was bombed at 3:38 AM on October 12, 1958. A man identifying himself as "General Gordon of the Confederate Underground" called Wayne Chester, of the United Press International, to claim credit for the explosion and to threaten further violence.

That same afternoon the police arrested George Michael Bright, a 35 year old draftsman, and four additional arrests were made within a few days. Bright had a long history of racist activities and threats against Jews. His trial, which began in December, ended in a hung jury, and in a second trial Bright was released on insufficient evidence. A star witness for the defense at the second trial was Marilyn Craig, a legally insane patient at the Milledgeville State Hospital, who claimed to have been with Bright the entire night of the bombing. The crime is still unsolved.

For Further Reading:

Arnold Shankman, "A Temple is Bombed — 1958," AJA, XXI II, 1971, pp. 125–153.

Q. Has shechita (kosher slaughter of animals) ever been forbidden in the U.S.?

A. Laws forbidding the kosher slaughter of animals have been in force, whether on religious or humanitarian grounds, at various times in European countries. The matter of shechita was under public discussion in the U.S. as early as the 19th century and had been raised in Congress. In 1958, a humane slaughter law passed through Congress requiring that animals be slaughtered in a manner that would not cause pain. Methods of ritual slaughter were specifically exempted from the law.

R. Joseph B. Soloveitchik, of Yeshiva University, served on a 12 man advisory committee assembled by the U.S. Department of Agriculture. He and R. Eliezer Silver, a leading Orthodox rabbi from Cincinnati, inspected a new device developed in Canada for restraining the animal before the slaughtering and declared it permissible according to Jewish Law. The fact is that the traditional Jewish shechitah performed by a shochet is almost entirely painless to the animal.

For Further Reading:

AJYB 1958, 59, and 1960, 61.

Q. Who is the greatest authority on American Jewish History?

A. The answer to such a question must, of course, be highly subjective. However, few would argue against the selection of Dr. Jacob Rader Marcus. Born March 5, 1896 near Connellsville, Pennsylvania, Marcus attended Hebrew Union College and the University of Cincinnati. After active army service during World War I, he went on to earn a Ph.D. at the University of Berlin. His first book dealt with the German Jewish leader, Israel Jacobson, and other writings on German and Medieval Jewish History followed.

In the 1940's Marcus developed an interest in the history of American Jews. He published prolifically in that field too. One of his greatest works is a four volume series, *United States Jewry*. Marcus emphasized collection of massive amounts of source material and built the American Jewish Archive at Hebrew Union College. Blessed with a good sense of the human aspect of historical events, he generally succeeds in avoiding mere pedantry and pounding on unimportant issues. He also authored two books on American Jewish women and a three volume set on Jews in early America.

For Further Reading:

Bertram Wallace Korn, ed . *A Bicentennial Festschrift for Jacob Rader Marcus*, New York, Ktav Publ. House Inc., 1976.

Q. How many Jews have served as U.S. ambassadors to foreign countries?

A. Jews have served the U.S. as ambassadors, ministers, or consuls to many foreign governments, beginning with Mordecai Noah's mission to Tunis in 1813, and Henry Barnet, consul at Gibraltar in 1833. The sample list offers some view of the work of Jewish ambassadors:

Herman Baruch	Portugal	1945- 1947
Herman Bernstein	Albania	1929- 1933
Lewis Einstein	Costa Rica	1911- 1913
	Czechoslovakia	1921- 1930
Walter Annenberg	England	1969–1974
Benjamin Peixotto	Romania	1870- 1876
	France	1877- 1885
Joseph Kornfeld	Persia	1921
Henry Guggenheim	Cuba	1929–1933
Simon Wolf	Egypt	1881- 1882
Ira Morris	Sweden	1914- 1923
Maxwell Rabb	Italy	1981- 1989
Milton Wolf	Austria	1977–1980
Marvin Warner	Switzerland	1977–1979

One of the busiest was Laurence Steinhardt, who served in six posts: Sweden, Peru, Turkey, USSR, Czechoslovakia, and Canada between 1933- 1950. In 1885, Anthony Kieley was rejected by Hapsburg Austria because his wife was Jewish. (Jesse Straus, Marcus Otterbourg, and several representatives to Turkey are noted in greater length elsewhere in these pages.)

For Further Reading:

Who's Who in American Politics, Bowker, New Providence, N.J., 1991

Q. What was served at the first cabinet meeting of the Kennedy administration?

A. The Sunday prior to the 1961 inauguration, the cabinet held an informal get acquainted session at the home of Labor-Secretary designate Arthur Goldberg. They brunched on bagels and lox. Goldberg went on to serve as a Supreme Court Justice and UN Ambassador.

A second Jew in President Kennedy's cabinet was HEW Secretary Abe Ribicoff who, as governor of Connecticut, had been the first major political figure to endorse John Kennedy as a possible vice-presidential running mate for Adlai Stevenson in 1956. Treasury Secretary C. Douglas Dillon, a Republican from a famous Wall Street banking family, had one Jewish grandfather.

For Further Reading:

Theodore Sorensen, *Kennedy,* New York, Bantam Books, 1965.

Q. What American Jewish territorial governor held a degree from Hebrew Union College?

A. Ralph Paiewonsky (1907–1991), Governor of the Virgin Islands, was awarded an honorary Doctorate for Humane Letters by HUC in 1969, one of several honorary degrees that he held.

A cousin of Paiewonsky's parents was emigrating from Lithuania to Brazil in the 1890's. Very careful in his observance of kashrut, the cousin nearly starved on the voyage. When his ship made a stop at the Virgin Islands, he got off, found a friendly Jewish community and stayed on. Within a few years, other members of the family joined him, including Ralph Paiewonsky's parents.

Successful in business and experienced in public affairs, Paiewonsky was appointed governor of the Virgin Islands by President John Kennedy in 1961, and served until 1969. He carried through an ambitious program which included attracting new businesses, improving hotel and transportation facilities to draw tourism, and providing better housing and medical care. Paiewonsky felt that the most notable accomplishment in his term was the founding of the College of the Virgin Islands, the Islands' first real institution of higher learning.

In 1968, Paiewonsky visited Israel with a group of American governors led by John Volpe of Massachusetts. He was surprised to learn that Israel President Zalman Shazar had gone to school with his uncle Julius Kushner in Lithuania. In his autobiography, *Memoirs of a Governor,* Paiewonsky describes his visit to Israel as "the capstone of a lifetime as a practicing Jew."

Once at a meeting of the Conference Group at the Virgin Islands University, Glen Davis, the student representative, rose and delivered a tirade about the long enslavement of Blacks and demanded the repayment that he felt was due them.

Paeiwonsky's response was notable. The Jews too, he said, had spent centuries in Egyptian slavery, and even after the exodus many wanted to return. They were kept in the desert 40 years so that they could learn to face the responsibilities of freedom. They had to replace slave-dependency with self-reliance. He went on to say that in another biblical story, Lot and his family escaped from the destruction of the evil cities Sodom and Gomorra. But, they were warned not to look back. When Lot's wife did look, she was turned into a pillar of salt. These biblical stories, he went on, teach two important lessons: we must not expect others to do for us what we can do for ourselves, and we should not always look back at the bitter things that happened in the past or we will never become anything but pillars of bitterness.

For Further Reading:

Ralph Paiewonsky, *Memoirs of a Governor,* New York, New York University Press, 1990.

Q. How is New Square, New York unusual?

A. In 1956 a group of 20 Skvirer Hasidic families, led by Rabbi Jacob Joseph Twersky, lived in Ramapo, NY. In 1961, they gained the legal right to set up a separate village in Ramapo. The Skvirers reject what they see as the banality and materialism of the general society and lead a strictly Hasidic lifestyle.

Some commute to work in New York City on a bus equipped with Torah Scrolls and separate seating for men and women, so that they can pray in a minyan while en route. In their schools, secular studies are minimal and the students concentrate on Torah. There were about 1200 residents by 1971.

For Further Reading:

Marc Raphael, *Profiles in American Judaism,* San Francisco, Harper and Row, 1984.
New York Times, July 14, 1961, p. 20 and July 18, 1971, p. 48.

Q. What unusual connection helped Arthur Goldberg to get some of his proposed labor laws passed through Congress when he was Secretary of Labor?

A. House Speaker Sam Rayburn of Texas was able to help President John F. Kennedy's labor legislation through the House by telling House leaders that Labor Secretary Goldberg was a Texan and should be given all the help he needs. Goldberg grew up in Chicago. But his father had spent two years peddling goods in Texas in the 1890's when he first came to the U.S., speaking Yiddish and Russian but hardly a word of English.

For Further Reading:

Howard Simons, *Jewish Times,* Boston, Houghton Mifflin Co.. 1988.

Q. What was the reaction of the mother-in-law of Arthur Goldberg upon learning of his appointment to the Supreme Court by President Kennedy in 1962?

A. Wonderful? Yes, but who cares anything about Arthur? Everybody knew something like this would happen to him, but that it should happen to me, that's more wonderful. That I'm the mother-in-law of a Supreme Court Justice. Arthur Goldberg did indeed have a distinguished career in public life, serving also as Secretary of Labor and as Ambassador to the United Nations.

For Further Reading:

Dorothy Goldberg, *A Private View of a Public Life*, New York, Charterhouse 1975.

Q. About which American presidential candidate was it said that he was barred from a golf course for religious reasons?

A. Senator Barry M. Goldwater (R-Ariz.). "Mr. Conservative," was defeated in a landslide by Lyndon Johnson in the presidential election of 1964, having frightened American voters with his extreme right wing views. In that same year, so the story goes, barred from playing on a restricted golf course because of his partly Jewish heritage, he quipped to the management, "Since I'm part Jewish can I play nine holes?" In his autobiography, Goldwater claimed the tale to be apocryphal.

Barry's grandfather, Mike Goldwasser, was a Jewish peddler who emigrated from Poland to the western U.S. in 1852. Mike, or Don Miguel as the Mexicans called him, gained success in business over the next decades. In June 1872, Goldwasser and several traveling companions were attacked by about 40 hostile Apaches. They escaped without loss of life, but not before Mike had a bullet pass through his hat. He topped off his career by becoming mayor of Prescott, Arizona in 1885. Barry's uncle Morris was also mayor of Prescott.

Although grandson Barry spoke about Mike fondly, he seemed reluctant to refer to his Jewishness, usually calling him a Pole. During his long Senate career (1953–1965 and 1969–1987), Barry was usually unsupportive and highly critical of Israel.

For Further Reading:

Barry M. Goldwater with Jack Casserly, *Goldwater*, New York, Doubleday, 1988.
Kenneth Libo and Irving Howe, *We Lived There Too*, New York, St. Martin's Press, 1984.

Q. With which American Jewish comedian did poet T.S. Eliot correspond?

A. T.S. Eliot, one of the 20th century's most prominent poets and playwrights, had an anti-Semitic streak. A series of anti-Semitic lectures delivered at the University of Virginia in the early 1930's was printed in *After Strange Gods*.

Nevertheless, Eliot could befriend his Jewish students. He also exchanged a number of letters with Groucho Marx, the famed Jewish comedian. Groucho's letter to Eliot on November 1, 1963 includes a hilarious dissertation on his name "Tom". Groucho visited Eliot at his home in London and describes how he tried to impress Eliot by quoting from Eliot's poem, "The Waste Land," while the poet seemed more interested in discussing old Marx Brothers movies.

For Further Reading:

Groucho Marx, *The Groucho Letters,* New York, Simon and Schuster, 1967, pp. 154–164.
T.S. Mathews, *Great Tom: Notes Toward the Definition of T.S. Eliot,* New York, Harper Row Publ., 1973.

Q. What is the OU?

A. Quite probably some Americans in small towns with minimal Jewish presence have noticed the OU symbol on food packages and wondered what strange new chemical process or food additive it indicated. They might be surprised to learn that the OU stands for Orthodox Union, or in its full title Union of Orthodox Jewish Congregations of America. When seen on a package of food, the symbol indicates that a food product was supervised and certified as kosher by a rabbi or kashrut supervisor representing the Union. The OU is involved in a variety of religious, educational, and political activities. Its yearly convention draws huge crowds. *Jewish Action,* its periodical, deals with Jewish views on religion, psychology, politics, and more.

The Orthodox Union was founded in 1898 by Rabbis Bernard Drachman, Henry Mendes, and several others. Orthodox in Jewish practice, but also more willing to work within the world of western society and thought, the Union entered into a period of growth in the 1950's as Orthodox Jewry began a significant expansion. Hundreds of synagogues became involved with the OU, and several very active organizations were formed, including National Council of Synagogue Youth (NCSY), Yavne (for college students) and the Association of Orthodox Jewish Scientists.

The OU's opening declaration stated its purpose "to protect Orthodox Judaism whenever occasions arise in civic and social matters .... and to protect against declarations of Reform rabbis not in accord with the teachings of our Torah." On a practical level this meant trying to accommodate to American life and to salvage the younger generation from assimilation without changing Orthodox practice. The OU also acted toward removing restrictions on Jews in public life: for example, opposing Sunday blue laws, and opposing the celebration of Christian holidays in public schools.

A second Orthodox rabbinical organization with a different and, at times, conflicting approach was the Agudath Ha-Rabbanim (Union of Orthodox Rabbis of the U.S. and Canada). Formed in May 1902 in Boston on the very day of the funeral of Rabbi Jacob Joseph, this group of European born rabbis sought to check the drift of the immigrants toward assimilation by encouraging rigorous adherence to the Torah in the European manner. They felt different from more liberal rabbis like Bernard Drachman whom they saw as a force for Americanization, and they sought to establish in America the sort of Judaism they had known in the yeshivot of Eastern Europe. The Agudath Ha-Rabbanim helped to found many of the first Jewish day schools in the U.S. It organized the Ezras Torah charity in 1915 and the Va'ad Hatzalah, an effort to rescue European Jews, particularly scholars, during World War II.

For Further Reading:

AJYB, LXVI, 1965, pp. 21–91.

Q. How many Young Israel synagogues are there in the U.S.?

A. Formed in New York in 1912, the Young Israel movement represented an American approach to Orthodoxy at a time when young Jews in the U.S. were deserting Orthodoxy in droves. By 1965, Young Israel numbered 95 synagogues and 23,000 families, consisting mostly of American born, college educated members .

For Further Reading:

Marc Lee Raphael, *Profiles on American Judaism*, San Francisco, Harper and Row, 1984.

Q. Why was there a Rosh Hashanah service in the Capitol Building in Washington DC in 1965?

A. An important vote in Congress was scheduled for Rosh Hashanah, 1965. Speaker John McCormack heard that Representative Herbert Tenzer of New York, an observant Jew, would not be present to vote because of the holiday. McCormack pressed him to come, even offering him the use of the House prayer room for Rosh Hashanah services. Tenzer agreed and the room was properly set up for the High Holiday services with a separation between men and women. Senator Abraham Ribicoff was among the 22 worshippers as was McCormack himself, wearing a yarmulke and a talit. Tenzer prayed with the minyan in the Capitol and stepped out for a few minutes to cast his vote.

On another occasion, Tenzer refused to join President Lyndon B. Johnson on a campaign motorcade through Tenzer's home district because it took place on a Saturday. Instead, Tenzer stayed in a nearby motel and walked to the Saturday luncheon. Johnson greeted him warmly and said "I want to commend you for observing in the traditional way as you do."

For Further Reading:

Jean Baer, *The Self-Chosen*, New York, Arbor House, 1982.

Q. Stanley Fields, a Jew from New York, was instrumental in saving one of the great wonders of the Ancient World. What was it?

A. Stanley Fields directed tourism and industrial development projects for countries like Mexico and Bolivia as part of his work for Hamilton Wright, a New York based public relations firm. In 1964, the building of the Aswan Dam in Egypt threatened to drown the ancient and magnificent buildings and statues of Pharaoh Rameses II at Abu Simbel. Hamilton-Wright was concerned over the probable decline of tourism in Egypt and appointed Fields to save Abu Simbel. Fields raised $48,000,000 from all sorts of sources, including Israeli and American Jews, even though Egypt and Israel were still in a state of war until Anwar Sadat's visit to Israel in 1977. Egypt's relations with the United States were also testy in those years.

In 1965 archaeologists successfully moved the huge stone monuments to safety. The grateful government of Egypt later invited the Fields' family to celebrate their son's bar mitzvah in Cairo. Ironically, it is probable that the Abu Simbel monuments were originally built by Hebrew slaves of Rameses II. Thus, Fields may have been saving the work of his own ancestors.

For Further Reading:

Miami Jewish Tribune, January 29, 1993, p. 3b.

Q. Which world renowned non-Jewish opera tenor received important early experience in the Tel-Aviv Hebrew National Opera?

A. In the 1960's, a young Placido Domingo sang with the Tel Aviv opera company. Working under unsophisticated stage conditions, but in front of knowledgeable and appreciative audiences, Domingo developed the resources that helped turn him into one of the top tenors of the era. He also added Hebrew to his language repertoire.

For Further Reading:
Placido Domingo, *My First Forty Years*. New York, Knopf, 1983.

Q. Why did the New York Grand Dragon of the Ku Klux Klan commit suicide?

A. On November 1, 1968, twenty-eight year old Daniel Burros, Klan leader in New York, shot himself dead after the secret of his Jewish birth and childhood was revealed in the *New York Times*. Several high officials of the Klan who witnessed the suicide said that Burros had returned in a wild rage to their apartment after seeing the *Times* article. He destroyed a bed with karate kicks before taking a gun and shooting himself. Burros had completely hidden his Jewishness and was strongly anti-Semitic.

Born in New York to Russian Jewish immigrants, Burros had a bar mitzvah and was an outstanding student at John Adams High School in Queens. His I.Q. was measured as 154. He later joined the American Nazi Party and several other neo-fascist groups, as well as the Klan. He had been arrested four times, once for defacing the B'nai Brith building in Washington. Four days after his suicide the National Renaissance party, another Neo-Nazi Jew-hating group, deposed Robert Burros, their National Secretary, when they learned from a local newspaper that his father was Jewish. The two Burroses were not related.

For Further Reading:
New York Times, Nov. 1, 1965, 1:3 and Nov. 5, 26:2.

Q. Why did an Orthodox Jewish girl jump from a ski lift?

A. In 1969 a Brooklyn Jewish girl was awarded $37,231 in a lawsuit. A ski lift on which she was riding with a male escort stalled. She leaped from the car rather than violate Jewish law, she thought, by being alone with a man in an inaccessible place. She fell 25 feet and suffered a broken nose and bruises. It turned out later that the apparatus was not broken. Attendants had turned off the power not realizing anyone was still in the cars.

For Further Reading:

New York Times, 1-22-69, 49: 1.

Q. How did young Jews respond to the radicalism of the Viet Nam era?

A. Many Jews were strongly attracted to radical groups, whether in politics or religion. However, some found themselves uncomfortable in the New Left and sought for some sense of Jewish identity. A variety of efforts tried to bridge the old and the new in Judaism. Two very different approaches were exemplified by Rebbetzin Jungreis and the college havurot. Sometimes called the Jewish Billy Graham, Esther Jungreis, wife of an Orthodox rabbi, began speaking to student groups in the early 1970's hoping to draw them back to Jewish observance and away from the cults and radical social movements. A survivor of concentration camps, Rebbetzin Jungreis appealed to all Jews, on a strongly emotional level, to find meaning in their own unique identity.

Another unusual response was the formation of Jewish student communes, often called havurot, on a number of college campuses, e.g. Case Western in Cleveland, Cornell, University of Michigan, and University of North Carolina. Individual communes offered their own blends of traditional and untraditional in Judaism and varied greatly in size and outlook.

Q. Did any Jews win the Congressional Medal of Honor in the Viet Nam War?

A. While some American Jews were leading anti-war protests, others were fighting in Asian jungles. Lieutenant Jack Jacobs was serving in the 16th Infantry of the 9th Army in the Kien Phong area. On March 9, 1968, his unit came under heavy fire from Viet Cong forces occupying well fortified positions. Jacobs directed air strikes against the enemy, so that his men could reorganize. The senior officers were all killed or wounded, so Jacobs, although himself wounded, took command. Under heavy fire, he made repeated trips into the open to save fourteen wounded soldiers and drove off several enemy attacks. For this, he was awarded the Congressional Medal of Honor. He also earned seven additional medals for his achievements in other incidents.

For Further Reading:

Seymour Brody, *Jewish Heroes in America,* New York, Shapolsky, 1991.

Q. What was the influence of Nathan Mnookin, a Kansas City Jew of Orthodox parentage, on the space program?

A. Mnookin was a graduate in chemical engineering from University of Kansas. He and Dr. J.C. Patrick established the Industrial Testing Laboratories, which led to many advances in chemical engineering. One of them was thiokol, a synthetic rubber, which was later used as the binder in the rocket fuel that powered astronauts to the moon.

Mnookin also helped organize the Aleph Zadik Aleph, the junior B'nai Brith, in Omaha in 1922. AZA became the largest organization of Jewish youth in the United States. The letters stood for ahavah (brotherly love), zedakah (benevolence) and achdut (harmony).

For Further Reading:

Phillip Klutznick, *Angles of Vision: A Memoir of My Lives*, Chicago, Ivan R. Due, 1991.

Q. When did the synagogue havurah movement begin?

A. The first havurah was founded in Somerville, Massachusetts by Rabbi Arthur Green in 1968, and the movement grew quickly under the guidance of leaders like Rabbi Harold Schulweis. The havurot were small groups of Jews that would meet for prayer or other activities and that emphasized individual and informal freedom of expression beyond what mainstream congregations would follow. Many affiliated with established congregations, usually Reform. People who were too far removed from traditional and institutional Judaism to feel comfortable with it and who yet sought some Jewish experience in their lives often found a place in the havurah movement.

For Further Reading:

New York Times, 9-13-77, page 35.

Q. Few Jews voted for Richard Nixon in his various campaigns for political office. How did this influence his policies as president toward the State of Israel?

A. A complex man, associated with right wing views and Communist baiting early in his political career, Richard Nixon never was popular with Jewish voters. Nevertheless, he was very supportive of Israel in its problems with hostile neighbors. Nixon did not approve of the pressure exerted on

Israel by President Eisenhower and Secretary of State John Foster Dulles to give up its gains in the Suez War of 1956.

It was again Nixon who, as president during the Yom Kippur War in 1973, pushed a recalcitrant Defense Department into supplying the Israelis with the military equipment they so desperately needed. The U.S. was soon sending 1000 tons a day to Israel, a project bigger than the famous Berlin Airlift of 1948. And the shipments continued despite the imposition by the Arabs of an oil embargo on the U.S.

Why was Nixon so helpful? Several speculations may be offered. First, Nixon admired the toughness and independence of the Israelis, surrounded as they were by enemies, a situation with which he could personally identify. Second, Nixon had a very warm relationship with Israeli Prime Minister Golda Meir, whom he described in his memoirs as "combining extreme toughness and extreme warmth." Also, the fact that Jews never voted for Nixon gave him, he wrote, greater flexibility to do what he thought was right without feeling that he was politically beholden to them. Nixon was also pleased at the feeling that he had fulfilled his moral obligations to the Israelis and that he was entitled to their trust.

For Further Reading:

Richard Nixon, *RN: The Memoirs of Richard Nixon* New York; Grosset and Dunlap, 1978.
Richard Nixon, *The Triumph of a Politician*, New York, Simon and Schuster, 1989.
Stephen Ambrose, *Nixon: The Education of a Politician*, New York; Simon and Schuster, 1987.

Q. How many American Jewish institutions were bombed or burned during the 1960's?

A. There were 19 bombings and four attempted bombings from 1960 through 1969. Eight of these happened between 1960 and 1963, and 11 occured from 1967 through 1969. There were 45 incidents of arson, with 15 in 1969 alone.

These acts were committed by individuals or lunatic fringe groups. While most were in the New York area, there were incidents or threats also in places like Gadsden, Alabama; Dallas, Texas; Trenton, Michigan; Cheyenne, Wyoming; Los Angeles; and Seattle. In 1967, a temple in Jackson, Mississippi and the home of its Rabbi, Perry Nussbaum, were bombed several months apart. In May-June 1970, five fires were set in three Dorchester, Massachusetts synagogues. There seem to be no known acts of this sort in the U.S. before 1951.

For Further Reading:

Report of Anti-Defamation League to U.S. Senate Subcommittee on Investigation of the Committee on Government Operations, August 4, 1970.

Q. Were there American Jews living below poverty level even after the period of the great immigration wave?

A. A 1972 issue of *Jewish Week* debated the number of Jews living in poverty, i.e., with income below $3,000. One report put the total number at 250,000. Another argued that there were 250,000 poor Jews in New York alone, and perhaps as many as 800,000 (about 12% of the total Jewish population) through the United States. Miami Beach, widely thought of as an affluent resort, included the South Bay area, which in the 1960's was home to almost 30,000 elderly Jews. 85% of whom had incomes below $2,500.

Jews and money are easily associated in the public mind, and many people take seriously the old canard that Jews control world banking and finance. However, many people might be surprised to learn that there are American Jews living in poverty, at times entirely beyond the reach of Jewish charitable institutions.

For Further Reading:

Abraham Lavender, *A Coat of Many Colors,* Westport, Conn: Greenwood Press, 1957.
Thomas J. Cottle, *Hidden Survivors: Portraits of Poor Jews in America,* Prentice-Hall Inc.: Englewood Cliffs, NJ, 1980.

Q. What periodicals did American rabbis read?

A. In the late 1970's Allan Maller conducted a study regarding the reading material of over 400 Reform and Conservative rabbis. He found that forty six percent of Reform rabbis and fifty four percent of Conservative rabbis read scholarly journals. "American Jewish History" was very popular, along with the "Biblical Archaeology Review," and the "Israel Exploration Journal". Young Reform rabbis also liked popular magazines like "Rolling Stone" and "Mother Jones". Among Conservative rabbis, fifty percent read periodicals in Hebrew, while among Reform rabbis 29% of of those over age 50 and 15% of those under age 37 read Hebrew periodicals.

For Further Reading:

Allen S. Maller, "Report from the Magazine Rack: What are the Rabbis Reading?" *AJA,* XXXI, 131–141.

Q. How did Jewish group reactions to urban problems differ between the early twentieth century and the 1960's and 1970's?

A. By 1970 a new activism, almost a militancy, seemed to have surfaced among some groups of Jews. One example was the large Hasidic communities in New York City that were faced with the daily problems of living in mixed urban neighborhoods where violence was a fact of life. Jews did not hesitate to respond actively to violence. For example, in December 1978, a large group of Jews invaded and took over a police precinct station in Borough Park, Brooklyn, demanding greater police protection after the murder of an elderly Jewish man in a street robbery. For days the press was filled with accusations and counter-accusations from Mayor Edward Koch, the police, and Jewish leaders. Eventually two men, Jose and Jimmy Julber, were arrested, tried, found guilty of murder, and sentenced to long prison terms.

Stories of New York Hasidim speaking up and acting for their own protection fill the pages of newspapers from the 1960's on. Demonstrations and protests were determined and not infrequent. The Lubavitch Hasidim of Crown Heights organized neighborhood patrols in the mid-1960's that came to be known as the Crown Heights Maccabees. Many Jews who came over as post-World War II refugees brought with them both an unwillingness to be patient in the face of threat and an uncompromising self-awareness. Although they were peaceable enough citizens in their daily affairs, they did not hesitate to react against street crime or anti-Semitic ideologues.

America, in the 1960's and 1970's, sprouted all sorts of groups and ideologies who could not easily identify with Middle America. Among Jews the new mood was strikingly in contrast to the great drive toward Americanization that characterized the immigrants of earlier generations. The Hasidim in particular were often easily identifiable by their appearance and seemed not at all self-conscious or shy about it.

Such militancy was far less common outside New York than in it. However, there was at least one incident. In San Francisco in April, 1977, a group called the National Socialist White Worker Party opened the Rudolf Hess Bookstore. The store, which sported a swastika on its front and sold anti-Semitic literature, was situated across the street from Temple B'nai Emunah. The membership of the congregation was largely older immigrant Jews and included many survivors of the concentration camps. The martial music blaring from the store and the brown shirted party workers finally proved too much to endure. On Passover evening, about fifty people came out of the synagogue after services, broke into the store, and burned it. Ironically, the owner of the premises was a survivor of Auschwitz, who was at first unaware of the Nazi affiliation of his tenants.

For Further Reading:

New York Times, April 6, 1977, p. 15.

Q. Who was "Rabbi Sally?"

A. In 1972, Sally Priesand (1946-) became the first woman to be ordained by Hebrew Union College. After serving as a student rabbi in Hattiesburg, Mississippi and Jackson, Michigan she took a full time position as assistant rabbi in the Stephen Wise Free Synagogue in New York. Her first full rabbinic position was in Monmouth, New Jersey in 1981. Her book *Judaism and the New Woman,* accepts the widespread view that Jewish women have historically been treated as secondary to men and that women should take a larger role in Jewish leadership.

Q. When did Conservative Judaism begin to include women for a minyan?

A. Conservative Judaism became more liberal in the 1960's and 1970's, with the counting of women in the minyan. In September, 1973, Conservatism's Rabbinical Assembly voted to count women as part of a minyan (prayer quorum). Women's groups hailed the decision as a recognition of women's status in Judaism and as an important step toward rabbinic ordination for women. The Assembly did not actually require its member synagogues to conform to the new ruling. It simply authorized them to count the women if they wished.

Orthodox leaders opposed the innovation as contradicting established Jewish law, with Rabbi Irving Greenberg about the only Orthodox rabbi to express approval of the Conservatives' move. Nor were all Conservative leaders pleased at the new declaration, some seeing it as too radical a break with tradition.

For Further Reading:

New York Times, Sept. 16, 1973, IV:7:5

Q. What unusual school was attended by director Mike Nichols, Treasury Secretary W. Michael Blumenthal, and a number of other highly successful Jewish Americans?

A. In Berlin in 1932, twenty three year old Lotte Kaliski founded Privat Judische Waldschule Kaliski school, covering from first grade through high school. Although not initially restricted to Jews, it soon became a haven for Jewish children brutalized in the public schools after the Nazi take over in 1933.

The Kaliski school offered an unusual curriculum, preparing students for British and American universities, and teaching also Hebrew and agriculture, as some students might wish to go to kibbutzim in Palestine. Student turnover was constant, as many Jews were fleeing Germany as quickly as they were able. At its peak, the Kaliski school taught 400 students. It provided a relatively stable atmosphere for children living in a horrifying world. The school closed after Kristallnacht in 1938.

Ms. Kaliski accomplished all this despite being disabled by polio. In 1992, seventy former students from half a dozen countries, gathered for a reunion with Lotte Kaliski in New York's Mayflower Hotel.

For Further Reading:

New York Times, Nov. 10, 1992 A12.

Q. What member of the U.S. House of Representatives studied at the Jewish Theological Seminary?

A. Bella Savitzky Abzug, Congresswoman from New York's 19th district (1970–1976), had taken evening classes at the JTS after graduating from Hunter College. Daughter of Russian Jewish immigrants, Abzug was a member of Hashomer Hatzair, and later taught in the Hebrew school of the Kingsbridge Heights Jewish Center in the Bronx. A longtime activist in liberal causes, Abzug was an early critic of the Viet Nam War and a strong supporter of women's rights. In 1972 she sought to introduce impeachment charges against President Richard Nixon.

For Further Reading:

Bella S. Abzug, *Mrs. Abzug Goes to Washington.* New York, Saturday Review Press, 1972.

Q. What changes in Reform Judaism were pointed up in the "San Francisco" platform of 1976?

A. The San Francisco platform, composed largely under the guidance of Professor Eugene Borowitz, expressed confidence in Reform Judaism. It states, however, that the 19th century faith in human progress was shattered, and Jews must depend less on the values of society and more on their Judaism. The Jew has ethical obligations and also the need to live a Jewish life involving life-long study, prayer, and the Sabbath. Reform Judaism committed itself to aliyah and to the State of Israel.

Rabbi Borowitz, in his many writings, also called upon Reform to pay more attention to Jewish ritual as a way of maintaining close contact with God, of achieving a rootedness in personal life and of strengthening links with both past and future generations.

For Further Reading:

Michael A. Meyer, *Response to Modernity: A History of the Reform Movement in Judaism,* New York, Oxford University Press, 1988.

Eugene B. Borowitz, *Liberal Judaism* New York. Union of American Hebrew Congregations. 1984.

Q. Who was often known as the Hippie Rabbi?

A. Shlomo Carlebach (1926 -1994), descended from a prominent rabbinic family, was born in 1926 in Berlin and escaped to the U.S. in 1939. He studied both at the Beth Medrash Govoha in Lakewood, NJ and at Columbia University.

In the late 1950's he began to develop a unique reputation within the Orthodox world as a guitar playing rabbi, making appearances at Jewish schools and the like. After a few years, Carlebach began to connect with the Jewish youth who were caught up in the social, political, and cultural turbulence of the time. Adapting himself to the style of the new movements, he sought to draw the drifting young Jews back to Torah. His teachings seemed an unusual fusion of 1960's and 1970's style love with traditional Judaism. He established centers in Israel and California. He wrote hundreds of songs, which are still enjoyed around the world today.

Q. How many Jewish vegetarians were there in the U.S. in the 1970's?

A. The North American Jewish Vegetarian Society numbered 300 members in 1977. It was affiliated with the world-wide Jewish Vegetarian Society, whose headquarters were in London, England . There were, of course, Jewish vegetarians outside the Society. Vegetarianism has never been enjoined by Jewish religious law, although several famous Jews have abstained from meat, including Nobel Laureate Isaac Bashevis Singer. Society members accept vegetarianism for a variety of reasons — sympathy for the animals or the feeling that meat was unhealthy because of modern methods of treating it.

For Further Reading:

New York Times, 9-14-77, C4.

Q. How did President Jimmy Carter once serve as marriage broker for twelve Jewish girls?

A. The Jews of Syria have been subject to harsh restriction and discrimination by the Syrian government ever since the creation of the State of Israel in 1948. Many young men fled the country, despite fear of punishment if they were caught. For women, escape was more difficult, and by the 1970's there were about 500 young Jewish women who could have little prospect of finding Jewish husbands.

In 1976, Congressman Stephen Solarsz (D-NY) and Stephen Shalom, a leader of the Syrian Jewish community in the United States, met with both Syrian and U.S. officials about the problems of the Syrian Jews. U.S. President Jimmy Carter expressed concern for the plight of the Jewish women and raised the issue in a discussion with Syrian President Hafez Assad in Geneva in 1977.

Assad agreed to allow 12 women to be married by proxy to American men and then to emigrate to the U.S. More women would follow at a later date. Since U.S. law did not recognize proxy marriages, the women could settle in the U.S. without actually going through with the arranged marriages. The story aroused considerable media attention at the time, but Syrian policies shifted and the program never went beyond the original dozen.

For Further Reading:

Joseph A.D. Sutton, *Magic Carpet: Aleppo in Flatbush*. New York, Thayer-Jacoby, 1979.

Q. What rock and hillbilly music star was once awarded a prize by the Jewish Defense League?

A. Kinky (Richard} Freedman, head of a band called the Texas Jewboys which gained fame in the 1970's, has written and performed songs like "Ride 'Em Jewboy" and "Ol' Ben Lucas Who Had A Lot of Mucus." Freedman was a former Peace Corps worker and once was Republican candidate for mayor in Kerrville, Texas. A hard-swearing iconoclast in a thoroughly Texan style, Freedman overcame a battle with drugs to gain renewed success as a singer. He then added a career as a writer of detective novels, whose hero is also named Kinky Freedman. His hard line views on Israeli foreign policy earned him the attention of Meir Kahane's super nationalist Jewish Defense League.

For Further Reading:
Ze'ev Chefets, *Members of the Tribe,* New York, Bantam Books, 1988.

Q. What famous Jewish comedian was ordained by R. Moshe Feinstein?

A. Comedian Jackie Mason, known for his rapid fire humor, was indeed ordained by R. Moshe Feinstein, head of Mesivta Tiferes Yerushalayim and one of the leaders of Orthodox Jewry. But the rabbinate was not for Mason, and in the late 1950's he turned to a career in show business.

Q. What Jewish diplomat of President Jimmy Carter's administration would read books to Elihu Root, who had been Theodore Roosevelt's secretary of state?

A. There was little comparison between Teddy Roosevelt's "Speak softly and carry a big stick" diplomacy and Jimmy Carter's vacillations. However, it is an oddity of history that Elihu Root, Teddy Roosevelt's secretary of state, helped launch the diplomatic career of Ambassador Sol Linowitz. Linowitz held several major positions in the 1970's including U.S. Representative for Middle East peace negotiations.

As a student at Hamilton College in Clinton, New York in 1930, Linowitz used to read aloud to Elihu Root, who was by then in his eighties and dim of sight. Root once asked Linowitz about his career plans. Linowitz replied, "I'm not sure. Maybe a rabbi or a lawyer." Root told him, "Be a lawyer. A lawyer needs twice as much religion as a rabbi."

One can imagine the effect on a young man of close contact with an illustrious personage like Root. Linowitz went on to Cornell Law School and later became chairman of the board of Xerox Corporation. His first major diplomatic post was as U.S. ambassador to the OAS under President Lyndon Johnson. From 1975 to 1980, he also served as lay head of the Jewish Theological Seminary.

For Further Reading:
Jean Baer, *The Self-Chosen,* New York; Arbor House, 1982.

Q. What was particularly unusual about Frank Collin, leader of the National Socialist Party of America, who attempted to lead a march in the heavily Jewish area of Skokie, Illinois in the late 1970's?

A. Collin was really Frank Cohen, a Jewish son of a Holocaust survivor. Other Nazi organizations shunned him. He had been a member of the American Nazi Party but was ousted when his heritage became known. Collin's ACLU lawyer was a Jew named David Goldberger. The ACLU executive director, Aryeh Neier, who also became involved in the case, had himself escaped from the European Holocaust with his parents in the late 1930's.

For Further Reading:

Aryeh Neier. *Defending My Enemy: American Nazis. The Skokie Case and The Risks of Freedom*, New York, Dutton, 1979.
David Hamlin, *The Nazi-Skokie Conflict: A Civil Rights Battle*, Boston, Beacon Press, 1980.

Q. What internationally renowned architect has been acclaimed for buildings he designed in Saudi Arabia, as well as for synagogues in the U.S.?

A. Born in Seattle to poor Japanese immigrants, Minoru Yamasaki (1913–1986) has become one of the world's best known architects, particularly for his design of the original World Trade Center in New York.

The first religious building he designed was the North Shore Congregation of Glencoe, Illinois, completed in 1964. Yamasaki attended a High Holy Day service to comprehend better the needs of a synagogue building, and he promised "a structure that is an interlacing of daylight and solids ... with a spacious contemporary feeling that is inspiring and neither raucous nor intrusive." The Temple Beth-El building in Bloomfield Township, Michigan, completed in 1974, was shaped so as to give the feeling of the biblical Tent of Meeting which the Israelites constructed in the Sinai Desert.

On the other side of the international fence, Yamasaki designed the Saudi Arabian Monetary Agency to house the Saudi national bank, aiming for a building that was highly functional and yet reflected Islamic traditions. Yamasaki also built the Dharan Airport for the Saudis, in 1961, and was called upon to plan a massive expansion in the 1980's. A picture of the earlier building appeared on a Saudi banknote.

For Further Reading:

Minoru Yamasaki, *A Life in Architecture*, New York; Weatherhill, 1979.

Q. Were there still Crypto-Jews or Conversos in the U.S. in the late 20th century?

A. For years scholars had debated the extent, if any, of the settlement of Conversos in New Mexico under Spanish rule. In the 1960's information began to surface about Americans who live in the southwest and are of Hispanic background. They trace their ancestry to Spanish Jews and still practice quietly certain Jewish customs passed down through the generations. A few are now openly returning to Judaism and have joined synagogues.

For Further Reading:

Henry J. Tobias, *A History of the Jews in New Mexico*, Albequerque, University of New Mexico Press, 1990.

Q. What is a mini-kollel?

A. A kollel is an institute in which adult students of Talmud devote their time entirely to study and teaching. Most major yeshivot in America or in Israel were supporting kollels by the 1980's. They ranged in size from a few scholars to several hundred, the largest in the U.S. being in Lakewood, New Jersey.

In the late 1960's the concept of the mini-kollel was first formulated. Small groups of young married couples settled in a number of American cities and set up small kollels independent of the larger yeshivot. In addition to long hours of study, the scholars of these kollels offered classes for the general community and provided a strong center of a Torah oriented lifestyle.

As of 1990, mini-kollels were functioning in 13 U.S. cities across the country, and the numbers continue to grow. Almost invariably, these kollels have been successful both in attracting local people to study and also in attracting Orthodox families to settle in their communities. They were a major factor in the growing strength and visibility of Orthodox life by the turn of the century.

Q. What gentile baseball superstar not only wears a "chai" chain but always drew a "chai" with his bat in the dirt at the batter's box each time he steps up to the plate?

A. Professional athletes are well known for the great variety of superstitious rituals they use to bring them good luck, and it is not uncommon for a baseball player to make the sign of a cross on home plate when he comes to bat. Wade Boggs, one of baseball's great hitters, was the one who used the "chai" sign. He was delighted to hear that his friend, Jewish talk show host Larry King, has a daughter named Chaia. *Chai* is Hebrew for life.

Q. What Jewish roommate of Babe Ruth was still a major league baseball coach over 60 years later?

A. Jimmy Reese, born James Herman Soloman in 1905, roomed with the great Babe Ruth while playing for the New York Yankees in 1930–1931. He continued in a variety of professional baseball jobs after his playing career ended in 1932. As of 1991, he was still coaching for the California Angels. Reese was greatly respected by players. Pitcher Nolan Ryan even named his son after Reese.

For Further Reading:

The Baseball Encyclopedia, New York, MacMillan Publ. Co., 1990.

Q. Who was called the man of a thousand voices?

A. Mel Blanc (1908–1989) supplied the voices for hundreds of cartoon and other characters during a long career in Hollywood. These included Porky Pig, Daffy Duck, Bugs Bunny, Elmer Fudd, Woody Woodpecker, Speedy Gonzales, Barney Rubble, Wile E. Coyote, Foghorn Leghorn, Yosemite Sam, Tom and Jerry, Sylvester and Tweety and many more. Blanc was hired by Warner Bros. in 1936. Porky Pig had already appeared in a number of short cartoons, but the studio wanted a better voice for him. They called on the newly hired Mel Blanc who joked, "You want me to be the voice of a pig? That's some job for a Jewish boy." Blanc went to a pig farm to study the pigs' grunts and came back with some good ideas of how a cartoon pig like Porky might sound. He then added Porky's stutter. I.e. Porky would find it impossible to say exactly what he wanted to say and after several failed attempts would say something altogether different. Soon after, Blanc received his first paycheck from Warners. It was the biggest paycheck he had seen so far in his life — two hundred dollars.

In his autobiographical *That's Not All Folks: My Life in the Golden Age of Cartoon and Radio* (1988), Blanc attributes some of his skill with speech to his growing up in a Jewish quarter in Portland Oregon, where he heard a lot of Japanese, Spanish and British as well as Yiddish.

Perhaps Porky's best-known expression is "Th—uh — the—uh—th— that's all folks." Porky can speak for us too as this book ends, "Th—uh-th— uh-th-that's all folks.

Index

Aaron, Israel, 123
Abraham, Chapman, 14–15, 20
Abraham, Isaac, 23
Abrahams, Abraham, 15
Abrahams, Rachel, 28
Abravanel, Isaac, 5
Abzug, Bella, 280
Ackerman, Paula, 252
Adams, Franklin Pierce, 159
Adams, John x, 27, 34–35, 56
Adams, John Quincy, 35–36, 55
Adler, Cyrus, 155
Adler, Joseph, 183
Adler, Nathan, 114
agricultural settlements, 148–149
Agudath Harabbonim, 271
Alamo, 34–35
Aleichem, Sholom, 179
Alexander, Moses, 187–188
Allston, Washington, 44
Alonso, Hernando, 6
Alter, Pinhas (Gerer Rebbe), 192
ambassadors, 265–266
Anderson, Gilbert, 174
Anderson, Marion, 152
Andersonville, 95
Ando, K., 188
Ararat, 50–51
Arnold, Benedict, 125
Arnold, Matthew, 195
Asen, Abraham, 158
Ash, Abraham, 73–74
Ash, Michael, 74
Askenazi, Moses, 25
Audet, M., 33

Baker, Adolph, 56
Balfour Declaration, 188–189
Bamberger, Earnest, 181
Bamberger Simon, 180–181
Bar Simon, Jacob, 10
Baron, Nahum David, 150
Barnard College, 133
Barnwell Ring, 225
Baruch, Bernard, 186, 228
Baruch, Simon, 130
baseball, 165, 258
basketball, 257
Belmont, August, 86
Ben Gurion, David, 185, 246, 249
Ben Hassan, 30
Bendell, Herman, 103
Benderly Samson, 176–177
Bendix, William, 156
Benet, Stephen St. Vincent, 14
Benjamin, I. J., 86
Benjamin, Judah P., 79, 83–84, 89, 97
Berg, Gertrude, 253
Berg, Moe, 203
Bergson, Peter, 237
Berkowitz, Henry, 237
Berlin, Irving, 196
Berliner, Emil, 118
Bibo, Solomon, 90
Blackstone, William, 135–136
Blatt, Sol, 225
Blanc, Mel, 286
Blaustein, Louis, 173
Bloch, Charles, 245
Bloom, Sol, 225
Bloomfield, Solomon, 143

287

Bloomfield-Zeisler, Fanny, 143
Board of Delegates of American Israelites, 81
Boggs, Wade, 285
B'nai Brith, 61, 232
Booth, John Wilkes, 97
Borowitz, Eugene, 280–281
Bougainville, Count, 17
Bouquet, Henry, 20
Brandeau, Esther, 16
Brandeis, Louis, 180
Breitbart, Zisha, 198
Breuer, Joseph, 248–249
Brice, Fanny, 192
Bright, George, 26
Brown, Benjamin Gratz, 103–104
Browne, Edward B. M.147
Browning, Robert, 255
Brownlow, William, 84
Brundage, Avery, 220–221
Brunswick, Ruth Mack, 24
Bunche, Ralph, 152
Burrows, Millar, 248
Burrus, David, 273
Burrus, Robert, 273
Bush, George, 27, 229
Bush, Lewis, 24
Bush, Solomon, 31
Buteau, 28
Butler, Benjamin, 91

Cahan, Abraham, 111
Cameron Dragoons, 87
calendar reform, 207
Canada, 15–18
Cardozo, Benjamin, 233
Cardozo, Francis, 115
Cardozo, Jacob, 49
Carillon, Reverend, 63
Carlebach, Shlomo, 281
Carter, Jimmy, 282–283
Carvajal, Luis de, 8
Carvalho, Solomon Nunes, 74
Catherine the Great x
Celler, Emanuel, 244
Chafetz Chaim, 163
Channing, Mr., 26
Cherokee, 4

Chicago Fire, 109–110
Chicago Jewish Training School, 131–132
Cincinnatus Society, 28
citrons, 69
Claiborne, William, 43
Clay, Henry, 79
Clemens, Clara, 186
Clemens, Suzy, 110
Cohen, Jacob, 50
Cohen, John Sanford, 211
Cohen, Joseph
Cohen, Joshua Falk, 78
Cohen, Morris (two-gun), 235
Cohen, William S., 211
Coleman, Beatrice, 194
Collen, Frank, 284
Columbus, Christopher ix, 4–5
Columbus Platform, 199
comedy, 254–255
Cone, Etta & Claribel, 156–157
Confirmation, 63
conversos, 285
Cordova, Jacob de, 69
Cotton, John, 4
Coughlin, Charles, 259–260
cowboys, 125
Cresson, Warder, 66–67
Cromwell, Dan, 221
Crown Heights Maccabees, 278
Cuming, Alexander, 14

Damascus Libel, 59–60
Daniels, Josephus, 186–187
Damrosch, Leopold, 108, 118
Davidson, Herman, 65
Davis, Abel, 183
Davis, Jacob, 106
Davis, Varina, 97
day schools, 229
De Leon, Daniel, 148
De Leon, David Camden, 88
DeLeon, Edwin Thomas, 89
Dead Sea, 67
Decatur, Stephen, 42
Dembitz, Louis, 140
Democrat-Jewish vote, 218
Des Moines speech, 231–232

Dillon, C. Douglas, 266
Dewey, Melvil, 163–164
Dickens, Charles, 53
Dickstein, Samuel, 218, 222–223, 239
Displaced Persons Act, 244
Dittenhoefer, Sam, 212
Dohla, Johann, 27
Domingo, Placido, 273
Drachman, Bernard, 46, 145
Dreben, Sam, 168
Dreyfus, Alfred, 75
Dropsie, Moses Aaron, 154–155
duels, 57–58
Dulles, John Foster, 276
Dunbar, David, 16
Dyer, Leon

Eastman, George, 207
Eban, Abba, 253
Edelstein, Michael, 231
Edward VIII, 225
Einhorn, David, 85
Einstein, Albert, 253
Eisenhower, Dwight D., 236, 240, 245, 247, 248, 276
Eitz Chaim, 239
Eliot, T. S., 270
Elizabeth I, i, 7
Elkus, Abraham, 162
Elliot, Mama Cass, 260
Ellis, Max, 169
Emanuel, David, 37
Enelow, Hyman, 46
Epstein, Ephraim, 37
Epstein, Moses Henry, 108
Etting, Henry, 5, 92
Ewing, Samuel, 46
Eytinge, Rose, 99
Ezekiel, Moses Jacob, 95–96

Fawcett, Rachel, 29
Feinstein, Moshe, 183
Fels, Joseph, 161
Feibleman, Uriah, 95
Felsenthal, Bernhard, 85, 140
Felt, David, 33
feminism, 137
Ferber, Edna, 146–147

Fields, Stanley, 172
Fiersohn, Reba, 179
Finkelstein, Louis, 244, 246
Fish, Hamilton, 194
Fischel, Arnold, 88
Fischel, Harry, 170–171
Flexner family, 152–153
football, 108–109
Ford, Henry, 190, 209, 242
Foreman, Milton, 183
Fort Ontario, 239
Foote, Henry, 84
four chaplains, 233
Franco, Solomon, 8
Frank, Leo, 181–182
Frank, Ray, 143
Frankfurter, Felix, 228, 233
Franklin, Benjamin x, 1, 27, 31
Franklin, Sidney, 204
Franks, Benjamin, 10–11
Franks, David, 25
Franks, David Salisbury, 25
Franks, Phila, 48
Frederick the Great, ix, 4
Freedman, Kinky, 282
Fremont, John, 74
Frey, Joseph S. C., 36
Fuqua, Galba, 54
Fuson, Robert, 5

Gabrilowitsch, Ossip, 186
Gadsden, Christopher, 37
Galveston Plan, 172–173
Garrick, David, 117
Gant, Love Rosa, 137
Gaunze, Joachim, 7
Gersoni, Henry, 141
Gerstle Lewis, 107–108
Gideon, Rowland, 8
Gillet, Francis, 194
Gillette-Reger Bill, 237
Gimbel, Jake, 169
Ginzberg, Eli, 167
Ginzberg, Louis, 150, 167, 244
Gleitzman, Isaac, 93
Gluck, Alma, 179
Glueck, Nelson, 203
Gold Rush, 65–66

INDEX

Goldberg, Arthur, 266, 268–269
Goldberg, Charles, 96
Goldberger, David, 284
Goldberger, Joseph, 190–191
Goldwater family, 269
Golden Harry, 172, 261
Goldhurst, Leib, 172
Goldwyn, Sam, 233
Goode, Alexander, 233
Gomez Isaac, 13
Gomez, Lewis, 13
Gordin, Jacob, 164
Gradis, Abraham, 16
Grahl, Ann, 47
Grant, Cary, 251
Grant, Ulysses, 91, 103, 105–106, 111
Granzotti, Gianni, 5
Gratz, Rebecca, 45–46, 103
Gratz, Richia, 36
Green, Arthur, 275
Greenberg, Hank, 225–226
Greenberg, Irving, 279
Gruenberg, Sidonia, 207
Grusd, Edward, 232
Gutheim, James, 86–87

Hahn, Michael, 89
Hamilton, Alexander, 29, 32
Harburg, Yip, 259
Harby, Isaac, 34, 49
Harby, Levi Myers, 92
Hart, Aaron, 17, 202
Hart, Cecil, 202
Hart, David, 203
Hart, Emanuel, 74
Hart, Jacob, 19
Hart, Moss, 196–197
Hart, Samuel, 19
Hart Trophy, 202–203
Hatikvah, 137
havurah, 275
Hayes, Rutherford, 100
Hays, Isaac, 104
Hays, Moses Michael, 8
Hazen, Moses, 18
"Hebrew Maiden's Lament", 89–91
Hebrew Union College, 129, 156
Helfman, Hessia, 128

Hendricks, Harmon, 23
Hendricks, Uriah, 22–23
Herzog, Isaac, 246
Heschel, Abraham Joshua, 246
Heydenfeldt, Samuel, 65, 80
Heyneman, Henry, 98
Hildesheimer, Azriel, 93
Hirsch, Emil, 108, 136, 139
Hirsch, Samson Raphael, 67
Hirsch, Solomon, 162
Hirshell, Solomon, 64
Hitler, Adolph, 220–221, 224, 227
Holy Stones of Newark, 82
Horner, Henry, 217
Horwitz, Jonas, 64
Horwitz, Jonathan Phineas, 65
Houdini, 146
House, Edward, 106
Howells, William Dean, 110–111
Humphrey, Hubert, 244, 248
Hunter, Robert, 11
hurricane, 265–266
Hyams, Henry, 89
Hyams, Isaac, 87
Hyamson, Moses, 207
Hyde, Ida, 151
Hyneman, Elias, 95

Illowy, Bernard, 85, 92
Imber, Naftali Herz, 137–138
Immigration Acts, 1923, 198
Immigration Restriction League, 140
immigration: views, 118
Intellectuals immigration, 1930's, 215–216
Irving, Washington, 46
Isaac, Isaac, 23
Isaac, Jacob, 30
Isaac, S. M., 15
Israel, Edward, 124

"Jacob and the Indians", 14
Jacobs, Abraham, 142
Jacobs, Jack, 274
Jacoby, Philo, 117
Jackson, Andrew, 43
Jaffa, Nathan and Henry, 212
Jaffe, Shalom, 135

Jastrow, Marcus, 84, 130–131
Jefferson, Thomas x, 18–19, 25, 27, 30, 33–34
Jeffries, Jim, 172
Jehudah, Tobias ben, 23
Jewish Theological Seminary, 129, 154, 202, 243
Jewish War Veterans, 141
Johnson, Alexander Bryan, 56
Johnson, Edward Isaac, 54
Johnson, Jack, 172
Johnson, Lyndon Baines, 230, 272
Jonas, Joseph, 46
Joseph, Jacob, 132, 172
Judah, Samuel, 34, 54

Kahn, Charles, 206
Kahn, Florence and Julius, 155–156
Kahn, Otto, 191–192
Kahn, Reuben, 207
Kalakaua, David, 129
Kaliski, Lotte, 279–280
Kalisher, Zvi Hirsch, 93
Kalmanovitz, Avraham, 237
Kaplan, Mordecai, 116, 195, 202
Karajan, Herbert von, 252
Karigal, Chaim, 26
Karpeles, Leopold, 87
Kaufman, David, 59
Kaye, Danny, 233
Kennedy, John F., 246–247, 266–267–268–269
Kennedy's Jew Baby, 150
ketubah, 256
Key, Francis Scott, 41
Kidd, Captain William, 10–11
King, Phil, 109
Kiss, Max, 159–160
Kohler, Kaufman, 126, 156
Kohut, Alexander, 131
Kook, Hillel, 237
Kotler, Aron, 237, 240, 263
Koussevitsky, Sergei, 184
Krauskopf, Joseph, 123, 144
Kuhn, Charles, 36
Kursheedt, J. B., 60

LaFargue, Jacques, 11

Lafitte, Jean, 43
La Guardia, Fiorello, 224
Lahr, Bert, 228
Lansky, Meyer, 223–224, 245
Laskau, Henry, 256
Lee, Robert E., 94, 96
Lehman, Herbert, 214, 244
Leeser, Isaac, 64, 71, 76, 155
Lehman, Marcus, 92, 117
Leinsdorf, Eric, 230
Leon, Lewis, 94
Levin, Judah, 195
Levin, Lewis Charles, 68–69
Levine (Lavien), John, 29
Levy, Asser, 9
Levy, David, 76
Levy (Levis), Henri, 16, 18
Levy, Isaac, 27, 64
Levy, Levi Andrew, 39
Levy, Moses, 55
Levy, Samuel, 29
Levy, Simon Magruder, 39
Levy, Uriah Phillips, 41, 50, 55
Liebermann, Judith, 255
Liebermann, Saul, 241, 255
Lilienthal, Alfred, 248
Lilienthal, Max, 15, 62–64, 76, 79, 85
Lincoln, Abraham, 86, 89, 91, 97
Lindbergh, Charles, 231–232
Lindo, Moses, 18–19
Linowitz, Sol, 283
Littauer, Lucius, 109, 160–161
Locke, John, 13
Lodge, Henry Cabot, 140, 194
Loeb, Sophie, 174
Loewenthal, Isidor, 76–77
Long, Huey, 214
Lopez, Aaron, 26
Lopez, Rodrigo, 7
Lubin, David, 157
De Lucena, Abraham, 11
Ludwig, Emil, 232
Lynch, William, 66

Mack, Julian, 211
Maduhy, Haim, 20
Magnes, Judah, 156, 169, 190
Maimonides College, 76, 155

Malbim, Meir Leibush, 236
Malki, Moses, 20, 26
Maller, Allen, 277
Malter, Henry, 150, 156
Manhattan Project, 237–238
Manischewitz, Dov Ber, 114
Mann, Louis, 217
Marcus, Jacob, 261, 265
Margolis, Max, 156
Mariaga, Salvador da, 6
Marion, Francis, 24
Marshall, Louis, 175
Martin, Abraham, 18
Marx, Groucho, 270
Marx, Karl, 75–76
Mason, Jackie, 283
Mason, Samuel, 188
Massena NY, 286?
Massias, Abraham, 41
Mather, Cotton, 12
Mayer, David, 93
Mayer, Helene, 221
mayors, 193
McCarran, Pat, 233
McCarran-Walter Act, 244–245
McCormick, John, 223, 271–272
Mcdonald, James, 249
McGee, Suspender Jack, 177
Mclane, David, 33
Meier, Joseph, 160
Meir, Golda, 249, 276
Meltzer, Samuel James, 144
Mendelsohn, Saul, 76
Mendes, H. Pereira
Mendlowitz, Shraga Feivel, 163, 206, 236
Merrick, Joseph, 44
Merzbacher, Leo, 61
Meyer, Jacob, 116
Meyer, Julius, 104–105
Meyers, Elias, 21
Meyers, Mordecai, 41
Michelbacher, Maximillian, 94
Michener, James, 237
Michtom, Morris, 164
Milan, Gabriel, 10
Minhag America, 79
mini-kollel, 285

Mitchell, Jacob, 74
Mnookin, Nathan, 275
Monis, Judah, 11–12
Monroe, James, 42
Monsanto, Isaac, 21
Montcalm, Marquis De, 16, 18
Montefiore, Moses, 58
Morais, Sabato, 129
Morales, Gonzalo de, 6
Morgenthau, Henry Jr, 237
Morgenthau, Henry Sr., 162, 192
Morrison, Samuel Eliot, 5
Mortara Case, 81
Moscowitz, Bella, 210
Moses, Franklin, Sr. & Jr., 106–107
Moses, Isaac, 27
Moses, Raphael, 98
Mozart, Wolfgang, 47
musical plays, 259–260
Myers, Abraham,
Myers, Hyam, 20
Myers, Mordecai

Nadrimal, Abhorad, 44
Nadrimal, Maria, 44
Nathan, Anne, 133
Nathan, Benjamin, 165
National Council of Jewish Woman, 139
National Farm School, 144
Naumkeag, 4
Nehemiah, Moses, 10?
Neier, Aryeh, 284
Netter, Jacob Mordecai, 79
Neuberger, Richard & Maureen, 160
New Deal, 215
New Square, 268
Newman Case, 80
Niles, David, 215, 240
Nixon, Richard, 275–276, 280
Noah, Mordecai Manuel, 21, 33–34, 36, 42, 50–51, 135
Nones, Joseph, 41, 51
Nordheimer, Charles, 24
Nordheimer, Isaac, 54
Nussbaum, Chaim, 235–236
Nussbaum, Jacob, 212
Nussbaum, Perry, 276

O U, 270-271
Obookiah, Henry, 40
Ochs, Adolph, 142, 194
Offenbach, J. J., 112
Older, Fremont, 166
Olympics, 220-221
Oppenheimer, J. Robert, 238
Ordronneaux, John, 41
O'Reilly, Alejandro, 21
Otterbourg, Marcus, 101

Paiewonsky, Ralph, 267
Paine, Tom, 23
Paraguay, 161
Parkman, Francis, 17
Patton, George, 236
Payne, John Howard, 48
Pearson, Drew, 237
Peck, Gregory, 251
Pehle, John, 237
Peixotto, Daniel, 52
Peixotto, Moses Levi, 52
Penja, Joseph de la, 10
periodicals, 271
Pershing, John, 108
Phillip, Philip, 49
Phillips, Naphtali, 28
Phillipson, David, 123, 194
Pickens, Thomas, 24
Pickering, Timothy
Pinto, Abraham & Solomon & William, 23
Plitt, Henry, 242
Polack, Louis, 65
Polachek, Solomon, 204
Pollak, Cushman, 24
Pond, Samuel, 60
Da Ponte, Lorenzo, 47
Pound, Ezra, 234-235
poverty, 277
Presley, Elvis, 260-261
Priesand, Sally, 279
Prohibition, 209-210
Pulitzer, Joseph, 123-124
Purple Gang, 201

Rabbi Isaac Elchonen Rabbinical Seminary, 150

Rabinowitz, Shalom, 179
Rappaport, Solomon Judah, 68, 87
Rankin, John, 23
Raphall, Morris, 84=85
Rayburn, Sam, 258
Reese, Jimmy, 286
Reform: Charleston, 48
Revel, Bernard, 176, 203
Revere, Paul, 22
Rhine, Alice Hyneman, 95
Ribicoff, Abraham, 266
Rice, Abraham, 64, 73
Rodkinson, Michael, 133
Rodriguez, Rafael Cristiani Gil, 40-41
Rogoff, Hillel, 150-151
Roosevelt, Eleanor, 227-228
Roosevelt, Franklin, 111, 200, 221, 223, 227, 234, 240, 260,
Roosevelt, Nicholas, 22
Roosevelt Theodore, 147, 154, 173, 175, 177, 233
Root, Elihu, 283
Rose, Edward, 40
Rose, Moses, 55
Rosenberg, Elias, 129
Rosenblatt, Yossele, 184
Rosenfeld, Joseph, 135
Rosenthal, Ida, 194
Rosenthal, Joseph, 135
Rosenthal, Julius, 151-152
Rosenwald, Lessing, 248
Rowson, Susannah, 30
Rubenstein, Helena, 206
Rudman, Warren, 114
Ruef, Abraham 166-167
Ruffner, Henry, 53
Runyon, Damon, 168
Rush. Benjamin, 33
Russell, Richard, 245
Russo-Japanese War, 165

Sabath, Adolph, 182
Salant, Shmuel, 135
Sale, Kirkpatrick, 5
Salomon, Edward, 99
Salomon, Edward, 99-100
Salomon, Hyam, 22
Salzburger, Meyer, 143, 155

Samuel, Wolf, 45
San Francisco Platform, 280–281
Sanchez, Gabriel, 6
Santillan, Gonzalo Diaz, 9
Santangel, Luis de, 6
Sarner, Ferdinand, 94
Sarnoff, David, 196–197
Schechter, Solomon, 140, 155, 169
Schereschevsky, Samuel, 77
Schiff, Jacob, 165, 173, 175
Schlessinger, Louis, 75
Schlessinger, Sigmund, 102
Schloesser, Max, 156
Schneeburger, Henry, 117
Schneersohn, Haim Zvi, 111–112
Schneersohn, Joseph Isaac, 212
Schoenberg, Arnold, 216
Schomberg, Alexander, 17
Schultz, Dutch, 219–220
Schulweis, Harold, 275
Schumann-Heink, Ernestine, 158
Schwab, Shimon, 275
Schwartz, Benedict, 58
Schwimmer, Rosika, 209
Scott, Walter, 45
Seixas, Gershom, 32, 52
Seligman, Arthur, 212
Seligman Henry, 116
Seligman, Jesse, 96
Seligman, Joseph, 72, 115–116
Sequeyra, John de, 19–20
Shakespeare, William, 7, 53
Shalom, Stephen, 282
Sharrett, Moshe, 249
Shearith Israel, 15, 27, 31, 53
Shechita, 264–265
Sheftal family, 11?
Shelby, Joseph, 97, 104
Sherman, William T., 43, 91
Sholom, NY, 57
Shushan, Abe, 214
ski-lift, 273
Da Silva, Gonzalo Diaz
Da Silva, Maldonado, 6
Silver, Abba Hillel, 199, 223
Silver, Eliezer, 265
Silver, Nathan, 109
Sloss, Louis, 107–108

Siegel, Bugsy, 223–224, 246
Simon, Joseph, 160
Simons, Abraham, 52
Simons, Uncle Billy, 83
Simpson, Earnest & Wallis, 214–215
Singer, Isaac Bashevis, 281
Sinykin, Louis, 253–254
slavery, 82, 85
Sloss, Louis, 107–108
Smith, Alfred, 110
Smith, S. Hosford, 66
Snow, Samuel Sussman, 65
socialists, 148
Society of Canada, 16
Solomon, Hannah Greenbaum, 65
Solomon, Ikey, 53
Solomon, Levy, 24
Solomon, Louis, 89
Solomon, Mr. & Mrs., 34
Solomons, Adolphus, 121
Soloveitchik, Joseph Dov, 204, 265
Soloveitchik, Moshe, 204
Sonneschein, Solomon Hirsch, 127
Spanier, Louis, 72
Spanish-American War, 147–148
Spanish Civil War, 222
Spector, Phil, 260
Spektor, Yitzchok Elchonen, 122
Spiegel, Marcus & Joseph, 100–101
Spiegelberg, Solomon, 212
Spingarn, Joel and Arthur, 178
Steinberg, Paul "Twister", 109
Stein, Jacob, 14
Stevenson, Adlai, 245, 261, 266
Solarsz, Stephen, 282
Stiles, Ezra, 26
Straus, Isidor, 177–178
Straus, Jesse, 221
Straus, Levi, 106
Straus, Nathan, 177–178, 181–182
Straus, Oscar, 138–139, 162, 173, 175, 177–178
Strauss, Joseph, 183, 229
Strauss, Joseph (Admiral), 229
Sulzberger, Arthur, 233
Sulzberger, Meyer, 138, 162
Sumter, Charles, 24
Sun-Yat-Sen, 135

Sunday Sabbaths, 125–126
Susman, Moses, 14
Sylvester, J. J., 60
synagogue bombings, 264, 276
Szilard, Leo, 238
Szold, Henrietta, 167

Taft, William Howard, 175, 177, 180
Teller, Edward, 238
Tenzer, Herbert, 271–272
terefah banquet, 123
Thompson, Dorothy, 248
Todres, Abraham, 240
Torres, Luis de, 5
Touro, Judah, 56
Travis, Sarah, 176
Trilling, Lionel, 212
Trotsky, Leon, 185
Trott, Nicholas, 37
Truman, Harry, 239, 246, 247
Tucker, Richard, 260–261
Tucker, Sophie, 213
Turner, C. C., 66
Tuska, Simon, 77–78
Twain, Mark and family, 110–111, 186
Twersky, Isadore, 161
Twersky, Jacob Joseph, 268
Twiggs, David Emanuel, 36
Twiggs, John, 36

Unitarianism, 127–128
university quotas, 200
Unterman, Sigmund, 78
urban life, 28

Valentine, James, 87
Vallandigham, Clement, 89–90
Van Buren, Martin, 60
Vance, Zebulon, 112–113
Varick, Richard, 26
Vaudreuil, Pierre, 16
vegetarianism, 281
Viet Nam, 274
Villa, Pancho, 118
Voltaire, 35
Vorsanger, Jacob, 1212

Waco, 69

Wallace, Lew, 121–122
Walsingham, Lord, 7
War Refugee Board, 237
Warburg, Eric, 241–242
Washington, George, 1, 19, 24, 32
Waterman, Sigmund, 78
Watson, Elkanah, 44
Watson, Tom, 181–182
Webster, Daniel, 67, 79
Weill, Abraham, 97
Weinstein, Lewis, 246–247
Weiss, Carl, 214
Weiss, Seymour, 214
Weizmann, Chaim, 246, 253
Whitecaps, 136
Whittaker, Benjamin, 37
Wiener, Leon, 250
Wiener, Norbert, 250
Wiesenthal, Simon, 5
Wigner, Eugene, 238
William of Orange, 10
Williams, Ezekiel, 41
Willowski, Jacob David, 171–172
Winchell, Walter, 127
Winthrop, John, 4
Wise, Isaac Mayer, 63–64, 67–68,
    72–73, 76, 79, 85–86, 90, 105,
    147, 150
Wise, Stephen S., 162, 192, 199, 219
Wittkowsky, Samuel, 113
Witmark brothers, 128
Wolf, Simon, 97, 140
Wolfe, Antony, 54
Wolfe, James, 18
Wolfson, Harry, 161
Wollenberger, Paul, 147
Workmens' Circle, 189
World War I, 183
Wyrick, David, 82

Yamasaki, Minoru, 284
Yellen, Jack, 213
Yeshiva University, 202
Yeshivahs, 182–183, 263
Young Israel, 169–170, 271
Yulee, David Levy, 62

Zangwill, Israel, 173

Zemurray, Samuel, 207
Zimbalist, Efraim, 179
Zion College, 76
Zuckerman, Michael, 254

Zunser, Elyakum, 145
Zuntz, Alexander, 27
Zussman, Raymond, 240

www.ingramcontent.com/pod-product-compliance
Lightning Source LLC
Chambersburg PA
CBHW051630230426
43669CB00013B/2240